Fundamentals of Level Three Leadership

Fundamentals of Level Three Leadership

How to Become an Effective Executive

James G. S. Clawson

BUSINESS EXPERT PRESS

Leader in applied, concise business books

Fundamentals of Level Three Leadership:
How to Become an Effective Executive

Cover design by Charlene Kronstedt

Interior design by Exeter Premedia Services Private Ltd., Chennai, India

First published in 2021 by
Business Expert Press, LLC
222 East 46th Street, New York, NY 10017
www.businessexpertpress.com

ISBN-13: 978-1-63742-040-9 (paperback)
ISBN-13: 978-1-63742-041-6 (e-book)

Business Expert Press Human Resource Management and Organizational Behavior Collection

Collection ISSN: 1946-5637 (print)
Collection ISSN: 1946-5645 (electronic)

First edition: 2021

10 9 8 7 6 5 4 3 2 1

Description

What does it take to become an effective executive?

Anyone with that dream goal will want to know the answers to the six questions around which this book is organized: Who are you? What's your strategic story? Can you sell your story? Can you organize to help not hinder? Are you a Change Master? Can you transform intangible asset pools into tangible financial results?

For easy apprehension, this unusual volume presents 140 concepts, one per short chapter each with an explanation, examples, visual diagrams, and challenging questions. Participants in 200+ three to five day seminars worldwide (US, Canada, Europe, Africa, Asia, South America and the Middle East) have been energized by these concepts and their applications to their careers and personal lives. Check out the Table of Contents and see if you aren't engaged by multiple titles.

Keywords

leadership; human behavior; strategic thinking; organizational design; change; balanced scorecard; organizational culture; problem solving; management; executives

Contents

Preface

What does it take to become an effective executive? Trait theory has long since been discredited. Intelligence has many faces and it seems obvious that the smartest person may not be the best leader. Experience is important, yet age is no guarantee of wisdom. Legal authority carries with it some power yet title is no guarantee of effective leadership. So are there any commonalities in the skill sets of effective executives? Can those skills be taught and learned? Are they transportable from one situation to another?

Yes and yes are the answers I have gleaned from over forty years of study, teaching, researching, consulting, and writing. During that time, I have continuously updated and revised my understanding of what it takes to make an effective executive and assembled them here. I never thought that any one person or model was accurate or comprehensive enough to hang your hat on. Consequently, you will see here broad inclusion of the ideas of many others along with my own. I believe in integrating and building on what we already know about various topics rather than asserting a narrow personal view—which I also include. Some of the chapters provide summaries of major works in each section, by which I simply introduce those frameworks and invite the serious student to read the original sources.

Some of the concepts here might be *familiar* to you—in my experience, that usually means "I've heard the term before" but does not extend to explaining it cogently without coaching. Often I will ask you your opinion on a thing and leave space for you to note it. If you don't do that and after reading say, "I knew that" I invite your serious reflection on what it was that you already *knew*. I have taught these principles to CEOs, C-level executives, company presidents, division heads of business, managers, supervisors and students of business at the MBA and doctoral levels. And done that all over the world from the United States to China to Japan to Australia to India to South Africa to Bahrain to Egypt to Italy to Germany to Sweden to Brazil and Costa Rica and many countries in between. *The concepts are tried and true in the crucible of active debate among business executives at every level in every region of the globe in a variety of industries.*

In my experience, executives vary widely in the amount of reading they do. Further, all the other books I have seen, with the exception of the works of Ken Blanchard and Spencer Johnson (*One Minute Manager* series, *Who Moved My Cheese?*) and John Kotter's *Our Iceberg is Melting*, have required long bouts of focus wading through multiple examples and verbiage chapter after chapter. No metaphors here, just short, focused two to five page chapters each presenting one concept, an example, a visual diagram, and a series of challenges. My goal, that is, every chapter will provide readers with a clear, powerful idea, and stimulation to think about its application to your life, work, and career.

The ~140 concepts presented here are organized around a **flexible, powerful model of leadership** I developed while at the Harvard Business School. Here are the questions that form a diamond shaped framework for this model:

1. What are the basic concepts that we must understand in order to *get* the rest of the book.
2. Who are you? Do you understand why people including yourself behave the way they do?
3. What is your strategic story? How does one develop a strategic story that one can offer to would-be followers?
4. Can you sell your story? Do you know how to influence people, who are influencing others, and can you improve your abilities to sell your story to others?
5. Can you organize to help not hinder? Do you understand how to organize people in ways that energize them rather than suck energy out of them?
6. Are you a Change Master? Do you understand how the change process works? Or are you doing the best you can with what you *know*?
7. Finally, can you convert intangible asset pools into tangible results? How does one recognize the essential intangibles like people, relationships, and processes, and transform them into financial returns?

My hope is that you will find **a significantly valuable idea in every chapter**. If so, this volume will provide a valuable introduction and reference for executives, managers, and business students worldwide. The format allows one to pick and choose what they want to read or assign to be read without extraneous verbiage. One man responsible for sales in half a continent encountered one of the ideas here and immediately left the program saying "I've been searching for this idea my whole career. I can't take any more!" I hope you find such an experience in this book.

James Clawson

Charlottesville, VA

January 2021

Acknowledgments

This book presents the research and ideas of hundreds of people in academe and practicing business organizations. They all have contributed to the ideas in this book. I have tried to acknowledge them throughout in the text, diagrams, and endnotes. For quotations, I have almost always tried to include a public domain photograph of the person quoted so readers can *see* the person they are *listening* to.

I am especially indebted to **Ed Schein's** work and conversations; he is one of my heroes, a man with a broad scope of influence, great productivity, and provocative insights. He introduced me to the example of Central American pyramids. These, the pyramids, were physical artifacts of ethereal rituals that were conducted there based on a culture's underlying beliefs. And that single triplet of ideas spawned in me a profound set of thoughts that affected my entire career. This book is the last of some two dozen books that explored that triplet and as such is the culmination of my life's work. I dedicate this book to **Ed Schein** and offer my thanks to him for his generosity of intellect that he shared with us all.

My deep gratitude to the professionals at Business Expert Press (BEP), to Mike Provitera for his encouragement and enthusiasm, to Scott Isenberg for his trust, to Charlene Kronstedt for her guidance and excellent support, to Sheri Dean for her marketing skills and to Exeter Premedia.

Finally, I thank my patient wife for tolerating my work habits and extended isolations while working, recently and throughout our wonderful (for me) 44 years together.

SECTION I

Basics

This section introduces some basic concepts that apply throughout the other sections of the Level Three Leadership framework. Consider these the basic building blocks upon which we will build going forward.

1. Leading Strategic Change

Concept

People want to talk about leadership, but before long they, or we, have to ask, "Leadership to what end?" Where are we going? And that's the strategy question. I asked a CEO once what his strategy was and his answer was, "Our strategy for the next six months is cut costs." I waited, but he was done. It didn't seem strategic, certainly not long term, and surely omitted many areas of important concern.

So, to talk about leadership requires one to talk about strategy, or its component, vision. Who decides where we are going and what we should emphasize? Without clarity about direction or end point, how do we know how to lead? So, I say, you cannot talk about leadership without talking about strategy.

What about leaders who are implementing someone else's strategy? These people are "managers" unless they have a bigger view of what's going on and how they can inspire their people to work to that end.

If you ask "to what end," the implication is we are going from here to there. Strategy demands an answer to the "there" question, so strategic thinking is a key leadership skill set.

Further, "going from here to there" implies the change question, "how are we going to get there?" So really, when we talk about leadership, necessarily we are talking about three things, direction or end point, leadership, and managing change, or more briefly, "leading strategic change." One very successful CEO of a $30B business, once told me, "I'm a *change master*. You ask me to maintain an organization in its current state, I can't play there. I always think there's a better way." I was impressed with his comment.

We call the people who maintain things the way they are "bureaucrats." They certainly aren't leading strategic change. In this view, would-be leaders need to know and manifest a lot about leadership and *also* strategy formulation, and they also need to be "*change masters*." While this is a book on leadership, you will find elements of all three in this volume.

Visual Capitalist (on 11/30/18) displayed a chart of what CEOs do. In sum, they reported that Chief Executive Officers spent about 25 percent of their time on people and relationships, 25 percent on business unit reviews, and 21 percent on strategy. Those data give us a good overview of what three-fourths of an executive's day/week/year looks like: people, unit performance reviews (what do you measure?), and strategy. Leading strategic change.

Example

Hans Von Luck was the German panzer commander assigned to defend the critical bridges over the Orne River during D-Day, June 6, 1944. Later in his career, he was assigned to defend against the Russian tide on the Eastern Front. Without reinforcements, out of ammunition, and surrounded by the Russian army, Von Luck assembled his troops and made this statement:

> We are here now, and I think it is more or less the end of the world. Please forget all about the Thousand-Year Reich. Please forget all about that. You will ask, "Why then are we going to fight again?" I tell you, there's only one reason you are fighting, it is for your families, your grounds, your homeland. Always think about what will happen when the Russians overcome your wives, your little daughters, your village, our homeland.
>
> *Pegasus Bridge*, Stephen E. Ambrose, e-page 2255

Von Luck had a bigger picture fed by his conversations with Rommel, earlier in which Rommel declared in Africa, "the war is lost." Von Luck was not buried in the details, in the bogs, in the reeds, he could transcend his immediate situation and see the broader picture and articulate a vision that would more than motivate, rather inspire his troops.

Diagram

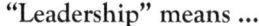

"Leadership" means ...

Challenge

1. In whatever leadership role you have or aspire to, think about what that part of the organization is trying to accomplish.
2. What's the purpose of that organization?
3. Where do you imagine it to be in 10 years?
4. What would be your strategy for getting there?
5. Rate yourself on a scale of 1 to 10 on how well you understand and can lead a change effort.
6. Create a time chart of how you spend your weekly time (164 hours) on average especially with regard to time spent leading, strategizing, and managing change.

2. Levels of Human Behavior

Concept

This is a very important chapter. To begin, may I ask you a short series of important questions. First, how old are you? _____ Thank you. If this were a personal conversation, we could start with a bit of accurate sharing, yes/no? I am 73 as of this writing, born in 1947.

Now, in your x years of experience, given *all* the people you have met in your life, **what proportion of people's Visible Behavior (what you can capture on film) would you estimate to be habitual?** By habitual, I mean "unthinkingly repetitive." People express or show their habits when they repeat behavior over and over again. Frequently, habits are so ingrained that they too become semi- or pre-conscious.

What's your personal estimate? How much of people's Visible Behavior is habitual?

WRITE YOUR ANSWER HERE: _____%

Now, in your experience, given *all* the people you have met in your life, what proportion of **the way people think** would you estimate to be habitual? We can't see what people are thinking only as they reveal it to us in their Visible Behavior. Yet, after a while, can you begin to predict what someone will say? What's your estimate? How much **of the way people think** is mindlessly repetitive? _____%

Finally, consider what I will call "Level Three" our *semi-conscious, pre-conscious Values, Assumptions, Beliefs, and Expectations about the way the world is or should be.* We can call these **VABEs** (rhymes with babes) for short. We say these are *semi-* or *pre-conscious* because we are often not really thinking about them yet they emerge in our judgments, conclusions, thoughts, and behaviors.

In your experience, given *all* the people you have met thus far in life, what proportion of people's VABEs are habitual, mindlessly repetitive?

WRITE YOUR ESTIMATE HERE: _____%

So, we can think of human behavior as occurring at three levels. Level One is visible behavior, the things that people say and do that we can capture on film. Level One behavior is available to us everywhere we turn if we observe.

Level Two is conscious thought. Clearly, we all have conscious thoughts. We are aware of our thoughts. Further, we choose whether or not we will reveal our thoughts to others. Sometimes our thoughts and emotions *leak* to others when we sigh, frown, smile, or roll our eyes. Sometimes we choose to say what we are thinking and this becomes the basis for honest communication. Level Two also includes our conclusions, that is, our judgments about what's happening around us, about what others say and do and about events in the environment.

Level Three is our VABEs. VABEs are similar to the concept of "memes" introduced by Richard Dawkins in the UK. He called them units of cultural transmission, that is, how people, mostly children, learn what's right and wrong in a culture.

Genes are *tangible* packets of information passed around societies and from generation to generation. Memes, by contrast, are *intangible* packets of information passed around society and down generation after generation. John Brodie called memes "viruses of the mind" and asserted three types: identity, value, and instrumental. Identity memes name something or someone. "Virginia" and "Europe" are identity memes. Identity memes can also label an ethereal concept like a stirrup, chair, or the wheel. Value memes assign a moral value to a concept. "Stealing is bad" is a value meme. So is "cleanliness is next to godliness." Value memes relate to what's good or bad, right or wrong, moral or immoral. Instrumental memes are "if-then" statements that label a cause-and-effect link. "Hard work brings success" is a strategy meme. So is "if you eat properly, you will lose weight."

The emotional component of memes is clearer in the concept of VABEs. The things we value by definition are what we prefer versus what we don't prefer. "Honest conversation" might be valued by one person and not by another. Our assumptions include those linkages or labels that we have come to accept without questioning. "Young people should be seen and not heard" would be one such assumption. Beliefs are closely linked to values and assumptions. "God loves me" is an example of a belief. Expectations are equally as powerful as values, assumptions, and beliefs. People have learned over the course of their lives to expect certain things. "Polite people shake hands" or "polite people bow" or "polite people don't touch you with their left hand" are examples of expectations. We can think of Values, Assumptions, Beliefs, and Expectations as different windows into the same core concept.

VABEs are semi- or pre-conscious because they are so familiar to us, they are like water to a gold fish, we don't think about them so much unless we encounter a **VABE-abrasion**, that is, when something happens that annoys, angers, or irritates us. Typically, our emotions are *reactions* to almost instantaneous comparisons between what the world is presenting to us and what our VABEs are. What we value, assume, believe, or expect is in a broad sense what we "want." What the world presents to us, what is happening around us is what we "get." So moment by moment, we are constantly comparing what we have got with what we want and if they match up, things are good. If they don't match up we will likely experience a VABE-abrasion—an irritation or conflict with our VABEs.

Recent research into brain functioning has clarified the huge impact our pre-conscious VABEs have on our decision making. (See Daniel Kahneman's *Thinking Fast and Slow*, Joshua Greene's *Moral Tribes*, and Jonathan Haidt's *The Righteous Mind*.) Humans tend to make very fast judgments about even large and important situations. The field of evolutionary psychology explains why this might have been a Darwinian advantage. If we are taught, for example, to be cautious of strangers with weapons, that VABE can save one's life. So when we observe and deal with others, we can choose to, or not, pay attention to all three levels of human behavior. Clearly, we can only "see" what's happening at Levels Two and Three by what we observe at Level One. Think of Level One behavior as the tip of the iceberg and the surface of the water the boundary between Level One and Level Two. You can see what's above the waterline and what's at the waterline, but very little of what's below.

Sometimes, but not always, people will tell us what their thoughts and VABEs are. Those who do tell us may be authentically accurate, deceitful, or lacking in self-awareness. Frequently we have to infer what people are thinking or assuming by signals they send at Level One. Frowns, sighs, rolling of the eyes, shouting, laughter, facial expressions in general, use of words like "should, have to, good, and bad," noises in general (grunts, growls), all give us some insight into what people are thinking and feeling. When people get angry or conflicted or emotional, they are often reacting to a VABE abrasion and we may try to assess what the VABE might be that caused that irritation or anger.

While the research to answer these questions would be difficult to conduct, I have asked these questions to managers all over the world. On average, they will say **75 percent, 85 percent, and 95 percent plus** respectively. Do those numbers match your experience? If we look at Northern Ireland, the Balkans, Central African tribal conflicts, India and Pakistan, US race relations, China and Tibet . . . Pick your part of the globe, the lingering, residual, omnipresent influence of VABEs is evident.

If those numbers are anywhere near reality, think of the implications. What are the odds in any situation that a person will learn something behaviorally, cognitively, or emotionally that will change their habits, their lives? The answer would be somewhere between 25 and 0 percent. In the vast minority. Which of course begs a major question: Are you open to learning, that is, to changing some of your Level One, Level Two, and Level Three habits?

William James once noted that "genius is the art of non-habitual thought." Hmmm.

Example

One person curses when someone else cuts in front of them in traffic. Another person slows down and smiles. What's the difference?

One person on his way in to work is thinking, "What do I have to do today?" while another is thinking, "What am I going to create today?" What's the difference?

One person opens a present and sighs and frowns. Another opens a present and is elated. What's the difference?

One person always looks for what's missing while another admires what has been done. What's the difference?

Diagram

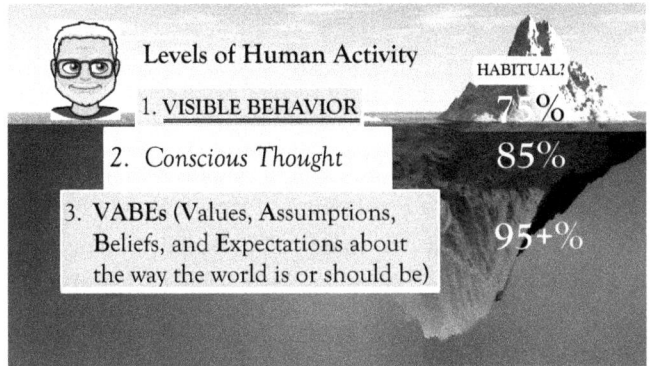

Levels of Human Activity

1. VISIBLE BEHAVIOR — HABITUAL? 7 %

2. *Conscious Thought*   85%

3. VABEs (Values, Assumptions, Beliefs, and Expectations about the way the world is or should be)   95+%

Source: https://gettyimages.com/detail/photo/tip-of-the-iceberg-royalty-free-image/157509282?adppopup=true

Challenge

1. Observe carefully what others say and do. What VABEs are they expressing? Try to identify another person's VABEs and write them down. Then, ask that person if they are accurate.

2. Listen for the "shoulds," "have-to's," and judgments of other people. Try to write down the underlying VABE. Don't just do that in your head. Write it down. There is a BIG difference between thinking you know something and articulating it or writing it down. FIND the words to accurately describe the VABEs of which you are vaguely aware.

3. Write down a list of your top 20, most important VABEs. Then show that list to someone who knows you well and see if they agree based on your Level One behavior.

4. Develop a sensitive *VABE radar*. Be aware of the signals when other people let you see a glimpse of their underlying VABEs.

3. Leadership Point of View

Concept

We introduced above the concept of human habituality. People manifest over time their habitual points of view, that is, how they look at the world. People may or may not be aware of their points of view. We introduce here three common habitual points of view for your consideration.

Many people take what we could call a "Follower's Point of View" or FPV. We infer this from the things that people say and do, that is, by observing their Level One behavior. People with an FPV tend to say things like "What do you want me to do?" "How do you want me to do it?" "When do you need it done by?" And so forth. They expect (the "E" in VABEs) others to guide them, to tell them, to instruct them.

Other people take a "Bureaucratic Point of View" or BPV. Again, we can observe this because people will repeatedly say things like "That's not my job." "That's not how we do things around here." "That's not in the operating manual." "That's not acceptable practice." Or "Have you filled out the form yet?"

Some people have developed a "Leadership Point of View" or LPV. They manifest three characteristics at Level One: they SEE what needs to be done, they UNDERSTAND all the forces at play, and they have the COURAGE TO ACT.

Have you ever noticed people who in conversation seem to have a knack for cutting to the heart of an issue while others are milling around in the peripheral weeds? They *see* what the real issue is. One popular example would be Steve Jobs's insight when he returned to Apple to become its new CEO. Reviewing the company's line of computer products, he saw that the proliferation of models had dissipated the company's development efforts. He refocused efforts by recognizing the need to consolidate and focus the company's efforts and product lines.

People with the LPV *understand* all the forces at play in an organization not just their favorite ones. Many general managers still hold an emphasis on the discipline of their past whether it be finance, marketing, or operations. An effective general manager with the LPV is less likely to be blindsided than a manager who remains focused on their original discipline (finance, accounting, marketing) because he or she understands how all the elements are essential to organizational health. A senior level manager in a $20B defense company once noted that people were surprised that his boss who came out of a finance background did not drive meetings from a financial point of view. Rather, he put emphasis where it was needed when it was needed, serving customers, fixing operational bottlenecks, ramping up marketing, or solidifying the company's equity structure.

Finally, I mention the *courage to act.* I say "courage" because it takes courage to make decisions and then live with their consequences. In my own experience as the CEO of a non-profit organization of 3,000 people, I learned that while many people will be quick to offer advice, in the end, someone must make a decision and if that person is the senior officer, he or she likely has developed an LPV.

That is not to say that "followers" and "bureaucrats" don't make it to senior ranks, they do. I've observed CEOs who were followers and relied on consulting reports and subordinate action to "administer." Likewise, I have seen CEOs who were bureaucrats so that their decisions were locked into the way things had been done historically—to the detriment of their firms.

Some will say that "I'll develop an LPV when I get the job that requires it." This is a mistake in my view. My own research into the relationship between vision and organizational level showed no correlation. People with vision had it early in their careers and kept it throughout. Likewise, some people without vision made it to the higher ranks. This suggests that one can and should develop the three skill clusters of the LPV early in a career. If you don't when the conversations turn to "what should we do" the FPVs and the BPVs will likely be listeners in the conversation; they will have nothing to say.

If you wanted to check your balance among these three skill sets, you might take the simple self-assessment tool at this location:

http://virginia.qualtrics.com/SE/?SID=SV_dnxICDUXE6QpbvL

Example

One CEO declares his dedication to staying the course and continuing the policies and strategies of his predecessors. Another hires multiple consultants to give her advice on what to do. Another thinks for a while and declares a vision for where he wants the company to be in 10 years. What's the difference?

Diagrams

What's Your Habitual Point of View?	
Point of View (POV)	Things They Say ...
Follower's POV	What do you want me to do? By when? How do you want me to do it? What's my authority? And so on.
Bureaucratic POV	That's not my job. That's not our way. Let me refer you. Have you filled out the form yet?

The Leadership Point of View

1. Do you SEE what needs to be done?
2. Do you UNDERSTAND ALL of the forces at play?
3. Do you have the COURAGE TO ACT to make things better?

Challenge

1. Pay attention to your words as you react to assignments and opportunities. Does your L1 language suggest an FPV, a BPV or an LPV?
2. Listen to the language of your leaders and managers. Which PoV is suggested by their language?
3. Observe your colleagues. Which ones have an FPV? Which ones have a BPV? Which ones have an LPV?
4. Reflect on your scores to the self-assessment tool above. Do they suggest an FPV, a BPV or an LPV?
5. Other than the phrases offered above, what other indicators of FPV or BPV or LPV can you imagine?

4. Seeing What Needs To Be Done

Concept

The first element in the Leadership Point of View is to *see what needs to be done*. Managers and bureaucrats wait for someone else to clarify what's important and what we should do about it. Leaders have the ability to cut through a fog of extraneous data and analysis and home in on the core issues. Some people seem to have this ability innately, but I suppose that virtually everyone has had to learn this skill. Clearly, toddlers cannot see the bigger picture and don't have the ability to cut to the chase.

The number of priorities that most organizations can deal with is limited. Leaders who see 10 things to work on will likely dissipate their energies and those of their people to the point that nothing gets done particularly well. Focus is important. Lou Gerstner, former CEO of IBM, in his book, *Who Says Elephants Can't Dance*, noted that "lack of focus is the most common cause of corporate mediocrity." The ability to find the two to three key issues is a critical leadership skill.

Some people outsource "sight" to consulting companies. They ask others to analyze their businesses and tell them what needs to be done. One big danger here, beside the cost of this approach, is that many consulting reports end up gathering dust on corporate credenzas because the executives either don't believe them or don't have the courage to implement them.

Sight is not easy to quantify. What is obvious to one is not to another. Good leadership sight is a function of a lifetime of learning and experience gathering. One may begin to see patterns in analysis, even consultants' analyses, in broader trends, and in one's world view.

Sometimes, the right questions can bring sight. "Who are our biggest competitive threats?" "What technology could disrupt our plans?" "What is keeping us from delivering on our customer value promises?" "What is the linkage between our people, our core capabilities, and satisfying our customers?" "What are the links in our value chain and how can we manage them better?"

Executives who have sight can see the way the organization works and how it delivers value to customers. They must be able to see and describe the transformation of intangible assets like human capital, social capital, and organizational capital through corporate capabilities to customer satisfaction that results in tangible assets that appear on income statements. Any executive who cannot trace those linkages is flying blind.

Example

When Steve Jobs was hired back to Apple he was confronted with a long list of problems and issues. The company had admittedly lost its way. The number of products had proliferated diffusing organizational energy. Jobs recognized this and in a meeting drew a simple 2x2 diagram with "corporate" and "retail" on one axis and "laptop" and "desktop" on the other. Then, he said, that the company would offer only one product in each cell—and instantaneously focused the corporation's considerable strength. Since then, Apple's products and business ventures have expanded, but at the time, Jobs's ability to see the confusion that a broad array of development projects was creating and his ability to focus the company's efforts were instrumental in Apple's resurgence.

	CORPORATE	RETAIL
DESKTOP	Mac Pro	iMAC
LAPTOP	MacBook Pro	MacBook

At Coca-Cola, Bob Goizeuta was confronted with a management team that was lamenting the company's success. The company had been so successful, they said, worldwide that they had succeeded themselves out of ways to grow. They thought the market was saturated. And for a brand recognized in more than 200 countries, it looked on the surface that they had a good argument. Goizeuta responded with two simple questions. "What is the average liquid intake of human beings worldwide? And what is the average intake worldwide of our products?" No one knew the answers, so they went off and did a little research. The answers came back "64 fluid ounces and 4 fluid ounces." It was clear to all that the company had enormous opportunity to raise that proportion by targeting the 60 fluid ounces (on average) that people were drinking that weren't Coca Cola products: 4/64 = 6 percent leaving a 94 percent market penetration opportunity. Now, let's not suppose that everyone wants their babies drinking sweet soft drinks, so this analysis also urged company executives to find other products with which they could "refresh the world."

Diagram

Do you SEE what needs to be done?

The greatest thing a human soul ever does in this world is to see something and tell what it saw in a plain way. Hundreds of people can talk for one who can think, but thousands can think for one who can see. To see clearly is poetry, prophecy and religion, all in one.

John Ruskin
English critic, essayist, & reformer
(1819-1900)

Source: https://google.com/search?q=john+ruskin+images&rlz=1C1GCEB_enUS910US910&sxsrf=ALeKk01uv3auX_HCsZA7NUEkyGl_z_Awcw:1611766150061&tbm=isch&source=iu&ictx=1&fir=NIkNGGhtbDg8xM%252CXKMweoD8FGn5TM%252C_&vet=1&usg=AI4_-kRGNX6Cz1_Gve812s9fqoqF-97Wfw&sa=X&ved=2ahUKEwii9dbmyLzuAhXEM1kFHetBC8gQ9QF6BAgNEAE&biw=1366&bih=578#imgrc=NIkNGGhtbDg8xM

Challenge

Practice developing your insight by:

1. Putting every problem in a broader context and relating it to the whole.
2. Clarifying inefficiencies of energy. "Where is energy being wasted in our organization?"
3. Constantly asking, "What's a faster, more efficient, more effective way?"
4. Asking, "What single thing would give us the most leverage?"
5. Asking, "What technology could replace us or ours?"
6. Asking, "What is our customers' perception of us?"
7. Asking, "How can I bring instant focus to this situation?"

5. Understanding All the Forces at Play

Concept

The second element of the Leadership Point-of-View (LPV) is "understanding all the forces at play." Many who are promoted out of a functional leadership responsibility continue to see the world primarily from their comfortable mental platform—their historical experience. Executives who come from operations are likely to be most concerned about efficiencies, productivity, fixed assets, and supply chains. Executives who come out of finance are likely to focus mostly on balance sheets, equity, operating ratios, stock price, and the economy. This will be exacerbated to the extent their contracts emphasize stock price (stockholders' interests). Executives who came out of marketing are more likely to focus on brand image, marketing campaigns, raising the top line (revenues), and advertising. Focusing on revenue generation is not necessarily wrong, it's just that more revenues without profits aren't worth much. Focusing on productivity isn't wrong, unless it is at the expense of generating more revenues. I know of companies who have managed their productivity into bankruptcy.

All of this is natural. People tend to be creatures of habit. People are more comfortable talking about and dealing with issues they have dealt with before. But becoming a general manager, an executive, demands a balanced perspective and attention on ALL of the key forces at play. Executives who rely too heavily on their experience are likely to be blindsided by issues and problems that lie outside their historical expertise.

Obviously, one way to overcome this tendency is to recruit experts in the areas that one is not strong in to be a part of the management team. Some people are better at this than others. Some are too proud to admit that they might not know what's going on or have an intimate feel for what's happening in the functional areas outside their past expertise.

This is one reason I am a strong advocate of the MBA degree for any manager and for any professor of business. Understanding the key issues and dilemmas of all the 10 or more functional fields in a business (finance, operations, accounting, marketing, strategy, human resources, leadership, ethics, economics, decision analysis, communications) is essential, in my mind and experience, to understanding how they all work together in an enterprise. Managers and teachers who rely too heavily on their functional field at the expense of an understanding of how they integrate do themselves and their organizations a disservice.

Imagine you were a doctor in a hospital emergency room (ER). Without warning, a gurney is pushed into your service bay. There is a human lying on the gurney. You have no background information, no medical history, nothing other than the person lying in front of you. What do you look for?

Readers are not likely medical doctors, nevertheless, you have a mental theory about what doctors look for. Write that down here. What is your semi-conscious ER triage model? (*Note: We ask you your view before we share ours in several chapters. We are inviting you to do your best thinking BEFORE you read about ours. It's too easy to not do that and then say, "oh I knew that."*)

It turns out that there are 13 systems that together create a fully functioning human being. Not all of these are critical for immediate survival, but many of them are. ER doctors will look for several things immediately:

1. Is it conscious and communicative? Can it talk to me?
2. Is it breathing?
3. Is it leaking blood? Any wounds?
4. Is the brain functioning? Eye and nerve responsiveness?
5. Is the heart functioning? Pulse and blood pressure?
6. Are the kidneys producing water?
7. Is the nervous system responsive?

Lesser systems like urinary tract function, glandular function, sexual function, and so on are important and can be considered after the critical ones have been attended to and confirmed.

What's your "ER TRIAGE" template for a *company*? That is, if you were assigned to be the new CEO of a company without any prior knowledge, what would be your "priors" about how to assess the health of that organization? Write that down here.

Having asked this question of managers all over the world, it's clear to me that active managers with significant responsibilities have widely varying implicit models. When asked to put those models on paper, the discrepancies between peoples' models becomes obvious. Even just sharing with one neighbor, most managers find things they had overlooked—and they modify their models.

As a budding executive, you have an implicit model in your head. You wrote it down in the box above. Did it include the following?

1. **Financial Status:** profitability, balance sheet stability, income statement health.
2. **Customer Value Proposition:** What do we promise? How well do we deliver on those promises?
3. **Corporate Capabilities:** Do we have the key capabilities needed to deliver on those customer promises? Raw Materials? Transformation processes? Channel management? Public Awareness/brand management?
4. **Human Capital:** What is the imaginary sum of what your people can do? A stack of resumes is a poor estimate of this pool.

5. **Social Capital:** How well do your people work together? How much are they ensconced in functional, location, or program walls and fiefdoms?

6. **Organizational Capital:** Are you organized to unleash your Human Capital potential or to dampen it? Is your IT system up-to-date and enabling or obsolete and hindering? How much bureaucracy do your people have to fight through to get things done?

7. **Executive Team:** Do you have a high-powered team who can all explain and are enthusiastic about your organizational charter? Do their talents and skills balance each other?

8. **Leadership:** Who can see all of these things and explain how they fit together? Who can describe without notes your mission, vision, values, strategy, and short-term operating goals?

Did your list include all of these essential business health factors? Would you/did you add anything else not subsumed by these categories?

Example

Walt Disney and his older brother, Roy, were a formidable force in the entertainment industry. Walt had the vision and values clearly in mind and could provide creative direction. Roy was more business oriented and practically focused. A former banker, he helped Walt channel his creative juices into a financially solid and sustainable corporation that has become a giant in the entertainment world.

Soichiro Honda and Takeo Fujisawa had a similar relationship as the Disney brothers, but one that expressed itself in the Japanese and global automobile industries. Honda was, like Walt, the creative force behind Honda (properly pronounced Hone-da, not Hawn-da) directing its engineering and product development functions. Fujisawa managed the financial side of the business—one that grew into a global conglomerate with products in automobiles, lawn care, motorcycles, and other segments. Fujisawa was known for his motto, "always tell the customer the truth," a VABE that many executives today do not behave.

Diagram

What's your corporate ER Triage Assessment Model?

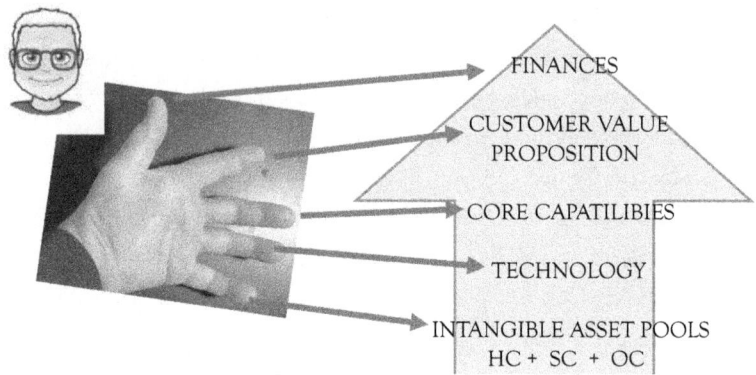

Challenge

1. Start now to expand your understanding of the various forces in a business, don't wait until you hope to get promoted, do it now so you are prepared and seen to be prepared.
2. Clarify your "take charge" map. Make sure it's complete; test it with others.
3. Use your "take charge" map with every new assignment. Analyze all the factors in play and get into the habit of assessing them all in every job even if you are assigned a narrow functional job. Refine your map with every experience.
4. Identify people who understand the various elements of your "take charge" map better than you do. Cultivate their wisdom by asking them questions and for explanations of their answers.
5. Press yourself to understand so that you can explain easily the linkages between and among all of the elements in your take charge map. Your ability to see how one function/system affects the whole will be critical to your ability to manage a whole enterprise.
6. Don't fake it. When you don't know, say so, then go find out, then add that insight to your box of wisdom. Remember, age is no guarantee of wisdom or judgment. Only those who learn from their "happenings" in life are adding to their reservoir of wisdom.

6. The Courage to Act

Concept

The third step in the Leadership Point of View is the courage to act. There are many people who can see what needs to be done. Most of them we call journalists. They are out there every day writing about all the problems they see and believe need attention. And there are many people out there who are studying all the forces at play. We call most of them professors. They are researching all kinds of issues and problems and reporting on their findings in a vast number of journals and books.

But people who have the courage to act are not so common, and the reason is the fear of rejection. Humans have had really only one major form of punishment throughout our history: exclusion. When people misbehave, we generally remove them from our society. We send our kids to their rooms. We send thieves to jail. We excommunicate people who don't follow the church's rules. We ignore those not in our clique. We meet in secret.

Over the millennia, humans have learned to conform or be excluded. We banded together to survive and thrive. And every group had rules. Every group today has rules. Things you can do and things you cannot do and still maintain your membership in the group. So we all have learned to do what is expected of us or risk being put out of the group. We will address this more in the chapter on Living Inside-Out versus Outside-in.

For now, though, realize that many—if not most—managers are afraid. They are afraid of censure and doing something that will offend the group. Some, a few, are so unconcerned about the judgment of others that they behave so unusually or outrageously as to not attract many followers. The effective executive has cultivated an inner boldness in which he or she can stretch the boundaries of what has been expected and accepted in the past while still maintaining enough traditional behavior as to not offend the majority of followers.

That said, no one can predict the exact outcomes of their attempts to lead. Leaders must believe in what they do—in fact, deep down, they all believe in what they do or they wouldn't do it. And we never know for sure that what we do will work out, will win the day, or lead the organization to success.

This is a great and powerful dilemma for executives: if you don't act, you will be seen as a past-promoting bureaucrat. If you act and fail, you will be seen as a bad leader. Effective leaders have the courage to overcome the fear of rejection, what some call the fear of failure, and act. They are not paralyzed by their analyses of all the forces at play, rather they are galvanized by them. Analyses give them greater confidence in their decisions.

Of course, deciding and implementing are two different things. But the decision to act must come first. Skill and wisdom in the how's of implementation are also important—a topic for another chapter.

Pause and think about how much you fear the judgments of others. And which others. Is your fear high medium or low? I doubt that it is non-existent. Some concern for the acceptance of others is essential to all good leaders. And in the end, effective leaders recognize that they must overcome whatever trepidation they may have about the uncertainty of the future and act. They do everything they can to gather the information they need to make reasonable judgments, they consider all of the options, and at last, they must exercise courage and do something.

Finally, note that bluster, impulsiveness, and foolhardiness are not the same as courage. Fools may indeed rush in where wise men fear to tread. Wise men will have done their homework, prepared, analyzed, utilized all their skills, and the skills of their advisors, and then with the odds stacked in their favor, proceed with confidence in the face of possible failure.

Example

Vijay Singh, the professional golfer once said that confidence doesn't come from winning, rather confidence comes from hard work and winning comes from confidence. His point is a powerful one. To have courage, one must have done one's homework and believe that that homework (whether it's mental or physical) has prepared them to perform. If you are untrained in martial arts and walking down the street, you may be, rightfully, fearful. If you have trained for years and are confident in your skills, you can walk down the street with some confidence. This confidence radiates from your being; people can sense it.

Diagram

Challenge

Courage is difficult to assess in the absence of a history of decisions. And it is something one can develop. Perhaps these exercises will help.

1. Consider how much of your life you live in fear of rejection. How much does how you dress, speak, and act reflect your own desires or the expectations of others?
2. Consider how much of your self-esteem depends on the judgments of others. How much do you define your value and worth by the feedback you get from others? If you care too much, you will be paralyzed. If you care too little, you will be seen as marginal and be rejected.
3. Identify people in your organization who you think have the right balance of conformity and innovation. How do they behave? How do they dress? What is different about them? What can you emulate and learn from them?
4. What is your weakest aspect? What can you do to make it a strength? Are you willing to do that?
5. What are your greatest fears? What would it take to overcome them? Again, are you willing to do that?

7. Leadership and Problems

Concept

What is the job of a leader? Take a minute, think about that question and note your answer.

For a long time, leaders were expected to *solve problems*. They were thought to be better educated, better prepared, better able to figure out what needed to be done.

As organizations became more complex, the problem became *finding* the problems. Then, the issue for leadership was how do I found out what needs to be fixed before it becomes a big problem? Internal information systems, that is, the ones the leaders used were critical to this effort. If the systems didn't capture or highlight issues that would become problems, however, the leaders might not know about the budding problems.

When leaders identified and tried to fix problems, they often ran into a bigger problem—resistance of the organization to the intended solutions. Habits, in the aggregate as organizational culture, often resisted making changes in the *way we do things*.

As organizations became larger and larger and the importance of the momentum of organizational culture became better understood, Hal Leavitt at Stanford and others suggested that maybe the job of leadership was to *create* problems. In other words, if the times are changing and the organization is not responding, perhaps leaders needed to help their organizations realize and respond to problems, creating perhaps significant emotional events (SEEs) as described by Morris Massey (*The People Puzzle*) half a century ago.

For many manager-leaders, this was a disturbing thought. How can my job be to *create* problems for my people? How can I turn a herd of *buffalo* from one direction to another? (*Flight of the Buffalo*) Standing at the back and shouting won't do it.

Did you think of the leader's job in terms of problem finding, solving, and creating? If so, you're not alone. Many others have the same view, even today.

But do you even know what a *problem* is? More on this in the next chapter.

Example

Mike Beer, a colleague at the Harvard Business School, once wrote, "… the starting point of any effective change effort is a *clearly defined* business problem."

If leaders and managers couldn't find and solve problems, what else would they do?

Diagram

Problems:
One Source of Change

"…the starting point of any effective change effort is a *clearly defined* business problem."

Beer, Eisenstadt , Spector - Why change programs don't produce change. HBR

What problems do you SEE?

What kind of problem is strong enough to motivate you to initiate change?

Source: https://hbs.edu/faculty/Pages/profile.aspx?facId=6421

Leadership and Problems

LEADERSHIP ACTIVITY	Questions	Answers
Problem Solving	Old	New
Problem Finding	New	Old
Problem Creating	New	New

Source: Adapted from *Pathfinding* by Harold Leavitt, Stanford GBS, 1995

https://google.com/search?q=images+hal+leavitt&tbm=isch&ved=2ahUKEwjniprKybzuAhW
HK98KHW4WCmMQ2-cCegQIABAA&oq=images+hal+leavitt&gs_lcp=CgNpbWcQAzoC
CAA6BQgAELEDOgYIABAIEB5QscIEWI_cBGC3ggVoAHAAeACAAT-IAfMEkgECMT-
GYAQCgAQGqAQtnd3Mtd2l6LWltZZ8ABAQ&sclient=img&ei=VpoRYOeHL4fX_AburKiY
Bg&bih=578&biw=1366&rlz=1C1GCEB_enUS910US910#imgrc=AYhPmgFHEHReIM

Challenge

1. Review your description of the leadership job with the text and make some notes about the differences.
2. What do you think a leader should do if not find and solve problems?
3. What's your definition of a problem? Write that down.
4. Reflect on how much of your time at work is spent on finding and solving problems. (If you are in customer complaints/service, this may be really simple.)

8. What's a "Problem?"

Concept

If you believe that leadership has something to do with finding, solving, and creating problems, then, I guess, you should understand what a problem is. What's your definition?

$$\begin{array}{|c|}
\hline
 \\
 \\
 \\
 \\
 \\
 \\
 \\
 \\
 \\
\hline
\end{array}$$

Hmmm. So, if you said something like "an obstacle to what you want," consider first "who's the *you?*" That is, if you asked the CEO, the VP of HR, the SVP of Marketing, and the CFO what the problems in the company were, would they agree? Probably, not. There would be variation in their answers. So the first challenge in identifying problems is to identify the key players in a situation. Can you list the stakeholders in a situation? Not 20 or 30 people, but the five or six people or groups of people who have an investment in the issue. This is an important part of *seeing what needs to be done* as described earlier.

The second step in identifying problems is figuring out accurately what those stakeholders *want*. In my experience, it turns out that "what do you want?" is a very difficult question. I once taught a second year MBA elective titled "What Do You Want?" to help graduating students figure out, before they hit the 40 year grind, what they were working for: Wealth? Power? Fame? Happy Family? Salvation? Good Health? Big Houses? Fine Cuisine? And so on. Most people struggle with that question—and believe that it will change from decade to decade. How well do 10 year habits change, I ask?

If you don't know what some key players want, perhaps you should go ask them. It's a good way to build relationships, offer your help, and fill out your organizational understanding—realizing of course that (a) they may not know and (b) they may not tell you the real things.

Then, you can construct a simple T-account sheet for each stakeholder and list out their problems. The WANTS are the debit side and you can note their GOTs on the credit side. If there is no gap between what one wants and what one has, then there's no problem. Only where there are want-got gaps are there *problems*. Yes/no?

Thus, problems are *want-got-gaps for somebody*.

Problems can be big ones, little ones, false ones, red herrings ... there are all kinds of problems. We want to see the big and relevant ones to the business situation we are in, yes?

Example

Here are a couple of simple examples. *George* wants to be on budget, but by the end of the third quarter, he's $20,000 behind. We could diagram it like this:

GEORGE	
WANTS	GOTS
To be on budget	-$20,000

Likewise, Mary wants to be promoted but the job went to someone else:

MARY	
WANTS	GOTS
To be promoted	Sandra got the job

You can see how we could easily develop these little T-accounts one for each stakeholder and analyze their situation and how it is contributing to our current situation.

This exercise requires one to see the world through other people's eyes. We have to let go of what we think they should want or what we would want and see the other persons' points of view. This also enhances our ability to *see what needs to be done* described earlier.

Finally, there is always the *universal* or *Providential* or *consultant's* point of view. We can look at a situation and try to think what an expert with total information would want in this situation.

ABC Consulting	
WANTS	GOTS
Client to have strong leadership	Weak leader

You can get a quick *topographical map* of your team's problems by using this technique making one T-account sheet for each person. And you may need to practice the empathy needed to make an accurate display as shown in the second diagram below.

Diagram

The Structure of Problems: Want-Got Gaps for Someone

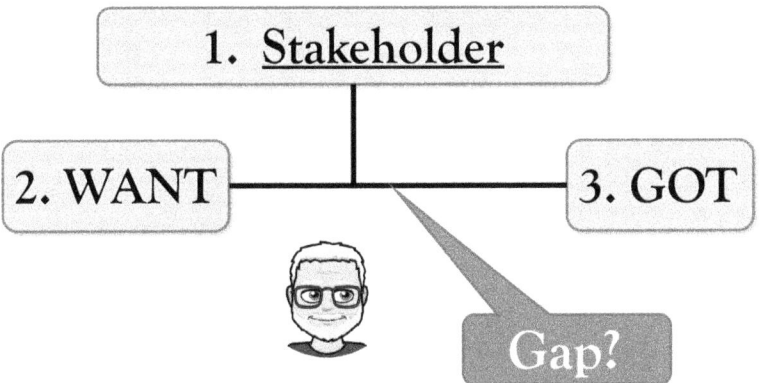

What are the problems here?
(LPV #1. Do you SEE what needs to be done?)

Boss		Subordinate		Work Associates		Family	
Want	Got	Want	Got	Want	Got	Want	Got

Universal "US"	
Want	Got

Challenge

1. Make a T-account list of your problems
2. Make a T-account list of your boss's problems
3. Make a T-account list of your significant other's problems
4. Make a T-account *Providential* list of your company's problems
5. If you are in a team or leading a team, make a list of your team member's problems as best you know them. What's missing? What do you need to learn?

9. The Problem with Problems

Concept

Wait a minute! There is a problem with problems. The problem with problems is that if you view your job, consciously or unconsciously, as finding and solving problems you are living outside-in. Someone else is driving your agenda. In this mode, you are in a reactive frame of mind, responding to issues that others have created.

Problem response is not all bad. Clearly, we have to deal with obstacles to what we want. And some problems are potentially lethal. Being able to sort out, to see, the difference between small problems and big problems is important. But how does one make those judgments? If we make those judgments based on our *elephant*, our Level Three VABEs, we may be making dysfunctional decisions.

But the big issue with problems is that a focus on them put us in a reactionary, outside-in frame of mind. And in that, we yield to the world around us the driving focus of our work.

The other issue with problem solving is that a focus on the problem often leads to short-term results that don't attend to the deeper sources of the problem. This short-term perspective can lead to a false sense of security. Take dieting for example. The problem is we want to be lighter (deeper, feel better), so we diet. We lose a few pounds and we are hungry. We fight the feelings, and for most of us, we think, "Ah, I've lost a few pounds, one piece of toast with honey won't matter THAT much." We don't notice any change, so we have another piece of toast. Or a bit of ice cream. Then we gain weight, and we are back where we started. Efforts to change have a certain negative resiliency—we tend to spring back to our former comfort zone.

This oscillation, back and forth, is a characteristic of efforts to solve problems: we work on them for a while, show a little results, feel good about it, relax, and go backward. In business, I have seen oscillations as companies swing back and forth from growth versus contraction, product focus versus customer focus, internal versus acquisition growth, centralized versus de-centralized, and more.

Example

Consider the company, let's call them Super Satellite Corporation, who built some of the world's most sophisticated satellites. Their focus on quality gave them a high cost structure. Eventually, that cost structure eroded their profit picture. So the board hired a new CEO known for his ability to manage costs. Immediately, the new administration began to implement cost-cutting measures. These measures were draconian and even included the requirement that cross-country flights would include at least one stop in the mid-West in order to get cheaper tickets. Eventually, those cost cutting measures cut so much *fat* out of the company that it couldn't function—and it went bankrupt. Surely there were other reasons for that result—and the focus on solving that one problem, the high cost structure meant that other issues of greater importance were neglected.

I know another organization that went back to its original organization after five years of moving to a new organization. Can you imagine the amount of energy and productivity that was lost by making those changes?

Diagrams

There is a problem with Problem Solving: OSCILLATION

- Recognizing the problem leads to action to solve the problem
  - → Leads to **less intensity** of the problem
  - → Leads to **less action** to solve the problem
  - → Leads to the problem remaining
- **False sense of security:** you know just what you
  If you didn't have problems, what would you think about? How would you spend your time?
- What drives the action is the intensity of the problem → **REACTIVE OSCILLATION.**

Source: Adapted from Robert Fritz, *The Path of Least Resistance.*

Structural Conflict leads to Oscillation

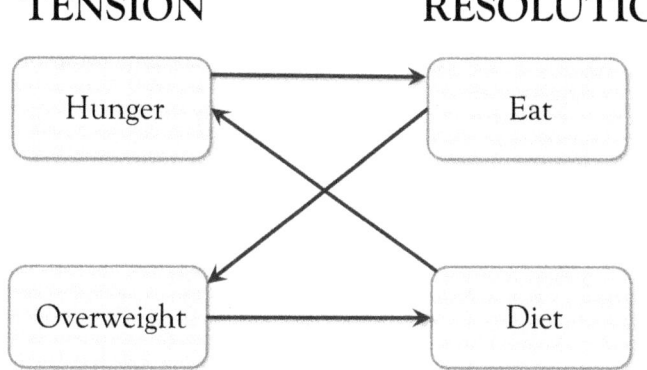

Source: Adapted from Robert Fritz, *The Path of Least Resistance.*

Organizational Oscillation drains energy

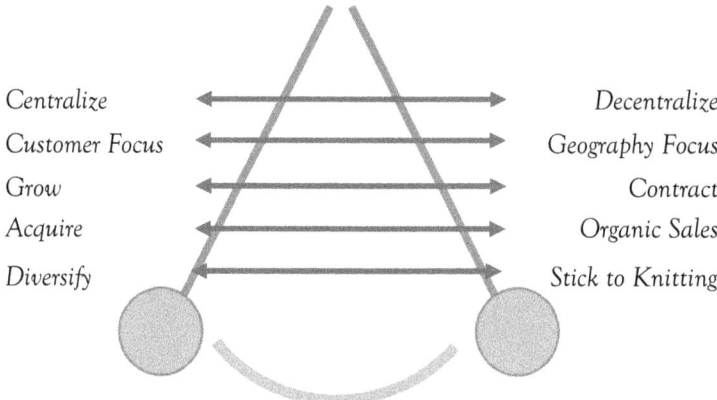

Challenge

1. Identify as many oscillations as you can in your own life. Include the opposing end points of the oscillations.
2. Identify as many oscillations as you can in your organization. What has been the impact on the organizational culture and energy level of those oscillations?

3. Identify the main problems in your life. Note who created them.

4. Identify the main problems in your organization. Who do you think created them?

5. How much of your time do you spend each day working on problems created by others? What percent of your time is devoted to these problems?

10. Leader as Creator

Concept

As we noted in the last chapter, the problem with a problem-oriented approach to leadership is that it is fundamentally reactive, outside-in. When one takes a problem oriented approach to leadership one lets the outside world set one's agenda and strategy. There is some theoretic basis for this. Organizations who can adapt to changes taking place in the world around them are more likely to survive. Darwin noted that it's not the strongest organism that survives, it's the most adaptable.

At the same time, depending on what problems that the world presents to you that the leader responds to, one may be doing exactly the wrong, and short-sighted thing.

The alternative, outlined by Robert Fritz in his book *The Path of Least Resistance*, is to take the point of view of artists like authors, sculptors, and painters—to **create**. Fritz's compelling logic is that problem solving leads to reactive oscillation, which we discussed in the last chapter.

Jung argued that none of the major problems in life could ever be solved, they were only supplanted by other more important life forces. This is a powerful idea. Rather than focusing on solving problems, why not focus on creating a bigger, more powerful force?

The creative force is one such force.

Fritz's approach begins with an accurate assessment of the situation at the moment. This is akin to Jim Collins's "confront the brutal facts" in *Good to Great*. Jack Welch proposed a similar VABE in *Control Your Destiny* when he wrote "accept reality as it is, not as it was nor as you wish it were."

The second step in Fritz's plan is to create a vision of where you want to be. This is a key step. You cannot buy a vision. Well, you could perhaps from a consulting firm. But then you wouldn't be leading, you'd be the executor, the implementer not the creator/author. Fritz's notion here is that like a composer, an artist, or a sculptor, you see in your mind's eye what you want to do, what you want to build, and then you begin to make it happen.

Actually, Fritz would say, just let it sit there. *If you want it bad enough, it will grow on you and begin to shape your behavior.* You will begin studying how to make it happen. You will run into obstacles (problems), but they won't be much more than speed bumps. Like the aikido principle of leading energy beyond the point of contact,[1] you will be extending your view beyond the immediate problems and with a direction and a focus.

So, one alternative to the problem-oriented leadership approach is the creative approach. The core question here is "what do you want to create?" If you can't answer that question, with regard to your own life, your current responsibilities or your organization, perhaps you're not ready yet for the leadership role.

Example

What is the energy difference between organizations that want to make as much money as they can and those that seek to serve a particular customer base?

Consider, for example, the goal of Google, "to organize all the world's information."[2] Truck load after truck load of books checked out of Stanford libraries being scanned into a gigantic database that will digitize as much of the world's written wisdom as possible. Here is one example of a clear desire to create something: a digital, online available library of all the world's books.

PROBLEMS	CREATION
Reduce Pollution	Create a healthy living environment
Increase Profits	Create a sustainable company
Hire (Fire) more people	Create a flexible company
Gain Control	Create a responsive company
Raise the Stock Price	Create lasting contribution to society
Lay Brick	Create a Cathedral
Increase Membership	Create an attractive learning company

---

[1] In aikido, one strives to meet (*ai*) or merge with the opponent's energy or force (*ki*), and then lead that force in a different direction. The point of contact between opponents is often the focus in other martial arts like boxing or taekwondo. Focusing on that point can produce lots of power and a more powerful opponent can then win. By focusing beyond the point of impact, one can often turn the opponent's force in a new direction and ultimately throw them to the ground.

[2] http://voanews.com/a/google-plans-to-put-all-the-worlds-books-online-80427622/416834.html

Diagrams

"Problems" are Insolvable

"All of the greatest and most important problems of life are fundamentally insoluble...they can never be solved, but only outgrown. This "out growth" proved on further investigation to require a new level of consciousness. One higher or wider interest appeared on the patient's horizon, and through this broadening of his or her outlook, the insoluble problem lost its urgency. It was not solved logically in its own terms, **but faded when confronted with a new and stronger life urge."**

~ Carl Jung

Source: https://google.com/search?q=images+carl+jung&tbm=isch&ved=2ahUKEwjG75Hyy
bzuAhVxneAKHYJsDBIQ2-cCegQIABAA&oq=images+carl+jung&gs_lcp=CgNpbWcQAz-
IGCAAQCBAeMgYIABAIEB4yBggAEAgQHJoCCAA6BAgAEB46BggAEAUQHICQmA
ZY9KMGYKCrBmgAcAB4AIABTogBqASSAQE5mAEAoAEBqgELZ3dzLXdpeilpbWfA
AQE&sclient=img&ei=qpoRYMbyH_G6ggeC2bGQAQ&bih=578&biw=1366&rlz=1C1G
CEB_enUS910US910#imgrc=mn9mpBrw6BoPMM

Fritz's Alternative to Problem Orientation: Orient to the Creative Process

1. **Describe** accurately where you *are*
   (Collins' "confront the brutal facts")

2. Make a *vision* of what you want to create with your life/work.
   Make sure it's something you want so bad, you are magnetically attracted to it.

3. Formally **choose** the result you want.

4. **Move** on (if you really want it, you will naturally 'flow' in that direction.)

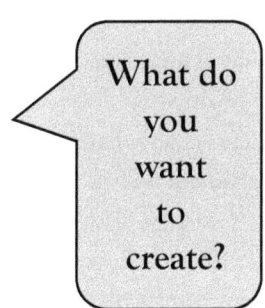

Challenge

1. What are you trying to create in your life?

2. What are you trying to create at work?

3. Practice thinking every day on your way into work, "What am I going to create today?"

11. Power and Leadership

Concept

There is, I say, a difference between *power and leadership*. All leadership exerts power, but not all power is leadership. Power is the ability to get others to do what you want them to do. So while leadership is to varying degrees powerful, some people with lots of power are not leaders. I say that because in my view leadership consists of the ability and the willingness to influence others so that they respond voluntarily. Without a voluntary response, we cannot call it leadership. It may be the use of power, or the *abuse* of power, but it's not leadership.

In order to understand more about power and leadership and the relation between them, let us first consider power and its sources. French and Raven (1959) identified five sources of power: legitimate, coercive, reward, expertise, and referent. **Legitimate** *power* means one has the title, the legal authority to influence. Legitimate power accrues to people who hold offices like chief executive, president, director, bishop, don, or any other recognized title of leadership will have some power simply because they hold the office, regardless of their personal abilities. They may or may not be effective leaders. People who rely on their titles to influence others are not developing their leadership skills, they are simply exerting power given to their offices. The underlying assumption related to legitimate power is something like "You must do what I say because I am the <fill in the box>." When parents say, do what I say "because I'm your father," they are relying on legitimate power.

Coercive *power* comes from the ability to threaten or hurt others so that they are forced to comply or in looser terms, *follow*. People will do what coercive people ask because they fear them. Threatening people with bodily harm, financial harm, the loss of their jobs, harm to their families or any other kind of harm are employing coercive power. The underlying assumption for such people is something like "I can and will hurt you unless you do what I ask." Sadly, for many people, coercive power is their primary means of influencing others.

Reward *power* refers to influence developed from exchange. If person A offers person B something that person B wants, they have influence over them. Most for-profit enterprises operate heavily on reward power, offering employees wages to do things they otherwise might not do. Parents often use this source of power too when they offer candy, toys, trips, or money to their children when they perform in a particular way. Rewards or exchanges only have influence when the "leader" offers something the other person wants.

Expertise power flows from a person's knowledge or skill in an area that someone else admires or wants. We listen to experts when they speak, and we listen more intently when they are experts in an area of importance to us. We may admire experts in fields unrelated to our own interests, but are not likely to model them. We are more likely to model or emulate people who are experts in areas that we value whether it be finance, sports, music, or careers.

Referent power is more ethereal. Referent power depicts the influence a person has over another who wants to be like them. While this may seem similar to expertise power, referent power has more to do with status and condition than expertise. We allow famous people or rich people or celebrity people to influence us because internally we want to be like them, to join their clubs, to go out in their circles, to bask in their presence, and in some sense feed off their beings. We may not want to do what they do or even know how they do it (expertise power), but we do want to be included in their circles.

TRADITIONAL BASES OF POWER	
LEGITIMATE	Based on you "legal" title, position of office (bureau)
COERCION	Based on your ability to hurt, intimidate, inflict pain, or punish
EXPERTISE	Based on your knowledge and expertise
REWARD	Based on your ability to give people something they want
REFERENT	Based on your status, fame, position, and the adoration of others

As suggested, power is not a necessary or sufficient condition for the emergence of leadership. Here, we distinguish power from leadership in the following ways to help shed insights into relationship between the two.

Power is not leadership. The five sources of power as articulated above are an example of one of the three identifiable forms of power: *power-over*.

The other two forms of power refer to *power-to*[3] and *power-from*[4] respectively. *Power-over* usually derives from an individual's position in a time and place that is regarded as superior over others (see Hollander and Offermann 1990). The basis for this form of power is also defined as the more or less enduring relationship between the leader and the led, which gives rise to the power in the first instance (e.g., French 1956). Power does not require goal compatibility. It only requires dependence. A leader's dependence on this form of power can lead to the undermining of relationships with followers. This form of power also takes as its starting point the notion of goal incongruence between leaders and followers: that the person with power and the person subject to it have incompatible objectives (Tjosvold, Andrews, and Struthers,[5] *Group and Organizational Management*, September 1, 1991).

Leadership in my view has three components: ability, willingness, and a voluntary response. Leadership ability refers to the capacity for influencing others. Leaders use a variety of, a mix of, power sources to influence others. People have different skills sets and may employ at different times and in different ways and in different strengths various mixes of legitimate, coercive, reward, expertise, and referential influences. The larger one's overall mix of influence skills is, the more powerful they are.

That does not mean in my experience that everyone with those skills will be eager, *willing*, to use them. I have met many people who would make good leaders but just don't want to do it. The reasons they offer include "not wanting to play god and muck around in people's lives," "fear of doing the wrong thing," "timid personality," and others. The president of our university once stated that he was looking for a new dean for one of our schools and had two candidates, one who did not want the job. It seemed obvious to him and to us that while a person might be well equipped to lead, they may or may not want to be put in a leadership position. Again, note that those in formal positions of authority have

---

[3] *Power-to* suggests the empowerment of followers or the sharing of power with followers.

[4] *Power-from* is the ability to resist the power of others by effectively fending off their unwanted demands. It can also be seen as having the ability to protect oneself.

[5] Power and Interdependence in Work Groups: Views of Managers and Employees,

some legitimate authority but may or may not be effective overall leaders. Incumbents we can call accurately and conservatively **authoritors**. Whether they are or can develop into leaders is an open question.

In leadership, rights are voluntarily conferred. This implies that leaders must be able to elicit voluntary response in others. As such, if a person has the skill set and the willingness to apply that skill set, the final element of real leadership is whether or not the intended followers *choose* to follow. Without that choice, how can we say the person is in fact leading as opposed to dictating? Are dictators leaders? Looking through historical and power lenses, perhaps. In the modern world, in my view, unless there's a voluntary response, you cannot call it leadership.

> # Power
> ## is the
> ## ability to get
> ## others to do
> ## what you want
> ## them to do.
> (outside-in)

Leadership is ...

1. The **ability** to influence others, and

2. The **willingness** to influence others

3. So that they respond **voluntarily**.
   (inside-out)

4. with positive **energy!**

Challenges

1. How do people exert power over you?
2. How do you exert power over others? Whom and how?
3. Which of the sources of power do you respect/admire the most?
4. Write down your list of favorite leaders—current and historical. What kinds of power did they use?
5. What kinds of power did your parents use on you?
6. How has that affected your own influence style?

12. The Diamond Model of Leadership

Concept

What's YOUR mental map of leadership? Do you have one? Take a moment and draw out your current thinking about what leadership is. What are the key elements? How do they relate to each other? Take a clean sheet of paper and sketch out your current formed or fuzzy model of leadership. C'mon, give me your best shot! After you do yours, I will share mine. No cheating now. It doesn't count if you say, "ah, I knew that" *after* the fact.

Leadership, I think, has several key components. These include personal characteristics of the leader, personal characteristics of the followers, something about the challenges the leader faces, something about the organizational context in which the leader is working, and, of course, something about results. If we simplify for the sake of a diagram, we have L for leader, E for employees/relationships/followers, S for strategic story, O for organization, and R for results.

A few thoughts about each element and the linkages between them. First, personal characteristics of the leader would seem to be obviously important. How you present yourself, how you speak, how you think, your priorities, your style, your beliefs about the way the world works, all of these things and more will contribute to or detract from your ability to influence others. Henry Mintzberg, a leadership guru, among others thinks that reflection or self-knowledge is one of the most important leadership characteristics. While we haven't identified a set of personal traits that define the effective leader (although many have tried for decades), clearly who you are makes a difference in your ability to lead. The big question here is "Who are you?"

Second, what do you believe you should spend your limited time and energy on? From all the possible options in the world of things screaming for your time and attention, which ones do you choose? How do you make that decision? I call this *vision* in the sense that people will work on things they think are important because they want to create something. Leaders have visions of what they want to do. What are yours? The linkage between you and your visions we could call your strategic thought patterns. The answer to the question "what's important to you to work on?" defines your *strategic story*. People want to know, if they are going to follow, "What's your story?"

Third, what are the characteristics of the people you intend to lead? What do you know about them? Where do they come from? What do they want? How can you get energy out of them? A *leader* without followers is of course no leader. So, now the question is, "Can you sell your story to others?" You may have a good story, but if you can't sell it, you won't have any followers. Further, if your story is weak, the bond between followers and strategy will be weak and diffuse as will the energy of the followers.

The fourth element in my mental map is the organization. You may know who you are, you may have a story to tell, and you may be good at telling it, but if you are laboring in a moribund, contradictory energy-draining organization, you won't likely be able to accomplish your goals. Also, if the organization if poorly designed, followers won't bind to it, loyalty will be low, and commitment will waiver. The importance of this element in leadership implies that good leaders are organizational architects. They know how to mobilize and organize their followers so that their energies are focused on the strategic vision. The question here is, "What's your design?"

All of these elements taken together—the leader, the vision, the followers, and the organization—produce some kind of results, good, bad, or otherwise. Most people think only of financial results. Profits are important, but they are not the only thing. In today's inter-connected world, *results* means we look not only at profits but also at long-term profits and that means we have to consider the impact of the leadership elements on the surrounding society, on the environment and on the sustainability of the enterprise. You probably have strong feelings about this assertion; most people do. If you're interested, there are a number of additional places you can look for more information.

The *south-west* axis represents the strength of the bond between employees and the organization. That bond is a function of several things including employee VABEs and organizational designs.

Finally, note that the *south-east* axis in the diamond shaped model below indicates the need to lead change. By the time you have figured out who you are, what your vision is, convinced others to follow you, and designed the right organization, the world has moved, things have changed. To lead, you have to be a leader of change. The mere fact of having a vision means you have to get from here to there, and that's change.

Diagram

So, my basic mental map of leadership looks like this.

Elements in Effective Leadership

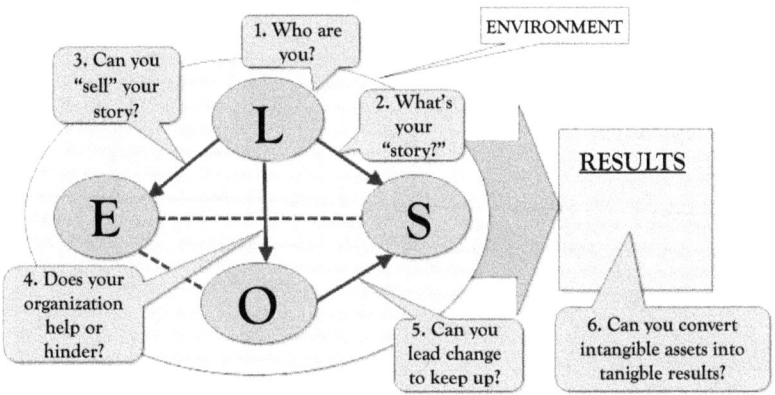

How does this compare with your mental map? What am I missing? What are you missing? Are there ways we could combine our models into a more accurate joint model?

Challenge

1. What things in your model must come together to produce good leadership results?
2. Do you believe that who you are makes a difference in your ability to lead?
3. Write a one sentence description of who you are.
4. Do you think a person can lead (not manage) without a strategic story?
5. Where would you like to take people?
6. Can you sell your story? What methods would you use to convince others to follow you?
7. Can you design an organization that will help not hinder your efforts to accomplish your vision?
8. Can you lead change? Do you understand the change process? Are you a change master?

13. Choice and Obligation

Concept

Imagine a continental divide between two lands, the Land of Choice and the Land of Obligation. When a person goes from the Land of Choice to the Land of Obligation, what happens?

What happens to energy level—up, flat, or down?
What happens to productivity—up, flat, or down?
What happens to innovation—up, flat, or down?
What happens to adaptability—up, flat, or down?
You pick your dimension, when people go from choice to obligation, bad things happen.

Some will say, "Wait a minute, many of us choose our obligations, like military service or marriage or children." Yes, AND review in one's mind the current thoughts about those previous choices. When we go from "I chose to do this" to "I *have* to do this," what happens to our energy, productivity, invention, and so on? Even though we made the choice, if we forget why we made that choice and simply view an activity or condition as an obligation, that mindset produces a reduction in positive emotions and behavior. Yes/no?

Example

Now, pick a typical work day. On your way into work, what is your most common, dominant thought?

Most people from my experience asking this question all around the world will say, "What do I *have* to do today?" Notice the obligatory nature of that thought. Doug Newburg first brought this to my attention. I assert that this self-imposed obligation is an energy draining event. It puts us in an obligatory mindset right at the beginning of the day. Because this thought is so common and so pervasive, it has become *non-conscious* for most people. This Level Two (Conscious Thought) habit (unthinkingly repetitive) is an energy drainer.

What's the alternative? "What do I *want* to do today?" or better "What do I want to *create* today?" *Merely* shifting one's thinking from obligation to choice infuses more energy, creativity, and excitement into our minds—and behavior.

Diagram

What happens when one crosses the divide between choice and obligation?

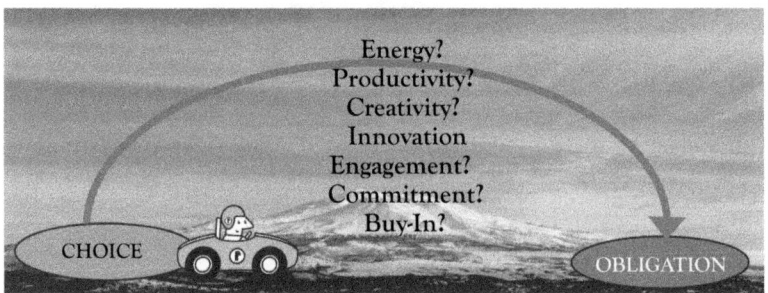

Challenge

1. I encourage you to think consciously about your thoughts at the beginning of each day. Are you putting yourself mindlessly into an *obligatory mindset* and perhaps unwittingly reducing your own energy level?
2. Can you develop a new and more productive habit of learning to think habitually, "what do I want to *create* today?"
3. How much of your life do you live in obligation?
4. How do you reconcile your daily lifestyle and energy with the obligations that you chose? For example, marriage, parenting, mortgages, military service, jobs taken, and so on.

14. Inside-Out or Outside-In

Concept

One question for would-be leaders to consider is "how much of your life do you live outside-in?" The *outside* world is everything outside of you. The *inside* world is everything inside of you. We live outside-in (OI) when we censor what we do (Level One Visible Behavior) because of our concerns about what others might think or say.

What others think and say is an important consideration. The ability of humans to work together has been a major factor in the success of the race. At the same time, living OI means fitting in, conforming, and obeying the rules of the group. We obey the rules of the group because of *the fear of rejection.* The fear of rejection is one of the main ways that humans have had to control the behavior of others.

The alternative is obviously to live inside-out (IO). When we live inside-out, we are willing to assert our point of view for the consideration of others. Consider a scale of inside-outness (on the left in the accompanying diagram) ranging from zero to 100 percent. At the bottom of the scale lie cowards, doormats, spineless, wishy-washy people with no opinions of their own, timid folks who always do what others say. At the top of the scale are self-centered, ego-centric, narcissistic SOBs.

Now, I invite you to consider two questions. The first is, "how much of your life do you live outside-in?" In other words, how often do you consciously or semi-consciously think "they won't like that" or "they won't approve of that" or "that's not how we're supposed to do things" before you speak or act? I know it varies from situation to situation, AND make an estimate on average how often you live outside-in. The inverse of course is your average life pressure inside-out.

Second question: "if you wanted to be a leader in society, where should your behavior be on the inside-out scale?" After some reflection and discussion, most managers worldwide, in my experience, would say in the third quartile, somewhere between 50 and 75 percent. By this they mean that good leaders should be willing to listen to others and yet on average are in the majority willing to assert their points of view.

I think that most people underestimate how much they live outside-in. And that is not all bad. Living OI is after all the basis for society. Without obedience to group norms, we couldn't cooperate or form societies. We rely on people to obey the law, to obey the speed limit, to listen to our community leaders in order to expect that *things* will move along in an orderly fashion. Those who don't obey—we chastise, send to their rooms, fine, imprison, or even kill.

Too much conformity however leads to a perpetuation of yesterday and a lack of innovation and progress.

Example

James Joyce in his anthology, *Dubliners*, tells a short story entitled "Clay." The young woman in that story has no opinions of her own. Every group she is in, every conversation she is in, she constantly tries to mold her views to fit those of the people around her. She is a social clay. She is living outside-in. I know a woman who lived her life like that. She was married to a man who had strong, uncompromising VABEs. At lunch once, this woman was sitting on the inside of the booth and asked her husband to let her out to go to the bathroom. He said, "No, you can wait 'til I've finished my lunch." And she complied. This woman was also living her life outside-in.

Diagram

The Conformity / Leader Dilemma

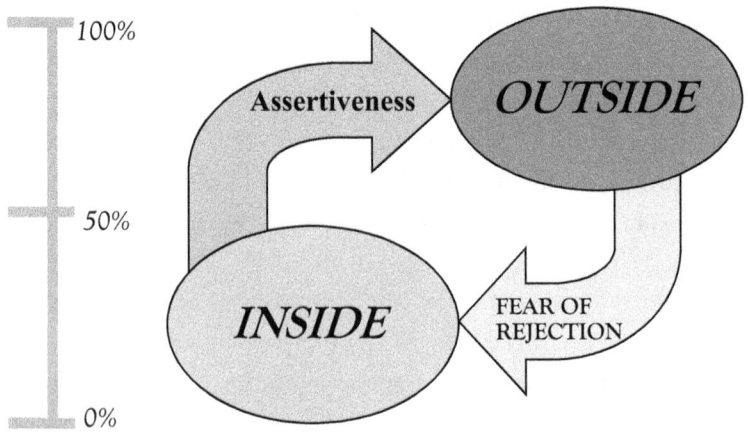

Challenge

1. So, my invitation here is to reflect on how much you conform and how much you assert your point of view (if you have one).
2. Of course, if you don't have a point of view on any particular issue, you will be consigned to the role of listener absorbing OI what others have to say.
3. A key element in leading is the development of new thoughts, new possibilities, and new action. That requires homework, study, reflection, analysis, and conclusions.
4. And the willingness to test the boundaries of what others think is right, correct, and acceptable.
5. How often do you strive to fit in as opposed to shape the environment around you?
6. How often do you allow others to express their opinions? Are you living too much inside-out?
7. Whose rejection do you fear?
8. Can one expect to live a life without rejection?
9. How should one handle rejection?

15. Buy-In

Concept

When you ask someone to do something, you could get a variety of responses. These responses, what many business managers call *buy-in*, range in analog not binary fashion from outright revolt to passionate acceptance. Consider the following possibilities:

At level 7 (see chart below), people might respond to your request with *active resistance*. This is the stuff of strikes, rebellion, revolt, and active antagonism. People who fight what you want are resisting you. They may organize a union, sue you, or do what they can in the market-place to undermine you and your company.

At level 6, people might respond with *passive resistance*. They don't fight you, but they go slow, lose the paperwork, drop a wrench in the gears, or drag their feet. Passive resistors are not willing to stand up and be counted, but they are willing to slyly sabotage the works. Passive resistors are a sea anchor drag on an organization.

At level 5, people can manifest *apathy*, they just don't care what you say or do. This often comes up in organizations where the senior leadership changes regularly but the lower levels continue on, such as large bureaucracies and civil organizations. They have seen leaders come and go, they know that each is trying to make their resume look good, and they know that "this, too, shall pass." So, they just continue doing what they have been doing, ignoring the leadership. Apathetic people keep their heads down, do just what they need to get by, and create a culture of mediocrity.

At level 4, we get a condition that I detest, *compliance*. Compliance means that people say they will do what you ask and all the while they are looking for ways around the rule or request. They say "yes," and then they look for ways to get around the rule. Compliant workers obey the letter of the "law" but not the spirit.

At level 3 we have *agreement* where the person says, "I will do what you ask me to do without reservation." They may not be energetic or enthusiastic, but they are willing to do the thing you ask.

At level 2, we have *engagement* where people not only agree to do what you ask, but they are actively and positively disposed to do it. They have a positive value for what you ask them to do. People with engagement *want* to do what you ask.

At level 1, we have *passion* where the person says or thinks or believes that what you ask them to do is the most important thing in life and they will sacrifice evenings, weekends, exercise, relationships, and vacations in order to strive to accomplish what you ask. They might even blow themselves up for what you ask.

BUY-IN	
1. Passion	What you ask is the #1 thing in my life.
2. Engagement	I **want** to do what you ask.
3. Agreement	Okay. I will do what you ask.
4. Compliance	I will do what you ask but I will be looking for loopholes and ways around it all the time.
5. Apathy	I really don't care what you ask one way or the other. Odds are I will be here after you're gone.
6. Passive Resistance	I don't like what you ask, so I will go slow, make mistakes, maybe lose some paperwork.
7. Active Resistance	I hate what you ask and I am going to fight you, maybe drop a wrench in the works, sabotage you or form a union.

We can think of this scale as *an energy scale* with the neutral line lying between apathy and compliance. The responses above that line are levels of increasing positive energy, the responses below that line are levels of increasing negative energy. So, what a leader is really trying to do with any endeavor is create, find, or release positive energy in those who are responding. Getting *buy-in* is not a binary event, it is an analog event. When you ask people to do something, pay attention to their level of *buy-in*. Don't assume because they say "yes" at Level One Visible Behavior that they mean it. Watch their energy level. The observant leader will note the levels of buy-in he or she is getting from others and adjust his style to compensate. *So, I note again, leadership is about managing energy, first in yourself and then in those around you.*

Diagram

Levels of BUY-IN

1. Passion ("What you ask is the #1 thing in my life.")   (+)

2. Engagement ("I **want** to do what you ask.")

3. Agreement ("I will do what you ask.")

4. Compliance ("Okay" but where are the loopholes?)

5. Apathy ("I just don't care.")

6. Passive Resistance ("Oops.")

7. Active Resistance ("No way in hell.")   (-)

What's in *your* wake?

Challenge

1. Every time you ask someone else to do something, ask yourself what *your* level of buy-in is to that task and how important it is.

2. When you ask someone else to do something, try to see and measure their level of buy-in to the request. If it's low, ask yourself if the way you delivered the request or the task itself contributed to their reaction.

3. Remember, in every conversation, you are affecting the energy level of the other person.

4. What's in your wake? What kind of energy level do you leave in the people behind you?

SECTION II

Who Are You?

The Northern Ball in our basic diamond model is about understanding human behavior. The premise here is that if leaders don't understand themselves or have an effective model of why people behave the way they do, how could they make good team or organizing decisions? The answer seems obvious to me, yet in my experience, most executives and managers have thought very little about who they are, who would complement their particular personality on a team and about a model of human behavior that includes what we have long known. This section is intended to enrich your understanding of why you and your colleagues do what they do. With a better understanding of human behavior, your attempts to influence them will be empowered—and less like groping around in the dark.

16. The Northern Ball: Who Am I?

Concept

The premise here is that who you are affects your ability to influence others. How you stand. How you dress. How you groom. Your speech. The volume of your voice. Your eye contact. Your facial expressions. Your body language. Your posture. The words you choose. Your sense of self-confidence. Your poise. Your polish. Your eccentricity. All of these things and more will affect your ability to get others to respond to you. If you expect others to obey you just because of your title, you are mistaken.

Taken together, these things make up what we call "presence." Some might call it "charisma." I don't like that term, only because it is so ethereal. Presence has components and one can deconstruct them and work on them. I say, your presence will affect whether people will listen to you—or not. Do you agree?

Example

People who knew him or were in a room with him say that Bill Clinton commanded the attention in the room. Not by his insistence. Just the way he walked in, began talking with people, his presence was felt throughout. Have you ever been around someone like that? Someone whose very presence in the room electrifies? Whom would you cite? Contrast that with some students I have had who, after raising their hands in a class of 65, would speak so quietly that no one could hear what they were saying.

Diagram

Who
are
you?

Challenge

1. How does the way you present yourself affect your ability to influence others?
2. What aspects of your public presentation would you like to improve?
3. Practice being confident. To do that, you need to have a thoughtful opinion. Confidence comes from preparation.
4. Stand tall. Don't slump.
5. Speak so everyone in the room can hear you.
6. Find the right pace—not too fast nor too slow.
7. Pay attention to your appearance, it matters.
8. Like a good stage actor, manage your facial expressions. Sometimes more dramatic.
9. Look at the people you are talking to not the floor or the sky.

17. Early Childhood Development

Concept

Much of our adult behavior is based on the foundations laid early in childhood. Freud once noted that we spend out adult lives dealing with the residue of our childhoods. Most psychologists have concluded that one's basic behavior patterns are established between the years of 0 to 6–10 years.

The first basis for our behavior is a gift we receive at birth—a set of genes. Genes are tangible packets of information passed on from generation to generation in our DNA. We live in a time unprecedented. We have mapped the human genome, some 40,000 genes, and are learning week by week what they all do and how they function.

What do you think genes determine?

Surely genes determine certain physical characteristics like eye color, hair color, height, skin color, and others. But genes can also affect our behavior. At birth, the human brain is growing at the rate of 250,000 cells per minute! Yes, per minute! Explosive growth. During the first year of life, 90 percent of nutrition goes into the brain. Eventually, a child gets a full complement of about 100 billion brain cells. Each of these can connect to 10,000 other cells! That is one quadrillion synaptic connections.

And amidst all of those brain cells and connections, floats some 300 known hormones, chemicals that allow the brain to function. If one gets a little too much of one and a little too little of another, bad things can happen. One might have a little, moderate, or a lot of bi-polar disorder, or of obsessive compulsive disorder, or attention deficit disorder, or attention deficit hyper-activity disorder, or some other mental variation. These variations can affect our behavior in correspondingly minimal, moderate or major ways. How many people do you know that exhibit any of these variations? Whatever those genetic gifts were, all of us face the existential question, "What am I going to do with the 'gene gift' I was given?"

In addition to the gift of genes, a new child begins at birth to receive a set of instructions. The new baby doesn't think about these instructions, she can't even talk or walk yet. But she is experiencing countless experiences daily that are "teaching" her what is okay and what is not okay. As she learns to control her arms and legs and tongue, she is also picking up signals about her place in the world and what she can and cannot do.

This second set of instructions are VABEs—Values, Assumptions, Beliefs, and Expectations—about the way the world is or should be. Parents may or may not be aware of the VABEs they are passing on.

In the meantime, every child is experiencing four fundamental questions: When I am hungry, will I be fed? When I am wet, will I be changed? When I am cold, will I be made warm? And when I am alone and afraid, will I be comforted?

If a child gets sufficient answers to these questions, he may grow up with a *whole* personality. If a child gets insufficient answers to these questions, it may grow up with *holes* in its personality.

So, the issue is, for every child, when—if ever—will they grow up? What's your definition of adulthood? Is a 30 year old an adult? They can drive, drink, go to war, marry, and so on. I have a different view. When, if ever, will they become mature enough to look at the childhood gifts—the genes and VABEs—they were given and *decide* consciously which of those teachings and habits will they KEEP, LOSE, or ADD to their adult repertoire. Most people never get there; they live and die simply replicating the gifts they inherited. "Gifts" here doesn't mean presents, rather the start in life given to them by their parents, the genes, and the VABEs.

Let me explain.

Example

There was a knock at my door one day. A woman stuck her head in and said, "Can we talk?" She came in and closed the door. Not a good sign. Then, she sat down in my visitor's chair and began to sob. Not a good sign. She explained, "You don't know me, I didn't have you for class. I'm graduating in a week, and I just got the job I've always wanted, working for the company I've always wanted to work for, making more money than I ever thought I'd make."

"Hmmm," says I offering her a Kleenex, "what's the problem?"

"Well, I called my mother to tell her about this. My mom volunteers at the hospital, and she is a member of the Garden Club and gets on TV and radio now and then. Within fifteen seconds she had turned the conversation from me to her. Wasn't I happy for her because she was going to be on television over the weekend. Wasn't I happy for her because she was quoted in the newspaper last weekend. And it's been this way my whole life!"

Time out. What should I say?

I was thinking about her mother. When her mother was a small child, I was wondering what kind of answers did she get to those four fundamental questions, sufficient or insufficient? What's your guess? If the answers were insufficient, she may have grown up with holes in her personality that she tried to fill in with her children. And how would she parent? With the focus on her needs rather than on her child's needs.

This might be manifest at Level One with statements like these: If you loved your mommy, you would toilet train sooner so I don't have to deal with this mess. If you loved me, you wouldn't interrupt me when I am busy. If you loved me, you would clean up after yourself so I didn't have to. I you cared for me, you would do the dishes without my having to ask you. And so on.

How many times a day would these messages be given? How many times in a year or ten years? So that at age 30 (is she an adult?), this graduating MBA student comes to a complete stranger, sobbing, at the pinnacle of her professional success to date seeking advice and some consolation.

The additional danger is that this student will marry, have a child, and parent her child in the same way,[1] not because she is mean or cruel but

---

[1] See Miller, A. 2008. *Thee Drama of the Gifted Child*, Klein, M. 2002. *Love, Guilt and Reparation,* Glasser, W. 1998. *Choice Theory,* Ellis, A., 1961. *A Guide to Rational Living,* Wilshire. and James, Oliver, 2002. *They F**K You Up* Bloomsbury. for starters.

because that's all she knows. So the psychological profile she "inherited" will be passed on from generation to generation just like genes.

Diagram

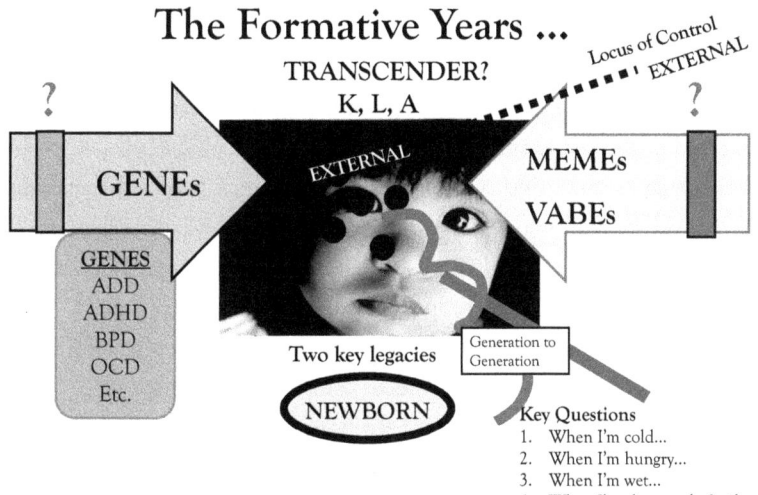

The Formative Years ...

Challenge

1. Reflect on and write down how you would assess how you have handled your genetic gifts.

2. Write down the ten major VABEs that your parents taught you. Which of them do you agree with and not agree with?

3. What, if anything, have you added to your personality since leaving home?

4. How does your current personality affect your leadership skills?

18. The Most Important Question in Life

Concept

Given the discussion of early childhood development in the previous chapter, we come to what I think is the single most important question in life. "Will you ever be anything more than a vessel transmitting the genes and VABEs of previous generations on to the next?" This is the underlying question that faces the young woman who came into my office as described in the last chapter.

In effect, I think this question determines the quality of being an adult. "When, if ever, will you *transcend* the genes and VABEs that were given to you by your parents and choose when you are no longer a defenseless child what you want to keep, lose, and/or add to who you are?"[2] Only then, I say, does one "become a person"[3] and take charge of their life.

This is a huge issue. How much does your upbringing shape who you are as an age-defined adult? If you had been born in a country half way around the world (pick one: Pakistan? China? Costa Rico? Uganda?), how would your world view be different today? How would your VABEs be different?

Viruses, as you know, have shells and limited internal information, relatively small amount of DNA. Yet they are inexorable in their effort to replicate themselves. Most humans are the same. Generation after generation. Yet VABEs are learned. Babies are not born with a set of VABEs. They acquire them from their environment. Mostly from their parents. Who intentionally and unintentionally shape a child's sense of worthiness, of space to be, of what's right and wrong, of whom to trust, and whom not to trust.

Example

My wife, for example, has significant ADHD. As a child, she fidgeted. This annoyed her parents. As a result of her behavior and her parents' VABEs, she was often beaten with a switch, which she had to choose. Her father, a public pillar in their church, kicked her down a flight of stairs while holding on to

---

[2] Read *The Evolving Self* by Mihalyi Csikszentmihalyi in which I found this concept. One of my top five all-time best books. Not easy reading, but dense and profound.

[3] See Rogers, C. n.d. *On Becoming a Person.*

her hair. He ridiculed her face, her body, her behavior. At age seven, she was taken to a doctor for a check-up. The doctor said, "This child is dying. If something doesn't change, I will have to call Social Services and have her put in a new home." Her mother said, "I know what's wrong; I'll fix it."

Later, she was viewed as a shy person by her peers in high school and college. She seldom spoke. She strove to think well of herself by getting good grades and by making herself attractive. She dreaded going home for holidays. When we married, her personality was "tiny."

One day, nine years later, I came home and she was curled up in bed in a fetal position, sobbing. I asked what the matter was. She said, "I was just talking to my mother on the phone. I asked her what happened that the doctor said they might have to take me away. She said, 'You were repulsive!'"

So, here was a 33-year-old mother of two lying in bed in the middle of the afternoon sobbing because her mother thought she was repulsive. Today, at 67, she still struggles with those feelings. She understands them better, and the underlying feelings of confusion—I *should* love my mother; my mother *should* love me; *what* is going on?—linger.

As we described earlier, current research confirms that people make fast decisions and judgments based on their deep, underlying VABEs, before they even "think" rationally. Changing, shaping, reviewing, altering, and even understanding those deep decision criteria are difficult things. Yet, without working on that, what will change?

Will you be anything more than a vessel transmitting the genes and VABEs of the previous generation on to the next generation?

Diagram

The Number One Question in Life

> *Will you ever be anything more than a <u>vessel</u> transmitting the GENEs and VABEs of previous generations on to the next?*
>
> **When you're no longer a defenseless child, will you become a transcender ?**

Challenge

1. Are you truly an "adult?"
2. How willing are you to review your core beliefs? Even the deeper ones that you don't even think about?
3. How much does your parents' approval mean to you and shape your life and decisions?
4. In what ways have you become your "own person?"
5. In what ways do you need to develop your own person?

19. Intelligence

Concept

Does one have to be intelligent to be a leader? Perhaps. If the key elements are clarity of purpose and vision, then additional intelligence may be superfluous. The ability to sell one's purpose and vision would help. As would the ability to analyze current data in creating purpose and vision. Yet sometimes, analysis paralysis sets in and too much thinking can cause potential leaders to stumble—hence, our assertion that the "courage to act" is a key one-third of the Leadership Point of View (LPV).

It turns out that there are many kinds of intelligence. Howard Gardner identified seven kinds (*Frames of Mind,* 1983). These included musical, visual-spatial, verbal, mathematical, kinesthetic (dance), interpersonal, intrapersonal (self-awareness and management), and natural. When we refer to management, I propose a four element model: intellectual capacity, emotional capacity (after EQ by Daniel Goleman), social capacity, and change capacity. Let's call these IQ, EQ, SQ, and CQ for short.

IQ is the historical index of brain power. Many have challenged this singular point of view, yet brain capacity seems a reasonable requirement of effective leaders. IQ is partly inherited, partly developed in early childhood (did your parents read to you?), partly born of curiosity (do you wonder why things are the way they are?), and partly of discipline (doing your homework).

EQ is the ability to recognize your own emotions (LPV Step 1: do you see?), the ability to understand your emotions (LPV Step 2: VABE analysis), and the ability to manage your emotions (LPV Step 3: the courage to lead yourself).[4] People can be "high jacked" by their emotions. (See example below.) The most common emotions that overwhelm us are anger, depression, fear, and apathy. Managing our way out of those emotions can be very challenging.

SQ is the ability to recognize the emotions in others (many self-centered people do not do this), the ability to understand other people's

---

[4] See Manz, C. n.d. *Self Leadership.* for more on this paradoxical concept of self-leadership.

emotions (VABE recognition and analysis), and the ability to help others manage their emotions.

Finally, CQ is change quotient, the ability to recognize the need for change (in one's self and in the situation around), an understanding of the change process (more on that in the module on Leading Change), and the ability to lead change, to be a Change Master.

Example

Have you ever seen someone whose face is red, the sinews on their neck are stretched, their jaw is clenched, and their fists are clenched. And you say, "Calm down!" And they say, "I AM calm!" This person probably has low EQ.

Or other people who don't notice the tear in another's eye? Low SQ.

We could rate individuals on these four kinds of intelligence as high, medium, or low. That profile would give us a little insight into how we might work with them.

Of course, we could also rate ourselves. And with that reflection decide that maybe we want to work on one or more of those intelligences.

At one time, I decided to work on my IQ. There are many ways to do this, I suppose. I chose to keep track of the number of books I read each year. My first goal was one a month. After the first year, I was reading at the rate of three a month—much more than I had before. Just setting that goal simmered in the back of my mind (like Robert Fritz suggested above), and I found myself reading about the origin of the universe, particle physics, evolution, evolutionary psychology, and much more. Did this make me "smarter?" Who knows? I certainly felt more aware of the world around me.

For some, a stronger EQ will require therapy or patient and honest significant others. For some, SQ improvements will hinge on coaching, feedback, and perhaps therapy. Improving one's CQ requires as Jim Collins put it, "confronting the brutal facts."[5] Jack Welch called it "dealing with the world as it is, not as it was or as you wish it were."[6]

---

[5] Collins, J. n.d. *From Good to Great.*

[6] Welch, J., N. Tichy, and S. Sherman. n.d. *Control Your Destiny or Someone Else Will.*

Diagram

<u>Four Key Intelligences</u>

- **IQ** Your mental processing power
- **EQ** Your ability to manage your emotions
    - **Highjackings**: anger, fear, apathy, depression
- **SQ** Your ability to see and help manage Others' emotions
- **CQ** Your ability to see the need to change and to do so.

Challenge

1. How well does your intelligence prepare you for leading other people?
2. How well can you manage your own emotions?
3. How sensitive are you to the emotions of others?
4. Can you help other people manage their emotions?
5. How open are you to re-examining your own VABEs and Level One Behavior?
6. Describe one or more events in your past where you, based on feedback or your own observations, decided to change your behavior and how that went.

20. Self-Awareness

Concept

The first element of self-understanding is enigmatic, self-awareness. We know what we know about ourselves, except if what we know about ourselves is incorrect, and except if what we know about ourselves isn't everything there is to know about ourselves. What can we know about ourselves? And is it even important.

Many people are disdainful about this issue. They know what they know about themselves and that's good enough for them. Anything further is useless "navel gazing." You can decide whether you are one of those or someone who wants to learn more about what you know about yourself and whether that may affect your ability to lead.

Alan Watts once noted, "Self-knowledge leads to wonder, and wonder to curiosity and investigation, so that nothing interests people more than people, even if only one's own person. Every intelligent individual wants to know what makes him tick, and yet is at once fascinated and frustrated by the fact that one's self is the most difficult of all things to know." *The Book: on the taboo against knowing who you are* (Alan Watts 1966, 139–140). Hmm. Perhaps. Do you think?

One way to think about this was developed a number of years ago by creating a two-by-two table comprised of things that Other people see and don't see and things that We see and don't see. The so-called Jo-Hari Window (have you heard of this before?) looks like this:

		OTHERS	
		SEE	NOT SEE
SELF	SEE		
	NOT SEE		

You can see that in the upper-left cell is the domain of things that both we and others agree on. We might call this *public* information. In the upper-right cell we have things that we see or *know* that others don't know or see. These would be our personal thoughts that we don't share, our secrets if you will. We could call this domain the *private* domain. The lower-right cell, domain that neither We nor They see or know, might contain some kind of psychological swamp of genetic, brain chemistry, and uncontrollable impulses.

THEN, in the lower-left cell, what Others see that We don't see, we have the domain that others observe in us that we are unaware of. This domain we could call our Blind Spots. In every seminar I have ever taught on six of the seven continents, every participant has agreed that they have blind spots. It's kind of a cheap joke to ask them, "how do you know?" Most reply that their spouses tell them what their blind spots are.

These blind spots could be any number of things. Things we say that annoy others. Perhaps that we tend to interrupt others. Or discount what they say. Or contradict others. Or condescend to them. Or contradict ourselves. Perhaps it's body odor. Or a tendency to exaggerate. Or to lie.

Then, there's the issue that if one becomes aware of one's blind spots, what do we do with them. We would like to think that if others were kind enough, or even if they were not so kind, to tell us what our blind spots are, especially our dysfunctional ones, we would want to reduce them, shrink them, become better people. Unfortunately, this is not what most of us see at family reunions, is it? I have a friend who defines aging as *more so*. That is, as people age, they just become *more so* as they were.

Most people do not become of aware of their blind spots, and if they do, they don't change them. That said, it's a choice. You can change your blind spots, your unknown habits, once and if you become aware of them. It won't be easy, *and* it's a choice. You can change your speech habits, your interpersonal habits, your assumptions about how people should behave.

On the other hand, if you never become aware of your blind spots, the ways in which your behavior is off-putting to others, you may never know why your attempts to lead, to influence, are not so effective as you believe they should be. If you want to continuously improve your ability to influence others, you must continuously learn how your behavior influences other people—and that means discovering your blind spots—and working on them.

Diagram

Self Awareness:
Beware your Blind Spots!

SEE OTHERS (SEE)

	PUBLIC	PRIVATE
SEE **SELF**		
(SEE)	BLIND SPOTS	

Challenge

1. How would you describe yourself?

2. What do you think other people think of you?
3. Do you have any friends who will give you an honest answer? If so, ask them.
4. What parts of your personality do you need to manage better to become a more effective leader?

21. The Rational-Emotive-Behavior Model

Concept

Our conscious and semi-conscious VABEs shape our Level One behavior. One person likes blue, another likes red and that shapes their choices. One child was taught that children are to be seen and not heard while another child was taught to speak up freely—and that shapes their Level One behavior. These and a thousand other comparisons make up one person's deep Level Three *elephant*, the criteria by which they make visible decisions. If to speak. When to speak. What to say. How to say it. What to do. How to do it.

For those of you who like mathematics, this is an insight into human behavior. In essence, Albert Ellis's theory (*A Guide to Rational Living*) and the variations therefrom give us an equation with one missing variable: VABEs. The equation is INPUTS + Level Three VABEs → Level Two Conclusions → Emotions → Level One Behavior. If one can identify the missing variable, the underlying VABE, one can understand and explain the resulting Level One visible behavior.

Inputs + L3VABEs → L2Conclusions → Emotions → L1Behavior

In this equation, INPUTS and Level One Behavior are observable. What happens in-between we can only infer. And what we can infer is that a change in VABEs changes everything else. If you believe that people should be courteous and you go into a deli in New York City, you are likely to be offended. If you believe that people should leave you alone, and you go into a greasy spoon in Kansas, you may be offended by the *friendliness* of the wait staff. It's all in the VABEs.

Modern research says, wait a minute, those conclusions are not *rational*, they are faster and deeper than that. Yet, those fast decisions (Kahneman, *Thinking Fast and Slow*) are based on deep preferences—preferences developed since birth. Surely, we will learn more about these cranial processes, stay tuned, but for now, it appears that whatever part of the brain is involved, those fast decision-making structures were not there nor informed at birth. And while no single theory of human behavior is comprehensive enough to hang your hat on, this one has immense practicality.

If you develop a *VABE radar* in which you watch for and note and register the underlying VABEs in what people say and do, you will have a very powerful tool for understanding behavior. You don't have to be a psychologist to do this; you only have to understand this equation and then develop observational skills that permit you to *see* why the person is doing what they are. This in turn will help you see that simply telling someone to change their behavior is largely ineffective. That approach doesn't address the underlying cause of that behavior. A wiser manager will identify the VABEs that drive someone's behavior and strive to influence there.

Examples

A man travels across the country to be by the bedside of his friend as he wakes up from pulmonary surgery. Why? What is his VABE?

A father beats his child with a switch when she disobeys. Why? What is his VABE? ("spare the rod and spoil the child?")

A man able to pay his debts, delays and delays repaying his debt to a friend. Why? What's his VABE?

A man borrows tools from his friends, often not returning them. Why? What's his VABE?

Another man buys new tools he needs never thinking to ask his friends if he can borrow their tools. Why? What's his VABE?

One man yells at an intern telling her to shut up and do what she's told. Why? What's his VABE?

Another account manager asks his intern what she was thinking when she did what she did and listens patiently. Then, he engages a discussion with her about her assumptions and his assumptions and how they might work together more efficiently in the future. Why? What's his VABE?

A woman stops by a homeless person walking and offers him a ride. Why? What's her VABE?

Another woman honks at the walking homeless person to get out of the way. Why? What's her VABE?

Diagram

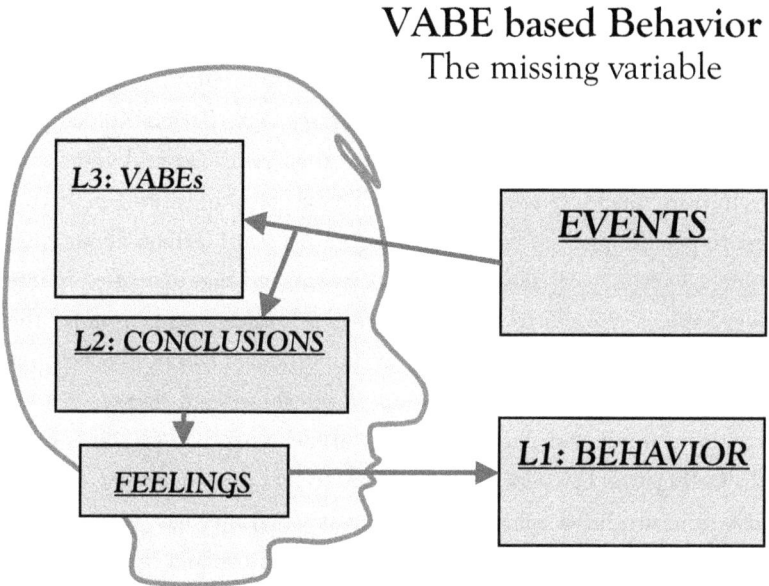

VABE based Behavior
The missing variable

L3: VABEs

EVENTS

L2: CONCLUSIONS

FEELINGS

L1: BEHAVIOR

Challenge

1. Develop your *VABE radar* by observing people's Level One behavior and trying to articulate (write down) their underlying VABEs.
2. Reflect on your own VABEs as they shape your behavior. Are they *functional* or *dysfunctional* in getting buy-in from those around you?
3. When you are angry or annoyed, pause and ask yourself "What are the underlying VABEs that are making me angry or annoyed? Can I revisit and perhaps refine those VABEs?" NOTE: Not all anger is bad. Much of it, however, is self-destructive and can actually harm the holder of anger.[7]
4. When someone else is angry or annoyed, ask yourself, "What VABE is generating this anger?" and see if you can't understand better and manage that relationship better.
5. When you think someone is being *irrational*, try to identify their underlying VABE and compare it with yours. In the REB model, all behavior is *rational* to the person who has a certain VABE. The VABEs are the difference in *rationality*.

---

[7] http://everydayhealth.com/news/ways-anger-ruining-your-health/

22. Leadership and Self-Deception

Concept

In 2000, the Arbinger Institute published a very interesting book, *Leadership and Self-Deception: Getting Out of the Box* (Berrett-Kohler, San Franciso), about how people often ignore their *conscience* and judge others, putting them in a *box*, a negative label or group of labels—perhaps a stereotype. The premise was that people have a set of feelings about what is the *right* thing to do (essentially a *conscience*) and that they often ignore those feelings in order to satisfy their own self-esteem and comfort. The consequence of this behavior is that we put others in *boxes* and others put us in *boxes* that erode or destroy our relationships. And that we do this to *justify* our own behavior. Only, they argue, when one examines one's own feelings and behaviors can one begin to let others out of *the box* and likely in return be let out of *their boxes* into which they have put us. They call on us all to reflect on how we put others in boxes and the things that we do that encourage others to put us in boxes and in so doing to resolve to *honor* our consciences and do the *right* thing. Three other concepts related to this model are: (a) the use of *always* that allows one to create a box, (b) focus on the Other's behavior rather than one's own, and (c) the dehumanization of the Other.

Example

A man's wife asks him in the middle of the night to let the dog out to pee. He thinks she's lazy and says "you do it," after which she thinks "he's lazy and doesn't care about me."

A boss tells an employee to do something and the employee rolls their eyes. The boss thinks "That employee is a stick in the mud and always trying to do less." The employee thinks "The boss is always giving me crap assignments and I hate it."

An employee tells their boss about a new idea that they believe could make the company millions of dollars. The boss says, "Look, just do your job and stop creating windmills." The boss thinks the employee is a pain in the neck. The employee thinks the boss is a dinosaur.

Diagram

Leadership and Self Deception

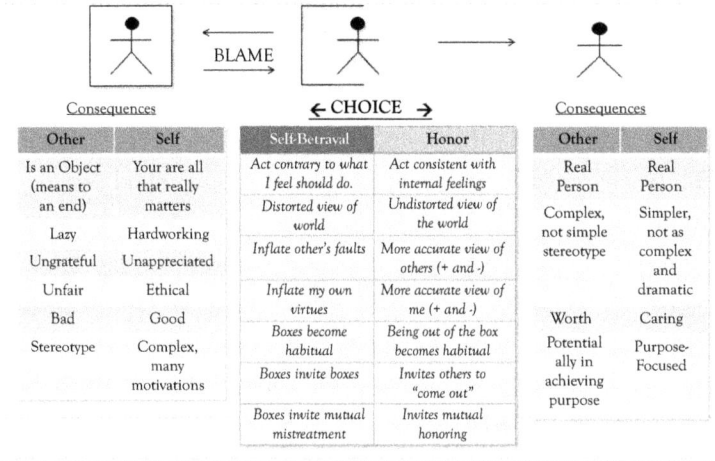

Consequences		← CHOICE →		Consequences	
Other	Self	Self-Betrayal	Honor	Other	Self
Is an Object (means to an end)	Your are all that really matters	Act contrary to what I feel should do.	Act consistent with internal feelings	Real Person	Real Person
Lazy	Hardworking	Distorted view of world	Undistorted view of the world	Complex, not simple stereotype	Simpler, not as complex and dramatic
Ungrateful	Unappreciated	Inflate other's faults	More accurate view of others (+ and -)		
Unfair	Ethical	Inflate my own virtues	More accurate view of me (+ and -)		
Bad	Good	Boxes become habitual	Being out of the box becomes habitual	Worth	Caring
Stereotype	Complex, many motivations	Boxes invite boxes	Invites others to "come out"	Potential ally in achieving purpose	Purpose-Focused
		Boxes invite mutual mistreatment	Invites mutual honoring		

Challenge

1. Do you think people have a *conscience*? If so, where did it come from? Deity? Early childhood environmental culture?
2. How reliable are the feelings associated with a *conscience*?
3. Identify a person with whom you are in a box. What is the box? How could you get out of that box?
4. Identify a person you have put in a box. How could they get out of your imposed box?
5. How does this model relate to VABEs?

23. Self-Concept

Concept

Earlier I asked you to write one sentence describing who you are. This is a rough summary of your self-concept. And our thoughts and feelings about who we are is more complex than that single sentence. And this has to do with our VABEs about who we *should* be. These self-concept VABEs were formed as we developed in our early childhood development environment.

Our self-concept VABEs, the principles we have ingested about who we should be, form together a definition of what we *want* ourselves to be. Remember our definition of a problem? *A want-got gap for somebody.* Well, our self-concept VABEs are the *want* side of that equation. The *got* side is how we see ourselves.

Humans have a distinct ability to watch ourselves. We can *see* what we say and do. We also get feedback from others who help us fill in our *blind spots*. If we listen to and pay attention to that feedback whether it is direct or implied in signals and hints, we get a more complete picture of who we are in the world than we can by simple self-observation. This self-awareness becomes our *got* side of the equation.

If we see ourselves (our self-image, what we have got) to be largely congruent with what we expect of ourselves (our ideal self—what we want), our self-esteem, the feelings we have about ourselves, is high. If there is a gap between our self-image and our ideal self, our self-esteem will go down.

Hence, we can modify the REB model described earlier by pointing out that what we *have* with regard to ourselves is our own Level One Behavior. Do you see how this is another example of the Problem Model? Another *Want-Got Gap* to manage.

Example

Andre believes he should be a good father. When his son interrupts him while he's working, he snaps at his son, "I'm busy now! Don't bother me!" His *fast thinking*, the elephant of quick VABEs based assessment, immediately ruled. A moment later, Andre feels guilty.

At this point, Andre's *slow thinking* will kick in and he will assess himself to be a *bad dad*, and feel guilty. This moment will then demonstrate a different concept, Andre's relative VABE system. Which VABE is more important? The first is, "I should be a good, loving dad." The second is, "I must be a productive, hard worker." These two VABEs are *competing*. Which one is more important to Andre? We will know in a moment as he either puts his work aside and apologizes and attends to his son OR continues working. Andre demonstrates his value structure, the relative strength of his VABEs, by his Level One Behavior.

Diagram

THE SELF CONCEPT

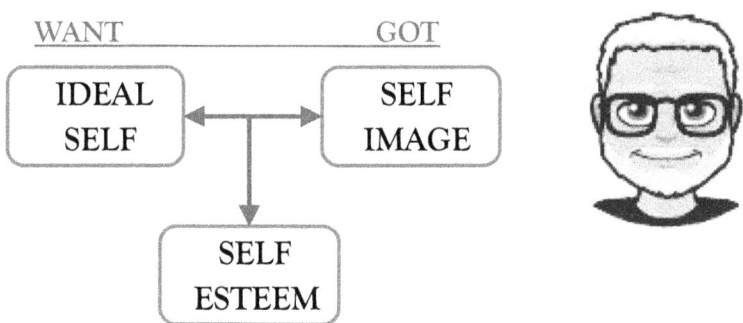

How we judge ourselves

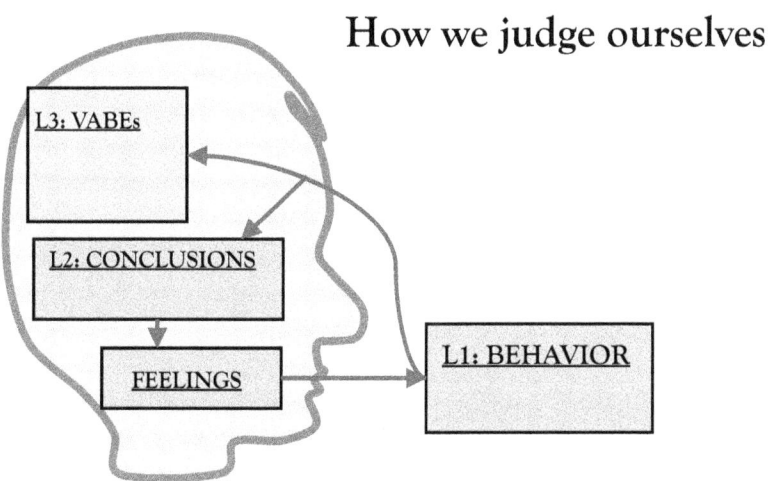

Challenge

1. What do you think of yourself?
2. What, if any, fears do you harbor about your worthiness?
3. How, if at all, is your self-image over inflated?
4. How, if at all, is your self-image under inflated?
5. List your weak points. Do you acknowledge these to yourself and others?
6. What are the consequences of thinking more highly of yourself than others do?
7. What are the consequences of thinking less of yourself than others do?
8. How does humility affect others?
9. How does false humility affect others?
10. How does over-confidence (arrogance) affect others?
11. How does justified confidence affect others?

24. Career Concepts

Concept

Mike Driver and Ken Brousseau at the USC business school developed the notion that people pursue different *ideal careers*. Not everyone wants to be the chief executive. As they studied this concept, they concluded that there are four naturally occurring career paths or *concepts* that people seemed to follow. Each of these paths has a different definition of intent and success. They named these patterns the Linear, Expert, Spiral, and Transitory.

The Linear *type* seeks to be promoted. Success means moving up the organizational ladder. The Expert *type* seeks to do a good job and has little interest in being promoted. Success is craftsmanship and perfection in execution. Experts include doctors, lawyers, teachers, carpenters, masons, and plumbers. Many Experts, because they do a good job, are seen by Linears to be *promotable*. In that, the Linears are assuming that everyone is like them, they *want* to be promoted, and even *should* want to be promoted. When I ask groups of managers, "How many of you have ever seen an Expert ruined by promotion into management?"—every hand in the room goes up. This is bad for the individual, bad for the company, and bad for the reputation of the manager who promoted him or her. Sadly, it continues to be a common problem.

The Spiral *type* seeks continuous learning. Spirals will even give up the power and status that Linears desire in order to enhance their learning and growth. The Transitory *type* have interests other than work and will work as long as they have to in order to pursue their more powerful passions—like sailing around the world, climbing tall mountains, and hiking across continents or on the negative side, alcohol, drugs, gambling, and other vices.

Each of these *types* make a useful contribution to an organization. Linears (good ones) bring drive, ambition, purpose, and vision. Experts bring talent, expertise, craftsmanship, and execution. Without the Experts, Linears would have no one to lead. Spirals bring new insight, learning, innovation, and change. And Transitories bring, to the enlightened HR manager, a chance to manage economic ups and downs. If they had hired 25 percent of their employees as

Transitories, when the next economic downturn and related layoffs came, they could choose those folks to lay off—and they would be happy because they could then sail around the world or go mountain climbing. When the economy turned up again, they would be happy to be rehired.

Tim Hall and others have suggested that a fifth Career Concept is the Warrior. It seems clear that there are people (career military, boxers, mixed martial arts fighters, football players, etc.) who love as General George Patton said, "the sting of battle." To me, Warriors are a specialized kind of Expert. They seldom want to be promoted, they would rather be in the fray. And they have specialized skills that they hone and rehearse so that in battle, they win.

Although this research is not new, it has been *new* to virtually every manager I have taught. I hope that you will be aware of these naturally occurring differences in people's goals and ambitions, and respect them as you make career decisions for yourself and others.

We have developed a short questionnaire to give you a little self-assessment profile of your career concept. Driver and Brousseau distinguished between Career Motives and Career Concepts. In this questionnaire, we just ask you to reflect on your interests. Because you now know the basic scoring for the instrument, your answers are likely to be sub-consciously biased by your VABEs about which Career Concepts are more *desirable*. Nevertheless, you can take this short instrument if you wish to generate some rough data about your own Career Concept.

http://virginia.qualtrics.com/SE/?SID=SV_e8Pdgv8sZERdluQ

Example

After explaining these concepts to one group, a fellow came up after class and asked me, "Why don't Linears listen?" Hmmm. Tell me more. "Well," he said, "I have only been to this company for six months. I used to work for one of their major competitors. I'm an engineer, a good engineer. Because I do a good job (Expert type, yes?), my former employers kept assigning me to leadership development programs. I kept telling them, 'I don't want to be promoted. I just want to do my job, do it well, and go home to spend time with my family.' But they didn't listen. It got so annoying that I quit—and came here. I've only been here six months and already they have put me in your fricking leadership development program! Why don't they listen?" True story.

What's your answer to this man?

I think it is because most of us especially Linears assume that anyone who does a good job is like them, desirous of moving up. I even had one COO in a client company slam his fist to the table and declare, "Absolutely not! If the janitor here doesn't aspire to be the CEO, we should fire his ass out of here! That's the American Dream! You lift yourself up by your bootstraps as high as you can!" Whew! If you were an Expert, a Spiral, or a Transitory working in that organization, how would you feel? Like a second-class citizen, unappreciated for who you are and what you contribute.

I read about a Transitory, a trained RN, whose primary goal was to hike around the world. She would hike as far as she could, until she ran out of money, then go to work (everyone needs more RNs) for a while and then trek off again.

Diagram

We can diagram these four concepts on a grid of power and status on the vertical axis over time on the horizontal axis.

Career Concepts: Each has Value

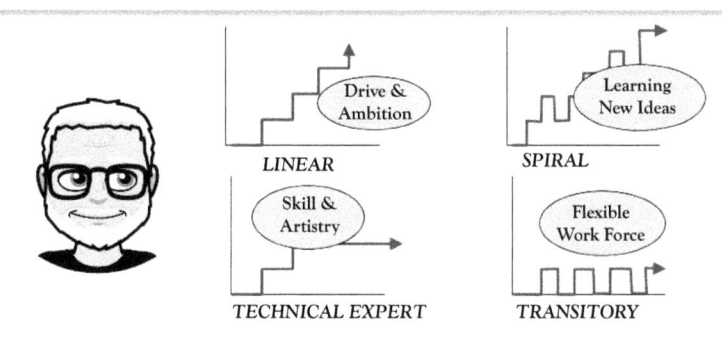

Challenge

1. What is your dominant Career Concept? (Reflection and the self-assessment test above)
2. What are the consequences of promoting an Expert into management?
3. What kinds of interview questions could identify these Career Concepts?
4. Identify at least one person of each type that you have known in your experience.
5. Given your Career Concept, what are the implications for your career decisions and plans?

25. Develop Your Opinions

Concept

Large numbers of people, in my experience, have few if any opinions. If one had not formed an opinion on a subject (profit vs. community contribution, debt vs. equity, immigration, minimum wages, health care system, product mix, current strategy, and on and on and on), one is likely to either waffle in discussion or rely simply on immediate emotional reactions (fast thinking, semi-conscious VABEs).

Much of what we do in business schools is an attempt to help students and executive education participants to form reasoned opinions (slow thinking). In this, we often create *expectation abrasions* in students so that they have an admittedly small and short space, the classroom, to consider whether their immediate thoughts are defensible, practical, applicable, and executable in the world of practical affairs.

In my experience, I found little more stimulating and growth-producing than struggling to form a reasoned opinion on every issue I encounter. By *reasoned*, I mean, one has read several sides of an issue so that one *understands all the forces at play* (the second step in the Leadership Point of View). Simple statements without some *homework* are nothing more than manifestations of one's past VABEs. Reasoned opinions can be substantiated with logic, evidence, data, history, and an apparent awareness of all the points of view.

This is one of the main reasons I strongly support and have used the case method as the *best* way of teaching, rather we should say, *facilitating learning*. In case of method instruction, we invite people to put themselves in the position of real, practicing managers (not made-up arm-chaired positions), and make in the safety of the classroom the decisions that face those people. This builds experience in analysis and persuasion one issue at a time three times a day, five days a week over two years.

When in discussion, I invite you to think about your opinions. Do you have one? If not, why not? (You haven't done your homework?) Are your opinions reasonable? (Have you done your homework?) Have you simply adopted the opinions (VABEs) of your parents or those around you? Are they *your* opinions or those of others that you have had embedded in you?

Example

During my career, I have had the opportunity or necessity of dining with hundreds and hundreds of groups of students and practicing managers usually seven at a time. I have often sat and listened as they set the focus of the discussion. Sometimes, no one has anything to say. I can usually start some kind of conversation by asking people about themselves. "What do you do for fun?" Is a good one. After doing that one hundreds of times, I began to want something more than superficial, trivial conversations. So sometimes, I would violate the *rule*, the *common VABE*, that we should not talk about religion, politics, or money in public. "What do you think, is there an afterlife?" (Shocked expressions.)

Many people are either unaware of their VABEs (opinions) or uncomfortable talking about their VABEs (opinions). We already know the reason for that: the fear of rejection from our discussion of living inside-out versus outside-in.

Recently, in a simple breakfast meeting with my wife and a friend, we were discussing among other things the impact of getting something for nothing. In particular, I was interested in bequeathing one's wealth to children. Should there be an inheritance tax? Or should children be able to enjoy the fruits of their ancestors' efforts? We had a mutual acquaintance who had inherited a very, very large sum of money at an early age. Arm's length observers could easily infer that this event ruined this person's life. The same has been reported by many lottery winners. SO, IF inheritance tends to undermine one's moral and societal development, should a government tax inheritance with the intent of (a) building a stronger citizenship and (b) sharing with those who for whatever reason have not been able to rise above a poverty level of living?

Do you have an opinion? What is it? Could you explain the logic of your thinking? Could you listen patiently to someone else's opinion? Is your opinion based on *fast thinking* or *slow thinking*?

Diagram

What issues have
you developed
reasoned,
evidence-based
opinions on?

Challenge

1. What is your opinion on the following?
   (a) Immigration
   (b) Health care
   (c) Your country's role on the international stage
   (d) Caring for the poor
   (e) Short-term profits versus long-term profits
   (f) International outsourcing
   (g) Free trade
   (h) Growth by acquisition versus organic sales growth
   (i) Your company's strategy
   (j) Afterlife
   (k) God (if yes, is your god *sentient*?)
   (l) Minimum wages
   (m) Nuclear proliferation—does a nation have the *right* to develop nuclear capability on its own?
   (n) The best form of government
   (o) How much should the government regulate businesses?
   (p) Why people behave the way they do
   (q) How to influence others most effectively?

(r) What any new leader of an organization should pay attention to (your corporate "vital signs" model)?

(s) How to manage the fight against terrorism?

(t) What constitutes *stealing*?

(u) The purpose of a private sector business

And so many more . . .

26. Balancing Your Life

Concept

The most commonly mentioned issue in my seminars world wide is work-life balance. Current pundits talk about *work-life integration*. Whether you think it as *balance* or *integration*, the way we move from our personal, home, family, and work roles has, with new technology, grown more complex. One CEO I know slept with his cell phone and would send out texts as he thought of them—and expected answers when he got in to the office early the next day. Some managers draw sharp lines between their work and personal lives, they *compartmentalize* their lives like the water-tight compartments of a submarine striving to keep the emotions and thoughts of one arena (work or home) separate from the other. Their VABE would be "don't take work home, and don't take home to work."

Whether we pay attention to them or not, we have a number of "–AL" aspects of life that are unfolding as we live. These include the physical, professional, financial, intellectual, emotional, social, marital, parental, familial, sexual, spiritual, and ecclesiastical aspects of life. We could sort these into four clusters: professional, personal, familial, and societal. Many observers today only want to look at those four clusters, but I feel it is important to look at each of the underlying –AL aspects individually.

Consider the condition of a newborn child. On all of these dimensions, their development is, shall we say, at zero. Over the course of time, depending on multiple factors, the child develops its physical, social, emotional, intellectual, and all of the other aspects. We could array these aspects on a radar chart with zero development at the origin (center) and subsequent development radiating outward on these 10 to 14 dimensions. Let's put *world-class* on the outer most ring; on a scale of 1 to 10, this would be 10.

World-class on the financial aspect would be about $75 billion (Bill Gates in 2017). World-class on the physical dimension would be Olympic gold medals or world championships. World-class on the intellectual dimension would be Leonardo DaVinci, Isaac Newton, and Albert Einstein. World-class on the spiritual dimension would be... pick your favorite: Dalai Lama? The Pope? Mohammad? And so forth. What's a world-class parent? You decide.

At birth, a person has no development. At age 10, what would the development of that no-longer newborn child look like? At age 20? 30? 50? You could, and I encourage you to do so, rate your development annually. That would be like a personal *balance sheet* similar to what a corporation does every year. It's a way of gauging progress. This would give you a traceable and more comprehensive way of making your New Year's resolutions.

You could also set some goals for each dimension. What do you want your net worth to be? Where is it now? Is there a want-got gap? And so on, for all of the –AL dimensions. You can draw this line on a radar chart (see below) and compare what you want with what you have got.

We use *world-class* on the outer circle to compare ourselves with the rest of humanity. Putting in your personal *ideal self* profile allows you to compete against your own goals, not necessarily against the best of human kind over the millennia.

You can download this Excel spreadsheet from my personal web-page that will do the calculations for you. https://nadobimakoba.com/managing-careers/

Example

The Balance Wheel of the subject of an often-used case on a 42-year-old general manager looks like this:

A Personal Developmental Balance Wheel

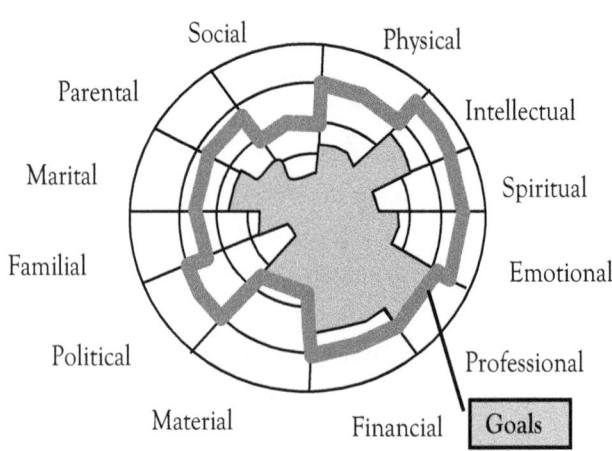

You can see here the person's self-assessment in the blue and his *ideal self* in the green. (Colors in e-book format only.) In some dimensions (e.g., Professional), he has reached his goal, while in other areas (e.g., Physical), he has not. Reviewing this profile annually, this man could manage or lead himself to become the person he wants to be.

Diagram

You can see in this screen shot of the spreadsheet/workbook that you can easily input your 1 to 10 rating of your development and then of your ideal self. The workbook will then automatically chart your radar chart shown below.

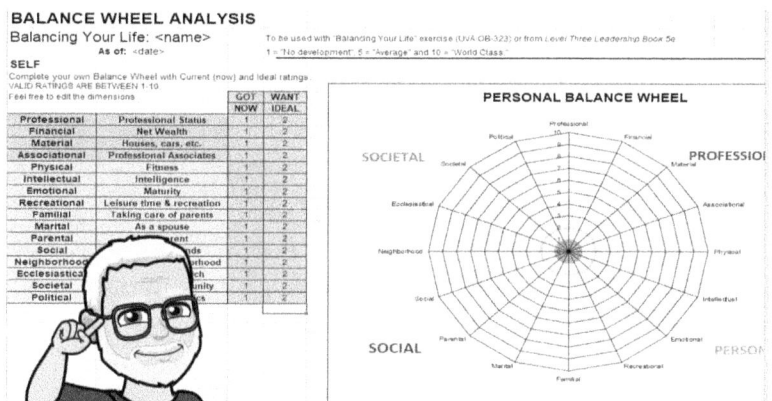

Challenge

1. Download the Excel Career Options Workbook (COW).
2. Fill in your current level of development as shown above.
3. Fill in your desired level of development as shown above.
4. Use this tool to guide your New Year's resolutions annually.
5. Print or save your annual profiles so you can compare them over the years.
6. Take control of the *balance* in your life.

27. Balancing Your Focus

Concept

There is another way in which we, I think, should pay attention to our *balance in life*. Most of us are aware of the balance between work and rest. This basic two-part cycle is what causes us to sleep, to *take a break*, and to go on vacation.

Please consider a third *station* or *mental focus*, learning. If we work, then we need a rest, and then go back to work, we are in danger of simply recreating every day in the same way, a kind of life-long *Groundhog Day*. (See the movie by the same name starring Bill Murray.) Only if we add a regular, habitual learning component to our regular routine do we have the chance of changing and of improving our situation in life.

So, now our *balance model* includes three stations of focus or activity: do, rest, learn. What proportion would you estimate is *good* for living a balanced life? 80/10/10? 70/10/20? 50/20/30?

In addition, we can consider that some people get *stuck* or shall we say *overly-focused* on one of these stations/positions. People who work too much can become *workaholics*. People who rest too much can become *lazy and non-productive*. People who learn too much can become paralyzed by analysis. Do, rest, learn. Each position has its own danger in excess.

Example

Workaholics may or may not get a lot of things done. Some work unproductively when they need to work smarter. Some workaholics can severely damage their health and their relationships. People who avoid work, who come late, go home early, who would rather lie around vegetating are not likely to produce much. Researchers and analysts who end their efforts with "We need to learn more and do more research," often struggle to get things done or make a difference.

Diagram

Common Daily Cycles
and Dysfunctional Whirpools

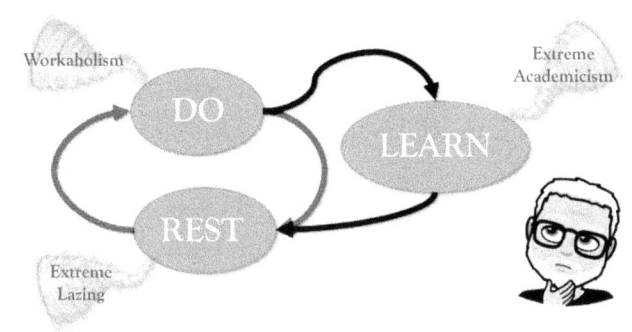

Challenge

1. Assign 100 percent to all your time. What percent of your time do you spend in DO, REST, and LEARN?
2. Which of these three would you like to enhance?
3. How would you plan to do that?
4. Do you have mild or moderate OCD? If so, what do you need to look out for?

28. Decision Making

Concept

People make decisions. Often they avoid making decisions; they waffle. Current research suggests that people tend to make quick decisions based on their established VABEs. In micro-seconds, we tend to judge a situation as safe or dangerous. Only when people *slow down* their thinking, do they—some of them—rethink their snap judgments and perhaps modify them.

Daniel Kahneman won a Nobel Prize for highlighting this phenomenon. (See *Thinking Fast and Slow*.) Jonathan Haidt in *The Righteous Mind* described this process as a small rider (our logical thinking process) on top of a large elephant (our quick, values-based snap judgments). Joshua Greene in *Moral Tribes* went through a painstaking analysis of research confirming this kind of decision-making process in humans. I recommend all three for your reading.

When executives make decisions in the business world, what are their key criteria? Are they also subject to this human tendency to make very fast decision based on VABEs? Of course.

So, if a business manager wants to slow down, how could they organize their thought processes at Level Two and strive to make better, more functional decisions? There are hundreds of ways scholars would answer this question. Here's mine.

I encourage managers to consider six elements around every business decision:

1. Does it fit our STRATEGY?
2. Is it PROFITABLE IN THE LONG RUN?
3. Is it LEGAL?
4. Is it ETHICAL?
5. Is it CULTURALLY ACCEPTABLE?
6. Is it, to me, MORAL?

Every decision should be clearly related to implementing one's *strategy* (more on this later). If you don't have a strategy, well, that's another issue. If the decision doesn't fit a strategy, why do it?

Every decision has *financial* consequences. Some are short-term and some are long-term. Frequently, short-term financial decisions can erode a company's long-term health. Delaying maintenance costs, for example. False advertising for another. Falsifying emission data for another. Outsourcing key technical skills for another.

Is the decision *legal*? Can we be prosecuted for doing this? What are our standards on obeying the law?

Is the decision *ethical*? Some professions, law, military, and medicine, for example, have ethical codes. Business not so much. Would this decision fit within the realm of "ethical behavior?"

Is this *culturally* acceptable? Does this fit the region of the world in which we are doing business?

Finally, if you can answer yes to all of the above, does this decision fit your personal *moral* standards? Are you compromising your standards if you make this decision?

Many managers don't use a conscious model, they act on their semi-conscious VABEs about what's right and what's allowed and whether getting caught is the same as being immoral.

Example

One global company delivers product to more than a hundred nations. In one very crowded country, the delivery truck double parks and takes the products inside the store. Outside, the policeman waits for the driver. Then he says, "I can give you a ticket for double-parking or you can give me a box of the product." What should the driver do? What should the company do?

(The company did an analysis and the data showed that giving a box of the product at wholesale prices was cheaper than paying the double parking fines.) Now what should the company do?

Diagram

DECISION MAKING CRITERIA

THINKING...

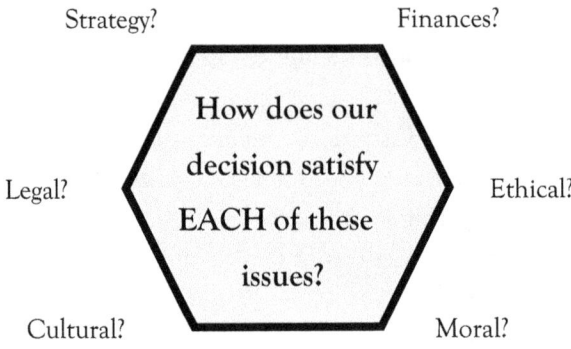

Strategy?   Finances?

How does our decision satisfy EACH of these issues?

Legal?   Ethical?

Cultural?   Moral?

**Most people think DEDUCTIVELY.
Recent Research on Decision-Making
explains why**

LOGIC

VABEs

- **Humans make very fast decisions based on their semi-conscious beliefs and preferences (VABEs)**
- **A <u>few</u> humans then reflect with their conscious minds (Level 2) and rethink their immediate judgments.**

Challenge

1. Have you ever been put in a business situation that challenged your moral thinking?
2. What did you do? Why?
3. Are the decision-making standards in your organization clear?
4. Does your organization adhere to its decision-making standards—does it walk its talk?
5. Where do you draw the line—what would you not do if your company asked you to?
6. What kind of decision dilemma would make you quit your job?

29. Decision-Making Pyramid

Concept

There are many different *ways* to make decisions. These include: majority (voting), hierarchical (tiered responsibilities), and consensus (we talk until everyone agrees). Toni Bauman adds proportional to this list; she argues that some people in a group may have disproportional influence on a decision.[8] McKinsey and Company argues for six dimensions of decision making, each with bi-lateral anchor points:

1. Ad-hoc versus Process driven
2. Action versus Caution
3. Broad data versus Narrow data
4. Corporate versus Personal
5. Continuity versus Change
6. Facts versus Stories.[9]

These axes, they argue, create five distinctive decision-making styles: visionary, guardian, motivator, flexible, and catalyst.

A major part of the issue of decision making is number of people involved. In autocratic processes, one person makes the decisions. In oligarchies, a small group of people make the decisions. In democratic processes, large numbers of people are involved. None of those involve consensus decision making in which everyone must *agree*. *Agree* here means that many must modify or compromise their original positions.

Autocratic decision making is faster if and when you have a decisive leader. The downside is that less data is considered and implementation can be a challenge if the *followers* don't buy-in.

Democratic/voting decision making serves the majority but can overlook or ignore the condition of the minorities.

---

[8] https://auroraproject.com.au/sites/default/files/common_decision_making_processes.pdf

[9] http://inc.com/erik-sherman/which-of-the-5-kinds-of-decision-maker-are-you.html

Consensus decision making takes a lot more time and may conclude with modest buy-in even though it is intended to create higher buy-in.

The ways to assess decisions include speed, participation, and buy-in. More participation takes more time but may enhance buy-in. Autocratic decision making can be faster but may omit key information from non-participants and can erode buy-in. Where do you draw the line between speed, involvement, and buy-in in your decision making? Is there a way to make fast, well-informed, highly participative, and highly energizing decisions?

Example

A father says at dinner after listening to his daughters argue over clothing, "There will be no more sharing of clothes! I can't stand all this bickering! You wear your own clothes. Period!"

The board of a non-profit organization with VABEs about respect for everyone debates for days the purpose of their organization.

A CEO reports the results of two years of executive committee of discussion for their four year strategic plan and ... not much changes.

A CEO listens to a custodian on his way out the door, and by using her advice, saves his company from virtual destruction.

Diagram

Balancing Decision Forces

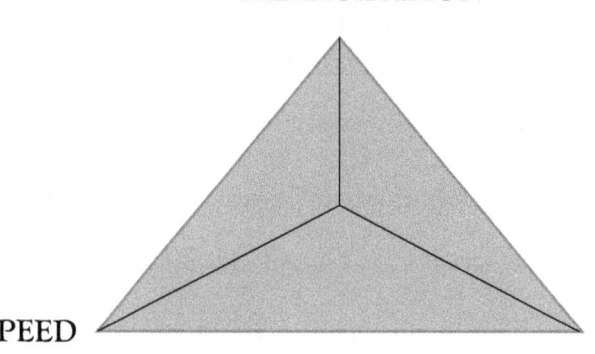

PARTICIPATION

SPEED   BUY-IN

What do fast, dictatorial decisions do?

PARTICIPATION

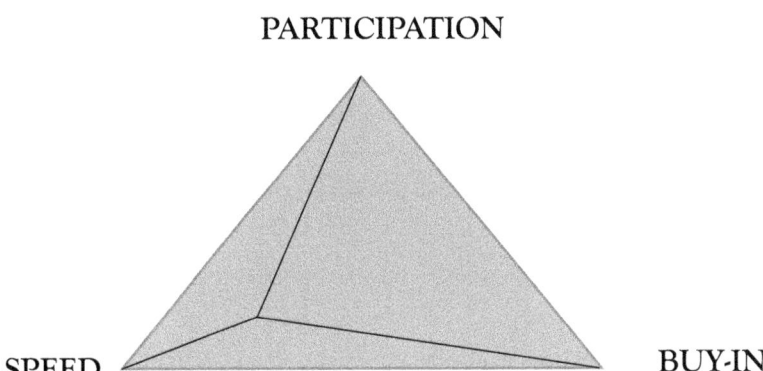

SPEED   BUY-IN

Challenge

1. How do you prefer to make decisions?
2. How would assess your preferred decision-making style on the triangle above? Where does the meeting point in the middle lie?
3. What are the downsides of your decision-making style?
4. What are the upsides to your decision-making style?
5. Do you have the flexibility to change your decision-making style?

The Unexplored Linkage Between Feel and Performance

Does how you feel affect your performance? If you say "no" then you can skip this section. If you say "yes" as has almost everyone in every seminar I have ever taught, then read on.

30. Feel and Performance

Concept

Consider this question, *Does how you feel affect your performance?* Yes? No? What do you think?

Pause . . . What's your answer?

In every room in which I have asked this question, every hand went up. People world wide believe that how they feel affects their performance.

Next, consider, *How many times in your career has your boss asked you how you wanted to feel?* What's the number for you?

In my seminars, people begin laughing. Laughing because the answer, 99 percent of the time, is zero. This was an absurd question.

If you believe that how one feels affects their performance, why wouldn't you, as a manager, want to know how people (a) *are* feeling and (b) *want* to feel?

Doug Newburg, PhD in Sports Psychology, introduced me to this concept and many related in the next several chapters. One day after a noon-time basketball game, he invited me to sit in on a lecture he was giving to a large undergraduate class that evening. During that talk, he asked the question "How do you *want* to feel?" I went home and I couldn't sleep. *How do I want to feel?* I had no idea. No one had ever asked that question before, not my father, not my mother, none of my teachers, none of my supervisors. They had always asked "What have you done? Did you mow the lawn? Did you clean the garage? Did you do your homework? Did you pass your exams? How many articles have you written? How many classes have you taught?" *No one* had asked me how I wanted to feel.

At first the question seemed irrelevant—until one thinks about whether how you feel affects your performance. It took me 18 months to answer that question. It came to me after a series of events following shoulder surgery. I had committed to give two talks on the West Coast and couldn't handle my luggage, so my wife accompanied me to help. I gave my talk in Los Angeles to a standing-room only conference session, then we loaded up and drive to San Francisco for my next event. That night removing my shoes, my back spasmed from all the off-kilter activity of the day and I was frozen in a fetal position. The next day, the hotel rented a wheel-chair and a portable elevator, and put me up on stage with a thousand people in the audience and huge screens spread throughout. I sat there and looked at my image thinking "there's something very wrong with this picture." After the talk, I canceled everything on my calendar for the next three months and went home to rest.

During that period the first edition of my book, *Level Three Leadership*, tumbled out. And I realized that I do my best work when I am feeling *light, unhurried, engaged, and connected.* Having that insight was just the beginning. (Thanks again, Doug.) I had at that point half a century of habits built up. I hung those words on my bathroom mirror and put them on my checks to remind me of how I wanted to feel and that if I could get that my performance and the *experience* of my performance would improve—dramatically. I came to realize, that if one manages or attempts to lead without attending to how their followers feel, one is ignoring huge amounts of energy and motivation.

Example

Dave Scott has won the Hawaii Ironman Triathlon six times. This is an extraordinary feat consisting of a 2 mile swim in the open ocean, a 110 mile bicycle race, and a 26.1 mile marathon footrace. He once noted that "during a race, I never wear a wristwatch and my bike doesn't have a speedometer. They're distractions." *What?* Wait a minute. How do most people compete? They check their watches and the mile markers and if they are behind their plan, they say to themselves, "I *have* to speed up." And that obligatory thought tightens the body, stresses the mind, and in the end, paradoxically, reduces performance.

Scott goes on to note, "All I work on is finding a *rhythm* that feels strong and sticking to it."[1] And by the way, he's blowing everyone else away.

Obviously, that kind of performance cannot just happen; it's the result of months of intense training. Training that is more than discipline; it's a love of the activity itself.

---

[1] *Outside* Magazine, September 2003, p. 122.

Diagram

Does how you feel
affect your performance?

- How many times have you been asked by supervision at work how you want to feel?
- How do you **WANT** to feel?

Focusing on Feel to Perform
Dave Scott
49, Six-time Ironman Hawaii Champion

"During a race, I never wear a wristwatch, and my bike doesn't have a speedometer. They're distractions.

All I work on is finding a rhythm that feels strong and sticking to it."

Source: Outside, 9/03, p. 122

Challenge

1. If you believe how you feel affects your performance, should you not begin thinking more carefully about how you feel?
2. If you could get more of your desired feel in life, what would happen to your performance?
3. Describe a time when you felt this high performing euphoria.

31. Connecting Feel and Performance: Flow

Concept

As a young teenager, Mihalyi Csikszentmihalyi survived/avoided the Nazi concentration camps. In them, he was surprised at how quickly so many died—but that there were a few, who despite the horrible conditions, not only survived but thrived. Beneath the overbearing formal systems, they had a hierarchy of command, rules and regulations, a black market, and processes for trying and punishing violators. He later came to the United States, studied psychology, became a department chair at the University of Chicago, and spent his career investigating this phenomenon of the few.

Over time, he named it *flow*. Flow he said was a collection of phenomenon:[2]

1. Time warped, either speeding up or slowing down
2. One lost a sense of self-awareness
3. One developed an intense focus on the moment
4. One performed at his or her absolute best
5. Surprisingly, this was not difficult, rather it simply *flowed* out
6. This experience felt really good
7. Afterward, one had a sense of growth and development

Have you ever experienced this? When? Where? What were you doing?

When I asked people all over the world if they had experienced this sometime somewhere, almost everyone raised their hands. They mentioned things like reading, singing, speaking, writing computer code,

---

[2] Mihalyi Csikszentmihalyi, *Flow*.

doing math (yes, even calculus), running, playing various sports (individual and team), giving birth (yes), playing musical instruments, and many, many more. Clearly, people experience these seven things from different activities and in different situations.

Example

A heart surgeon goes into a coronary bypass case. Five hours later, he emerges and says the surgery felt like 15 minutes, that he had an *out-of-body* experience as if he were hovering over the room watching his own and others' work, that his fingers were not his own, that it was a *transcendental* experience. (Twenty years later, a man he trained will perform a triple bypass on the author.)

Diagram

Have you ever been in FLOW? When ...

- ❖ Time warps (slow or fast)
- ❖ Lose sense of self
- ❖ Intense focus
- ❖ Perform at highest level
- ❖ Seems effortless (flow)
- ❖ Internally satisfying
- ❖ Regain larger sense of self

Source: Adapted from FLOW by Mihalyi Csikszentmihalyi

https://google.com/search?q=images+Mihalyi+Csikszentmihalyi&tbm=isch&ved=2ahUKEwjjwejBy7
zuAhUSPN8KHQSLDxgQ2-cCegQIABAA&oq=images+Mihalyi+Csikszentmihalyi&gs_lcp=CgN
pbWcQAzoECCMQJzoCCAA6BggAEAgQHlCf_wZYm7kHYIHCB2gAcAB4AIABYogBhAuSA-
QIyNJgBAKABAaoBC2d3cy13aXotaW1nwEEB&sclient=img&ei=XpwRYOOaA5L4_AaElr7AA
Q&bih=578&biw=1366&rlz=1C1GCEB_enUS910US910#imgrc=ptlcls32PMEKeM

Challenge

1. Identify specific incidents when you have been in *flow*.
2. Describe the feelings you had when you were in flow. Can you identify how you *felt?*
3. How often do you feel this phenomenon?
4. What do you think causes this to happen?

32. What Do You Think of Flow?

Concept

What do you think of *flow*? Does it come and go like the breeze? Is it manageable? Could you manage the frequency with which you experience flow? Could you live in a way to ramp up the percentage of time in life that you are in flow?

Or is flow something that *just happens* from time to time?

Could one design flow into one's life?

What if flow was something you could *take with you* wherever you went?

Imagine how your life would change if you could raise the probability of being in flow on any given day or week.

Example

A teenage girl sat down to practice the piano. She immersed herself in her session. She didn't notice that the family dog came in to lie beside her. She didn't notice when her siblings came in to listen. She didn't notice when her mom came in. She didn't notice when her father came in and sat down by the rest of them. When she finished her session, she looked up and said, "Whoa! Where did you all come from?" (true story)

Did this "just happen?"

Diagram

What to you think of FLOW?

- It seems to come from a variety of sources
- But can you repeat it regularly or is it "unmanageable?"
- Could you "design" it into your life?
- Even better, could you take it with you wherever you go?

Challenge

1. Try to identify *different* activities in which you have experienced flow. Are there any?
2. What made those different kinds of activities produce the similar experience of flow?

33. The Resonance Model

Concept

Doug Newburg in his research into the relationship between feel and performance interviewed some 500+ high performers: athletes in 29 different sports, Olympic athletes, world champions; touring musicians who like athletes had to perform at their best on demand; heart surgeons who held people's lives in their hands every day; executives in double digit growth businesses; and landing officers and pilots on aircraft carriers, another place where one mistake and people die.

In analyzing these interviews, Newburg identified a common pattern. All these people he said had a dream, put in intense preparation, dealt with obstacles, and had to find ways to revisit their dreams.

The *dreams* he mentioned were not the usual external dreams of achievement, rather the internal feelings of how they wanted to feel. The *preparation* was long and intense (think Malcolm Gladwell's 10,000 hour rule, *Outliers*). Newburg noted that for anyone to get really good at something, they must really love it. Otherwise, they wouldn't have the stamina required to practice that long to become expert.

Obstacles referred to speed bumps along the way where one tried and failed. When people fail at something, Newburg observes, they tend to tell themselves, "I have to practice more," and in so doing put themselves in a *duty cycle*, an obligatory mindset. Many people get stuck there and lose sight of the childlike feeling they had when they were performing at their best out of sheer joy and enthusiasm.

And "Revisiting the Dream" referred to how people reconnected with their *internal dream*, that is, how they wanted to feel.

Example

Doug worked with a runner from South America. Her friends had talked her into running in the national marathon. She had never done a marathon before and was nervous. In her conversations with Doug, he counselled her to focus on how she felt when she ran rather than focusing on her intermediate results.

After the race, she called Doug and they talked for a long time. She described her feelings during the race and how enjoyable it was. When the call was over, Doug didn't know how she had finished; he didn't ask and she didn't volunteer. He found out later she had won; her first marathon.

How many parents press their children to perform externally in sports? "How many runs did you score? How many touchdowns did you make? How many games did you win?" Perhaps parents should focus on their child's experience whether in sports, music, art, math, or whatever the subject is. When people enjoy what they are doing, they tend to get better at it.

Doug's lesson was a powerful one for me. Eventually, we co-authored a book focusing on this phenomenon, *Powered by Feel: How Individuals, Teams and Companies Excel* (World Scientific 2008).

Diagram

The Resonance Model

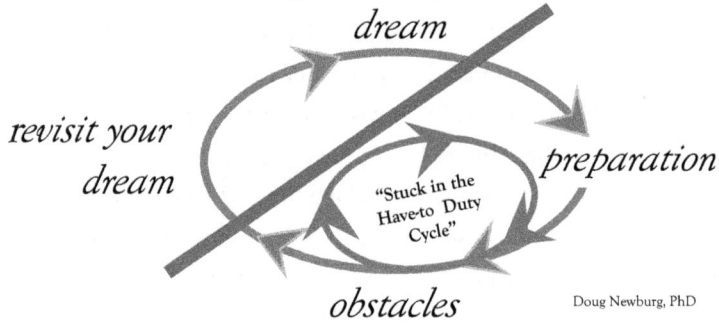

Doug Newburg, PhD

Challenge

1. Watch for the Resonance Cycle as you observe other high performers.
2. Pay attention to how much practice/preparation is required to perform at a high level.
3. Note how much *stamina*, that is, love for the activity is required to get to where you can perform at a high level.
4. Think about the obstacles you have encountered in life and how you responded to them.
5. Whenever you find yourself in a *have to* frame of mind, pause and use your "Resonance Radar" to reset your energy level. Why are you where you are? How many choices did you make to get there? What was it that made you choose what you did? Can you recapture that emotion when you first chose?

34. Managing Your Energy: External and Internal Dreams

Concept

Bill Gates once noted, "When people come to work, it's important that they be connected to a dream." This is an important principle of Level Three Leadership—that people are inspired and will give more energy if they believe deeply in what they are doing. Most managers don't understand this, they simply work at Level One using rewards and punishments to *motivate* their people. Most likely Gates was referring to an *external dream*, what people want to do or become. Newburg's subjects however talked about an *internal dream*, how they wanted to *feel*. If one is rich, powerful and famous, but feels miserable, what good is that external success?

The first element in Doug's resonance model is *dream*. By this he means something different from what most people think of as a dream. Most people think about what they want to do or become. "I want to be a pilot. I want to be a doctor. I want to be Senator. I want to build skyscrapers." And so on. Let's call these achievements *external dreams* because they are visible.

But what Doug's interviewees wanted to talk about was how they *felt*. The premise they discussed was that if you paid attention to how you feel, your performance, paradoxically, goes up. Remember Dave Scott's statement from the previous chapter.

We might call this one *internal dream*. They described how they wanted to feel. Jeff Rouse, nine years the world record holder in the 100 meter backstroke and Olympic gold medallist calls it *easy speed*, when he exerts 80 percent effort but gets 100 percent efficiency. It's not struggling and straining, rather it is a sense of harmony with one's surroundings and being at one with the world. Martial artists call it *mushin* to be without mind, a state in which one can be very dynamic, perform at one's best but without thinking about what one is doing. In aikido they refer to the unification of mind and body.

We could, I suppose, connect this concept to the *elephant* in Jon Haidt's *Righteous Mind*, already introduced. The pre-conscious *knowledge* of what to do and the ability to do it very fast. This *fast thinking* system must be built, however, it is not born with us. During our early years our preferences form and emerge. We gradually become aware of what we like and what we don't like. Newburg argues that the definition of success is, "when it's over, you want to do it again."

Example

Dawn Staley, two time NCAA women's basketball player of the year, WNBA all-star, Olympic gold medallist, and head coach described it like this: "Everyone wants to win, that's the goal. But that's not why I play. I play for the feeling I get when the game's on the line, and I've got the ball."[3]

What is that for you? I have only ever met one person who could answer that question immediately. He was a finance professor who said without hesitation, "Buoyant, connected mastery. I love being in the classroom when I can feel the rising tide of enthusiasm and learning, everyone in the room is attentive and connected and driving the conversation, yet underneath it, I know I'm in control of what's going on."

Diagram

Examples of Feel ...

❖ Easy speed (Jeff Rouse)
❖ Playing to win at the highest level (Dawn Staley)
❖ Out of my chest
❖ Being at one with my surroundings
❖ Peaceful, satisfied, alive
❖ Buoyant, connected mastery
❖ Light, unhurried, engaged and connected.

Source: https://google.com/search?q=images+Jeff+Rouse&tbm=isch&ved=2ahUKEwihr4D9y7zu AhXNi-AKHaEWDFEQ2-cCegQIABAA&oq=images+Jeff+Rouse&gs_lcp=CgNpbWcQA zoCCAA6BggAEAgQHlDqxQVY29QFYMTcBWgAcAB4AIABUogB4wSSAQIxMJgBA KABAaoBC2d3cy13aXotaW1nAEB&sclient=img&ei=2pwRYKHaCs2XggehrbCIBQ& bih=578&biw=1366&rlz=1C1GCEB_enUS910US910#imgrc=918TO3PePxSprM
https://google.com/search?q=images+Dawn+Staley&tbm=isch&ved=2ahUKEwjv8JuqzL zuAhXRneAKHZL6CcUQ2-cCegQIABAA&oq=images+Dawn+Staley&gs_lcp=CgNp- bWcQAzoECCMQJzoCCAA6BggAEAUQHjoECAAQHjoGCAAQCBAeUO6XBFirqARggLI EaABwAHgAgAGkAYgBnQaSAQM5LjKYAQCgAQGqAQtnd3Mtd2l6LWltZ8ABAQ&sclie nt=img&ei=OJ0RYO_0PNG7ggeS9aeoDA&bih=578&biw=1366&rlz=1C1GCEB_enUS910U S910#imgrc=uObajy2svjvw_M

---

[3] Close words to that effect as reported by Doug Newburg.

Challenge

1. Can you, before you die, figure out how you want to feel?
2. Make it one sentence or less. Remember "happy" is too broad, vague and non-differentiating.
3. Think back on the times when you have been in *flow*, when you were performing at your best and feeling good. Find the adjectives to describe those feelings. Most of us are not very good at describing our feelings. See if you can find the words.

35. Preparation

Concept

The second element in Doug Newburg's Resonance model is *preparation*. By that he meant that one cannot expect to realize an internal dream, how you want to feel, without preparing to recreate it. This means practice, rehearsal, lessons, study, and more. And lots of it. I have already mentioned Malcolm Gladwell's 10,000 hour rule.

How long does it take to get really good at something? My colleague, Alex Horniman, is wont to say, "Excellence is a neurotic lifestyle." Bud Greenspan once noted that "Excellence is attained by those who care more than others think is wise, who risk more than others think is safe, and who dream more than others think is practical." Vijay Singh, professional golfer, noted that confidence doesn't come from winning, rather, confidence comes from practice and winning comes from confidence. What do you think? Looking at the balance wheel, if you want to be world-class at something, will the other aspects of your life suffer? How much does one need to focus to be world-class?

Perhaps more importantly, how skilled do you intend to be? How often do you settle for *good enough*? How many cut corners when running laps? How many seek to do the absolute least they can to get by? How many can look back and say that every turn they got, they did their absolute best? Is excellence a habit? Probably one that fits people with a little obsessive compulsive disorder (OCD). Is excellence a matter of brain chemistry? What percentage of your assignments thus far in life have you done your absolute best on? Alex also used to tell me, "What if Peters and Waterman's book (*In Search of Excellence*) had been titled *In Search of Good Enough*?" It's a profound question.

Example

One CEO of a $20 billion company once told me, "In these 32 assignments I got, go here go there, six months, a year, not one of those came undone. (All finished in spec, ahead of schedule, and under budget.) So, I wanted to be able to look back and have the confidence, to know, that I had always done my best. So, fix it in the right way with the right people and the right processes, it just works."

Bruce Hornsby, one of the subjects in Newburg's study, noted that at one point, he wanted to be able to express his feelings seamlessly on the keyboard. So he put a piano in his backyard *shed* and began practicing scales and riffs for hours a day, day after day. His wife said it was awful, she was in the house trying to manage their new family, and he was out in the barn for endless hours. Hornsby said that after many months he could play whatever he wanted on the moment. So, he crossed his hands and started over again. Eventually, he could cross his hands mid-song and continue without missing a note. He would do this on stage and his band members would just gape in amazement. Excellence. World-class.

Diagram

Preparation

People ask me, "How do you play so well?" I practiced, intense "shedding." If you're willing to put in the time, you can do it to a certain level. Maybe I have a special talent that is intangible, but if you are willing to put in the time, you can really get it together."

Bruce Hornsby

Source: https://google.com/search?q=images+Bruce+Hornsby&tbm=isch&ved=2ahUKEwiH5_z MzLzuAhWKFN8KHYfwBUMQ2-cCegQIABAA&oq=images+Bruce+Hornsby&gs_ lcp=CgNpbWcQAzIGCAAQCBAeOgIIAFDe-gdYjpEIYJaZCCgAcAB4AIABdIgB0gaSAQQx MS4ymAEAoAEBqgELZ3dzLXdpei1pbWfAAQE&sclient=img&ei=gZ0RYMeiNoqp_AaH4Ze YBA&bih=578&biw=1366&rlz=1C1GCEB_enUS910US910#imgrc=n-QsAndilKJRJM

Challenge

   1. How often do you do your best?

   2. How often do you say to yourself, "That's good enough?"

   3. How important is it to you to be the best at what you do?

4. What is the difference between "be the best you can be" and "be the best in the world?" How does the pursuit of excellence affect one's work-life balance?

5. What is it that you love so much, if anything, that you can lose yourself in it and view practice as enjoyment rather than duty/obligation?

36. Obstacles

Concept

The third element in Newburg's model of Resonance is encountering *obstacles*, attempting and failing. His conclusion was that most if not all high performers run into obstacles and that how they deal with those obstacles determines whether they will go on to higher performance or sink into a kind of mediocrity. The choice is between a mindset of obligation versus a mindset of revisiting one's internal dream.

This choice is a big one. Most people it seems fall into what Newburg called a *duty cycle* or an *obligation cycle*. That is, they became *cut off* from their internal dream, they forgot what it was like, and began to focus on results instead of the feel that produces results and their performance eroded and their determination to practice, their method of practice, wavered. In essence, they began to think about what they *had to do* instead of what they wanted to do and how they wanted to feel.

Eventually, this *duty-cycle* mindset causes one to lose stamina and performance declines.

There are other kinds of obstacles to living in *resonance*. One, oddly, is success. When one *wins*, one begins doing other things than what puts them in the zone. Golfers who win go on television shows and give interviews and make advertisements and ironically, they are playing less golf and therefore reducing the time they are able to get in the flow. Success can be a big obstacle.

Example

Vijay Singh, a professional golfer, once noted how much he loved practicing golf. He even said sometimes he would just rather hit golf balls all day than play in competition. He said he just loved the way it *felt* when he hit balls flush on the sweet spot of the club. Feel.

On the other hand, consider the professional golfer Tom Weiskopf. He once noted that he remembered exactly the day that he stopped enjoying golf; it was the day he turned pro. What happened that day? The love of his life went from being a choice to being an obligation. Now, it was something he *had* to do.

Contrast that with another of Newburg's subjects, John Molo, Grammy Award winning musician/drummer. He said that people paid him a lot of money to be away from home, to eat rubber chicken, to ride on buses all night long, and to sleep in cheap hotels. But when he went on stage and the curtain went up and the lights went on, *THAT* he did for free. What a great lesson! If you go in to work every day, thinking, "What do I have to do today," you have put yourself in an obligatory mindset and this is a formula for reduced performance.

That single insight has had a huge impact on my own life. I strive now to always come back to, "What do I want to feel today? How can I make that happen?"

What do you think?

Diagram

OBSTACLES

Adversity has ever been considered the state in which a man most easily becomes acquainted with himself.

- Samuel Johnson

Source: https://google.com/search?q=images+Samuel+Johnson&tbm=isch&ved=2ahUKEwjyuc ONzbzuAhVHON8KHbwRCXYQ2-cCegQIABAA&oq=images+Samuel+Johnson&gs_lcp=C gNpbWcQAzIGCAAQCBAeOgIIADoGCAAQBRAeUMO8Clit2ApgheAKaABwAHgAgA FfiAG2BpIBAjE0mAEAoAEBqgELZ3dzLXdpei1pbWfAAQE&sclient=img&ei=CZ4RYLKRE Mfw_Aa8o6SwBw&bih=578&biw=1366&rlz=1C1GCEB_enUS910US910#imgrc=gnqQLUOZ NApkxM

Avoid Getting Stuck in the "Have-To Duty Cycle"

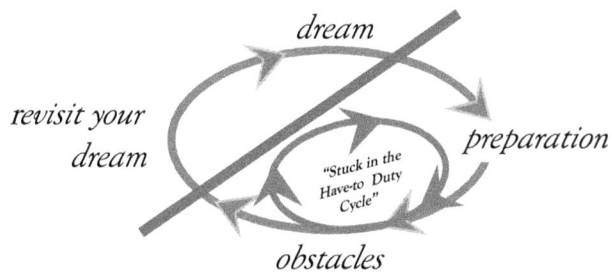

Source: Doug Newburg, PhD

Challenge

1. What's your dominant thought on your way into work on an average day? "What do I have to do today?" Beware.
2. Identify the major obstacles you have encountered in life.
3. How did you deal with them? Did you give up? Try to practice harder?
4. How much stamina to practice do you have when you are thinking that you *have* to go practice?
5. What do you love so much that doing it is just pure pleasure?
6. How could you turn your *job* into productive and enjoyable *work*?
7. Separate the things that *people pay you for* (grading exams) from the things you do for *free* (teaching classes).

37. Revisiting the Dream

Concept

The last element in Newburg's Resonance Model is *revisiting the dream*. By this, he means regaining intimate contact with one's early, feel-based choices in life. Somewhere along the line, we get told what to do, how to do it, and to put our feelings aside.

"Revisiting the Dream" means finding those feelings again, paying attention to them, and managing your life and career accordingly. For many, this means a deep re-evaluation of where they are and what they want. It means a shift in focus from external outcomes to internal experience—which by the way leads to better external outcomes.

When you find yourself in a *blue funk* and aren't happy with your life, I encourage you to stop, think about how you want to feel, get that down and on paper, and then begin working on how you can get that on a regular basis. And *that* may mean changing some long-established habits around speech patterns, VABE recognition, diet, exercise, sleep, and life planning.

Example

One of Doug's subjects was a thoracic surgeon who one morning had a patient die on the operating table. This man went back to his office and sitting there in a *blue funk*, depressed, thinking about what had happened. And he had another procedure scheduled right after the lunch hour.

Now, if you were the patient scheduled for after lunch, is this information you would like to have? I would. Say, Doc, are you on your game today? Are you feeling confident? If not, maybe we should re-schedule.

Doug was aware of this situation and went to visit the surgeon. The doctor said, "Go away, I want to be alone." Doug's reply was, "Hmm. Not going away and we need to talk. This may seem like a dumb question, but why did you become a heart surgeon?" "What?" replied the MD. "Go away!" "Humour me," Doug said. "Why did you become a heart surgeon?"

The doctor thinks for a second and says, "I was good with my hands and it looked like a profitable career." "Okay," says Doug. "Go back further. Why did you become a doctor?" "My mother thought it was a good thing and I did well in pre-med." "Okay. Go back further. Why did you go to med school?" "Well, I did well in organic chemistry, so it seemed normal." "Okay. Go back further. Why did you take pre-med classes?"

At this point the doctor, pauses, thinks more deeply, and then says, "Hmmm. When I was six, there was a commotion in the middle of the house. I remember padding down the hallway in my pyjamas and seeing my grandfather lying on the floor in the living room. My dad was kneeling over him and trying to revive him. My mom was crying and on the phone calling 911. I felt so helpless. The truth is that's the moment I vowed I would work to never let that happen again. That's the moment I decided to be a heart surgeon."

The hair on Doug's neck stood up. And there it was. The core emotional, feel-based choice that put that man on the path to that morning.

So, Doug says, "Come with me." And he led the doctor down to the room of the elderly man awaiting surgery that afternoon. Doug says, "Hello. You don't know me, and I understand you are going to have a quadruple bypass this afternoon." "Yes that's right." "Okay. You know that they are going to crack your chest, stop your heart, pour buckets of ice in to your chest cavity, strip a vein from ankle to hip, and then stitch that vein in pieces onto your heart. That's very, very invasive. Why would you want to do that?" "Well, the doc here says I'll die if I don't."

"Okay, this may seem like a dumb question, but why do you want to live? These grafts will on average give you another ten years of life. If it works what would you want to DO with those years?"

The old man thought a moment and then said, "I have two grandchildren, boys. I'd like to go fishing with those boys."

At this point the surgeon jumps in to the conversation and said, "That's great. And we are going to do everything we can scientifically and medically and team-wise to make that happen! And I want you to fight for that with everything you have!" And the grandfather said, "Uh, okay, Doctor!"

Six hours later when Doug went to see the doctor, he said, "It was weird. It was like I was watching my own fingers from above the table. We were in there for five hours, but it felt like minutes. Everything went swimmingly. Wow."

Doug just smiled and went home. He had helped this surgeon go from a depressed likely to be dangerous operating condition to an emotionally high and high performing mental state that focused on the feelings he had when he first decided to become a heart surgeon. By bringing the doctor back to that state, he significantly enhanced his odds of performing at a very high level. He helped him revisit his dream.

The surgeon soon learned to manage this part of the Resonance Model himself. Going forward, he asked his patients what they wanted to do with their renewed life span. "Play with the grandchildren. Mow the lawn. Go sailing. Fly my plane again." And then he asked them to send him a picture doing that after they recovered. And they did. Soon he had a drawer full of photos. Whenever he got depressed because of whatever, he would take out one or two of those photos and they would remind him of why he was doing what he was doing and he would find new energy. Next, he loaded those photos onto his smart phone so they would be with him all the time.

This heart surgeon had become a self-leading manager of his own energy level and thereby a manager of his own energy level.

Diagram

Imagine a sleepy polar bear pushing himself across ice on his belly—tired, worn out, at the end of his rope.[4] Now imagine an adolescent male penguin during mating season dancing his way through the ladies, putting on his best moves, a veritable ball of energy?[5] Which would you like hire—polar bear or penguin?

---

[4] https://google.com/search?q=sleepy+polar+bear&rlz=1C1GCEB_enUS910U S910&oq=sleepy+polar+bear&aqs=chrome..69i57j0l3j0i22i30l6.3397j0j7&sou rceid=chrome&ie=UTF-8

[5] https://google.com/search?q=energetic+penguin+images&rlz=1C1GCEB_ enUS910US910&tbm=isch&source=iu&ictx=1&fir=1H3SSTEZl6ShiM%252 CUilbXdaeR8qZIM%252C_&vet=1&usg=AI4_-kR4aWz_vYgQ7-hv4pQnak VZ8MouaQ&sa=X&ved=2ahUKEwjIo_T7kOLuAhU-FVkFHXVlD1IQ9QF6 BAgOEAE#imgrc=1H3SSTEZl6ShiM

How do you approach your work?
Polar Bear or Penguin?

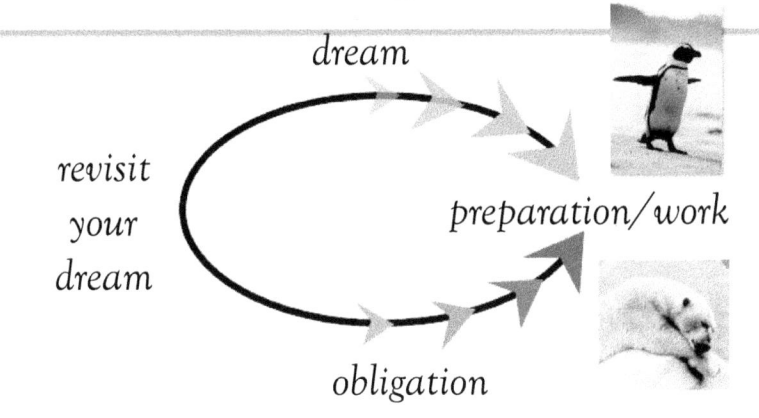

dream

revisit
your
dream

preparation/work

obligation

Do you approach your work like a sleepy polar bear or an energetic penguin?

Challenge

1. Have you clarified yet how you want to feel?
2. Can you remember when you first had that feeling?
3. How often are you getting that at work?
4. What mechanisms can you use to help you remember your (internal) dream?
5. What is the purpose of life? I think it is
   (a) To figure out how you want to feel before you die.
   (b) To invest in your capacity to recreate that on a regular basis.
   (c) To realize that when you are in *flow* it doesn't get any better than that.
   (d) To help others figure out they want to feel and to help them get that.

SECTION IV

Global Business Leaders

In this section, we explore the qualities that successful global business leaders need. Thanks here to Bob Johnson, former CEO of Honeywell Aerospace and of Dubai Aerospace Enterprises. Bob's book with Rob Oberwise, *Developing Global Leaders: A Guide to Managing Effectively in Unfamiliar Places* (Palgrave Macmillan 2012) and my conversations with him and the case we wrote and published on his life and career provide the basis for this section.

38. The Importance of Global Business Leaders

Concept

Many people malign large corporations. And there is much that needs improving in them, not the least of which is the proportional divide between extractors and contributors. Many scholars, consultants, ethicists, and observers have worked hard to bring Adam Smith's men of *good character* more prominently into the capitalist model.

That said, I don't see how the political and religious leaders will *save the world*. If anything, they contribute to most of the world's conflicts. I have become convinced that it is the global business leaders who are and have been most likely to knit the world together into a global economy that is tolerant of cultural differences, religious differences, and willing to compromise for the sake of a mutually beneficial deal. I say *mutually* beneficial. Historically, many corporations were political entities unto themselves and clearly took more than they gave. Witness the East India Company and its peers.

But today, business leaders who are willing to live in different cultures, tolerate them, adapt to them, and leave a fair share of the balance of trade in the foreign site are better ambassadors of world peace than zealots and political fanatics.

Sustainable trade makes friends of otherwise distrustful enemies. I say *sustainable*. Short-term extraction with unbalanced benefits is not a viable long-term strategy. Mutual benefit and related trust over time brings business people to each other's tables. They share food, the idiosyncrasies of their cuisines, their clothing, their drink, their manners, and their dreams. If those dreams are based on unbalanced extraction or control, the sustainability erodes.

So, I say that it is the business leaders who have the best chance of building world peace. Tranquility is a goal of the executive. Wars are bad for (most, non-defense related) business. Business people want stable markets, stable political environments, stable exchange rates, ... stability around the table.

What do you think?

Former CEO of Honeywell Aerospace, Robert D. Johnson, and a colleague wrote a book on global business leadership. See *Developing Global Leaders: A Guide to Managing Effectively in Unfamiliar Places* (Palgrave McMillan, 2012). *Kiss, Bow or Shake Hands* is also a great guide to working in different cultures.

The next several chapters will explore various aspects of the challenges involved in conducting business in different lands, countries, regions, and cultures.

Example

Many years ago, several international organizations criticized Nestle's for assertively marketing baby formula in under-developed lesser educated countries in Africa. These NPOs argued that breast milk was healthier for babies than formula and that the company was dumping unsold product on the uninformed. The arguments went back and forth.[1]

On the other hand Merck, a large pharmaceutical company, decided to distribute a cure for river blindness free of change including funding a significant distribution system.[2]

Many oil companies established operations in foreign countries that had reserves but lacked in technology or capital. In some of these countries, citizens felt that the bulk of the wealth had left them, that the oil companies were extracting too much.[3] Some countries nationalized the oil operations causing significant disruptions in the global petroleum system.[4] These were political upheavals.

Diagram

International Business Dinner in Beijing, China. Source: author.

---

[1] https://en.wikipedia.org/wiki/Nestl%C3%A9_boycott
[2] http://nytimes.com/1987/10/22/world/merck-offers-free-distribution-of-new-river-blindness-drug.html
[3] https://en.wikipedia.org/wiki/Oil_imperialism_theories
[4] https://en.wikipedia.org/wiki/Nationalization_of_oil_supplies

Challenge

1. What is your impression of global corporations?
2. If we lumped all of the war, conflict, and terror in the world, past and present, how much of that would you attribute to religion, politics or business interests? Total = 100 percent.
3. Write a draft of what you think the international code of business ethics should be. Be prepared to present this to your peers.

39. Cultural Tolerance

Concept

Former CEO of Honeywell Aerospace, Bob Johnson, named "cultural tolerance" in his book on *Developing Global Leaders*.[5] In today's interconnected world where raw materials, refining, molding, assembly, advertising, sales, and service might all be done in different countries, the need for an executive to have cultural tolerance seems obvious. The willingness to adjust one's own Level Three assumptions about how one travels, meets others, exchanges business cards, sits, speaks, eats, and dresses is essential for the modern executive.

Despite this, many business people hold deep biases for or against various parts of other cultures. In my experience, they tend to be more culturally tolerant, however, than political or religious leaders. It seems more likely to me that talented and culturally tolerant global business people are more likely to move the world toward global peace than their political or religious counterparts.

When people judge others by their own cultural VABEs, it will be difficult to conduct business. When people are willing to grant others some latitude in the relatively superficial aspects of culture like dress, cuisine, social interactions, and time, deals will be made and mutually beneficial relationships will form.

How willing are you to eat new kinds of food, to dress differently, and to spend time in ways you are not used to? If offered the honor of raw monkey brain (Indonesia), would you partake? Or snake? Or shrimp that were still moving? How willing are you to be driven out into the desert to who knows where to participate in a tent meeting? How willing are you to learn to shake hands or to place your hand over your heart or to allow someone to kiss the hem of your pants or to bow properly or to touch your palms and bow? How willing are you to learn to pause daily for prayer time, to eat with your fingers or a fork, to tolerate cars coming at you on your side of the road or to ride on a motorcycle?

---

[5] Johnson, R.D., and R. Oberwise. 2012. *Developing Global Leaders: A Guide to Managing Effectively in Unfamiliar Places.* New York, NY: Palgrave Macmillan.

Culture is a set of shared VABEs. And VABEs are deeply seated, closely held values, assumptions, beliefs, and expectations about how the world is or should be. Many, if not most people, are unwilling to make the compromises described above. They assume that their culture is superior to the cultures of others. They expect others to conform to their beliefs. This is not the foundation for successful global business dealings.

IF you want to manage raw materials in Costa Rica, machining tolerances in China, assembly in Mexico, refining in the United Arab Emirates, marketing in India or Japan, and customer service in Singapore, you must learn and embrace a robust tolerance of cultural differences.

There are a number of books that can help you in this regard. *Kiss, Bow or Shake Hands* is one.[6] *The Culture Map: Breaking Through the Invisible Boundaries of Global Business* is another.[7] *The Art of Crossing Cultures* is another.[8]

Better than reading is going. Travel abroad, with a tolerant and curious mindset, is a good way to test your cultural tolerance. Combining the two is even better. When you travel, you may not experience the full range of a culture—indeed, that may take years of curious residence. And travel is no guarantee of developing a cultural tolerance—for some, travel simply reinforces their (unexamined) belief in their own way of doing things. Traveling abroad and living in Little Tokyo, Chinatown, the American enclave, or the German neighborhood will stunt your cultural growth and tolerance. For many, the stigma of being a foreigner, not understanding the language and more, is overwhelming and so they clump together with people *like them*.

---

[6] https://amazon.com/Kiss-Bow-Shake-Hands-Bestselling/dp/1593373686

[7] https://amazon.com/Culture-Map-Breaking-Invisible-Boundaries/dp/1610392507/ref=pd_sbs_14_t_1?_encoding=UTF8&psc=1&refRID=JTGPDKQCMQEEMW2X3J7Y

[8] https://amazon.com/Art-Crossing-Cultures-2nd/dp/1931930538/ref=pd_sim_14_2?_encoding=UTF8&pd_rd_i=1931930538&pd_rd_r=JTGPDKQCMQEEMW2X3J7Y&pd_rd_w=eJ4ba&pd_rd_wg=s2TL8&psc=1&refRID=JTGPDKQCMQEEMW2X3J7Y

Example

A major American manufacturer used a Japanese supplier for a significant portion of the parts for their end products. After years of using this supplier, American management decided to move the supply of those parts to a domestic supplier. Management wanted to do that smoothly and courteously to their Japanese supplier, so they announced to their supplier a year in advance of the transition to give them time to manage their business and to provide time for the American plant(s) to make their adjustments as well. A month later, all shipments from Japan ceased throwing the Americans into turmoil as they scrambled to find parts to assemble. The Japanese viewed the announcement as an insult and a rupture of a long-standing trusted relationship. They *punished* their American, now distrusted, customer by stopping shipments immediately.

In January, 2016, Iranian president, Hassan Rouhani, made a historic trip to visit European leaders. Given his Muslim faith, Rouhani asked his Italian hosts to cover naked statues and refrain from serving wine at meals. The Italians complied. Rouhani made the same requests of his French hosts. The President of France replied that since Rouhani was visiting France, he would be asked to tolerate French cultural standards and refused to cover statues of naked women and also said he intended to serve wine at meals. The resulting irritation led to the canceling of Rouhani's visit to France.[9] [10] [11] [12]

What's your take? Where was the cultural tolerance?

---

[9] https://theguardian.com/world/2016/jan/25/hassan-rouhani-in-first-europe-visit-by-iranian-president-in-16-years

[10] https://rt.com/news/329300-iran-rouhani-europe-trip/

[11] http://aljazeera.com/news/2016/01/iran-rouhani-starts-historic-visit-europe-160125115232346.html

[12] http://newyorker.com/news/daily-comment/france-iran-and-the-affair-of-the-lunch-wine

Diagram

Abu Dhabi Falconry Festival   Giza Pyramid

Challenge

1. What aspects of other cultures do you find most disturbing?
2. What aspects of your culture are you least likely to adjust?
3. What have you learned from other cultures?
4. Which of your VABEs have been challenged by other cultures?
5. Are you willing to travel or even live abroad?

40. Humility to Learn

Concept

Humility is a controversial potential characteristic of the effective global executive. Controversial because some, like Jim Collins,[13] have argued that humility is an important characteristic of effective executives while others would argue that many, if not most, CEOs are highly self-confident and even narcissistically arrogant.[14] VABEs probably play big part here as researchers like all of us have preferences and ideal models in our heads.

Part of the issue here is semantics. By humility here, I mean openness to learning rather than self-effacement or a humble demeanor. Executives who are willing to learn from others are better prepared to foresee problems, to get better options for solutions, and be better prepared to ward off potential substitutions.

Many people in life find it difficult to listen to feedback, to contradictory evidence, to data that doesn't support their VABEs. And people who gain positions of power and influence often think or believe deeply that since I got to where I am, I must be *right*. Thus, powerful people may lose whatever learning humility they may have once had. Are you one of those?

Meanwhile, Bob Sutton at Stanford University described his experience receiving hundreds of e-mails about his article in the *Harvard Business Review* decrying the arrogant assholes that many saw in the ranks of business executives. He subsequently wrote a book entitled "The No Asshole Rule."

One may be able to get short-term results by using the Level One Techniques of intimidation, threat, and coercion. Fear is not respect.[15] When the threat is removed, those who *obeyed* will likely choose different paths.

---

[13] In *Good to Great*. See Level 5 Leadership: The Triumph of Humility and Fierce Resolve, HBR, July–August 2005.

[14] http://businessinsider.com/asshole-ceos-startup-founders-and-success-2014-11

[15] http://eqi.org/respect.htm

Example

Rick Pitino, head coach of the Louisville University men's basketball team, once noted,

> Humility is the true key to success. Successful people lose their way at times. They often embrace and overindulge from the fruits of success. Humility halts this arrogance and self-indulging trap. Humble people share the credit and wealth, remaining focused and hungry to continue the journey of success.[16]

William Pollard also said, "Learning and innovation go hand in hand. The arrogance of success is to think that what you did yesterday will be sufficient for tomorrow."[17]

Diagram

---

[16] https://brainyquote.com/quotes/quotes/r/rickpitino675705.html?src=t_arrogance

[17] https://brainyquote.com/quotes/quotes/r/rickpitino675705.html?src=t_arrogance

Challenge

1. What is your opinion of the arrogant, proud, self-aggrandizing people you know?
2. How do you want to be known? Does your reputation among your followers matter to you?
3. How can one avoid becoming more arrogant as one's power and responsibility increases?
4. What will you do to keep your openness to learning to be alive and healthy?
5. Do you think humility means a person is weak? Why?

41. Honesty

Concept

Should executives be honest? That may seem like a simple question. Yet when one reads about the World Com, Enron, Madoff, Tyco, and Nestle scandals over the last several decades, it is clear that many executives are not. One could argue that much of marketing efforts overemphasize product or service good points and underemphasize the bad points. Read the fine print. Listen to the rapid talking at the end of the commercial. Do marketers attempt to persuade potential buyers by ignoring or even mis-stating research data on their products and services? Witness the history of marketing of tobacco, alcohol, sugar, and soda drinks. Does it pay to be honest?

Should you tell the truth? Or only when others *need to know*? What if others *cannot handle the truth*? What if telling the truth compromises your competitive advantage? Should you tell the *whole* truth or can/should you just tell part of the *truth*? What if telling the truth would be harmful to yourself? Or cause your company to lose some money? What if the truth would hurt the other person?

Yogi Berra is reported to have said one time, "ninety percent of short putts don't go in the hole." That is a *true* statement. And it doesn't tell the whole story. What is the role of honesty in your reputation? In labor negotiations? In international weapons negotiations? In marriages?

There are cultures in the world in which it is expected that people will not tell you the truth or the whole truth. In some cultures, the measure of a good negotiator is how well he or she can manipulate the other person to get what they want. What expectations (VABEs) would you have going into those countries to do business?

Examples

I was surprised one time during a consulting assignment with a company's senior executives. In the middle of our discussion, these colleagues began shouting at one another. One senior vice president even stood up on his chair, and pointing emphatically with his index finger, began yelling at his colleagues across the room. The question in discussion was this, "Should executives tell the truth?" Half of the room was asserting that "If you tell the truth, people will take advantage of you!" The other half of the room just as firmly asserted that "If you don't tell the truth, people won't trust you."

The discussion raged. People began to try to find the *line* between truth-telling and competitive secrecy and *omitting* some relevant facts.

Waking up one morning, I saw my wife dressing in front of the mirror. She turned to me and said, "Does this blouse make me look fat?" Where do you draw the line between honesty and kindness? What would you say in this situation?

A seminar participant once told me that he was part of a management team called together to decide whether or not to close the plant they were managing. The GM announced that they were going to close the plant but that no one should say anything to anyone until the day lest worker production drop off. Everyone in the plant knew that management was meeting. One employee of my participant loitered around the conference room door. When the meeting broke, he asked his boss, "Are you going to close the plant?" What should the manager have said?

Once while having dinner during the Clinton administration with the CEO of a $2 billion business, I mentioned that my instructor in business school, Steve Covey, once noted that if a man would cheat on his wife, he'd cheat in business. The CEO replied, "Well, that's not true. I know most of the business people in the city and they all have mistresses and I'd trust them any day in a business deal." What's your VABE?

Diagram

Challenge

1. What were the biggest lies you have told? What was the impact of those incidents?
2. What lies do you tell your partner?
3. What lies do you think your partner tells you?
4. What lies do you tell yourself?
5. What's your VABE about honesty? "Tell the truth all the time?" What?
6. What role does *bluffing* play in the world? In business?
7. Would you lie a little if it meant saving yourself $1,000? $10,000? $1,000,000?

42. Patient Impatience

Concept

One of Bob Johnson's principles for managing effectively in unfamiliar places is what he calls *patient impatience*.[18] Bob wanted to get things done correctly and quickly. The faster one shows results, the faster the hemorrhaging would stop. When working in a new environment or a different culture, one can expect that (a) there might be a learning curve and (b) the host culture might not view time the same way one's home culture does. So Johnson advises being impatient for results but to expect the need to be patient while one's colleagues learn different ways of doing things and one's self learns to adapt to local time rhythms.

There is a similar principle in the martial arts. One may know how to make a middle block, for example, but if you block too soon OR too late, bad things happen. Timing is critical. One must be *in tune* with one's opponent in order to compete successfully. Forcing things to go faster than they otherwise might can lead to disaster.

So, here is another paradox. (There are so many, yes?) Be impatient to show results and at the same time, be respectful of the host culture, your colleagues, their VABEs regarding time, and nudge but not faster than can be tolerated. Yelling at slow colleagues in a different culture is likely to make things worse as people move into passive aggression on the Buy-In scale.

Remember that your frustration or irritation with the *slowness* of things is a function of your VABEs about the way the world should be. Clearly, it is not that way all around the globe.

Example

The Japanese culture, for example, is famous for going slow, slow, slow, and then BAM let's GO! In that culture, building long-term relationships is important and that takes time. Meanwhile, people are touching base with suppliers, employees, discussing and anticipating how the new approach will work. Once all of that checking is done, once the *dating* is

---

[18] http://palgrave.com/us/book/9780230337510

over, then they are ready to go and begin producing. North Americans often attempt to go fast in making the deal and then are not prepared for the execution that naturally follows.

Diagram

Really? Take a deep breath and work the culture/system in which you are living. Remember to "work yourself" at the same time. What VABEs do you need to adjust?

Challenge

1. What irritates you? What is the underlying VABE? Could you adjust that VABE?
2. Describe times in which you have been hurried beyond your preferences. What happened? What did you learn from that?
3. Describe times in which you have been forced to go slower than you want. What happened? What did you learn from that?
4. What happens when you stretch a rubber band farther than it will permit? Hurts, doesn't it?

43. Well Spoken

Concept

How you communicate will affect your ability to influence others. Yes/no? People who struggle to articulate their thoughts, their feelings, their goals, and their visions (if they have one), will struggle to get followers. Speaking in clear, memorable, authentic, and respectful ways is an important leadership tool.

Regardless of your past or current speech patterns, you can learn to speak more effectively. When I was in high school, I stuttered badly. I had a difficult time putting two words together, especially anything that began with an L, a D, or an M. Later in life, after a series of life changes and constant practice including learning foreign languages, I was able to articulate my thoughts much more seamlessly.

Have you ever said out loud or to yourself, "I know what I'm trying to say, I just can't find the words?" Be careful; don't fool yourself. As most writers will admit, the discipline of putting words to paper is a sharp edge. The same is true of speaking.

Becoming well-spoken is much more than simply eliminating one's "um's" and "you knows," "know what I mean?" (no, I don't) and "like's." It means being able to clarify your thoughts and then to use the right words to explain them. When things happen to us, we may or may not be aware (at Level Two) of our reactions. Most adults are not good at describing their experiential feelings. Clarifying in our minds what we are feeling and experiencing we might call Translation #1.

But then there is another translation required: getting your thoughts into words, moving from Level Two to Level One. Let's call this Translation #2. Because this translation involves moving the muscles of your brain and your mouth, one must practice this translation out loud. Practice, practice, practice. What if your boss asks for an unexpected performance review? What would you say? What if you got an unexpected call from a head hunter? What would you say? If your CEO asked you in the hallway what you thought the company should be doing, what would you say? Identify these and a hundred other possible and likely scenarios and practice them. In the car. On your commute. In the shower. While running. While walking. Practice out loud.

Carl Rogers in his seminal book, *On Becoming a Person*,[19] clarified these translations and the importance of becoming aware of one's experiences and feelings in order to understand one's VABEs. More importantly, speaking out loud helps one develop an opinion. As writers judge themselves by re-reading what they have written, speakers can judge themselves by listening to what they say. You can't do this well only in your head at Level Two. You can become ever more well-spoken if you practice and practice out loud.

Of course, if you haven't done your homework and created a charter, you won't have anything to say. Glib language won't compensate for having a story to tell, a story built on research, analysis, and good strategic thinking.

Example

There have been many, many great speeches in history. You can find them online.[20] Read some. Winston Churchill once noted, "Let each man search his conscience and search his speeches. I frequently search mine."[21] It's good advice for us all.

Later, at the end of that same speech, Churchill said, "Hitler knows that he will have to break us in this Island or lose the war. If we can stand up to him, all Europe may be free and the life of the world may move forward into broad, sunlit uplands. But if we fail, then the whole world, including the United States, including all that we have known and cared for, will sink into the abyss of a new Dark Age made more sinister, and perhaps more protracted, by the lights of perverted science.

Let us therefore brace ourselves to our duties, and so bear ourselves that if the British Empire and its Commonwealth last for a thousand years, men will still say, 'This was their finest hour.'"

Well-spoken, yes?

---

[19] https://amazon.com/dp/B00AD9YL6C/ref=dp-kindle-redirect?_encoding=UTF8&btkr=1

[20] http://historyplace.com/speeches/previous.htm

[21] http://historyplace.com/speeches/churchill-hour.htm

Diagram

Language of Leadership:
Two Key Translations

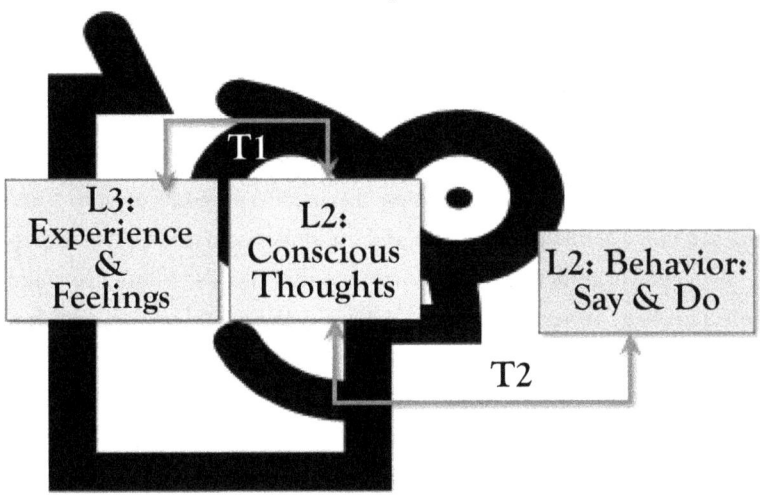

Challenge

1. Pick a topic, any topic. Do your research and identify three main points that you have come to believe to be true. Practice articulating those three points 20 times.

2. Pick another topic. Find five things about that topic that you believe and *why*. Practice articulating those five points 10 times. Don't stop until you can outline the points, describe why you believe them, and do so with conviction and power.

44. Presence

Concept

Many researchers have described the importance of first impressions and the sense of what it is *like* in someone's presence. Without speaking, people project a kind of aura about who they are and what they are feeling. This aura is no doubt a composite assessment of dress, grooming, posture, gestures, facial expressions, eye focus, and more. We observe from across a crowded room or within speaking distance or in conversation. One's aura can come across even on film and on long-distance virtual meetings.

An effective leader projects a presence that signals confidence, calm, understanding, power, and control. Less effective would be signals of fear, nervousness, confusion, weakness, and lack of control. How does one develop a leadership presence?

Confidence comes from expertise. If you know your subject, if you have done your homework, if you can anticipate the likely questions or concerns, the odds are you will feel confident in the presence of others. People new in their roles, people in minorities, and those who have not prepared adequately often feel nervous—and they project that nervousness in tiny signals on the channels mentioned above. Doing your homework and being even over-prepared is, in my experience, critical to feeling and therefore projecting confidence. Whenever you find yourself saying, "Hmm, this is okay, I can wing it," be careful! People will *smell* your nervousness and that invites probing questions, concerns, and lack of follower confidence.

Calmness is reassuring to listeners. Emotionality may well have roots in brain chemistry (and therefore genetics), reactions to diet (caffeine, etc.), and underlying VABEs (like "I have to be perfect."). That said, one can develop calmness in life—in fact this is often the focus of therapy sessions, behavioral counseling that examines underlying VABEs and unrealistic self-expectations. But you can work on your calmness in a number of ways: slowing down your speech, focusing your eye contact, monitoring any nervous tics you may have, removing useless phrases from your speech (e.g., *like, um, you know*) exercising, and meditating. People want to follow those who project a calm air of understanding and control, not those who are fidgety, ill-at-ease, and worried.

Your understanding of a situation will be reflected in your demeanor. Again, the importance of doing your homework, of developing your own reasoned opinions on how to manage a subject, of having ingested all the available data and analyzed it is critical here. Experience is important in understanding the world. That said, age is no guarantee of wisdom. Many live the same daily experiences over and over again and learn nothing new as the world changes around them. For them, their words and behavior lend an impression of *out-of-touch* or *clueless*.

Power and control project confidence to listeners. When a leader can outline the critical elements of a situation (remember "Do you SEE what needs to be done?" as part one of the Leadership Point of View?), explain the root causes, and describe a relatively simple plan of action (steps 2 & 3 of the LPV), people feel reassured that the person in charge knows what they are doing.

Example

During the U.S. presidential campaign of 2016, one candidate was asked how he would handle Aleppo, the Syrian city then submerged in civil war among multiple factions. The candidate expressed a perplexed look and said, "What's Aleppo?" That short incident was viewed around the world and greatly contributed to undermining that candidate's credibility.

Pick your favorite debate between competing political candidates. Observers and commenters will immediately home in on their *presence*. Which one projects the better presence? Which one behaves more leader-like? Often, the content of their messages is overshadowed by the unspoken nature of how they present themselves to the world. Presence.

Diagram

Challenge

1. Ask a few people who know you well to write down a few words that describe your presence, anonymously if they wish.
2. Describe your feelings about running for school, business, or political office. Why did you run/not run?
3. How much of your presence is based on the fear of rejection from others? How can you manage that fear?
4. Watch people in the meetings that you attend. Who has leadership presence and who doesn't? What is it about them that lends that impression? What can you do to emulate those characteristics?
5. Rate yourself on the speed of your speech. How does your talking pace affect your influence?
6. Go on YouTube and find someone with leadership presence and someone without.

45. Determination

Concept

The will to win is an important part of effective leadership. This will, desire, can be focused on beating the competition or on accomplishing an internally generated vision. The former may push one to becoming a highly effective manager, but the second will push one to becoming a leader. In the absence of vision, a determined person can play a powerful lieutenant role in getting things done—things that are imagined by the inside-out visionary leader.

We say in taekwondo, "a black belt is a white belt who never gave up." Persistence is every bit as important as vision. No matter how difficult the next step may seem, those who succeed choose to take that next step and conquer it.

Where does this drive come from? Perhaps some of it is brain chemistry— a little bit of obsessive compulsive disorder (OCD) can be helpful in pushing each project through to completion. A bit of attention deficit disorder (ADD) can divert one's determination with the allure of alternative projects. Early childhood training surely contributes. Children taught to finish what they begin may have more persistent behavioral patterns than those who were not imbued with that principle. And some people for whatever reason are possessed with what taekwondo-kas call *indomitable will*. Never, never, never give up.

Applied to business projects, this can be a good thing; applied to losing endeavors, it can be very dysfunctional. So, here is another paradox/dilemma. Be determined to finish and know when and where to apply this determination. Working hard to finish an uncompetitive project is just a waste of time and energy. Knowing the difference is part strategy and part wisdom.

Determined people tend to focus on the end result while those who give up focus more on the immediate hurdle. When you begin something, check your commitment to the end goal. How important is it to you? If it's really important, the short-term speed bumps that come along may be difficult, but they won't derail you. Whatever it takes.

Example

Malcolm Gladwell in his book, *Outliers*, explored the difference between North American and Chinese children in their determination to solve problems.[22] The research showed that Chinese children tended to spend more time striving to solve math problems than their North American counterparts. Gladwell asserted that this had to do with being raised in a rice culture in which significant determination and persistence are required to bring the rice crop to fruition—compared with the increasingly *sound bite* culture of North America based on cell phones, 140 character tweets, and handheld calculators.

Navy SEAL BUDS training is notorious for the ways that it tests one's determination. In the face of insurmountable obstacles, BUDS instructors want to know how far each person will go. Can they exercise their will over their bodies and the situation surrounding them? Can they impose their will on the world around them?

The story of the trans-continental railroad in America is a powerful one. President Abraham Lincoln in the midst of a terrible civil war had the prescience to support and nudge the development of a project that was too expensive, too difficult, impossible, and hard to even imagine. The leaders of the Central Pacific and Union Pacific railroads and those that worked for them demonstrated enormous determination in overcoming political, geographic, financial, engineering, labor, and business hurdles to link the east and west coasts by rail, reduce travel time from months to days, and secure the United States' claim to the territories of California, Oregon, and Washington.

Diagram

DETERMINATION

---

[22] https://amazon.com/Outliers-Story-Success-Malcolm-Gladwell-ebook/dp/
B001ANYDAO/ref=sr_1_1?s=books&ie=UTF8&qid=1488639420&sr=1-
1&keywords=malcolm+gladwell+books

Challenge

1. Describe the biggest project you have ever completed. What did it take to finish it?
2. Describe a time when you gave up. What happened and why?
3. On a scale of 1 to 10, rate your average level of determination. How often do you say, "Ah, that's good enough."
4. How much of your life do you spend working on other people's goals rather than your own? (time spent working on other people's goals/168. 168 = hours in a week.)
5. What is the biggest thing in your life now that you are determined to do?

SECTION V

What's Your Strategic Story?

Anyone who wants to influence others needs some kind of story, some rationale for getting them to do what they want. In the absence of a strategic story, influence devolves to coercive power based on rewards and punishments. There are dozens of traditional, established models for strategic thinking. I will introduce a few of them here and then the one I find to be critical to leading effectively at Level Three, a *charter*, and its six elements.

46. The Eastern Ball: Strategic Thinking: What's Your Story?

Concept

Given our assertion earlier that *leadership* really means *leading strategic change*, a big part of, the Eastern Ball, our leadership model is formulating a strategy. In easy to remember terms, "what's your (strategic) story?" IF you want to be an effective and inspiring leader, you will have to have a view of what your organization is about and where it is trying to go. If not, you will be a listener in the conversations—conversations that take place in the board room, in the hallway, in the rest room, in the office, and on the airplane or in the cab. If you have no opinion about what the company's purpose is, about where the company is going, and how the company should get there, you have relegated yourself to the role of implementer, manager, and follower.

It is not easy to develop a strategic story. There are multiple models, frameworks, and pathways for doing this. Some are clearer than others. Some have a particular focus while others have a broader, vaguer scope. But unless you do this intellectual homework, you are little more than a chip riding on the currents of everyday news and disjointed information sources. To have a strategic story means you are clear on what you are trying to build. Clear on what you are trying to create.

For many, the purpose is *simple*. They say, "You ivory towered academic! The purpose of business is to make money!" It is true that every successful organization is self-sustaining and turns a profit. But if that is your purpose, you will have a hard time motivating your employees. You will be stuck with Level One leadership techniques, rewards, and punishments. Who wants to work hard to make other people rich? Who will give their best efforts to people who cannot point to a future?

Example

Well, you say, how does one inspire people to make concrete sewer pipe or any of the hundreds of other *mundane* businesses necessary to keep society moving? Ah. Perhaps you know the story of the three bricklayers?

A reporter went out one day to interview some bricklayers. She asked the first person, "What are you doing?" The man answered, "I'm laying brick. Thousands and thousands of bricks. Day after day, brick after brick! The boredom is unending! I hate my job!" The reporter went to another brick layer and said, "What are you doing?" His reply was, "I'm building a wall. It's a big, long wall. Forty feet high, a hundred feet long, four feet thick. It's a big wall." Hmm, she thought.

Then she asked a third man the same question. His reply was,

I'm building a cathedral in which people are going to worship God. Every brick in this cathedral is going to contribute to or take away from the feeling of awe and inspiration that those people feel when they go into the building. I've got to make sure that my work contributes to that overall sense of awe and reverence.

Three men, three different perspectives. And where do those perspectives come from? From inside for sure, for each man comes from a different home and different set of VABEs imbued early in life. So what is the role of the leader? To make sure that the bricks are laid within the minimal standards of quality? To ensure that the men are paid on time? To replace men who are sick or quit?

Let's take an even more ordinary example, mentioned above, concrete sewer pipe. What is the leader of that organization likely to say to his or her employees? "Okay, y'all, show up on time, dig like hell, make sure the joints fit, and turn in your time sheets." What *could* the leader of that organization say?

Hey guys, do you know what cholera is? Probably not since you haven't had to live with it. Let me tell you about cholera and dysentery. These are horrible diseases that can kill people within hours. People with cholera have racing hearts, explosive diarrhea, they vomit, for hours on end, they lose all the fluids in their bodies, their skin goes hard and plastic, their blood pressure drops, and they have painful muscle cramps. And THEN they die, within hours. And you know what causes cholera? Contaminated water! What we are doing here today is creating a system that intends to remove diseases like cholera and dysentery from this neighborhood. What we do here today means a better, healthier life for the people who live here. So be careful! Make sure there are no cracks in the sections! Make sure every joint is tight and secure! Make sure the backfill is tight and fully supporting of the pipe. What you do here today will matter for years to come. Do it right the first time!

The first leader had a strategic story, but it wasn't inspiring. The second leader's story was much more likely to inspire the workers. Hmmmph, you may say. What concrete pipe team leader would say the latter? Exactly. That's why most people work for minimum wages and are only looking to get their wages and go home. In my view, it's a failure of leadership. Their leaders have no story to tell, or at least the story they tell or imply is "work your butts off to save this company as much money as you can so the owners can have big houses and fancy cars." THAT I say is a story that produces mediocrity—and leaders who come and ask, "How can I motivate my workers?"

Diagram

Challenge

1. Do your mental/intellectual homework and form your own opinions about the purpose of your organization and what you/it are trying to create.
2. Practice framing a story in your mind and articulating it—in the car, the shower, on your walks/jogs, while swimming, wherever.
3. Strive to uncover the implicit story in the employment contract you now have. What did they *sell* you to make you come work for them?
4. Like the third bricklayer, try to identify and articulate the bigger picture of what your job is supposed to do. Hold onto that every day.
5. Even if your employers don't do this for you, be different. Stand out. Create the worthwhile purpose and vision for your work no matter how mundane it may seem. You will be happier, you will do better work, and your chances of being promoted and gaining more responsibility will grow!

47. Hope Is Not a Strategy

Concept

"Hope is not a strategy." The source of this phrase is unclear. Rudy Giuliani and the Reverend Akande used it in 2009. I was making this comment in classes prior to 2000. Later, it became a comment in presidential campaigns.[1] Like many things, there may have been a parallel development; that said, early on I became distrustful of students' in-class statements like, "I hope so." and "Hopefully, they will respond." Students would propose something and then add on, "I hope that will do it." Usually, it was a substitute for more careful thinking like, "If I did that, what would happen? I might get A or B or C. How would I deal with each?"

This is a simple chapter—but it can have a deep impact. Whenever you find yourself saying, "Hopefully, …" pause and ask yourself, "How can I deepen my planning? How can I prepare for various outcomes? How can I make my own luck?"

I often use role-plays in my classes. I don't instigate them, I only use them when a student recommends going to talk to someone. Usually in that suggestion, they will either say or imply, "Hopefully, he will agree with me." The role-play allows the class to explore the Level One actuality of that conversation. Frequently, the conversation goes badly because the recommender hasn't thought through how they would manage that conversation. Or speech. Or meeting. They assume, superficially, that all will go well.

By the way, using role plays is very powerful. The instructor gets to hone his or her dramatic skills and his or her own thoughts about what's next, and then what, and then what? AND one gets to see the limits of the student's thinking very quickly. Role Playing is a great, quick way to get below the surface.

Example

"Let's put 10% into advertising. Hopefully, that will get us 20% more hits."

---

[1] Mitt Romney's.

"I'll go talk to the man and hopefully get his approval."

"Let's have a sit-down, face-to-face, and hopefully that will take care of the problem."

"Let's lower taxes and hopefully, the savings will trickle down to everyone."

"If we lower prices, hopefully they will follow."

"I'll buy my spouse a present, and hopefully that will smooth things over."

"Well, I'd talk to her, get her approval and then call a team meeting."

Diagram

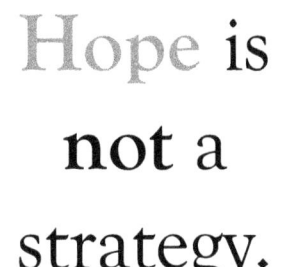 

Challenge

1. Be aware of every time you say "Hopefully, …"
2. When you are tempted to say "hopefully," or "I hope," stop, go back, play out the contingencies in your mind and devise plans to deal with each of them. Then, you can say, "If A, happens, I will do this. If B happens, I will do that."

48. Ansoff's Model of Strategic Growth

Concept

Igor Ansoff's model of strategic growth has been an enduring and influential framework for thinking about how to grow a company. The model is a 2x2 matrix with axes of products (and services) and customers. The end points on both axes are *old* and *new*. Presumably, a company begins the analysis with its existing products and services and customers.

The first analysis then is what proportion of the market do we have with our existing products and customers? No one has 100 percent of those elements, so the first strategy for growth is to expand one's share of the market defined by existing products and customers. This can be difficult for companies with established shares of market in stable markets, nevertheless this is the first place to think about how to get our existing customers to buy more of our existing products/services.

The second strategy for growth is to find new customers for our existing products and services. This may mean geographic expansion including going overseas. This is a *comfortable* strategy because we already know our products well and we have experience selling them, so in essence, we are *pushing the past* on new customers. In that sense, this is a more *seller-centric* approach. This approach does not require us to develop new technologies or manufacturing or servicing techniques. What may be uncomfortable here is learning to sell in new geographies including international areas. We may have to adjust our selling culture to fit each new area that we try to invade.

The third strategy for growth is developing new products and services for our existing customers. In this case, we seek to get more share of wallet from our current customers. What's comfortable here is we know our customers, we have established relationships with them and they have a level of trust with us based on our history. What's uncomfortable here is developing internal capabilities to produce the products and services that we don't have experience with but which our customers want. This approach is a *more customer-centric* approach in that it requires us to know not only what our customer wants from us, but from the world as a whole. In this approach, we need to not only listen to our customers, but to become strategic partners with them in helping them get what *they* need to grow.

The fourth approach, offering new products and services to new customers, is often called the *suicide strategy* because we are dealing with both products and customers that we don't know so well. Targeting this fourth quadrant of the matrix is a very bold, chancier, lower probability of success, higher risk approach.

Each of these four strategies can expand to multiple sub-layers of analysis. In this fundamentals volume, we will not expound on those deeper levels. If you wish, there are other volumes that treat those analyses. Here our purpose is simply to ensure that you have a clear, mental map of what the Ansoff model is and of the basic vectors of thrust in it.

Diagram

Every Business is a Growth Business

Ansoff's Model of Strategic Growth

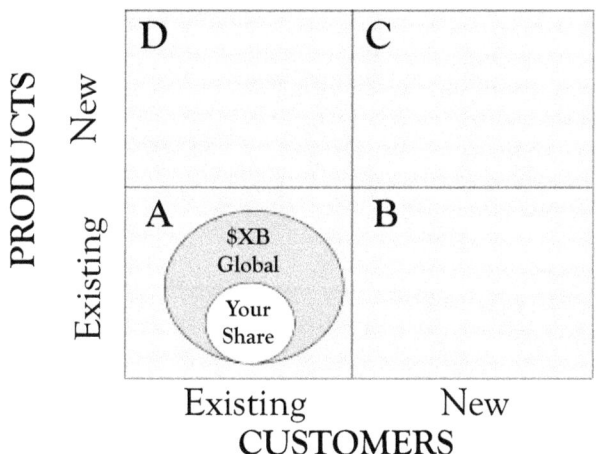

Source: Adapted from Charan and Tichy, Every Business is a Growth Business, 3 Rivers Press, 2000.

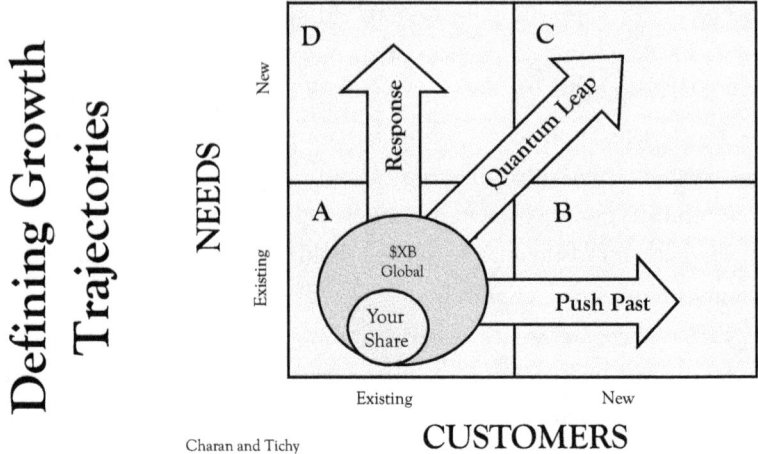

Defining Growth Trajectories

Charan and Tichy

Challenge

1. Identify which of Ansoff's strategies your company or organization has used. How well did they work?
2. What organizational core capabilities are necessary to implement Ansoff's strategies?
3. Identify the dangers of each of Ansoff's strategies.

49. Porter's Five Forces Industry Analysis

Concept

Michael Porter of the Harvard Business School has been one of the most influential strategic thinkers of the 20th and 21st centuries. He has written a number of highly influential books on strategic analysis.[2] In *Competitive Strategy: Techniques for Analyzing Industries and Competitors*,[3] he introduced the notion of *five forces* that can help executives understand their competitive positioning in an industry.

These five forces were competitive strengths, bargaining power of suppliers, bargaining power of customers, the threat of new entrants into the industry, and the threat of new substitutes that might actually kill an industry.

The starting place for identifying and analyzing an industry was to list and assess the major competitors in an industry. Who are your competitors and what are their strengths and weaknesses? What niches in the industry are defined by the strengths of your competitors collectively?

Suppliers also create forces in an industry. Their ability and willingness to provide the resources a company needs to function can and does shape what a company can and cannot do. Managing the supply chain has become a whole discipline in and of itself.[4] See the next chapter.

Customers also put pressure on an industry's competitors by demanding higher quality, better dependability, and lower prices. Yet giving in to all customer demands can be self-destructive. (See the chapter on Innovator's Dilemma.) When a small number of customers dominate a company's revenue stream, their power increases. The relationship between customers and supplying companies is a complex, and again, another focal point of intense investigation. Companies who ignore customer forces often go bankrupt—it is customers after all who pay the bills. Companies who over-react to customer pressure may also go bankrupt—they try to be all things to everyone and risk mediocrity.

---

[2] https://google.com/search?q=michael+porter+books&oq=michael+porter+books&aqs=chrome.0.0l6.13247j0j9&sourceid=chrome&ie=UTF-8

[3] https://amazon.com/Competitive-Strategy-Techniques-Industries-Competitors-ebook/dp/B001CB34J0

[4] http://investopedia.com/terms/s/scm.asp

When the analysis of competitors' strengths and of customer needs reveal gaps or niches in the industry, the danger of new entrants bubbles up. Who else, perhaps with bigger pockets, is also looking to gain advantage by filling those niches?

Ultimately, some technological innovation may make the whole industry obsolete. The carriage, buggy whip, cathode ray tube, projection TV, camera, dot-matrix printer, and countless other industries have all been supplanted by new, cheaper, more functional technological substitutions. Organizational innovation can also threaten whole industries (i.e., fast food, software leasing rather than sales, low budget airlines with a single airframe, etc.)

Example

Jack Welch used the industry competition lens to generate his famous dictum, if you aren't number 1 or number 2 in your industry, you are in danger of being sold.[5] His thinking was why would you want to compete in a game where you are not and are not likely to win? Either win or find another game.

Southwest Airlines revolutionized the airline industry by reducing supplier complexity through use of a single airframe, the Boeing 737, by engineering fun into the organization, and changing the whole flyer experience.

Diagram

Porter's Five Forces Model

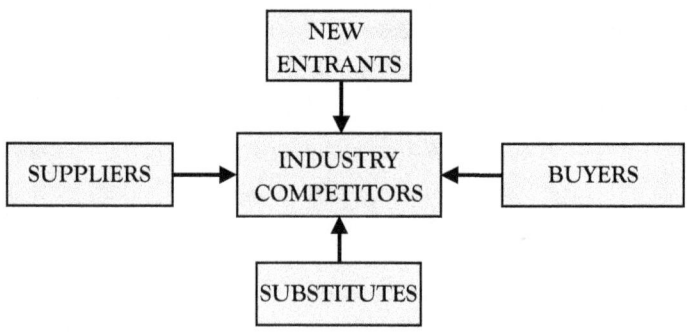

---

[5] *Control Your Destiny or Someone Else Will*, with Noel Tichy and Stratford Sherman, Harper, 1994, New York.

Challenge

1. Use the five forces model to analyze your organization's industry.
2. Diagram your organization's supply chain.
3. Describe the pressures that your organization's customers are putting on you.
4. What new entrants into your industry would upset the balance of power?
5. What kinds of substitutes would destroy your industry?

50. Value Chain

Concept

A concept close to the supply chain is the value chain. The value chain is the series of steps or links in the process that leads to customer satisfaction. If one analyzes the value chain for the profit and loss structures in each link, one can avoid the meta-thinking that goes along with *vertical integration*. In vertical integration, the thinking goes, "If we own all the steps in our value chain, we can control our costs and supplies better." That may or may not be the case and a value chain analysis addresses that issue.

A value chain analysis consists of identifying all of the steps involved from raw materials to maintenance. Then, one analyzes each step or link in the chain to determine the profit margins evident in those links. Each link represents a business, perhaps an industry, with all the issues identified in Porter's Five Forces already introduced. Some links are likely to approach the razor-thin margins of commodities, while other links might have larger margins based on any number of factors from technology to shipping to scarcity. Thus, a wiser supply chain management philosophy would be to assess the potential profit margins in each link of the value chain and then to decide to integrate backward or forward only into those links where the margins and the future expectation of margins were high leaving the thin margin links to others—who then become your suppliers.

Recognizing this link between industries, Porter identified a *generic* value chain that most manufacturers face and must deal with.[6]

Example

Henry Ford famously was enamored with the vertical integration concept and organized the Ford Motor Company so that they owned every step in the process to manufacturing an automobile. He went all the way to mining the ore, smelting it into iron and steel, then machining the parts, and creating a highly efficient assembly line that at one point could produce a new Ford automobile every 30 seconds: 3,000 cars a day! This required

---

[6] https://amazon.com/Competitive-Advantage-Creating-Sustaining-Performance/dp/0684841460

understanding each of the steps or processes involved in making an automobile; there were 84 steps in making Ford's most successful model, the Model T. The Model T cost $825 (about $20,000 in 2015) in 1908, but given the efficiencies found through the concept of a moving assembly line, the price had dropped to $260 (about $6,300 in 2015) by 1915. Ford's River Rouge and Highland Park plants were enormous flagships of a vertically integrated manufacturing system that produced some 15,000,000 Model T's. At one point, Ford was selling nearly half of all the cars sold in the United States.

Diagram

GENERIC VALUE CHAIN

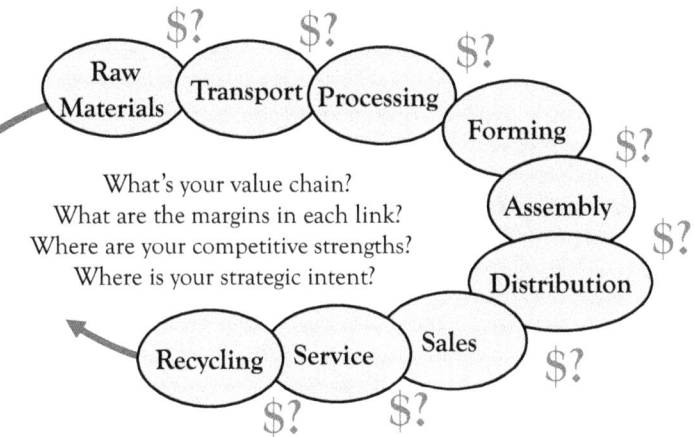

Porter's Generic Value Chain

FIRM INFRASTRUCTURE				
HUMAN RESOURCE MANAGEMENT				
TECHNOLOGY DEVELOPMENT				
PROCUREMENT				
Inbound Logistics	Operations	Outbound Logistics	Marketing & Sales	Service

MARGIN

Source: Adapted from Porter, M. 1985. *Competitive Advantage* 46. New York, NY: Free Press.

Challenge

1. Draw the value chain for your organization. Check your diagram with a couple of colleagues to ensure that you haven't left out anything.
2. Find estimates for the profit margins in each link in that value chain. (Generally, the average profit margin for the industry or the average of the profits of all major competitors in that industry.)
3. Given that (relatively superficial) analysis, which links should management consider integrating into and which links should management avoid entering?

51. Boston Consulting Group Model

Concept

The Boston Consulting Group created one of the more popular strategic analysis tools, the Product Portfolio Matrix. The premise of this analytic framework is that a company's market share in an industry is a rough measure of its ability to generate cash flow. The related concept was that taking market share away from others in the industry was expensive—because you were fighting against elements of the Ansoff Model, namely that companies that have existing products selling to existing customers have an advantage over competitors with those products and those customers. Established relationships are stronger than new relationships.

So, market share was a placeholder for available cash while market share growth was a placeholder for cash drain. BCG developed a matrix depicting these two concepts, the one side measuring market share and the other side the rate of growth in market share.

Companies in the high share and low growth cell were considered *cash cows* because while not growing, they generated lots of revenue. The high-high cell had high market share and a high growth rate. These companies were *stars*, that is strong and growing. Companies in the low share but high growth rate were *questionable*, that is, it wasn't clear yet whether the larger companies in the industry would move to crush them and if they could withstand the attacks. Their power in the market was not yet certain. The companies who had low share and low growth were considered *dogs* because their prospects, in the face of the competition, were weak.

A BCG Matrix analysis would then explore the likely movements among the cells. Cash Cows were the most stable, however, they were also vulnerable to innovation in the industry since they were long established and well entrenched—and therefore, likely to be less nimble and capable of re-doing the way they did business.

Stars were likely to become Cash Cows as their share continued to grow—at some point, growth must level off. Questionable firms might make it to the Star and eventually the Cash Cow cells but only time and management decision making would tell. Dogs were less mobile, working at a significant competitive disadvantage, and therefore, were candidates for divestiture.

Like all our model explanations in this introduction, there is much more to the BCG model and its application.

Example

The Cola Wars were a good example of this model. Coca-Cola and Pepsi fought fiercely for market share throughout the last half of the 20th century and continue fighting during the 21st century. The cost of these competitive fights was by one estimate more than $50 billion for Coca-Cola alone.[7] While the two behemoths continued to compete, many of the smaller soft drink firms struggled to maintain a position in the industry. Following Ansoff, both Coca-Cola and Pepsi added new products and then new markets. Coca-Cola is one of the most widely known brands in the world doing business in over 200 countries. Each of its individual brands could be analyzed using the BCG model by dividing the industry into its segments including sugar, non-sugar, water, sports drinks, juices, teas, and so on.

Diagram

BCG Model

		RELATIVE MARKET SHARE (Cash Generation)	
		HIGH	LOW
MARKET GROWTH RATE (Cash Use)	HIGH	STAR	?
	LOW	CASH COW	DOG

---

[7] http://marketrealist.com/2014/11/soft-drink-industry-dominated-coke-pepsi/

Challenge

1. Identify your organization's market share.
2. Identify your organization's rate of growth or decline in market share.
3. What do these figures imply to you about the future of your organization?
4. If you were on the senior executive team, what would you do with this information?

52. Design Thinking

Concept

The business world at the end of the 20th and the beginning of the 21st centuries was enamored with the concept of *design thinking*. Much of this interest was stimulated by IDEO founder Tim Brown's book, *Change by Design*.[8] Design Thinking can be an elusive concept to those not trained in schools of design. At its core, Brown argues that it takes a *human-centered* approach to helping people do things easier and better. At IDEO, on of their philosophies is that we can learn most about design by observing closely humans doing the thing we are interested in. Their *work arounds* and routines will instruct us if we look carefully and those observations can inform better designed solutions.

What was the most elegant design you have ever witnessed? Think a moment and note it here.

Now, please note all the items/aspects/elements that you can think of that went into that design. What made it so elegant? Why were you impressed? How did it make the world better?

---

[8] https://amazon.com/Change-Design-Transforms-Organizations-Innovation-ebook/dp/B002PEP4EG/ref=sr_1_1?s=books&ie=UTF8&qid=1486692894&sr=1-1&keywords=tim+brown+change+by+design

When we think of design, we can think of effectiveness and efficiency. Together, these denote elegance for me. An elegant design does a superior job and does it with the least use of resource, and by the way, it looks beautiful.

The concept of design applies, of course, to physical things, but also to services, to systems, to organizations, to processes and coding and regulations, to almost anything. Not just furniture.

Many people, if not most, are satisfied with *good enough*.[9] Herb Simon popularized this concept in *Administrative Behavior*. How many times have you said to yourself, "That's good enough"? What proportion of the time do you strive to do your absolute best?

Getting the job done is only part of design thinking. In fact, design thinking wants to be sure what the *job* is. Is it *getting more people to recycle* or something larger like *getting people to live sustainably*? Brown's design thinking process encourages people to think and discuss carefully what the project is really trying to do.

In addition to elegance, we can think of beautiful designs in terms of their efficiencies. How many times do you see people or companies or governments throwing money at something without apparent regard for the cost? Efficiency often takes a back seat to effectiveness in the satisficing world. In a design thinking environment, more time and energy would be put in up front, similar to the concept of concurrent engineering or integrated product development teams, in the design phase, in order to save cost and inefficiencies later in a product/process life cycle.

So, elegant designs are, I say, relatively simple, efficient, and beautiful as well as functional.

Brown thought of design in three phases: inspire, ideate, and implement. What would be the inspiring purpose of our work? What exactly is the real, core, inspiring goal of this project? The second phase consisted of steps to find multiple ways of solving the inspiring challenge. Finally, he argued, without implementation, ideas are just ideas.

Tim Brown's process for design thinking consisted of the following:

1. **Define the challenge carefully.** Be sure to get below the immediate and obvious and identify what you are really trying to do.

---

[9] https://en.wikipedia.org/wiki/Satisficing

2. **Observe People.** Spend time watching people who are living at the core of what you are trying to do. Take photos, interview, watch, reflect.

3. **Form Insights.** Use inductive logic to uncover what your observations are telling you.

4. **Frame Opportunities.** Look for ways that your insights can connect to create synergistic positive possibilities.

5. **Brainstorm Ideas.** Find as many associative ideas as you can to the core concept. While this technique has been around for a long time, most facilitators don't manage the process well. Non-judgmental, more is better than less, free flowing.

6. **Try Experiments.** Try lots of little experiments to see what works and what doesn't. Apply them in the field.

Example

Brown's organization, IDEO, offers the example up front of helping a large financial services company develop new products to serve women with children. They noticed in the observation phase that many customers would round their bills up to the nearest dollar so they didn't have to futz with small amounts and the difficulty of writing longer checks. Based on that observation, IDEO recommended a new product that allowed customers to put the small differences between actual bill and payment into a savings account—making it easier for households to add to their nest eggs.

The unusual and elegant designs of SAS of Cary NC has been the subject of case studies by Stanford professor, Jeff Pfeffer.[10] SAS has a number of interesting, superior design features including no performance reviews, on-site medical care, on-site schools, and park-like grounds.

On the other hand, there are many examples of bad designs. I had a client once who had a process that involved 13 steps to get a hammer out of the supply room. One could have manufactured a hammer

---

[10] Jeffrey Pfeffer, SAS Institute (A): A Different Approach to Incentives and People Management Practices in the Software Industry, HR6, Stanford Graduate School of Business, Stanford, CA, 1998.

quicker. I had another client who had 81 steps to fire someone. Jack Welch's "Work-Out" effort in the late 1980s and early 1990s was a 10 year and extensive attempt to get rid of bad process designs.

You may remember the "Rube Goldberg" cartoons showing odd, ill-conceived designs that make us laugh. See below for one example and its source. There are many images of such designs online.

Diagram

The Tim Brown/IDEO design thinking process adapted:

Adaptation of
Tim Brown's IDEO Design Model

INSPIRE   IDEATE   IMPLEMENT

Frame   *Brainstorm*
Opportunities   *Ideas*

Form Insight

Observe People

Define the Challenge   *Try Experiments*

Challenge

1. Identify some poor designs in your life and in your organization.
2. Attend an IDEO design thinking seminar.
3. Find a better design for one or more of the bad designs you have identified.
4. Read Tim Brown's book, *Change by Design*.

53. The Ecological Model

Concept

Warren Boeker at Columbia University[11] and others have been studying what they call the ecological model of organizational behavior and strategy. Essentially, they apply concepts from the fields of ecology and evolution to describe firm behavior within an industry. Organizations, like species, live in an environment and that environment affects the ability of the species or organization to thrive and persist. In nature, for example, studies have shown that the wolf and mouse populations of the northern tundra are highly dependent on each other for survival. If the wolves eat too many mice, the wolves will starve. If the wolves don't eat enough mice, the mice will over populate and over graze their grass food and the mice will starve. Likewise if the climate changes and the snow and ice cover melts, what will happen to the two species?

Observers in this field note that, as in nature, there are companies who compete at the expense of others, companies who have symbiotic relationships with other companies so that survival is in the best interests of both, and companies who cannot or do not adjust to changes in the environment, which leads to their extinction.

Iansiti and Levien[12] argue that the success of firms like Wal-Mart and Microsoft are largely attributable to ecological factors like the development of a global network of suppliers, distributors, loose and tight alliances within their industries, information sharing, and trends in the consumer markets. When companies begin to share their sales data, manufacturing data, and research data with suppliers and customers, they create a kind of ecosystem upon which all of the networked companies depend. The collapse of that ecosystem or any significant part of it would damage or kill off not only a subject company but any others that participated in that system.

The Ecological Model extends the value chain model as the value chain model extended the supply-chain model. This environmental approach now includes regulatory agencies for all the members of the industry, the

---

[11] Boeker, W. 1991. "Organizational Strategy: An Ecological Perspective." *Academy of Management Journal* 34, no. 3, pp. 613–635.

[12] Iansiti, M., and R. Levien. March 2004. "Strategy as Ecology." *Harvard Business Review*.

labor markets facing those companies, the financial markets that shape exchange rates, political contexts, and, of course, religio-cultural contexts.

The concept of an ecological model of organizational behavior is hard to define. Identifying the boundaries of any particular business ecology would be very difficult. Instead, Iansiti and Levien argue, one should analyze the entanglements that an organization has with other organizations so that one can better appreciate, study, and plan for the multi-vectored forces that pull on the organization. Some of those forces may be distant and subtle, others more proximate and prominent.

Even more difficult, many of the domains of a business ecosystem may overlap with the domains of multiple other ecosystems—as when one country's regulations affect more than one industry. Apprehending and managing such a diffuse and inter-connected sets of linkages is a huge and extremely difficult challenge of the modern executive. It requires an appreciation of economics, politics, cultures, religions, civil unrest, global financial markets, international trade balances, elections, and more.

Example

Iansiti and Levien report that Microsoft, for example, has system integrations with some 7,452 firms, 5,747 developmental services companies, 4,743 campus resellers, 3,817 independent software resellers, and dozens of other domains each with large numbers of participants. Can you imagine trying to understand and manage that kind of ecosystem?

Diagram

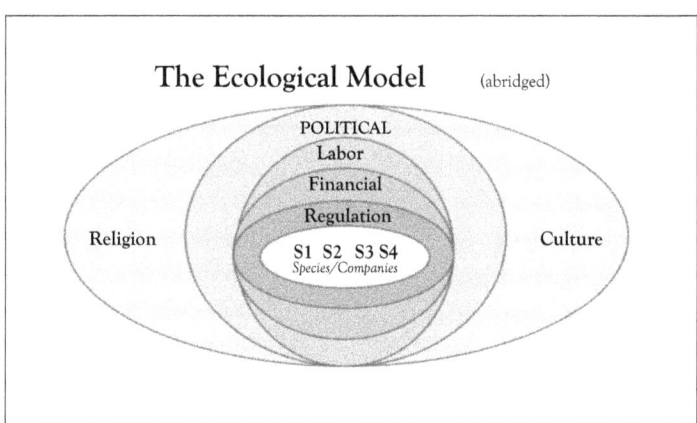

Challenge

1. Identify three ways in which your company would be affected by the sudden disappearance of the two largest competitors in your industry.
2. Identify three ways that changes in one of the domains in your company's ecological environment that would destroy your company.
3. Identify three ways that technological innovation would ruin your company.

54. Strategy as Revolution

Concept

Well-known strategic theory author Gary Hamel has written a number of books on strategic thinking. One focused on the concept of strategy as revolution—breaking the past and redesigning the future in revolutionary ways.[13] Revolution, of course, requires dramatic changes in thinking, planning, and executing. Hamel offered 10 rules to help people develop more revolutionary thinking.[14]

1. **Set unreasonable expectations.** The idea here is that creating seemingly impossible goals and demands will cause/force people to approach issues in dramatically new ways. The same idea appeared in Jim Collins's big hairy audacious goals or BHAGs.[15] Those who followed Collins's advice often found that BHAGs didn't work. Collins refined his idea later in the *hedgehog* concept, the notion that one could only set BHAGs at the intersection of Talent, Passion, and Marketability. Lacking passion, managers confronting BHAGs were more often than not, likely to fail. At the same time, I think we can agree that unreasonable goals can and often does force people to think in different ways.

2. **Stretch your business definition.** This concept invites executives to rethink what business they are in. Frequently, executives settle into an *assumed* business industry, segment, and model. This can limit their ability to respond to changes in the environment—technology, labor markets, consumer expectations, competition, and so forth. One might think, for example, one is in the *steel cap liquid closure* business—when competition in plastics attacks one's markets. Unless you could stretch that view of the business to say *vacuum sealed liquid closures*, you might miss the revolution brought

---

[13] Hamel, G. 2002. *Leading the Revolution: How to Thrive in Turbulent Times by Making Innovation a Way of Life.* New York, NY: Plume.

[14] "Reinvent your Company," by Gary Hamel, *Fortune*, June 12, 2000, p. 98

[15] Jim Collins, *Good to Great: why some companies make the leap … and others don't*, Harper Business, New York, 2011.

on by plastics. Coca-Cola held a less *stretchy* view of their business and missed the initial opportunities to enter the sports drink business created by Gatorade. They followed playing catch-up with Powerade.

3. **Create a cause, not a business.** I really like this one. It links to Collins's passion and my own Level Three Leadership. People will give you so much more energy when they are working on something they believe in. Simply defining a business as "to make as much money as we can" is perhaps *true* from an investor's point of view, but it ignores the impact on employees. Who wants to work hard—and innovatively—to make other people rich? Defining the societal contribution that an organization makes and inviting people to join in that contribution creates more energy and passion. Linking with employee's sense of purpose in life unleashes energy and innovation.

4. **Listen to new voices.** Executives frequently settle into habits of information collection as they manage their businesses. *Trusted sources*, explicit and implicit, get regular attention while other sources are ignored. The problem here is that one might miss trends and revolutions that aren't represented in one's usual data channels. So, finding unusual sources, listening to different people, reading different reports, and seeking out uncomfortable opinions can lead one to see important changes that they might otherwise miss. This is hard to do. We like to listen to our familiar voices. We, as a matter of human nature, seek confirmatory information. The danger is that we miss key sea changes.

5. **Design an open market for ideas.** Most companies are not good at this. Consider, for example, Hewlett-Packard missing the personal computer idea, Coca-Cola the sports drink, and American automobile makers the electric hybrid revolution (at first). Again, most people don't like to engage in ideas that are foreign to them. The discomfort, the disease, the fear that comes from recognizing contradictory ideas prevents us from seeking out alternative points of view. Closed-minded executives have difficulty creating open-minded cultures. This extends to all kinds of issues within an organization: how people speak, dress, communicate, work, and so on. Hanging a

suggestion box on the wall doesn't begin to address the need to create a culture in which people at all levels can get real hearings for their thoughts.

6. **Offer an open market for capital.** As you can tell, many of these suggestions relate to the central concept of *opening up* people's views of the world. Another way to do that is to create competition for internal investment funds. This would require in many if not most organizations a change in the processes by which they decide where and how much to re-invest in the company. These investments are major strategic moves—investments here preclude investments there and often have a long-term impact. Creating a regular process by which new ideas that require up-front investments can get a full and rigorous hearing raises the probability that the company will be able to see and assess multiple opportunities carefully.

7. **Open up the market for talent.** There is a big balance to be observed between talent and organizational design. Too much emphasis on freedom for talented people can lead to chaos, while too much emphasis on conformity to organizational guidelines can squelch talent. Allowing non-traditional paths for talented individuals can seed an organization with fresh, revolutionary thinking and influence. Most organizations however stick to their old step-by-step, channeled pathways to increasing influence. Finding regular ways to consider unusual candidates from inside and outside can help an organization springboard to a new kind of responsiveness.

8. **Lower the risks of experimentation.** Most people and companies punish failure in ways personal, emotional, social, political, and financial. This leads to a *fear of rejection* (that, by the way, is the foundation for most of our outside-in self-censoring behavior), which stifles experimenting. Most experiments fail. Edison famously failed more than a thousand times trying to find a workable light bulb. He argued that he didn't fail, rather the light bulb was invented with a thousand steps, each one narrowing and clarifying the way forward. Organizational cultures that severely punish experiments dampen their own innovation. In fact, making small

experiments is a key step in the modern process of design thinking developed by IDEO and Jeanne Liedtka at the Darden School, UVA.[16]

9. **Make like a cell—divide and divide.** If you try a small experiment and it works, then repeat it. Then repeat it. This kind of organic growth, properly fertilized will likely create a deeper and more substantial change than ordering/directing people to do it. Apply the successful experiment in location after location, function after function, department after department.

10. **Pay your innovators well—really well.** Pay is a big thing, the recognition that comes with it is perhaps even more important—but not sufficient. Rewarding innovation is the capstone to all the suggestions above—be public and serious about your commitment to revolutionary innovation.

Clearly, all of these suggestions imply the need to make deep seated changes in the way executives believe and think about their companies, their VABEs. The innovative revolution represents significant deviations from the tried-and-true, comfortable, traditional, *our way* pathway. Most people, creatures of habit that they are, simply don't do that. One might say they *choose* not to,[17] although most of these *choices* are made without awareness, rather made on top of the unexamined assumptions about the way we run our business.

Example

3M famously encouraged employees to spend 10 percent of their time working on innovative ideas—a process from which Post-Its for one emerged. IDEO in San Francisco has institutionalized the process of design thinking—innovation by design.[18] GOOGLE also actively encourages constant innovation and revolutionary thinking.

---

[16] Liedtka, J., and T. Ogilvie. 2011. *Designing for Growth: A Design Thinking Toolkit for Managers.* New York, NY: Columbia Business School Publishing.

[17] Glasser, W. 2010. *Choice Theory: A New Psychology of Personal Freedom.* New York, NY: Harper Collins

[18] Brown, T. 2009. *Change by Design.* New York: Harper Collins.

Diagram

Strategy as Revolution

- **Rule Makers**
- **Rule Takers**
- **Rule Breakers**

Source: Strategy as Revolution, Gary Hamel, HBR July-August, 1996, 96405, p. 69

https://google.com/search?q=images+Gary+Hamel&tbm=isch&ved=2ahUKEwjZ_tWAzr-zuAhXHZt8KHa6kCA8Q2-cCegQIABAA&oq=images+Gary+Hamel&gs_lcp=CgNpbWcQ
AzoCCAA6BggAEAgQHlCaugRYr8oEYN7SBGgAcAB4AIABQIgBvQSSAQIxMJgBAKAB
AaoBC2d3cy13aXotaW1nwAEB&sclient=img&ei=-p4RYNmZLcfN_QauyaJ4&bih=578&biw
=1366&rlz=1C1GCEB_enUS910US910#imgrc=JDsA4dOfy989mM

Challenge

1. Rate yourself and your organization on the following grid using Hamel's 10 guidelines to making revolution a way of life.
2. Get five to ten others from different levels to rate your organization on the grid.
3. Compare your answers and discuss.

Hamel's Guidelines	I do this 1-10	My company does this 1-10
1. Set unreasonable expectations		
2. Stretch your business definition		
3. Create a cause, not a business		
4. Listen to new voices		
5. Design an open market for ideas		
6. Offer an open market for capital		
7. Open up the market for talent		
8. Lower the risks of experimentation		
9. Make like a cell-divide and divide		
10. Pay your innovators well—really well		
TOTAL =		
AVERAGE =		

55. The Experience Economy

Concept

Pine and Gilmore's book, *The Experience Economy*,[19] introduces a very interesting historical overview of human economic activity with huge immediate implications. They tell a high-level story that goes roughly like this:

About 10000 BC, humans in large numbers changed their basic economic paradigm from hunter gatherers to farmers herders. Other sources suggest this occurred in significant part because humans had basically decimated all the large fauna.[20] Instead of killing animals and gathering berries, humans decided to stop wandering and plant food and grow herds of food. Taking grains and meats from the ground in large numbers, humans soon learned that the margins on grown food began to shrink. Essentially, grains, pork bellies, and other similar out-of-the-ground foods became commodities.

Then, about 1800 there was another dramatic shift in the common human economic paradigm. With the creation of mass production, the steam engine, the discovery of petroleum, the invention of steel and related processes, humans entered the Industrial Era in which they made things out of the things they took out of the ground. Over the course of the 250 years of the Industrial Era, the margins on durable goods declined, that is, durable goods became commodities characterized by shrinking profit margins.

Then around 1950, companies (IBM was perhaps the first) recognized that they were making more profit of the service contracts on their durable goods (360 computer main frames) than they were off the machines themselves. This ushered in the Service Economy based on legal contracts. The Service Economy was enhanced by advances in computer technology including electronic calculators (i.e., HP-80) personal computers (e.g., Apple II), the Internet, online shopping, and smart phones. And, more

---

[19] Pine, J., and J. Gilmore. 2011. *The Experience Economy*. Cambridge MA: Harvard Business Review Press.

[20] Only One Man. 2016. *A Song of Humanity: A Science-Based Alternative to the World's Scriptures*. Charlottesville, VA: L3L, LLC/Lulu Publishing.

rapidly now, the Service Economy also began to commoditize. Financial contracts, professional services, warranty contracts, service contracts, all began to lose the margins they showed in the last half of the 20th century.

So, Pine and Gilmore ask, where are the margins today? One might ask, "How much would you pay for a Rolling Stones concert ticket? A World Cup ticket? A Super Bowl ticket?" The answer of course is hundreds and thousands, yet when the event is over, all you have is the memory—no durable good, no service contract, nothing but the memory. People, therefore, they argued, I think persuasively, would pay premium margins for superior experiences.

Pine and Gilmore argue that the next high margin economy will be the Transformation Economy in which people will pay top dollar to those who can change us, transform us into something new. But, let's focus for a moment on the Experience Economy. How might this apply immediately to an existing business?

Example

At the age of 19, I had an experience that ruined my life. I went to live in Japan. After about a month, I needed a haircut. I had no idea where to go. Back in Idaho, men's barbershops usually consisted of an elderly gentleman with a translucent nylon smock and some rusty scissors, sheep shears, and a 10-pound electric vibrator would sit you down facing a tiny black and white TV playing football re-runs. After wrapping a tissue around your neck, he would clip a smock over you. Then zip, zip, zip, sheep-shear a taper up the back. Then, using his rusty shears, he would clip/pull hair off the top, sometimes drawing blood. Then he would rub your head for a minute with that huge electric vibrating motor that smelled like burning flesh (might have been). A quick blow from the dryer, a dab of butch wax and out the door you go, five dollars lighter. "Next!"

With no idea where to go in Japan, I picked a barbershop at random. I walked in and was greeted by five young women dressed in blue and white uniforms. IRASSHAIMASE! they chimed, "Welcome to our humble shop." The first young woman took me to the shampoo station where she shampooed my hair not once, not twice, but three times! After that,

I was melting. The second young lady took me to the clipping station where, instead of using electric clippers, she took a comb and scissors and somehow got a perfect taper right down to the nape of my skin. It felt like she was cutting each hair individually.

The third young lady took me to the shaving station where she laid me back and put a hot towel on my face. Then, I hear a very ominous sound, "Strop, strop, strop!" She was going to use a straight razor! I had never seen one before. She didn't look old enough to drive much less put a razor to someone's neck! Then, she put some hot lather on my face and shaved my neck, my cheeks, my chin and THEN to my great surprise, my forehead, temples, the space between my eyebrows, my nose, and my EAR LOBES. Then she did what even my wife won't do, she trimmed the hair out of my ears and nose. There was not an extra hair anywhere on my head!

The fourth young woman took me to the head and neck massage station—which I later learned was a distinguishing and differentiating feature of many shops. Some used the *air puff ball* technique making an airball with both hands and gently pounding tight shoulder and neck muscles. Some shops used the *limp finger* technique striking with the little finger, which then collapsed the ring finger and so forth, clump, clump, clump, clump. I never saw an electric vibrator—they all used the old-fashioned manual technique by placing their elbows on tight muscles and shaking their hands. Marvelous.

The fifth young lady took me to the grooming station and used a small vacuum on my scalp, thus avoiding that annoying prickly clipping feeling for the rest of the day. The vacuum was like another scalp massage. Then she placed something that smelled really good on my hair, groomed it and stepped away. They all lined up again, bowed and said, "One US dollar please. And please come back again!"

Wow. That experience ruined my life because ever since then I knew what a "haircut" COULD be. And I have been searching for one ever since. It's not to be had in America. In part because of our culture. In large part because Americans don't have the deep seated values of customer experience imprinted on their personalities, skill development, and orientation.

Are you in a commoditizing industry? Odds are you are. If a potential customer can get what you sell (goods and/or services) from one place with a kick in the shin and a poke in the eye and the same goods or services from someone else and get a Japanese haircut, where will they go?

Creating a *Japanese haircut* requires more than a bit of training. It requires a deep-seated, Level Three value for the value of experience. American theorists have talked about exceeding customer expectations for a couple of decades, yet the concept has not taken hold beyond a superficial level. Wall Street stock prices, *efficiencies*, and personal performance contracts that pay out even when goals are not met still dominate the North American economy.

Diagram

Economic Development
Where are the margins?
(Pine and Gilmore, The Experience Economy)

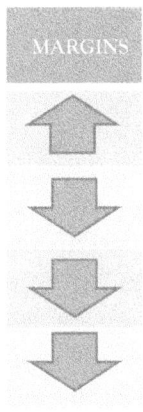

5. Transformations (pay for how time with you **transforms** me)

4. Experiences (**pay** for time with you)

3. Services supplant goods (what I do for you, and margins are ... declining, becoming commoditized)

2. Goods out of commodities (margins?)

1. Commodities out of the earth (margins?)

Challenge

1. Identify how you could give a *Japanese haircut* to your customers. How could you make those elements a part of your deep organizational culture?

2. How do financial performance contracts cause people to minimize customer experience?

3. What is the value of a Japanese haircut kind of customer experience on your top line revenues?

56. The Innovator's Dilemma

Concept

Clayton Christensen at the Harvard Business School (a former colleague and basketball junkie friend) identified a new idea, something every academic hopes to do. Clayton in his book, *The Innovator's Dilemma: When New Technologies Cause Great Firms to Fail*, focused on the percent utilization of product features.[21] Clayton's idea in sum was this: In order to add revenues, firms will naturally add features to their products and therefore gradually raise the prices of their products. Ultimately, they are vulnerable to attack by cheaper, less sophisticated new entrants. Thus, the percent utilization of this annual wave of new features defines opportunities for competitors—where there are lower percent utilizations. They can offer fewer features for lower prices, and gain a segment foothold, but then to gain revenues, they, too, begin to add features. So, the dilemma is that established firms who add features may find them unused and hence make themselves more vulnerable to attack.

Example

Honda begins to sell cheap, tiny, 50 cc motorbikes in California. Mercedes Benz and Harley Davidson hardly notice; they metaphorically *spit* on the cheap, tiny, unsophisticated Honda two wheelers. Honda gains a foothold. Then, to increase revenues, Honda begins to add features and even to create cheap four wheeled automobiles. Again, no threat to the established blue-chip owners of higher priced segments.

Honda adds features: bigger sizes, better engines, heated seats, and revenues grow. Before long, Mercedes Benz begins to notice the growing opportunity costs of sales going to Honda. Likewise at Harley Davidson. Daimler then decides to follow the classic GM strategy of filling out models for various socio-economic strata. They add an E class, a C class, and eventually a Smart car. The tiny Smart car however was built with Daimler culture in a highly automated, very expensive $2 billion dollar plant.

---

[21] Christensen, C. 2013. *The Innovator's Dilemma: When New Technologies Cause Great Firms to Fail.* Cambridge MA: Harvard Business Review Press.

Meanwhile, Honda adds more features and even a new *luxury* line of cars, Acura, into which they can insert even more features and charge higher margins. In Scandinavia, Volvo begins to work back down the price points with V80, V70, V50, V40, and so on.

Then Hyundai, an unknown Korean company introduces a cheaper, unsophisticated car with a 10 year, 100,000 mile warranty. MB and Acura metaphorically *spit* on their cheap construction, tiny wheels, thin metal doors, lack of features. And Hyundai gains a foothold. And begins to add features. Eventually, they introduce the Genesis, a *luxury* brand to compete with Benz and Acura (and now Infiniti and Cadillac).

Meanwhile, Kia, an unknown Korean automobile manufacturer, introduces a cheaper, unsophisticated car … and gains a foothold. And begins to add features.

Concurrently, in the personal computer industry, Steve Jobs is re-hired to try to save the declining fortunes of Apple. He finds a bewildering array of models with myriad features. He simplifies the business by declaring they will focus on four products, retail and commercial and desktop and laptop in each. The company regains control of costs, recovers, … and begins to add features.

Diagram

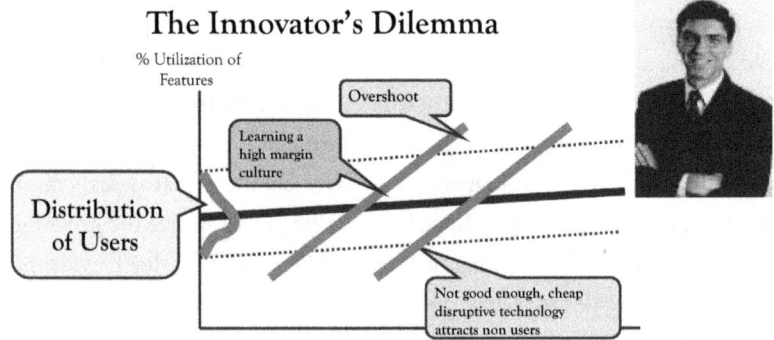

The Innovator's Dilemma

Source: https://google.com/search?q=images+Clayton+Christensen&tbm=isch&ved=2ahUKEw iHx8-lzrzuAhWng-AKHRlRCj0Q2-cCegQIABAA&oq=images+Clayton+Christ ensen&gs_lcp=CgNpbWcQAzoECCMQJzoCCAA6BggAEAgQHlDxoAdYuLsH YLa_B2gAcAB4AIABXYgBuQiSAQIxOZgBAKABAAoBC2d3cy13aXotaW1nwAE B&sclient=img&ei=SJ8RYleDDqeHggeZoqnoAw&bih=578&biw=1366&rlz=1C1G CEB_enUS910US910#imgrc=_ZGbuPEaVDvCCM

I find an interesting connection in Clayton's insights to energy in the workplace. What if we looked at "percent utilization of employees' energy pools?" Every person has an imaginary *pool of energy* that they can apply to an activity. How do companies seek to gain access to higher percentages of that pool of employee energy? They add features like bonuses, gold stars, promotions, and so on to *incentivize* employees to give more to the company. This becomes more and more expensive.

Then, along comes a non-profit with no wages to promise gets people give up evenings and weekends and with full energy. Habitat for Humanity, Red Cross, Salvation Army, Rescue Squads, and so on, get people to dedicate large amounts of personal time with full energy to achieve the organization's goals.

Challenge

1. Try to identify the marginal value added by each of your company's products features.
2. How does your company protect itself against cheaper, *unsophisticated*, substitutes?
3. What features is your company planning on adding to its products?
4. What features are you adding to your personal skill set and how does this affect your expected salary/wage?
5. What cheaper threats do you see to your salary/wage job security?

57. Good to Great Model

Concept

Jim Collins sold six block-buster management books that together sold over ten million copies. *Built to Last* was translated into 25 different languages while *Good to Great* (GTG) sold over 2.5 million copies and was translated into 32 languages.[22] The Good to Great project took five years and involved an extensive research team of 20 who reviewed data from some 1,435 companies, read over 6,000 articles and created interviews with 2,000+ pages of transcripts.[23] The results said that there were seven characteristics of companies who went from mediocre to great when compared with competitors in their industries. This pair-wise design touched on pharmaceuticals, retail electronics, groceries, banking, steel, pharmacies, and more.

Collins's team said that the differentiating factors were:

1. Level Five Leadership
2. First Who, Then What
3. Confront the Brutal Facts
4. Hedgehog Concept
5. Culture of Discipline
6. Technology Accelerators
7. Flywheel Concept.

Level *Five* Leaders were at level five from employee, to supervisor, to manager, to executive to a special kind of executive who had both humility and persistence. I once had a colleague say, "You must be disappointed because you have Level Three Leadership and Jim Collins just came out with Level Five Leadership." When I looked at the five levels, I was shocked at the simplicity of the levels; they had nothing to do with stratified leadership skill sets or characteristics. So, no, not disappointed at all, totally different measures and scales. I also had conversations with Jim Collins in which he noted that his team wrestled to find the "cut-points"

---

[22] https://en.wikipedia.org/wiki/James_C._Collins
[23] https://en.wikipedia.org/wiki/Good_to_Great

in the data that would separate the Great and Also-Rans. He noted that he didn't like Jack Welch's style and set the cut-point to move GE out of the *great* group. For me, this was another example of how VABEs dominate our behavior and thinking, even in science. As Tversky, Thaler, and Kahneman have shown, it's a common phenomenon among humans. Collins believed that executives with a *never give up* determination and coupled that with a reasonable degree of humility were more successful than their more arrogant, self-centered, demanding counterparts. See for example, Bob Sutton's book, *The No Asshole Rule.*[24] Both Sutton and Collins were at Stanford although I don't presume there is something about humility at Stanford (my beloved alma mater).

The "First Who, Then What" principle was that companies should hire the *best athletes* and give them more latitude rather than hiring smart people and shoe-horning them into constrictive jobs. Stephen Covey used to teach this same principle (in my MBA program) with the *ill-fitting suit* story, in which he described how companies tended to hire bright young people and then put them into constrictive jobs (ill-fitting suits) and expect them to perform. After a while, the innovation and energy had been *beaten* out of the new recruits.

"Confront the Brutal Facts" brings to mind Jack Welch's dictum: Face reality as it is, not as it was nor as you wish it were.[25] In this principle, Collins's team was urging resistance to the fast-thinking phenomenon by telling managers to deal with the reality of facts, not their semi-conscious hopes and wishes. *Brutal* makes the point that most people find this difficult to do.

Collins classified these first three principles as the *run-up* to takeoff, that is, necessary foundations or pre-cursors for dramatic changes in performance.

The Hedgehog Concept was taken from the animal that protects itself by curling up into a ball of spines—and that it does very well. Collins argued that a kind of synergistic power was unleashed at the nexus of

---

[24] https://amazon.com/Asshole-Rule-Civilized-Workplace-Surviving-ebook/dp/B000OT8GV2/ref=sr_1_1?ie=UTF8&qid=1512769990&sr=8-1&keywords=the+no+asshold+rule

[25] Welch, J., N. Tichy, and S, Sherman. 1994. *Control Your Destiny or Someone Else Will.* New York, NY: Harper.

passion, skill, and a viable economic model. In *that* space, one could set *big hairy audacious goals* (thus modifying his advice from *Built to Last*). I find this to be a powerful idea because it identifies the key elements of *love of work* (see my book *Powered by Feel* for example), real skill in that work (see Malcolm Gladwell's *Outliers* on the "10,000 hour rule"),[26] and passion and skill in something that people actually want to buy.

"A Culture of Discipline" was concept five, the idea that unless a person or an organization had the discipline to follow through on their efforts, things would fizzle out and die. Colllins liked to describe what he called the kind of extreme discipline shown by triathletes (he was married to one) who were obsessive about their diets and training, to the point of rinsing their cottage cheese to get just the protein without any other counterproductive substances.

The sixth concept was "technology accelerators," systems that allowed high energy employees to lever their impact and get more done with less. Exchanging ideas, finding research results, sharing financial results and more were key to giving employees the right information at the right time. (See also my description of *infocracies* in my article "Leadership in the New Infocracies."[27])

Finally, Collins suggested that when these six factors were in place, not only would a company *take off*, but it will also experience an enhanced momentum similar to an engine's flywheel. This momentum would give the company more power and longevity.

Despite the worldwide popularity of Good to Great, there have been those who have disputed the results of the pair-wise research as *generic* and non-replicable.[28] Some researchers have taken serious issue with the GTG findings.[29]

---

[26] https://amazon.com/Outliers-Story-Success-Malcolm-Gladwell-ebook/dp/B001ANYDAO/ref=sr_1_3?s=digital-text&ie=UTF8&qid=1512770911&sr=1-3&keywords=outliers

[27] Clawson, J. May–June 2000. "Leadership in the New Infocracies." *Ivey Business Journal.*

[28] http://businesspundit.com/why-good-to-great-isnt-very-good/

[29] Niendorf, B. and K. Beck. November, 2008. "Good to Great, or Just Good?" *Academy of Management Perspectives.*

Example

Collins listed Abbott Laboratories (vs. Upjohn), Circuit City Stores (vs. Silo), Fannie Mae (vs. Great Western Bank), Gillette (vs. Warner-Lambert), Kimberly-Clark (vs. Scott), Kroger (vs. A&P), Nucor (vs. Bethlehem Steel), Philip Morris (vs. R.J. Reynolds), Pitney Bowes (vs. Addressograph), Walgreens (vs. Eckerd), and Wells Fargo (vs. Bank of America) as the companies who went from good to great.

Subsequent to the publishing of GTG, many of the companies included in the *great* category above did not do well, in some cases going bankrupt or falling back into *goodness* or mediocrity.

Nevertheless, some executives called the book the best business book they had ever read and GTG did have worldwide impact.

Diagram

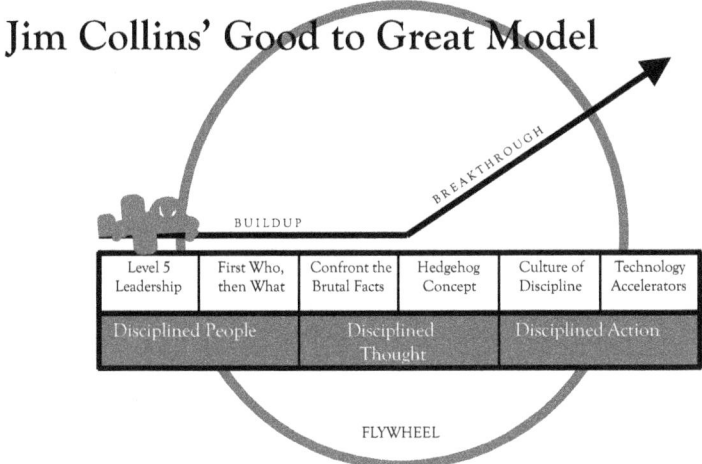

Jim Collins' Good to Great Model

Challenge

1. Assess your organization on each of the seven GTG principles/concepts. Rate each from 1 to 10.
2. What, if any, gaps or pitfalls do you see in the GTG model?
3. Why would so many people around the world want to buy and read this book?
4. Read the two refuter references in the endnotes and discuss with your team.

58. Strategy Maps

Concept

Bob Kaplan of the Harvard Business School and David Norton published a wonderful book in 2004, *Strategy Maps*.[30] In it, they explored the ways that a *balanced scorecard* could be used to guide strategic decisions. The Balanced Scorecard[31] is a model they developed as a way of connecting mission, vision, values, and core strategic areas. In many ways, the Balanced Scorecard and the Charter concept introduced earlier, attempt to do the same thing: provide an integrated frame for organizing one's strategic thinking.

The Balanced Scorecard has often been compared to a baseball diamond where individual skills were first base, organizational processes were second base, customer orientation was third base and financial results were home plate.[32]

Kaplan and Norton also present the balanced scorecard as a vertical step model, where we start at the top and deconstruct downward to understand where our financial results come from. In that approach, we begin with financial results (rather than first base). It's an appropriate place to begin since most executives are hyper-focused on financial results. There is a way, however, in which hyper-focus on finances can urge people to make short-term self-defeating decisions. This idea was in fact one of the main reasons Kaplan and Norton developed the balanced scorecard in the first place. The central idea is that finances are *results* not causes. To have better financial results, one must understand where financial results come from and in a more sophisticated way than simply revenues minus expenses.

Revenues come from customers. To enhance our top line, we need to satisfy customers better than anyone else. (See our discussion of a Japanese Haircut introduced earlier.) This depends on managing expectations, that is, what do you promise your customers? Quality, low price,

---

[30] Kaplan, R.S., and D.P. Norton. 2003. *Strategy Maps*. Cambridge MA: Harvard Business Review Press.

[31] http://balancedscorecard.org/BSC-Basics/About-the-Balanced-Scorecard

[32] http://josephlogan.com/baseball-and-the-balanced-scorecard/

dependability, warranty, more features, brand identity, and so on.? If you exceed your customers' expectations, based on your promises to them through advertising and experience, they are likely to be repeat customers and give you more money.

The third level then is do you have the capabilities of fulfilling those promises you make? If you promise superior quality, do you have the processes that allow you to deliver superior quality—or is it just lip service? Most companies have a handful of core capabilities. These might include procurement, machining, and marketing.

The fourth or foundational layer in this view consists of three pools of intangible capital: human, social, and organizational. Human capital is the sum of what everyone in the organization can do. A stack of resumes is a poor estimate of this since we all know that an MBA is not an MBA is not an MBA. Yet we can imagine the cumulative set of skills that all our people have.

Social capital is the marginal value added by how our people work together. That means the incremental value added by how we work across site, functional, program, and other organizational, geographic, and technological boundaries. Social capital can be positive or negative. Organizations who don't integrate well as they grow,[33] will have a negative social capital. Organizations that have Collins's flywheel spinning are likely to have positive social capital.

To this, we can add the concept of *organizational capital* including our IT infrastructure. Some organizations inhibit progress, some organizations make it easy to accomplish its goals. Bad organizational design drains energy while good organizational architecture creates paths of least resistance to performance.

The broad overview concept here is that effective executives know how to transform intangible asset pools (human + social + organizational) into tangible financial results. The strategy map then invites careful attention to any strategic investment at each level. Unless a training program, a hire, an organizational reorg contributes directly to a key core capability that enhances our ability to meet our promises to our customers, it's a

---

[33] http://faculty.babson.edu/krollag/org_site/org_theory/Scott_articles/lawren_lorsch_cont.html Lawrence and Lorsch on integration and differentiation.

waste of time and money. Effective executives therefore will *see* this map and make their investments carefully *on paths* that lead to the top level.

Example

Consider Starbucks (again). At the second level, customer satisfaction, Starbucks promises (a) a third place to wind up or wind down, (b) free WIFI to continue connecting, (c) majorly customized drinks (18,000 options) made with the best raw materials, and (d) a different kind of experience.

To fulfill those promises, Starbucks must (a) have the best beans, (b) prepare/roast those beans in the best way, (c) provide a unique store/venue, and (d) manage real estate carefully. Four core capabilities without which they could not meet their mission or vision. Starbucks has invested millions in a Central America bean growing school. They wanted to teach local growers how to grow the best beans in return for which they would purchase their crops. They have a proprietary roasting facility that is as closely guarded as the Coca-Cola formula. Then, they have developed a store management system that is so carefully designed that they measure inches in barista movements as they prepare drinks and serve customers. Finally, given the number of stores and their desire to *be there*, convenient, and available to commuters everywhere, Starbucks must manage real estate carefully. It's the kind of capability that could kill the company. Partnerships with grocery stores, book stores, and others have augmented Starbucks' ability to be there for an increasing customer base.

Starbucks hires a lot of part-time and short-term employees. Not many are career baristas. To attract the best—and because of an early childhood event—Howard Schulz offered comprehensive medical insurance and stock option programs to ***part-time*** employees, a major investment in human capital. While social capital within stores is limited to a few people, it is positive. And the organization of the stores and the company make it easy for employees to do their jobs, giving Japanese haircuts to their customers.

Diagram

Strategy Maps and Investment Linkages

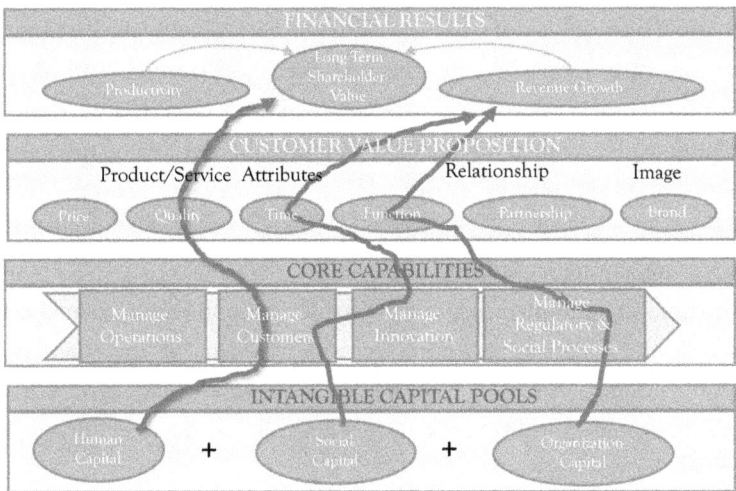

Note the small red pathways in the diagram above. Those pathways represent direct linkages between investments in the layer below to the layer above. If there is no direct linkage, the proposed investment should be trashed, it would be a waste. Each company will have a unique set of details in a strategy map. And a more detailed exploration of strategy maps would include tables that list proposed investments (i.e., initiatives, programs, trainings, acquisitions, etc.) and their major elements and expected contributions. See *Strategy Maps* (obviously) for greater detail.

Challenge

1. Describe what your organization promises its customers.
2. Describe what handful of capabilities are necessary to fulfill those promises.
3. Assess from 1 to 10 the readiness of each capability to fulfill your customers' value proposition.
4. Assess from 1 to 10 the readiness of your intangible asset pools to strengthen your core capabilities.
5. What investments would you make or initiatives would you take to strengthen your company at each level?
6. Have this discussion with your colleagues.

59. Scenario Planning

Concept

"Scenario Planning" is not what one thinks of immediately, the best case, most likely case, and worst case scenarios. Scenario Planning is not that. Rather it's a process developed at the Royal Dutch Shell (RDS) strategic planning department when RDS was near the bottom of the *seven sisters* in the oil industry. Arie deGeus, Pierre Wack, Peter Schwartz, Les Grayson, and others developed this process to deal with the uncertainty of long-range strategic planning.

In sum, scenario planning is the careful development of a small set (perhaps three) alternative future scenarios that are, at the moment, equally plausible. These scenarios are not best/likely/worst cases, rather futures that could plausibly happen depending on how the world develops along key decision points.

Once one develops the three or so scenarios, one then identifies what kinds of events would signal that the world was moving in one direction, not another. Then, one scans the environment for those signals and when they appear, adjust their long-term investments accordingly.

The careful development of the scenarios is important. This is not back-pocket brainstorming, rather the identification of trends in multiple avenues of human endeavor that might affect one's business. Technology trends, financial trends, political trends, economic trends, scientific trends, and more. To those descriptions we add "What if..." alternative pathways/scenarios. And by assigning probabilities to those, we settle on three or more likely or highly possible alternatives. There's a lot of analysis and work in this endeavor. The RDS team named the three scenarios they came up with and began scanning for the harbinger signals that might inform them which scenario was developing.

The use of scenario planning can help a company think strategically and long-term. Many of the trends take years even decades to unfold allowing a company with the foresight afforded by scenario planning time to restructure and rethink their core capability investments.

Note how many of the concepts introduced in this module (the Eastern Ball or strategic thinking) overlap or relate to each other. For example, Kaplan and Norton argue for the importance of core processes. Hamel and Prahalad focus on the long term development of core capabilities. Stalk argues for the importance of timing. Jack Welch said, "change before you have to." SWOT says pay attention to what you can do and what you need to be able to do. Since it takes time to develop the handful of important core capabilities a company needs to excel, it behooves executives to *do their homework* and prepare for the changes they see coming. Not to do so is, in my view, negligent. Not to do so is to live in the present reactively, responding to outside-in pressures.

Example

One of the scenarios the RDS team named was the Cartel scenario. In the early 1970s, they envisioned a possible future in which the oil producing countries of the world would coordinate to control oil supply and prices. In a Global economy scenario, each oil producing entity would compete in a free market. In a Nationalistic scenario, countries would compete against other countries for revenues and political advantages. The RDS team then *sat back* and began scanning the news reports from hundreds of sources intentionally looking for the events they thought would signal one scenario or another. Of course, seeing and interpreting the signals was and is a subjective phenomenon. Having a set of alternatives (with somewhat fuzzy boundaries) and a set of indicators to watch for made that effort much easier.

One day, they noticed a short article buried deeply in one of the business newspapers in which it was reported that several of the Middle Eastern oil producing countries were meeting to discuss the global oil supply. BINGO! Here was a nondescript short newspaper article that was *shouting* CARTEL, CARTEL, CARTEL!

Shell then began shifting their investments to enhance their ability to produce their own oil—buying oil fields, ramping up exploration, securing a backwardly integrated supply chain. As a result, they catapulted over a decade from near the bottom of the seven sisters to near the top, a huge industry shake-up.

Military strategists also wrestle with the challenge of predicting the future. Are we trending toward a global nuclear holocaust? A series of smaller more tactical regional, cross border *tribal* conflicts? A more nationalistic world in which each country tries to "go it alone?" Each of these scenarios imply different kinds of military investments. The diplomacy, hardware, technology, politics, economics, and more are all different for each scenario. Of course, one might get two or more scenarios happening at the same time. We cannot plan for everything. But using scenario planning, we can dramatically reduce our uncertainty about the future and make reasonable plans and investments to deal with it.

Diagram

Scenario Planning

1. Identify **possible** future pathways in your industry/society.
2. Identify key success factors for each scenario.
3. Identify early indicators of each scenario.
4. Watch for the early indicators.
5. Adapt company investments to build success factors for the indicated scenario.

Challenge

1. Identify the major trends that might affect your industry/business.
2. Develop three alternative but equally plausible scenarios for the future based on those trends.
3. Identify the key indicators that would imply movement down each of the scenarios.
4. Read and scan and watch.
5. Adjust your investments to match your new likely scenario.
6. Read the reference list below.

References

Schwartz, P. 2012. *The Art of the Long View*. Crown Business.

deGeus, A. 2002. *The Living Company*. Harvard Business Review Press.

Wack, P. November 1985. *Scenarios: Shooting the Rapids*. Harvard Business Review.

Grayson, L., and J. Clawson. 1995. *Scenario Planning*. G-0260, Darden Business Publishing.

Jeanne Liedtka, et al. 2007. "Scenario Planning." G-501, Darden Business Publishing.

60. Chart Your Course

Concept

I am surprised repeatedly how many conversations about direction or strategy in companies are laced with confusing, conflated, misunderstood words. Executives regularly interchange words like vision, mission, strategy, goals, and purpose. The net effect of imprecise leadership language is confusion and the resultant disengagement.

Here's a simple but powerful model for organizing your thoughts about your enterprise. By *your enterprise*, I mean any and all of the following: nation, corporation, division, current job/team, and yourself as an individual. Leaders of all these entities should have, I believe, a clear statement of purpose.

This model, which I call a *charter*, has six elements: mission/purpose, vision, values, strategy, and short-term operating goals. That's five. I will introduce the sixth below at the end.

Mission and purpose are synonymous. Many, if not most, people go through life and their work life without thinking about or defining a purpose. In my experience, clarity of purpose, though, is critical to focusing energy and making progress. I invite you to think carefully about purpose and mission and to do that in an inspiring way rather than a numbing way. Corporate committees will, after six months of deliberation, come back with something like "we deliver world-class goods and services that delight our customers beyond their expectations and deliver an above-industry-average return on investments." Most people find a statement like this bland, boring, and unmoving. Much more powerful would be something like "keep Virginia moving," or "we protect those who protect us," or "we make education affordable for everyone." A powerful purpose is short, memorable, powerful, and inspiring.

The second element is vision, that is, a picture of where you want to be at some point in the future. You pick the time horizon whether it be five or fifty years. If you don't know where you are going, how can you get there? If you have no destination, any place will suit. Good visions are typically somewhat complex because you need a financial vision, a strategic vision, a competitive vision, an operational vision, and so on. Whether you look at a corporation (the various disciplines) or an individual (the various "—AL" aspects of life), a complete vision will include detailed imagery and measures of where you want to go. A vision is a definition of what success looks like. In the absence of a clear vision, how would you ever know if you have *succeeded* or not?

The third piece in a charter is values. Your values statement defines your principles of operation. What's important to you? How will you treat your people and your customers and suppliers? I had one client who had 24 *core* values. I thought that was way too many. Brain research suggests that human short-term memory is limited to about seven items. Can you list your values, what you stand for, your guidelines for operation, in seven short statements or less? My first one is "Work for what you want; there is no free lunch."

The fourth piece, strategy, is often the longest and most involved. Your strategy statements define your plan for how you plan to get from today to your vision. I say *strategy statements* because you need a financial strategy, an operational strategy, a marketing strategy, and so on. for a company charter, and a physical strategy, an intellectual strategy, a social strategy, and so on, for an individual charter. By the time you have worked through all these pieces, you may have 30 or more pages of dense thinking.

The fifth element of the Clawson Charter model is short-term operating goals (STOGs). Many managers mistake STOGs for a strategy. They are not. They are simply measures of whether you are making progress toward your vision. Accordingly, your STOGs should be measures of things that are included in your vision's definitions of success. Be careful of what you choose to measure though. Too many and you will paralyze people. Inappropriate measures and you will get people doing unproductive things. For example, one company wanted to increase customer satisfaction by reducing the time customers spent waiting for a company representative to answer the telephone. So they instituted a new measure: we want 80 percent of calls to be answered within 20 seconds. After they implemented that measure, customer satisfaction went *down* because employees were putting customers on hold so they could answer new, incoming calls within the 20 second guideline.

Here's a drawing of the Clawson Charter model below. I invite you to consider using it to organize your thoughts about your nation (if you are a president), your company (if you are a president), your division (if you are a president), your program (if you are a program manager), your team (if you are a team leader), your church (if you are a pastor), and eventually, yourself (if you are a self-leader).

The sixth element in the charter model is *leadership*. Consider this question: If you don't decide the answers to these basic questions, who will?

1. What is your purpose for existence?
2. What is your vision? What do you want to look like in 30 years?
3. What are your core values? What do you stand for in action not just words?
4. What are your strategies for reaching your various visions?
5. What are your short-term operating measurements to see whether or not you are making progress?

You may be working in an organization or a part of an organization where these elements are fuzzy and unclear. That's okay. You can fill that vacuum. *You* could decide that you will answer those questions for yourself and begin working to make them happen. Making that decision would require you to do some mental homework. These are not easy questions to answer. Consulting firms charge millions of dollars to answer a few of them here and there. Unless you begin practicing seeing the need for these answers and seeking the answers, you probably won't become proficient at it. I encourage you to begin at the individual level and write your personal charter. You might also write one for your current work group or team that you are responsible for. If you are not the leader, you might do it anyway. That way, when the next opportunity comes along, you will be prepared to participate in the "who's next?" conversation instead of sitting back on your heels and stammering.

Example

Missions: "To help people find themselves," "To Refresh the World," "To cause people to think" "We make education affordable for everyone." "We protect those who protect us."

Visions: Financial: By 20 years from now, we will have a sustained profit margin of 10%+, a debt/equity ratio of Y%, ACOC: of 4.3%, and so on.

Marketing: By 20 years from now, we will have a market share of X%, be spending Y on advertising with a return of Z, and others. Operations: By 20 years from now, we will have a dependability index of 99%, operating efficiency of Z%, and so on and so forth.

Values: J&J: We believe our first responsibility is to the doctors, nurses, and patients, to mothers and fathers … and so on. We are responsible to our employees, the men and women who … and so on. We are responsible to the communities in which we live and work and to the world … and so on. Our final responsibility is to our stockholders.[34] Four values by which J&J manages some 350+ companies.

Strategy Statements: Link a strategy to each Vision above. Financial Strategy. In order to get sustainable profit margins of 10%+, we will a. b. c. d. e. f. g. h. and so on. Market Share: Analyze competitors and beat them at their own games with superior core capabilities.

Short-term Operating Goals: We will measure the following as indicators of our success on each of these strategies. Finance: operating profits, total profits, and so on. Marking: SOM, share growth, and others.

Leadership: WHO is going to make these decisions? We the executive C-suite incumbents in conjunction with our colleagues make these statements and stand by them.

Diagram

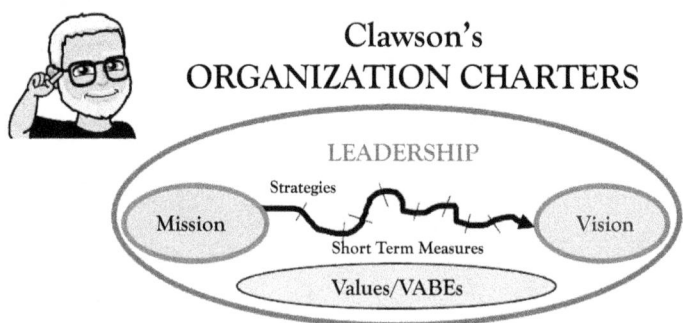

Clawson's
ORGANIZATION CHARTERS

LEADERSHIP

Strategies

Mission

Short Term Measures

Vision

Values/VABEs

1. **Mission** Statement (one inspiring senence)
2. **Vision** Statement (~5 pgs, clear picture of future)
3. **Values** Statement (1/2 page, what we stand for)
4. **Strategies** (~30 pages, linked to each vision)
5. Operating **Measures** (beware!)
6. **Leadership** (WHO makes these decisions?)

---

[34] https://jnj.com/about-jnj/jnj-credo

Challenge

1. Draft a personal charter.
2. Draft a charter for the department/team you now manage.
3. Draft a charter for your company.
4. Draft a charter for your nation.

61. Mission Statements

Many C-level and below executives interchange strategic language with the effect of confusing people and obfuscating what's really going on. Leaders, should, in my view, work to be:

1. Clear
2. Memorable
3. Authentic, and
4. Respectful

… in their language and communications. Strategic conversations in particular demand, I believe, *clarity*—else all those listening and employed and invested come away confused about what we are doing, where we are going, how we are going top's going on.

A clear mission statement or statement of purpose is essential to developing a high-energy business. In my experience, a good mission statement is one inspiring sentence. If you give the charge to develop a mission-statement to a committee, they will wrestle and wordsmith for weeks and return with something very close to "We deliver world-class goods and services that delight our customers beyond their expectations and deliver an above-industry-average return on investment to our share-holders." Perhaps true in some broad sense, but utterly uninspiring. And usually, disingenuous at best since the definition of *world-class* is seldom defined or compared with leaders.

There are those who decry the value of mission statements and the effort to define them as wasted energy. I see the argument. In its early days, Hewlett and Packard made all kinds of reactionary changes to their products until they found something customers would buy. It's clear that an organization, for profit or not, needs to serve a clientele or it will wither and die. One could infer from that that mission statements are secondary to a broader strategy of "finding something that people want to buy." Many people run their businesses that way. Okay. In my experience, that approach ends up in a place with weakly motivated employees who have a hard time getting energized to bust their buns to make other people rich.

The alternative is to, as has been said, create a cause, not a business. This concept is not just connecting your business to a social cause as say advocated by Olivia Khalili at CauseCapitalism[35] or by Jerry Welsh in the Harvard Business Review.[36]

In my explorations of the relationship between feel and performance,[37] I concluded that most businesses use motivation processes that leave large amounts of employee energy fallow and untapped. When one compares the energy and passion of volunteers in the non-profit sector, one wonders how if at all private sector businesses could tap into that pool of energy.

I agree that some people are chronically low energy and low motivation. Some proportion of that group have been taught to be that way. Some are perhaps never under any circumstance going to be passionate about productive activity. That said, I have come to believe that businesses could tap into that unused pool of energy in a number of ways. The book Doug Newburg and I wrote, *Powered by Feel,* was one attempt to explore that possibility.

At a deeper level, it seems to me that people seek purpose in life. They want their lives to mean something. Especially when they spend long hours, weeks, months, years, and decades at work. I have come to believe that it is the leader's *job*, the leader's *responsibility* to clarify why we are here and what we are doing, and that in fact, leaders who don't or can't do that are, in a word, negligent or incompetent or both.

I have also come to believe that since people seek meaning, the best way they can do that is to settle on a purpose in and of their lives. Some people are waiting to be told what that is, perhaps from God or the clergy or some mysterious mechanism including the occult. Some people with ADD or ADHD may have brain chemistry issues that make it even more difficult to settle on a mission in life.

---

[35] http://causecapitalism.com/why-your-company-should-have-a-social-mission/

[36] https://hbr.org/1999/09/good-cause-good-business

[37] https://amazon.com/Powered-Feel-Individuals-Teams-Companies/dp/9812818928/ref=mt_paperback?_encoding=UTF8&me=

So, ask yourself, what's my purpose in life? Can you answer that question? If so, great. If not, I urge you to think seriously about that. To what end are you spending your on average roughly 700,000 hours in this life? If you don't have a central purpose or mission, the odds are that you will slump into what I would call shallow attempts to entertain yourself with food, drink, television, sports, or some similar sedentary outside-in activity. If you want to energize your life, pick a purpose and begin working on it. The related question is "what do you want to create?" What will be the legacy of your life? Will it have any focus? Will there be a created or built result?

That is not to say that any endeavor to create is *better* than one or the other. People who build fences and dig ditches serve a valuable purpose in life as much as doctors and lawyers and engineers. There is honor in all honest work. If one has spent one's life plumbing, building fences, driving trucks, or whatever, one can look with pride on what they have accomplished, especially if they see the mission or purpose they have fulfilled.

Some people have no stated purpose in life, yet year by year they continue to allocate their weekly allowance of 164 hours per week. One could examine those allocations and infer what one is investing in—"what you do is what you love, and what you love is what you do."

The same is true of companies. Let's consider some examples.

Example

Consider this example from *USA Today*, December 7, 3B, in which an executive vice president stated, "This is an important step in (company name)'s mission to become a global airline." If a company's mission to become something (a) that's a vision, not a mission, and (b) what does that have to do with any kind of service to customers? I believe an organization's reason for living should be something around contributing to society and its needs—unless of course the organization is organized only to serve its members. In that case, it is, to me, not a company but a self-serving club—of which there are many. Private golf clubs, for example, exist only to serve their members. Fraternities. Sororities. Home Owner Associations. And so on.

Back to the more usual private sector company, let's consider a *mundane* one. Suppose you own a company that repairs automobiles. Most people would look at that and say, "Not very sophisticated, it's a low wage, low tech, marginal business. No interest." Managers with that set of assumptions would hire people and focus on wages, hours, and doing a *good enough* job.

One could take a different view. This would require understanding the underlying value of automobiles. This would require understanding laws governing automobile safety, rates of auto theft in the area, number of automobile deaths and the value of dependability to customers. That understanding (which would require doing a little homework—easily done in today's world with a desire to do so) would allow one to explain to employees the value of automobile safety, owner identity, convenience of travel and dependability. Such a leader might conclude that "Our mission is to 'keep people moving' or 'keep people safe and moving' or 'renew your wheels.' Let me show you some slides of what unsafe automobiles look like. When we do a good job, we can go home at night proud of what we do. Every fender, every circuit, every system must be done perfectly to prevent possible damage, destruction and death. Hold your head high and do a good job!" What do you think? Could you create a single sentence inspiring summary of the purpose of your company or organization?

Here are some other examples of powerful one sentence mission statements.

1. We protect those who protect us. (BAES USA)
2. We make education affordable for everyone. (Sallie Mae)
3. We keep Virginia moving! (VDOT)
4. We refresh the world! (Coca-Cola)
5. "To help people find themselves" (the author based on having had three last names)
6. "To build ever more powerful and efficient rockets(?)" (Werner Von Braun)

I find these statements powerful, clear, and inspiring. Anyone in any job in those organizations could connect what they do to that one sentence, be easily able to remember it, and have pride in how they are spending their working lives. Contrast these statements with the committee-designed statement above.

I believe that leaders of nations should also be able to declare the mission of their countries. What is the purpose of India? China? Japan? Germany? The United States? Mexico? Could one declare a purpose that would inspire all citizens? Or do many leaders simply want to stay in power? In which case, there's no tapping into that latent pool of citizen energy. The personal mission "to be in control and suck my comfort out of the populace" perhaps not stated but behaved is not one that inspires others.

Many individuals seemingly live their lives around the purpose of *maximizing my leisure time.* A life without purpose, though sucks energy. Coming in late, avoiding work, going home early, sitting on the couch drinking, and watching TV may be what some people want or think they want, and it's not a productive lifestyle. Sadly, movies, plays, books, and articles tease about and accept this *lazy* lifestyle and make it funny and attractive. See the earlier chapter on balancing the DO-REST cycles of daily life.

Alternatively, consider these mission statements of individuals:

1. I cause people to think. (professor)
2. I protect the poor and under-served. (defense attorney)
3. I bring the facts of key events to the world. (journalist)
4. I entertain and educate people by creating powerful stories in film. (producer)
5. I create safe, comfortable transportation for millions. (highway contractor)
6. I nurture healthy, productive, well-rounded citizens. (parent)

Lily Tomlin once noted "I always wanted to be somebody ... I guess I should have been more specific."

Diagram

What's YOUR purpose in life?

Contain and include professional, familial, personal all aspects of your life.

- *What's the purpose of your life?*
  - On average, 675,000 hours to live.
  - ½ to 2/3 of it spent at work
  - How do you want to spend it?
  - Consider the educational principle of the Matsushita Leadership School in Japan: how could you presume to lead others if you have no purpose in life?

The Importance of Purpose

..the single most critical improvement anyone can make in brain function, and in character, is **to find his mission in life.** Passion heals; a whole -hearted commitment to a calling, or a career, or an avocation focuses the mind and the soul.

And neuropsychiatry tells us that idleness is indeed the devil's playground. It is well known that idleness increases psychiatric and physical symptoms of all kinds; this is true even of schizophrenics. Psychotic patients report that while they are working they don't hear voices. The effect is so pronounced that some authorities speak of work as a wonder drug.

Source: John Ratey, Shadow Syndromes, p. 363.

https://google.com/search?q=images+John+Ratey+harvard&tbm=isch&ved=2ahUKEwiO1NTgzr zuAhXlqXIEHfzTBGwQ2-cCegQIABAA&oq=images+John+Ratey+harvard&gs_lcp=CgNpbWc QAzoECCMQJzoCCAA6BggAEAgQHlDJjwlYqq4JYPSvCWgAcAB4AIABfogBgQySAQQxNC 40mAEAoAEBqgELZ3dzLXdpei1pbWfAAQE&sclient=img&ei=xJ8RYI7iAuXTytMP_KeT4AY &bih=578&biw=1366&rlz=1C1GCEB_enUS910US910#imgrc=OOpFEe9993dk8M

Challenge

1. Draft your one sentence view of the purpose of your nation. (Here's mine for the USA: "To be a robust democracy that provides opportunity, liberty and justice equally for all.")

2. Draft your one sentence view of the purpose of your company or organization.

3. Draft your one sentence view of the purpose of your life.

4. Assess these drafts in terms of their clarity, power to inspire, and memorability.

62. Vision Statements

Concept

Your mission or purpose for existing is not a vision. A dream can be a vision.[38] A vision is a definition of what you think the future will look like or what you want to **make** it look like. A vision can be chronologically indeterminate, however, I assert it's better to set a time horizon. You may or may not hit that target; if you don't, you can reset the timeline so long as you maintain your view of what you are trying to create.

How far out should you attempt to see/look/envision? Six months is not strategic. Five years seems minimal—and was often used by many Asian countries as their strategic planning horizon. Ten to twenty years seems realizable within one person's tenure. Jack Welch was CEO at General Electric for 20 years, for example. If an executive isn't planning on the long haul career, rather is looking only at short-term stepping stones for his or her own career, they are not likely to be thinking strategically. Konsosuke Matsushita at Panasonic Electronics (Matsushita Denki KK) famously developed 10 25-year plans, extending 250 years out. That's long-term thinking. You choose. For me, I think 10 to 20 years is a good range. In other words, can you describe what your company (or you for that matter) should look like in 15 years?

What's the difference between a goal and a vision? Time. A goal is short-term. A vision is broader, longer, bigger, more pervasive.

The importance of vision in business is related to the issue of living inside-out or outside-in. Problem solvers are essentially living outside-in because they are allowing things that come up to dominate their action. Problems for those living inside-out with a vision are secondary speedbumps along the path. Robert Fritz makes the point well, if sometimes obtusely, that to live inside-out one needs to think about what they want to create rather than finding and solving problems.[39] Creators have

---

[38] Martin Luther King, "I have a Dream." https://archives.gov/files/press/exhibits/dream-speech.pdf

[39] Fritz, R. 1984. *The Path of Least Resistance: Principles for Creating What you Want to Create*, DMA.

problems, sure, and they are not the main focus—the long-term vision is the dominant perspective.

While mission statements, I say, should be only one sentence, a vision statement is longer, maybe 10 pages. This is because if you make a detailed picture of your vision, you will be describing what your financial, operational, marketing, human resources, government relations, expansion overseas, and so on, will look like. The same is true for an individual vision statement. What do you want to look like in 10 to 20 years—or by the time you turn 65? This requires attention to each of the –AL aspects of life: physical, social, marital, intellectual, professional, and so on.

Many people say it's impossible to develop long-term visions because things are changing so rapidly and unpredictably. This is an outside-in way of looking at the world. It is true that things are changing rapidly on almost every front, technology, politics, and so on. At the same time, unless one has a vision of what they want to create, they will spend their lives and careers responding, reacting, living outside-in.

Further, there are ways of dealing with uncertain futures. A powerful one was developed by the strategic planning department at Royal Dutch Shell in the mid- to late-20th century. This was *scenario planning*, a process by which careful analysis identified predictable indicators of the direction change might take.[40] If one knows what to look for, one can *see* indicators that will point this way or that way. This is not the usual *scenario planning* of the best case/worst case. Not at all. It involves developing three very plausible alternative futures, then watching for the harbingers that would signal one path over another as we described above.

Example

As mentioned earlier, the Royal Dutch Shell company was in the 1970s the seventh of the seven sisters of the oil industry. Then the strategic planning department developed three plausible scenarios. When a little

[40] See Schwartz, P. 2012. *The Art of the Long View.* Crown Business. for latest edition, written much earlier. See also *The Living Company* by Arie deGeus. And "Scenario Planning," technical note, G-0260 by Les Grayson and James Clawson, Darden Business Publishing, 1994.

observed newspaper article appeared signaling the development of one of those scenarios, the company began to position itself for that future—and jumped to number two among its competitors.

A corporate vision statement might look like this: By 2030, our debt/ equity ratio will be X, our EBIT will be running at Y, our net profits will be Z, our operating ratio will be F, our revenues will have grown at B percent per year on average, and so forth. What do you WANT your financial picture to look like? How detailed do you want to be in your financial analysis?

By 2030, our share of market will be A, our global penetration will include Y countries with at least Z sales, our advertising will be running about E percent of sales, our customer base will have grown to BB million, and so on. What do you WANT your marketing function to look like? What are the important elements of your marketing function—as you see it? How detailed do you get when you analyze your marketing function?

And so on for operations, government relations, research and development, product/program management, accounting, information technology, and all and any other functions that are essential to running your business.

Martin Luther King had a vision for the United States; he described that in his famous, "I have a dream" speech. You can see the full text easily online (see endnotes). Jack Welch had a vision of the kind of company he wanted to create; he spent 10 years restructuring the company buying and selling several hundred companies. During his second 10 years, he focused on reducing inefficiencies in his new structure, driving out *organizational cholesterol*. Under his tutelage, GE was ranked in the Fortune 5 annually.

Brigham Young had a vision of a safe place in the Rocky Mountains where his followers could practice their religion in relative peace and quiet. There were enormous obstacles to achieving this vision, huge problems, which he and his followers overcame.

Genghis Khan had a vision of dominating the various Mongol tribes and their enemies. Alexander had a vision of conquering the known world.

Creative vision, I have come to believe, dominates advances in human endeavor. Those who simply look for problems and solve without a bigger vision are what we might call managers, bureaucrats, or maintainers. Creating vision takes effort. If the thought of going through the exercise at the beginning of this segment is daunting, ask yourself, "What do I want to create? How much effort am I willing to put into making that happen?"

Mahatma Gandhi had a vision and like so many of his ilk, that vision dominated his life. Creators tend to be a bit obsessive, even neurotically so. My colleague, Alex Horniman, is wont to say, "Excellence is a neurotic lifestyle."

At the individual level, vision statements revolve around the various –AL aspects of life. "By the time I'm 65, I will have weighed X pounds annually." "I will have run A marathons." (physical) "I will have Y degrees or read ZZ books." (intellectual) What is your vision for how you want to look at +20 years on EACH of the –AL aspects?

You can see how this might take 10 pages or so.

Diagram

Your IDEAL SELF VISION @ 65

ASPECT	VISION
PHYSICAL	
FINANCIAL	
MATERIAL	
INTELLECTUAL	
EMOTIONAL	
SPIRITUAL	
MARITAL	
PARENTAL	
SOCIAL	
And so on.	

Challenge

1. Write your vision for your country in 30 years.
2. Write your vision for your company in 20 years.
3. Write your vision for yourself in 30 years.

63. Values Statements

Concept

Consciously or unconsciously, mindfully or mindlessly, explicitly or implicitly, people value some things and not other things. The chapter on VABEs explains this. What do you stand for? What does your company stand for? Ed Schein,[41] Albert Ellis,[42] Ellen Langer,[43] and Chris Argyris[44] among others have described how some VABEs are conscious while many are not. They all made a distinction between what we think we are doing and what we actually do. That is, we may state our values and beliefs and yet behave in different ways reflecting other even opposing values.

So, the question, "What do you stand for?" they would suggest has two answers, what you think you stand for and **what your behavior says** you stand for. That said, if we don't *strive* to stand for something, our thoughtless behavior will define us.

What does your company stand for? What are the values that guide decision making in your organization? Stanford psychology research on short-term memory suggests that seven is about maximum for most people. Consequently, I assert that a person's or a company's value system should be short enough for people to see and remember. Perhaps, half a page max. I had one client that had 24 core values. Way too many. No one could remember them and consequently, although the company taught them and advertised them, employees just did what they did. Too many values means basically none.

That is not to say that each of our hundreds of VABEs is not a value, it is. But we need a core group on which to focus. Something memorable and inspiring. If an organization's primary value is "make as much money as we can," it will be led to make unethical and perhaps even illegal decisions. There are big margins in illicit drugs and adult movies, yet most

---

[41] Schein, E. 1985. *Organizational Culture and Leadership.*

[42] Ellis, A., and R. Harper. 1961. *A Guide to Rational Living.* Prentice-Hall.

[43] Langer, E. 2014. *Mindfulness.* Da Capo Lifelong Books.

[44] Argyris, C. 1982. (several references including) *Reasoning, Learning and Action: Individual and Organizational.* Jossey-Bass.

organizations shy away from these activities out of moral or values-based considerations.

SO, I say, a clear listing of your core VABEs is an important part of a charter.

Example

One of the most famous values driven companies is Johnson & Johnson, which is really a confederation of some 300 companies. Their four main values, they say and history confirms, (noted briefly above) are the glue that holds those companies together in spirit and operating patterns. Those four values are, condensed, responsibility to the medical personnel and customers who use their products, second responsibility to employees, third responsibility to the communities in which they work, and finally, responsibility to their shareholders.[45] One could point out the parallelism with Kaplan and Norton's balanced scorecard noting that devotion to customers brings financial results (for shareholders) while attention to employees generates energy to serving customers. It's a loose connection, nevertheless it seems similar to me.

Coca-Cola lists seven core values: leadership courage, collaborative genius, accountability, passion, diversity, and quality.[46]

General Electric says passion for customers, meritocracy, global growth, every person, be on the offense, fast excellence, and respect for former leaders.[47]

British Aerospace USA (BAES) posts to be Trusted, Innovative and Bold.[48]

---

[45] https://jnj.com/about-jnj/jnj-credo

[46] https://google.com/search?q=coca+cola+core+values&oq=coca+cola+core+values&aqs=chrome..69i57j0l4.5334j0j4&sourceid=chrome&ie=UTF-8

[47] https://ge.com/annual01/values/

[48] http://baesystems.com/cs/Satellite?c=BAEMedia_C&childpagename=UK%2FBAELayout&cid=1434554636657&pagename=UKWrapper

Diagram

Charter #3. Values

- What do you stand for? Believe in?
  - List them.
  - Many are "pre-conscious"
  - Gaps between espoused and behaved?
  - Constant discovery process
  - Which did you inherit?
  - How many are core?

THINKING...

Challenge

1. Write down your personal most important core values.
2. Write down what you think your company behaves in terms of its core values.
3. What do you think your company's core values should be?

64. Strategy

Concept

A strategy is a plan for how to reach a vision. We start *here* and we want to go *there*, and the strategy is a description of how we plan to do that. Vision is not strategy—although visions imply or suggest strategic foci. Mission is not strategy although mission implies or suggests strategy foci.

Because a complete vision statement includes long-term goals for multiple aspects of the business including financial, marketing, accounting, public relations, government relations, human resources, research and development, IT infrastructure, and so on, the strategy statement will be the longest section in a charter, as much as 20 to 30 pages. What is your financial strategy? Your marketing strategy? Your human resource strategy? What is your growth strategy? And others.

I once asked a CEO what his corporate strategy was. He said, "Our strategy for the next six months is to cut costs." I waited. That was all he had to say. I concluded that he was a short-term manager, not a strategic thinker, not particularly excited about his business, and not at all inspiring.

Example

Suppose a domestic company wants to have a global presence. It may have a vision statement something like, "By 2040, we will have a profitable and growing presence on six continents." The strategy for achieving that vision might look like this:

1. We will identify the most promising countries on the other five continents for our industry/business line.
2. We will develop domestic areas of competence in marketing for each of those countries.
3. These areas of country competence will study and understand the marketing and sales nuances of each country.
4. We will make adjustments to our products that fit each country identified.
5. We will consider and evaluate the pros and cons of making joint ventures or alliances with companies in those countries.

6. We will develop sales offices in those countries to distribute our products. Some will be joint ventures and some will be wholly owned.

7. We will work hard to satisfy and surprise every customer in each of those countries. Our new reputation is prime to developing local brand equity.

8. We will maintain constant and intimate contact with each marketing/ sales office. This will include constant travel as well as technological contact.

9. We will rely on a combination of local talent (in development) and domestic management to grow each office. The local leaders must have real opportunities to grow within our company culture.

10. When demand reaches a level that could support local creation of products and services, we will begin to develop local competence in product creation.

11. We will continue to reinforce our corporate values and culture throughout local growth phases.

12. We will share the rewards of growth with our local leaders.

13. As demand for our products and services grow within the initial target country, we will begin to explore marketing and sales in neighboring countries in the continent.

14. We will repeat the above processes in each new country that we open.

15. In this way, our company will grow like plugs of zoysia grass: we plant a plug and water it and when it grows, it will extend in its region.

You can see that if this were a simple outline of a global growth strategy, the details for each company in each industry would quickly expand this one page list into several pages.

Then, if you do this for each of the vision statements, one quickly has 20 to 30 pages of analysis and planning.

In 2017, the new CEO at General Electric, John Flannery, announced a new strategy for the company, a "smaller, simpler, and more efficient" company.[49] His predecessor, Jeff Immelt, had changed the strategy of the

---

[49] https://nytimes.com/2017/10/20/business/general-electric-strategy-report. html

company when he took over from Jack Welch on September 10, 2001. Welch had emphasized a limited number of industries, superior performance in each industry, and a financial *engine* (he called it) that included using GE Capital to hit his financial targets year after year. Gary Hamel once called Welch the ultimate *juice squeezer*. Immelt took a different strategy what Hamel would have called an innovator. Innovation is less efficient than juice squeezing. Immelt announced 10 new innovative initiatives for the company, designed in his view, to make the company a leader in new technologies and industries in the 21st century. The stock performance of the company did not, over the succeeding decade, improve, but in fact declined. Jack Welch was a hard act to follow. Flannery's statement (referenced above) sounds more like Welch's rhetoric, focusing on immediate performance—perhaps at the expense of leadership in new emerging industries. Flannery mentioned restructuring the constellation of GE companies—much as Welch did in the 1980s—buying and selling companies to fit his view (vision) of what the company should look like.

Timing is a big issue here. Growing a $120 billion company is hard to do in small, emerging industries. And BCG, Hamel and Christensen might argue, I surely would, that finding the right balance between Cash Cows and Rising Stars is delicate and difficult. My guess is Jeff Immelt would agree.

Diagram

Strategy connects today with tomorrow

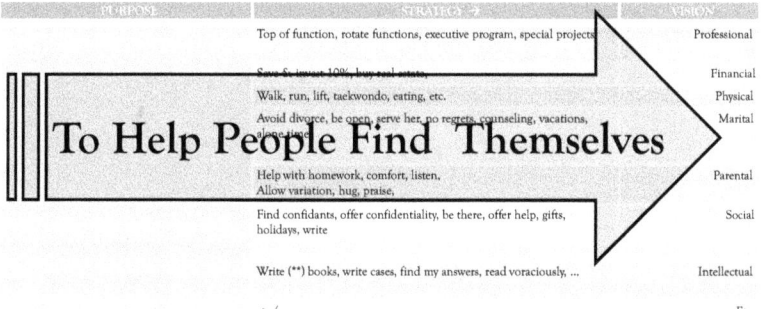

Challenge

1. Select one of your company vision statement elements from your earlier draft and develop an outline of your strategy as given in the example above.
2. Do the same for your personal vision statements.
3. Can you see that spending a day on developing a draft of charter could structure two decades worth of intense, passionate, inspiring work either in your life or in your company?

65. Short-Term Operating Goals

Concept

Once one has vision and strategy statements in place, the challenge is to find ways to measure progress along your strategic path toward your vision. Let's call these *short-term operating goals* (STOGs). In other words, what are you going to *measure* to assess your progress? Many executives focus on measurements before they think about vision or strategy. For me, that's bass-ackwards.

You have to be careful about what you measure lest you actually damage or destroy your strategic efforts. You will see in a couple of examples below how that can happen.

Identifying measures depends on some kind of control or accounting system. If you don't collect data, you cannot measure progress. Hip pocket assessments are susceptible to self-deception and fantasy. By the same token, too many controls can stifle innovation and creativity. Another paradoxical balance that successful executives must navigate. See the chapter on Control.

Tim Gallwey, you will see in the chapter on him in the Change module used measurements as a central element in his change theory.[50] The adage, "people pay attention to what you measure" is the core principle there.

Example

I had a client once for whom about 80 percent of their business came in over the phone. A few people complained that it took too long to get through to a customer service representative (CSR). Management was concerned about this, so they decided to fix the problem. In order to raise customer satisfaction, they decided to measure time-to-answer for each CSR. They put a device on each CSR's phone that would measure

---

[50] Tim Gallwey, *The Inner Game of Work*, https://amazon.com/Inner-Game-Work-Learning-Workplace-ebook/dp/B000FC1IT0/ref=sr_1_3?ie=UTF8&qid=1513182659&sr=8-3&keywords=tim+gallwey

this and instituted a new *rule,* the 80/20 rule (not the Pareto version but perhaps inspired by it): they expected that 80 percent of calls would be answered within 20 seconds. What do you think happened to customer satisfaction ratings?

Yes, they plummeted. And the reason was that CSRs were putting people on hold so they could answer the phone within the 20 second guideline. That's an example of how management's choice of measures can actually damage or destroy their stated goals.

There was a plant manager in one of my seminars who said his management put 64 measures on him. He said he felt like Gulliver strapped down by the Lilliputians, unable to move, paralyzed. A linear program with 64 constraints would leave a very small field of choice. Clearly that's what management wanted, virtually complete control.

On the individual level, I included *reading books* in my Intellectual strategy. As an STOG, I chose to keep track of the number of books I read in a year. This was consistent with my VABE, "Read or you will have nothing to say." I started with an STOG of one book a month. After a couple of years, I was up, to my surprise, to 48 books a year. This, I thought, was pretty good, four books a month, done simply by reading 20 to 30 minutes a night before falling asleep. I mentioned this once in a class I was teaching. I asked people how many books a year they read. Most people said one or two or none. (That alone was a revealing insight.) One man raised his hand and said, "600." I was shocked! Really? Yes, he said. It turned out he was an astro-physicist working at Oak Ridge labs. He didn't watch television. He sat in his easy chair at night while his wife knitted. He had a stack of *unread* books on the left and *read* books on the right. He would *read* a book in an hour, skimming each page, capturing the main ideas, absorbing them, integrating them, and then repeat the process. Two books a night. 600 a year! Wow. I realized, as usual, that my efforts were quite humble by comparison!

Diagram

Short-Term Measures of Progress

HOW ARE WE DOING

Financial Strategy
Marketing Stragery
Sales Strategy
Operations Strategy
Safety Strategy
Environmental Strategy
Government Relations Strategy
Human Resource Strategy
Talent Development Strategy
... and so on

Challenge

1. Write down what you think the short-term measures of progress should be for EACH strategy in your personal and corporate charter drafts.
2. Think through the implications of each measure and whether they will produce unintended consequences if applied.

66. The Importance of Having a Story

Concept

When you are in the presence of an executive, perhaps the CEO, and the talk turns to company strategy, are you a listener or a participant? Most people are listeners. They haven't formed their own opinions about what the company should be doing.

IF you aspire to be an executive, I believe you must develop your own story about what the company should be doing. This will require work, homework, analysis, using the tools introduced in the Strategy module, especially the Charter. It's not easy.

If you have a charter in mind, if you are clear in your own mind what the purpose of the organization is, if you have a vision of what it could and should become, if you are clear on what the company stands for, and if you have strategies in mind for reaching your vision, you can **participate** in the strategic conversation.

Humans have had from pre-history a strong oral tradition. We like to tell and listen to stories. We remember well-told stories. Powerful stories move us, inspire us, energize us. The same is true in business. We love powerful stories.[51] We are instructed by stories. We need good, clear, memorable stories.[52]

What's your story? Do you have a personal story? Do you have a corporate story? If not, how will you convince others to give you more responsibility? Simply asking for it, believing you somehow deserve it, isn't enough. You need a story, a charter. Of course, this is primarily true of Linear types (see the chapter on Career Concepts). If you are an Expert or Spiral, the odds of you becoming a senior executive are diminished. That said, if you rise in the organization, again, you need a story. You need one to share with investors, with analysts, and with your people. It

---

[51] https://shannonturlington.com/2010/06/03/why-are-stories-so-important/
[52] See for example, Loehr, J. 2007. *The Power of Story*. Free Press. https://amazon. com/Power-Story-Rewrite-Destiny-Business-ebook/dp/B000VM9ZJ4/ref=sr_1_ 1?ie=UTF8&qid=1513204118&sr=8-1&keywords=the+power+of+stories

is important to have a story and know it well and be able to tell it well at the right time and right place.[53]

If you don't have a story, you have nothing to sell. For me, that story is best framed in a Charter. Can you sell a purpose, a vision, a set of values, and a set of strategies? If you don't develop a story, how could you hope to influence others? What do you give them?

Example

Suppose you are asked to explain your company to a group of Wall Street analysts. What would you say? Could you articulate your company's charter?

Suppose you are interviewing for more responsibility in your company. Could you describe the future you see for your company and the role your new job would have in that vision?

Diagram

CONCLUSION

- What's your charter?
- What competitive advantage will achieve your charter?
- Are you internally consistent?
- Nurture your revolutionaries.
- Create problems that build the future.
- Take the Leadership Point-of-View

---

[53] Rosen, H. n.d. The Importance of Story, https://jstor.org/stable/41405427?seq=1#page_scan_tab_contents

Challenge

1. Write your personal charter.
2. Write a charter for your current responsibility.
3. Write a charter for your company/organization.
4. Practice telling your *stories* in the mirror, the shower, while driving.

67. Analyzing Ethics

Concept

The *standard* method of ethics analysis is to identify the harms and benefits for various stakeholders[54] and then to make decisions by balancing all those consequences. This is a relativistic approach—what's right and wrong is relative to each stakeholder and how one balances the overall effects. While this system is widespread and commonly taught in business schools, it leaves, for me, the question of are there any absolute principles? Religions of course argue for absolute values and principles. Many of those we would agree or argue are self-serving for that religion. The ideas, for example, that "every knee shall bow" or "every infidel shall submit or die" are absolute principles that are ego-centrically self-serving to their promulgators.[55]

The relativistic approach helps people examine and review their VABEs and thus, perhaps, invites people to rethink their judgments and biases. On the other hand, we could argue that the relativistic approach allows people to use their biased VABEs (as all VABEs are biased) to create the *balance* on which they make their decisions. See the chapter on the Decision Hexagon.

The relativistic approach begins with the identification of the key stakeholders. This analysis invites a broader view of who will be affected by an initiative. We must, for example, consider community residents not just corporate shareholders as we assess the impact of toxic discharge into a local stream. Research on authoritarianism suggests that society is *rigged* in favor of those in power—they make the rules, they enforce the rules, they make the rules to benefit themselves.[56] The experiential exercise, *Star Power*™,[57] illustrates this concept dramatically.

---

[54] Schwartz, P. 2012. *The Art of the Long View.* Crown Business.

[55] Haidt, J. 2012. *The Righteous Mind: Why Good People are Divided by Politics and Religion.* Vintage.

[56] For example, Snyder, T. 2017. *On Tyranny: Twenty Lesson from the Twentieth Century.* Tim Duggan Books.

[57] Available from simulationtrainingsystems.com. https://simulationtrainingsystems.com/schools-and-charities/products/starpower/

Second, we attempt to identify the *harms* and *benefits* of the initiative to each shareholder. This may involve interviews or speculation or both.

Finally, we attempt to balance that matrix of consequences as we make a decision.

Careful analysis is necessary at each step. Our first impressions may be mistaken as we allow our VABEs to screen or bias our data-gathering and consideration. Our analyses are further clouded by the bias in most humans to yield to people in positions of authority. This tendency is an important basis for society and civilization and it contributes to a power-centric pattern of decision making that can lead to disastrous results. The tendency to obey leads to big questions of what's ethical, what's legal, what's *right*, and how and when should one protest or disobey.

Example

A carpet manufacturer is discharging several dozen chemicals into the local water shed as a result of its manufacturing processes.

A coal-fired electricity plant discharges various particles into the air.

A stock with increasing price invests in exploitative businesses in Africa.

Large investors in medical marijuana make double digit profits while small quantity distributors languish in jail.

Caveat Emptor, "Buyer Beware."

And the classical ethical dilemma (with many variations), a person standing by a switch sees a train barreling down on his or her baby on the tracks and a group of townsfolk standing at the end of the switched spur.[58]

A professional athlete refuses to respect the national anthem and flag before a sporting event.

A company sells inventory of baby formula prohibited in industrialized nations to less-informed people in third world nations.

---

[58] Greene, J. 2014. *Moral Tribes: Emotion, Reason, and the Gap between Us and Them.* Penguin, New York.

Diagram

A *typical* stakeholder analysis.

STAKEHOLDER	HARMS	BENEFITS	NET COSTS
Management			
Employees			
Shareholders			
Community Residents			
Natural Environment			
Unions			
… Others?			

Challenge

1. Pick a key initiative in your organization.
2. Identify the key stakeholders. Be sure to include those who are *peripherally* affected.
3. Identify the *harms* to each stakeholder if this initiative is implemented.
4. Identify the *benefits* to each stakeholder if this initiative is implemented.
5. Identify the net cost to each stakeholder if this initiative is implemented.
6. Assess those consequences and decide what YOU would do with regard to this initiative.
7. Be prepared to speak to each stakeholder group and describe why you chose the way you did.
8. What core VABEs of yours are dominating your decision? Do any of these VABEs need to be revisited?

68. Ethical Leadership

Concept

Given the traditional method of ethics analysis introduced in the last chapter, executives decide, consciously or not, what they will do—and those decisions have big ethical implications. We all *balance* the consequences to stakeholders with our own VABEs.

Rich Teerlink, former CEO of Harley Davidson, had a powerful *moral foundation* for his leadership. He asserted that moral leaders exhibited four characteristics: truth-telling, promise-keeping, fairness, and respect for the individual.

Truth Telling is the beginning of transparency and authenticity. How often do you tell the truth? How often do you fudge the truth? Withhold it. Distort it. Bend it.

Promise Keeping is similar. If you break your promises, what will that do to your trustworthiness?

Fairness is equally as difficult to define. We talk of distributive justice, to each as they have *earned*. What is fair to one person may not be fair to another. Our stakeholder analysis would be useful here.

Respect for the Individual is something that many if not most people in power lose. They begin to see people as (like one colleague calls them) the *little people*. Or not people at all, simply replaceable assets.

I have come to believe that one can give speeches, introduce incentives, do periodic performance reviews, and hand out gold stars and extra stripes, but if they don't have this four cornered foundation of *moral leadership*, his or her people will not be moved.

If you told your people the truth half of the time, would they follow you?

If you kept your promises to your people half of the time, would they follow you?

If you treated people fairly half of the time, would they follow you?

If you showed respect for individuals (at all levels) half of the time, would they follow you?

If you agree with me that the answers are "No," then how often is *good enough* to motivate/move people?

Let's put these four dimensions on a 1 to 100 point scale where 50 equals *half of the time*. Then you could ask your people to rate your organization and your leadership (anonymously) on them. I assert that if you aren't getting "Olympic Gold Medal" ratings, 9.9, 9.7, 9.8, and the like on these four concepts, you won't be able to raise the bar for your people. They simply won't trust you.

Example

I once had the senior leadership of a large mid-western company in the room. At one point, we were debating the ethical question, "Should one tell the truth in business?" To my surprise, these suited executives were soon shouting at each other. One even stood on his chair and was shouting and pointing at his *colleagues* across the room. On the one side, people argued, "If you tell the truth, people will take advantage of you." On the other side, people argued, "If you don't tell the truth, people won't trust you." Hmmm.

A participant in one of my seminars once noted that his company was going to shut down his plant. His boss, the plant manager, called an executive meeting. In that meeting, he said, in essence, "We are going to shut down the plant. I don't want you to tell anyone lest productivity drop off." As the participant left the meeting, he was met by one of his subordinates in the hallway (who *happened* to be getting a drink of water from the nearby water fountain) who asked him, "Are we closing the plant?" To whom does this man owe his allegiance? If he reports the *truth*, "I cannot tell you that," what will the message be?

I have reported earlier, the freeway construction company owner who sold his company for $200 million and immediately gave $1 million to each of his 100 employees. Most people were astounded by this. He saw it as simply being *fair*. "They did all the work," he said. "And I still have $100 million!"

Ikujiro Nonaka describes the plant manager of a new state-of-the-art chip-factory who was struggling with rejection rates. His team worked hard for months and could not get their rejection rate into an acceptable range. One day, an elderly woman, a custodian, stopped him on the way into work and said she thought she had a solution. Now, how many plant managers in high tech industries would stop and listen to an elderly custodian? In my experience, most would not. The vast majority would not. She said that she noticed that when the local commuter train went by, the ground shook a little. She thought building a moat around the factory would dampen those shock waves and reduce the reject rate in the miniscule circuits on the chips. This manager listened, he had respect for the individuals at all levels in his organization, built the moat, and his reject rate dropped immediately.

Diagram

The case for change ...
The Moral Foundation of
Extraordinary Performance

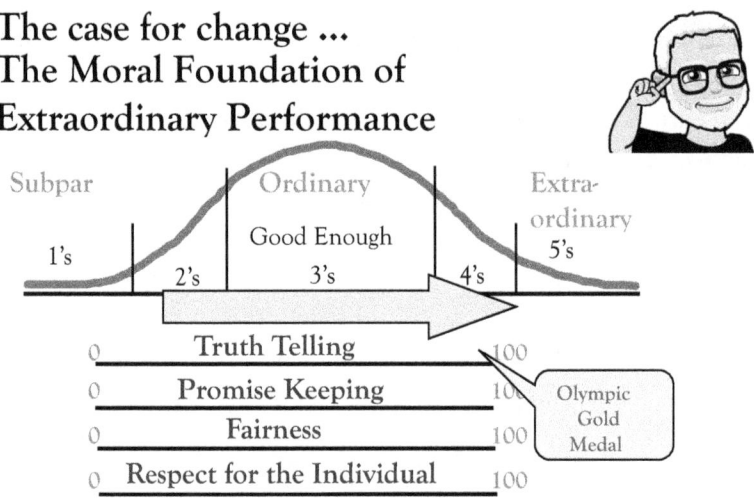

Source: Rich Teerlink, CEO Harley Davidson

Assessing the Moral Foundation of Your Leadership

(Copy and use with your team anonymously—adapted from *Level Three LEadership*, pp. 395) After you have discussed the moral foundation of leadership, use this form to begin your leadership team assessment. First, make copies of the form and give one to each member of your team and have them assess your team. Second, answer each question according to your view of your current management team and its interactions. Third, collect each team member's answers (anonymously if you wish) and summarize the data. Fourth, hold a team meeting in which you discuss the results (average scores, variation, difference from expectations, or hopes) and make joint plans for how to improve your scores. To answer, circle the number that represents the percentage of the time that each principle describes your leadership team.

Cornerstone Principle	Percentage of the Time That This Principle Describes Our Team									
1. **Truth-Telling:** We tell the truth to each other and don't hide things or talk behind others' backs. We know where each person stands.	10	20	30	40	50	60	70	80	90	100
2. **Promise-Keeping:** We keep our promises to each other no matter how large or small.	10	20	30	40	50	60	70	80	90	100
3. **Fairness:** We treat each other fairly and do not try to take advantage of each other.	10	20	30	40	50	60	70	80	90	100
4. **Respect for the Individual:** We show respect for each other and other members of our organization in our speech, action, and courtesy.	10	20	30	40	50	60	70	80	90	100

Team Scoring	Team Average	My Assessment	Difference
Truth-Telling			
Promise-Keeping			
Fairness			
Respect for the Individual			

Note again that each of these principles is really only a different window onto the same central concept. In other words, if you tell the truth, you have to keep your promises. If you are fair, you will have respect for the individual.

Challenge

1. Complete your ratings on this assessment page on your team.
2. Distribute this assessment page to your team.
3. Have your administrative assistant gather and average the results.
4. Compare your assessment with the average of your employees.
5. Address any gaps. How can you raise the numbers?

69. Leadership and Diversity

Concept

Leaders set the tone for diverse inclusion. Leaders like everyone else have VABEs that shape their views on diversity, inclusiveness, and the value of engaging people who aren't like them. In my view, leaders should make decisions based on merit and morality. The natural tendency for all humans is to be more open to people who are like them.[59] John Bradley, formerly of JPMorgan Chase, once noted that "A system left to its own devices will recreate itself." Let's assert this as a natural human tendency— but one that has a number of negative consequences.

First, this tendency builds boundaries and enmity between groups. Lack of understanding leads to speculation and rumor mongering.

Second, this tendency precludes all groups from learning from and benefitting from the insights and traditions of the *others*.

Third, this tendency produces internal schisms and distrust that can lead to disruption and chaos.

Fourth, this tendency precludes the development of larger business activity that transcends the boundaries.

Fifth, this tendency abrades a reasonable analysis of the values of fairness.

You may be able to think of additional pitfalls to the preservation of non-merit based biases and prejudices.

If executives are truly willing to engage merit and talent and value, they will take an open-minded and diversity engaging view of the world. See the chapters on global leadership introduced earlier.

One of the first issues that comes up in discussions of diversity is proportional representation. If there are 50 percent women in a society, the argument goes, there should be 50 percent representation in business leadership. We know, however, that the world is moving slowly, one can easily argue too slowly, from a male dominated global society toward a more gender balanced, fairer society.

---

[59] Byrne, B. 1997. "An Overview (and Underview) of Research and Theory within the Attraction Paradigm." *Journal of Social and Personal Relationships.*

The Institute for Women's Policy Research notes that while 50 percent of the American workforce is female, and while more women get college degrees than men, men are still paid more for equivalent work and that gap is 20 percent or more.[60] The IWPR also predicts that the gender wage gap will not close until at least 2059 for white women, 2233 for Hispanic women and 2124 for black women. Should a person be paid similarly for similar work? That would be fair.

The results for racial minorities is no better. Fortune reports that there have only been 15 black CEOs among the Fortune 500.[61] They also report that blacks hold only 6.7 percent of the 16.2 million management jobs in the United States. Despite billions spent on diversity training, old biases and prejudices seem to continue to block the advancement of qualified women and racial minorities.

Malcom Gladwell's work on *thin slicing*,[62] and research on stereotyping[63] suggest that people make judgments about others in split-seconds. Anciently, this may have been beneficial to survival; today, non-merit based quick judgments have become unfair and unjust and dysfunctional.

Effective executives who understand the value of diverse opinions and viewpoints and want to avoid the pitfalls mentioned above will work hard to include diverse demographics, diverse viewpoints, and diverse expertise in their strategic councils. Window-dressing won't be enough. They will also have to listen to and engage those voices. And make decisions with them.

Diversity for diversity's sake may have a benefit of creating the appearance of fairness, but the true benefits of diversity and diverse thinking won't accrue unless the executive values multi-faceted points of view.

---

[60] https://iwpr.org/issue/employment-education-economic-change/pay-equity-discrimination/?gclid=Cj0KCQiAgs7RBRDoARIsANOo-HiEC02v6Fdk-CIqlyrB6qiPGiRYaZ5_vE3I4V4uWs-xVTL-SxywqJHYaAlvDEALw_wcB

[61] http://fortune.com/black-executives-men-c-suite/

[62] Gladwell, M. 2007. *Blink: The Power of Thinking Without Thinking*. Back Bay, Boston.

[63] For a broad overview, see Wikipedia: https://en.wikipedia.org/wiki/Stereotype

Most just don't. In the end, those who eschew diversity end up in self-defeating group-think.[64]

Clearly, one cannot begin to explore the issues in leadership's influence on diversity and fairness in a couple of pages. We *can* point to the importance of leadership's influence on merit-based systems within their organizations and challenge *you* to become more aware of how your decisions may lead you to recreate yourself rather than to create a more diverse and more functional you/organization going forward.

Example

Reuter's has developed a Diversity & Inclusion Index (D&I) to spotlight firms that are leading the way in capitalizing on diversity in their organizations.[65] The 2016 list included Clorox, Microsoft, Proctor & Gamble, Cisco, Colgate-Palmolive, Eli Lilly, and at #1, Johnson & Johnson. Reuter's publishes a D&I score for companies based on a number of factors including supplier diversity programs, training programs, mentor-protégé programs, participation in gender and minority networks, and leadership behavior (e.g., John Chambers at Cisco required all managers to read Sheryl Sandberg's *Lean In* book).

Martin Davidson's book, *The End of Diversity as We Know It*, has influenced many managers to rethink the way they approach managing diversity and changing their corporate cultures.[66] Davidson argues for a shift in the way managers think of diversity from *managing it* to *leveraging it* for the benefit of their organizations.

---

[64] See Wilcox, C. 2010. *Groupthink: An Impediment to Success*. Xlibris.

[65] http://businessinsider.com/here-are-the-top-7-most-diverse-and-inclusive-companies-in-the-us-2016-9

[66] Davidson, M. 2011. *The End of Diversity as We Know It: Why Diversity Efforts Fail and How Leveraging Diversity Can Succeed*. Berrett-Kohler.

Diagram

Beware of Homogeneity
Leverage Diversity

> "A system left to its own devices will recreate itself."

Source: John Bradley, JPMC

Challenge

1. Describe the merits of the women you work with.
2. Describe the merits of the minorities you work with.
3. Describe the degree of diversity in your organization.
4. What could you do to improve the way your organization deals with diversity?
5. What could you do to be more inclusive in your behavior? What VABEs would you have to change in order to do this?

SECTION VI

Can You Sell Your Story?

If one has developed a strategic story, in my view, a robust, clear, and inspiring charter, then the question is can they sell that story to others, convince them of its validity and worthiness? This section is about influencing others and building teams, world-class teams that will embrace and execute your strategic story.

70. The Western Ball: Can You Sell Your Story?

Concept

Managers of all stripes have asked me and thousands of others, "How can I motivate my people?" Enormous energy has been expended in the academic community trying to answer this question. Multiple theories have emerged from researchers like Maslow, Alderfer, McClelland, Cialdini, Skinner, Lawler, Ellis, Herzberg, Damasio, and many others.

The question facing us represented by the Western Ball in our Diamond Model is "Can you sell your story?" This, of course, presumes that you have a story to tell. More accurately, do you have an effective, explicit, and inspiring story? For most leader/manager/authoritors, the implicit story is, "If you do what I ask you to do, I'll pay you this much." This is a simple transactional story, based on the exchange of work for pay.

How do you attempt to sell your story? It seems to me you have three basic options with multiple variations. Level One Techniques include rewards and punishments, techniques that focus on managing visible behavior. Level Two Techniques include techniques designed to influence another's thinking: logic, analysis, data, statistics, charts, theories, and rationality. Level Three Techniques include tactics designed to influence another's values, assumptions, beliefs, and expectations. These include clarity of purpose, clarity of vision, clarity of values, symbols, music, and stories. Do you have a characteristic technique?

You could take this simple questionnaire to generate some broad data on your characteristic style:

https://virginia.ca1.qualtrics.com/SE/?SID=SV_1RCmSEI7nmt4TyJ

Your dominant influence style will affect what kind of *buy-in* you get from your potential followers.

Recent research on brain imaging, decision making, and evolutionary psychology show that humans make fast decisions based on their preferences and biases—most of which were developed early in life. (Kahneman *Thinking Fast and Slow*, Greene *Moral Tribes*, Haidt *The Righteous Mind*.) More on this later. For now, realize that there are at least three different levels that one might *target* in one's efforts to influence others—to sell one's story.

Example

About five to six centuries BC, Darius and Xerxes pushed across Asia Minor (present day Turkey) conscripting soldiers as they marched on Greece. They forced these conscripts to fight for them on the pain of death. They built an *army* of some one million men. Xerxes, after heavy losses, finally *won* the battle of Thermopylae and continued his march on Greece. Clearly, he was employing Level One Techniques.

Thomas Kuhn in his book *The Structure of Scientific Revolutions* demonstrates how the presentation of *irrefutable* data about whether the sun revolved around the earth or the earth revolved around the sun was not necessarily convincing to most people even fellow scientists who were committed to recognizing and responding to data. Today, the same kind of debate rages over the issue of global warming.

Thirdly, consider the amount of energy and enthusiasm the world's non-profit organizations generate—without paying their people or offering clear data on their results. SOMETHING is motivating these millions of people to do what they do for no pay or tangible reward.

Diagram

Leadership Technique → Consequence

BUY-IN

1. Level One Techniques:
Pay, rewards, punishments, threats, coercion, intimidation

2. Level Two Techniques:
logic, data, evidence, reason, statistics, charts, analysis

3. Level Three Techniques:
vision, purpose, values, stories, music, symbols, strategy, TPOV

1. Passion
2. Engagement
3. Agreement
4. Compliance
5. Apathy
6. Passive Resistance
7. Active Resistance

Challenge

1. Try to observe and understand your dominant, implicit theory-in-action for influencing others? Do you tend to rely on Level One, Level Two, or Level Three techniques?
2. Watch yourself and others to identify the styles of influence that are in play.
3. Pay attention to the kind of buy-in each of those dominant styles get.
4. Resolve to ramp up your buy-in reactions by managing the way you try to sell your story.

71. Control

Concept

If you owned the company, if your **name** was over the door, how much control would you want? (Yeah, yeah, yeah, what about this and that? On average, how much control would you want?) Write that number down, a number between 0 and 100 percent.

Your answer:

[ ]

I have asked this question of people all over the world. The answers range from 5 to 110 percent. Many people choose 51 percent. I haven't kept a distribution, and you can imagine that the answers were, I would guess, roughly normally distributed. Every time I do this, I am amazed at the variety.

If you choose a number like 5 to 20 percent, you might ask yourself, "How would I know what our sales were? How would I know how many employees we have? How would I be able to control costs? What would keep us from going bankrupt?"

If you chose a high number like 90 to 100 percent, you might ask yourself, "What would this do to creativity? What would this do to innovation? What would this do to speed of decision making?" I had one woman once say 110 percent. Really? "Yes," she said. "If it's my name on the door, I want to know what my employees are doing on Thursday nights and on the weekends. I don't want them doing anything that would embarrass me." Wow.

Consider the premise "The more control you have, the less innovation you will get." Control implies compliance and conformity. As long as you have a winning formula and things don't change, perhaps you can survive. When things in the world around you begin to change, however, your organization comes in danger. Who will notice the changing signals? Who will respond? How will people overcome their habits? Are you willing to bet your future on *your* insight alone?

The mechanisms of control are many. They include hiring processes, work design, organizational design, accounting (control) systems, budget controls, authority levels, reporting structures, and much more.

Example

In the early 90s, the Chicago Park District was paying bills alphabetically out of a shoe box.[1] They also didn't know how many employees they had. This would be an example of 10 percent or so control.

Fascism would be an example of *very high* levels of control. Some religions, the military, monasteries, abbeys, and prisons would be examples of very high levels of control. They control your sleep, your daily schedule, your dress, your diet, your activity, and attempt to control even what you think and believe.

Diagram

If your name is on the door, how much CONTROL would you want?

100%

What is the impact of the level of **control** on innovation and creativity?

0%

Challenge

1. Estimate the level of control exhibited in your own organization.
2. What changes do you think need to occur for your organization to succeed?

---

[1] See "Chicago Park District (A)," UVA-OB-618, Darden Business Publishing by James Clawson.

72. What Is Trust?

Concept

Trust is central to leadership. If people don't trust you, they won't follow you. You might force them. I argue leadership is only leadership if people choose, *voluntarily*, to follow. Otherwise, it's coercion or manipulation.

Volumes and volumes have been written about trust.[2] What an executive needs to understand, I believe, is a simple powerful framework for understanding the role of trust in leadership. (Obviously, the model of this whole volume is about simplicity and memorability.)

Consider this series of questions.

1. Would you trust your life's savings with someone who could not manage money? Of course not. To trust such a person, we must have confidence in their competency.
2. Would you trust your life's savings to someone who didn't care about your well-being? Even if they were competent, and were self-serving, you wouldn't.
3. Would you trust someone who cared about you one day and didn't the next? Of course not. You expect consistent competence and consistent caring.

So, competence, caring, and consistency. In the absence of any one of those, trust is undermined, eroded, and ultimately, destroyed.

You might compare this assertion with the irregular reinforcement patterns in behavioral conditioning. That is, people tend to respond more strongly when the reward patterns are irregular. This is the premise behind gambling, especially with the lottery and slot machines. Maybe, just maybe, the next roll will be the big one![3] This insight grows out of B.F. Skinner's theories of behavior (Level One) modification.[4] How can we reconcile irregular reinforcement schedules with my assertion that

---

[2] For example, Kramer, R.M., and T.R. 1996. Tyler, *Trust in Organizations: Frontiers of Theory and Research,* Sage, Thousand Oaks.

[3] https://verywell.com/what-is-a-schedule-of-reinforcement-2794864

[4] For example, Skinner, B.F. 2014. *Contingencies of Reinforcement: A Theoretical Analysis.* B.F. Skinner Foundation.

consistency is an essential condition of trust? Well, would you want your boss to treat you like the lottery? Would you want your financial advisor to treat you like a slot-machine? I think not.

The discussion of trust also takes us back to the "moral foundation of leadership" (truth-telling, promise-keeping, fairness, and respect for the individual) introduced earlier. Would you trust people to lie to you? Who break their promises to you? Who treat you unfairly? Or who disrespect you?

Example

Consider for example the case of Bernie Madoff who got scores of wealthy people to trust him and then bilked them of their money.

Con men who prey on people's willingness to trust what people say. You might enjoy looking up the stories of Frank Abagnale, Victor Listig, Charles Ponzi, George C. Parker, and Joseph Weil.[5] Natwarlal, Mithilesh Kumar Srivastava, was an Indian who repeatedly duped people into buying the Taj Mahal and other famous sites and venues. He used disguises, aliases, and convincing rhetoric to convince people to *invest* in his projects.[6]

FDA litigation against companies who make unfounded (in science) claims about health or weight results from using their products. In 2015, Medtronic, Inc., for just one example, paid $2.8 million in resolution of claims made against its "SubQ" stimulation procedure in which physicians charged for procedures that didn't work.[7]

The widow of a successful real estate developer, unskilled in financial affairs, relied on her husband's accountant to manage her new seven figure estate. Over the next few years, he embezzled all of her funds and left her penniless.[8]

---

[5] https://en.wikipedia.org/wiki/List_of_con_artists
[6] https://en.wikipedia.org/wiki/Natwarlal
[7] https://fda.gov/ICECI/CriminalInvestigations/ucm434212.htm
[8] Personal experience of family members.

Diagram

Trust and Trustworthiness

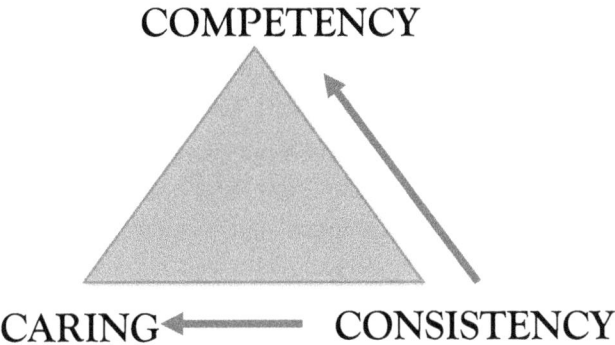

COMPETENCY

CARING ←——— CONSISTENCY

Challenge

1. What does it take to become trustworthy in your mind?
2. What does it take to lose your trustworthiness?
3. How can people manage their tendency to trust what others say?
4. What do you have to do to become more trustworthy?
5. How could you implement the Russian proverb, "trust, but verify" in your life and career?[9]
6. How well do you trust your senior management? Why?

---

[9] https://en.wikipedia.org/wiki/Trust,_but_verify

73. The Language of Leadership

Concept

Language is one of the leader's most important tools for influence. What you say and how you say it makes a big difference on how you lead, influence, and persuade other people.

As mentioned above, I think leader-like language has four main characteristics: clarity, memorability, authenticity, and respect.

Have you ever come out of a meeting and wondered what the main message was? In my seminars, every hand goes up. If you are speaking to a team, a group, your company, your message should be unequivocally clear. If people don't understand what you are saying, you might as well not say it.

Have you ever come out of a meeting and a week later you can't remember what the message was? Again, every hand goes up. Leaders who can send a message in a way that is unforgettable will have a bigger impact than those who cannot.

Have you ever listened to an executive speak and thought, "That's BS. That's not what he/she is or believes?" You get the feeling or sense that the speaker is acting or pretending? And the impact on your trust is up, flat, or down?

Finally, like me, you have probably listened to powerful, clear, memorable speakers who were evil people. People who can persuade and not for good purposes. Hitler comes to mind. So, I argue, effective leaders should be respectful of their audience and of humanity.

If you are clear in your communications (you have a story/Charter), and you communicate in a memorable way, and it's really you, not some act, and you are respectful of your audience and all of humanity, then you are likely to have an impact for good on people.

To be clear means you know what you are trying to say. Too many people try to figure that out while they are speaking and the result is mass confusion.

To be memorable means you use some drama in your style. You use pauses effectively. You use emphasis effectively. You might even take a beginning drama class to learn how to be more powerful in your style. People tend to remember stories, particularly powerful stories. Review the chapter on Life's Stories to find mini-stories from your own history to illustrate your key points.

To be authentic in your communication means that you aren't hiding anything, that you are who you are and don't try to be something you are not. That doesn't mean if you are introverted or flat in your delivery that you can't try to be more memorable. It just means that you don't blow smoke, you don't lie, you don't pretend to be something or somebody you are not.

To be respectful means you respect all humans and all walks of life and strive to be aware and courteous to all people regardless of their backgrounds, race, gender, ethnicity, religion, age or background.

Example

There are a number of powerful speeches in history and in literature.[10] Some of these include: Teddy Roosevelt's "Duties of American Citizenship," Winston Churchill's "We Shall Fight on the Beaches," Chief Joseph's "Surrender Speech," John Kennedy's "Inauguration Speech," Martin Luther King's "I have a dream," and many more. You can find these and more in the reference/end note.

You can also find "22 of the Best Motivational Speeches of All Time," here:

https://blog.hubspot.com/marketing/best-motivational-speeches

Or the "10 Greatest Leadership Speeches of All Time" here:

https://opencolleges.edu.au/careers/blog/10-greatest-leadership-speeches-of-all-time

Steve Covey told the story of *ill-fitting suits* (see the chapter on Ill-fitting suits) in class when I was 24. Forty-five years later, I still haven't forgotten that story. With the right story, you can have a similarly powerful impact.

---

[10] https://artofmanliness.com/2008/08/01/the-35-greatest-speeches-in-history/

Diagram

The Language of Leadership:
Can you find the words to be ...?

1. Clarifying?

2. Stimulating & Memorable?

3. Respectful?

4. Congruent & Authentic?

Practicing in the shower, car, where ever. The ability to articulate an inspiring "charter" is the language of leadership.

Challenge

1. Before you speak, write down the three or less main messages you want to convey.

2. Think about stories from your past you can use to illustrate your point(s).

3. Practice telling those stories—in the car, the shower, wherever.

4. Use silence, pauses, to add drama.

5. Show emotion—along with evidence—as you speak.

6. Take a drama class to learn how to present your ideas more memorably.

7. Watch your audience to gauge their energy level. If it's low, become more dramatic.

74. Level One Techniques

Concept

Level One Leadership or Influence techniques are any techniques that attempt to affect the way people behave, what they say and do. Level One techniques include rewards and punishments.

Rewards include incentives like gold stars, green jackets, recognition schemes, bonuses, raises, praise, vacation trips, wines, meals, and so on. Rewards are reinforcements in the Skinnerian sense. The premise, to repeat, is that people will respond, that is change their behavior, to rewards.

Punishments include reprimands, demotions, humiliation, threats, intimidation, physical and verbal abuse, fines, beatings, whippings, cutting off hands, seizing assets, and more. The premise is that if you punish behavior you don't want, it will cease.

People who use Level One Techniques don't care whether it changes people's thinking (Level Two) or beliefs (Level Three). They just want people to do what they want them to do. Perhaps there is a deeper semiconscious belief that if we can control behavior, it will affect thinking and belief.

Some people argue that managers *shouldn't* worry about what people think or believe, only about what they do. What's your view?

It seems that most managers worldwide use Level One Techniques primarily. It seems to be the simplest. It's visible. You can observe the *results*. People either do or don't do. When they don't do, however, the Level One manager may not understand or even have a model for trying to understand why.

The core VABEs associated with Level One Techniques include the following:

1. People will do almost anything for money.
2. Subordinates should do what they are told, they should obey.
3. You should reward wanted behavior and punish unwanted behavior.

Example

Military trainers working with new recruits will shave their heads, change their clothing, control their sleeping hours, control their diets, and daily activities. If the recruits don't comply, they are punished with verbal and physical abuse, push-ups, running laps, and so on. In this way, recruits are behaviorally conditioned to do what they are told without question.

Many parents will say, "Do what I say. I'm your (parent). Just do it!" Similarly, many managers will say, "Just do it."

Many companies will give high performers trips to vacation spots, public recognition, bonuses, and so on.

Diagram

Level One Techniques
(Rewards and Punishments)

Challenge

1. Describe Level One managers that you have seen or worked for.
2. What kinds of rewards and punishments do you respond to? How do you respond?
3. What would you do for a million dollars? What would you not do?
4. Which of the VABEs or stories listed above do you agree with?
5. When you think about rewards and punishments, what is the thing in between?[11]
6. Read Alfie Kohn's book *Punished by Rewards*, Mariner, 1999.

---

[11] Levinson, H. 1973. *The Great Jackass Fallacy*. Harvard Business School Publications.

75. Level Two Influence Techniques

Concept

Level Two Techniques are any techniques that attempt to influence one's thinking. These techniques include logic, data, statistics, charts, evidence, scientific studies, surveys, and so forth. The premise here is that people, especially mature rational adults, will be persuaded by evidence. This is a wide-spread belief, only recently (1960–2020) disproven by research into behavioral economics among other fields.

Level Two managers are interested in collecting evidence. They do surveys. They do focus groups. They ask for employee feedback. They hire technical consultants. They like equations and studies. They read scientific journals. They look for trends. And when they speak, they cite evidence to make their points. Jack Welch asserted this principle: "Face reality as it is, not as it was or as you wish it were."[12] Jim Collins argued we should "confront the brutal facts."[13]

The central VABEs of Level Two techniques include the following:

1. People should be and will be persuaded by evidence.
2. Truth is reflected in data, evidence, and science.
3. Evidence trumps beliefs.
4. Data and logic are irrefutable.
5. Science is more accurate than superstition and tradition.
6. You cannot argue with data.

Example

Thomas Kuhn's book, *The Structure of Scientific Revolutions* is a powerful case in point.[14] In the first half of the book, he explores the global transition from the Ptolemeian view that the sun revolved around the earth to the Copernican view that the opposite was true. Once Copernicus and

---

[12] Welch, J., N. Tichy, and S. Sherman. 2005. *Control Your Destiny or Someone Else Will.* HarperBus, reprint edition.

[13] Collins, J. 2011. *Good to Great.* Harper Business.

[14] Kuhn, T.S. 2012. *The Structure of Scientific Revolutions.* University of Chicago Press.

Galileo had gathered data using Tycho Brahe's invention, the telescope, that proved that the earth revolved around the sun, how long was it for the *scientists* of the day to change their view?

Most people when asked that question will say, 100 years, 200 years, and similarly large numbers. IF humans were data-based and rational, we would expect the answer to be two to five years or whatever the communication cycles of the era might have been. In fact, Kuhn showed, it was about 30 years—basically one generation. In other words, the old duffs had to die off literally before the new perspective became widely accepted.

In the second half of the book, Kuhn argues, in essence, "Well, you might think that the medieval scientists weren't that smart, so that if we looked at a paradigm shift in the 20th century, we might see a faster turnaround." He then explores the transition from Newton to Einstein in the first half of the 20th century. And it turned out that the old duffs had to die off before the new physics were accepted.

In other words, while we claim to be creatures of science and evidence, by and large humans rely more heavily on their beliefs than on data.

Suppose a CEO asks his or her team to put together an analysis of whether or not to buy a private jet. They go off and in six weeks return with their analysis. And they report that it's much more cost effective to fly first class than to bear the expense of the corporate plane. Of course, they acknowledge they had to make assumptions about the value of time and convenience. What do you think the majority of CEOs would say?

My guess is that they would say, "Do it again." No?

Diagram

Level Two Techniques
(Logic, data, evidence, statistics, science)

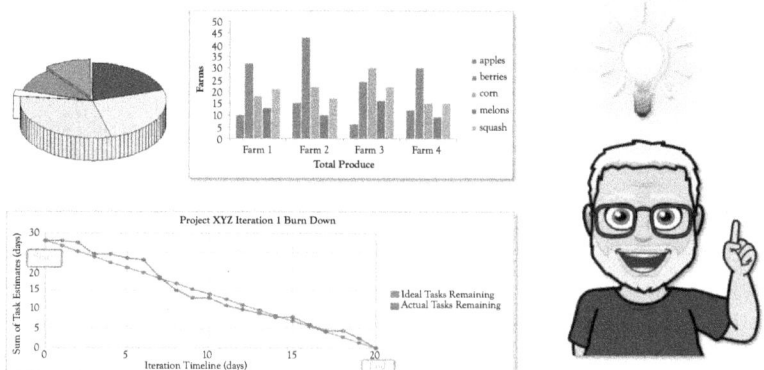

Challenge

1. How do you explain the debate on global warming?
2. How is the globe responding to the world's population growth?
3. Why do companies go bankrupt?
4. What is your favorite statistic? What should be your favorite statistic?
5. What trends do you find most important?

76. Level Three Influence Techniques

Concept

Level Three Influence Techniques are those that attempt to change what people believe, value, assume, expect, feel, and take for granted. The main techniques are clarifying purpose, clarifying vision/direction, and the use of identity symbols like badges, uniforms, flags, logos, songs/music, and phrases. Level Three techniques inspire and move deeply. The kind of deep inchoate influence that charisma and inspiration generate is Level Three.

Clarity of purpose or mission is empowering and energizing. People want to know what they are doing and why. They want to have a purpose in life, something that moves them. Leaders who can clarify what we are doing and why we are doing it are likely to have a deeper and more powerful influence on their followers.

Clarity of vision or direction is as important as mission. First, we need to know what we are doing and second, where we are going. Vision extends to mission into the future. When we know what we are trying to create, we are more likely to either leave (because this is not what we want to spend our lives doing) or dig deep to make it happen.

Music touches us deeply. Music can *make* us euphoric, deeply patriotic, sad, and nostalgic—music touches us at the emotional level. Look at how many people go to music concerts. Music is a powerful motivator.

Symbols like uniforms, flags, badges, and logos also move us. First, we need some kind of identification with the symbol so that when it is used, we connect with something, a larger group, a *family* as it were of like-minded people. Symbols are used widely in the military and in religions but also in businesses. Think about the coffee mugs, the logos on the corporate building, the polo shirts, and insignia imprinted pens that employees see over and over again and connect with. Think about all of the time and money that goes into the development of new corporate logos and the advertising spent to get people to connect with them.

Think, too, about the amount of energy people devote to non-profit organizations—without pay. They will donate evenings, weekends, months, even years of their lives giving everything they have for the purpose of their chosen organization.

The core VABEs associated with Level Three techniques include:

1. People will give everything, even life itself, for causes they believe in.
2. When people believe in something, they will go above and beyond.
3. Belief in purpose is more powerful than mercenary commitment in exchange for money.
4. When organizations create VABE abrasions for employees, they will resist mightily.
5. Many people believe that Level Three influence takes longer, but in fact, it can occur quite quickly.
6. Most people want a purpose in their lives.
7. Most people want to know where they and their employer are going.
8. People who know what they are doing and where they are going need less supervision.

Example

Volunteer rescue squads in which people spend hours and hours in training and service.

Habitat for Humanity, Red Cross, Volunteers for America, Mormon missionaries who serve without pay.

During World War II, the employees in the various top secret and non-communicating departments of the Manhattan Project were getting disgruntled, complaining, going slowly, and dealing with unhappy families who had been moved to the desolate desert in New Mexico. When Peter Oppenheimer got permission, he called them all together and explained that they were building an atomic bomb and that it could save over a million American lives in the event of an invasion. The clarity of mission and vision galvanized the program almost instantly and energy surged throughout the organization.[15]

---

[15] https://en.wikipedia.org/wiki/Manhattan_Project

Diagram

Level Three Leadership

1. Clarity of Mission/Purpose
    2. Clarity of Vision
        3. Identity

Challenge

1. Write down your purpose in life (one sentence).
2. Write down the purpose of your employer (one sentence).
3. Write down what you want to look like on all the –AL aspects of life at age 70.
4. Write down what you think your company should look like in 20 years.
5. Take the simple survey at https://virginia.az1.qualtrics.com/jfe/form/SV_1RCmSEI7nmt4TyJ to get a rough assessment of your balance of use of Level One, Two, and Three influence techniques.

77. The Relationship between Leadership Style and Buy-In

Concept

If you took the self-assessment instrument at

https://virginia.az1.qualtrics.com/jfe/form/SV_1RCmSEI7nmt4TyJ

you have a rough assessment of your preferred, self-aware, style, that is, the balance among Level One, Two, and Three techniques.

We might then ask, "What is the relationship between those three styles and follower buy-in?" Which style gets more buy-in from followers?

My view, and this is *my view* based on observations of the organizations who tend to use one style or another, is that when people use Level One techniques, they can get anything from passion to active resistance but that the modal (most common) responses are on the lower end of the buy-in scale. Coercion and other forms of punishment lead to resentment.[16] Rewards lead to a mercenary mindset that ignores underlying values around purpose and vision.[17] And that when one uses Level Two techniques, one tends to get mid-range, "begrudging" buy-in.[18,19] And when one uses Level Three techniques, one tends to get higher levels of buy-in including passion to the point of death.[20]

I don't have empirical data to support this claim—it's based as I said on informal observations of the kinds of organizations that exhibit those modal leadership styles, various research references (see endnotes), my own consulting experience, my personal experience in various kinds of organizations, and the 200+ cases I have written on various kinds of organizations.

What do you think?

---

[16] See, for example, the relationship between turnover rates and organizational performance, e.g., http://psycnet.apa.org/record/2012-33461-001

[17] See Kohn, A. 1999. *Punished by Rewards: The Trouble with Gold Stars, Incentive Plans, A's, Praise and Other Bribes*, Houghton Mifflin Harcourt.

[18] Levinson, H. 1970. "Management by Whose Objectives." *Harvard Business Review*.

[19] Herzberg, F. 1966. *Work and the Nature of Man*. Oxford.

[20] Lawler, E.E., and J.L. Suttle. 1973. *Expectancy Theory and Job Behavior*. Elsevier.

Example

Religious zealots or fanatics will spend years of their lives at their own expense working for their cause. Buddhist monks and other religious fanatics have committed suicide because of their beliefs.[21]

Beliefs in best practices are often inaccurate and inconsistent with known evidence.[22]

Even scientists tend to reject new evidence in favor of their beliefs.[23]

Diagram

Leadership Technique → Consequence

BUY-IN

1.Level One Techniques:
Pay, rewards, punishments, threats, coercion, intimidation

2.Level Two Techniques:
logic, data, evidence, reason, statistics, charts, analysis

3.Level Three Techniques:
vision, purpose, values, stories, music, symbols, strategy, TPOV

1. Passion
2. Engagement
3. Agreement
4. Compliance
5. Apathy
6. Passive Resistance
7. Active Resistance

Challenge

1. What evidence do you find skeptical? Global warming? Population bomb? Importance of balanced budgets? Impact of diet on health?
2. Read Pfeffer and Sutton's book, *Hard Facts, Dangerous Half-Truths, and Total Nonsense: Profiting from Evidence-based Management.*
3. Read Alfie Kohn's book, *Punished by Rewards: The Trouble with Gold Stars, Incentive Plans, A's, Praise and Other Bribes*

---

[21] For example, Taylor, M., and H. Ryan. 1983. "Fanaticism, Political Suicide and Terrorism." *Terrorism* 11, pp. 91–111, Crane, Russak & Company, http://tandfonline.com/doi/abs/10.1080/10576108808435703?journalCode=uter19

[22] Pfeffer, J., and R.I. Sutton. 2006. *Hard Facts, Dangerous Half-Truths, and Total Nonsense: Profiting from Evidence-based Management.* Harvard Business Review Press.

[23] Kuhn, T. 1996. *The Structure of Scientific Revolutions.* University of Chicago Press.

78. Identifying VABEs

Concept

If one is going to work and lead at Level Three, one must be able to identify the underlying Values, Assumptions, Beliefs, and Expectations about the way the world is or should be (VABEs). In one's self as well as in others. We all have hundreds even thousands of VABEs. See the chapter on VABEs.

Here, we focus on how to recognize and *see* VABEs. First, whenever people judge, they are using their VABEs. When people imply or say that something is right or wrong, good or bad, correct or incorrect, moral or immoral, ethical or unethical, they are revealing the iceberg tip of a VABE. Many of these VABEs are so deeply ingrained in us that we find contradictions abhorrent. Cannibalism is, to most cultures (a collection of shared VABEs), abhorrent. Yet there are some cultures in which cannibalism was/is *normal*. Some people would not eat another human even if it meant staying alive. Other people would. Most people find female *circumcision* abhorrent, yet it was practiced in 23 nations in 2017. These are more extreme examples.

On the more *trivial* end of the distribution, some people eat with fingers, others with sticks others with utensils. Some people leave their shoes on in the house, others take them off. Some people shake hands, others bow.

All of these behaviors are based on assumptions about the way the world is or should be. VABEs.

The second way to identify VABEs is to watch for *should, have to, good ones …, must, really oughta wanna …*[24] These words and many like them belie an underlying assumption. Can you articulate what that assumption might be?

A third way to identify VABEs is to observe behavior and reflect on why that person did what they did. For a person to do that, what must their underlying assumption be?

---

[24] See Mager, R., and P. Pipe. 1997. *Analyzing Performance Problems: Or, You Really Oughta Wanna—How to Figure Out What People Aren't Doing What They Should Be, and What To Do About It*, 3rd ed. Center for Effective Performance.

262 FUNDAMENTALS OF LEVEL THREE LEADERSHIP

A fourth way is to observe what makes people angry or irritated. Usually, they are experiencing a VABE abrasion, that is, something that counters one of their VABEs and rubs them the *wrong way*. Not all VABEs are equally important. We have peripheral VABEs and central or core VABEs and intermediate VABEs. Similarly, VABE abrasions can be mild, moderate, or major. When you or someone around you expresses anger, you might ask yourself or them "What assumption of yours is being attacked or abraded here?"

Once you have identified a VABE, and by this I mean, you have written it down on paper (there is a huge discipline in translating from thought to paper), you can reflect on whether it is functional or dysfunctional. I say *functional* in contrast with *right, wrong, correct,* or *incorrect*. Note that all VABEs make sense within the cultures in which they are embedded. It is only to the outside observer that behavior and the VABEs that underlie it are surprising or shocking or abhorrent.

When you are clarifying a VABE, try not to use single words that can be interpreted in multiple ways. State the proto-VABE (or draft or proposed VABE) in a phrase or sentence. *Integrity* is much vaguer than "People should tell the truth all the time" or "People should tell the truth except when it hurts someone" or "People should tell the truth most of the time" or "People should tell people what they want to hear."

Having identified a VABE (written it on paper), you can discuss it with the other person. If you do this without an accusatory tone, you might be able to work through to a mutually agreeable solution. That won't mean that the VABE abrasive behavior will stop—we are creatures of habit after all. And this discussion *could* mean the first steps toward understanding each other and working toward a more functional relationship.

Some VABEs, many of them very deep and very important, become the source of *irreconcilable differences*. Consider Northern Ireland, Ruanda/Burundi, India/Pakistan, China/Tibet, Sebia/Croatia, and so on. Many of these differences are religious in some sense. Others are ethnic or racial or language/culture based. Simply identifying the differences in VABEs is no guarantee of resolution.

It seems clear to me that simply working at Level One, telling people what is *acceptable* and *unacceptable* will not lead to long-term solutions.

Unless we can identify VABEs and then discuss and debate them, we are not likely to get below the surface of human behavior and conflict. And ultimately to some lasting change.

Example

What's the assumption when a driver cuts you off and crams into the space in front of your car? Perhaps something like, "My needs are more important than the person who's leaving a car length or more in front of them." Or "People shouldn't leave more than one car length in front of them."

What's the assumption when someone takes a package off someone's doorstep? Perhaps, "It's okay to take what you don't have, even if you haven't earned it." "It's a dog-eat-dog world. Take what you want like everyone else."

A boss says, "Just do your job and stop whining." Perhaps the VABE is, "Subordinates should obey without questioning."

The Thirty Years' War in central Europe was one of the most destructive wars in human history.[25] Nearly eight million people died as a Catholic emperor tried to dictate religious conformity throughout his *realm*. Protestants protested, vigorously. We can add to this example wars between Christians and Muslims, Hebrews and *pagans* in the Old Testament, and the modern conflicts around religious terrorism.

Consider Israel and Palestinians. What are the VABEs on both sides?

Consider a dual-career couple. What are the VABEs in such a relationship that might lead to conflict?

---

[25] https://en.wikipedia.org/wiki/Thirty_Years%27_War

Diagram

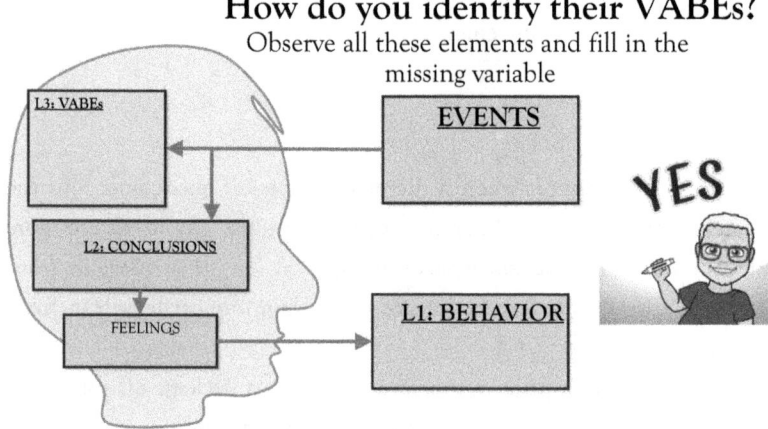

How do you identify their VABEs?
Observe all these elements and fill in the missing variable

Challenge

1. Write down your *top ten* VABEs.
2. Write down the top ten VABEs of your organization's culture. These may be stated or implicit based on the way people behave.
3. Listen for *should* in your daily conversations.
4. Listen for judgments in your daily conversations.
5. When you or someone around you is angry or annoyed, try to identify the underlying VABE abrasion. What is the VABE that is being rubbed the wrong way?
6. Watch for VABEs in the media including movies, news, editorials, and so on. Try to state them clearly using phrases or sentences.

79. A Formula for Mediocrity

Concept

There are a number of common VABEs in the world. A few of them are:

- I am right and you are wrong.
- Parents know what's best for their children.[26]
- Parents are responsible for teaching their children.
- Parents have a right to punish their children if they don't obey.
- My religion is true; yours is false.
- My way of life is better than yours.
- You should do things my way.

And more. Do you recognize any of these VABEs in the people you meet? In yourself?

There is another VABE common in managers worldwide. I have observed this in my consulting around the world. The VABE is

> **Professionals will do what they *have* to do regardless of how they *feel*.**

This VABE is, to me, a formula for mediocrity. And it has two major flaws. First, it puts people in an **obligatory** mindset. And as you read in the chapter on Choice and Obligation, obligation drains energy, motivation, initiative, productivity, and creativity.

The second flaw is that it takes ***feel*** or *emotion* off of the table. See the chapters on Resonance and the relationship between Feel and Performance.

So, if you tell people what to do, tell them to do what they are told, and to leave their emotions at the door, you are basically asking them to be robots. Henry Ford famously once said, "I keep trying to hire a pair of hands and they keep showing up with heads and bodies attached." He would have preferred robots. And indeed robots have taken over many manufacturing jobs.

---

[26] Glasser, W. 2010. *Choice Theory*. HarperCollins. (later edition)

When it comes to management, however, robots are not so good at managing people—who have heads, bodies, hands, and hearts.

If you believe this VABE, PWD WTHTD ROHTF, I invite you to think about the consequences of your behavior. Will it generate energetic, passionate, and creative employees? What are your VABEs about how much innovation and creativity and energy you want at each level of your organization?

We begin to teach this VABE to our children when we send them off to school. "I know you don't want to go, my dear, but it's time for you to grow up and be a big girl/boy and do what you have to do. I know you don't want to, but you have to put your feelings aside and go to school. This is what big people do!" When we say things like this, what are we teaching our children?

Example

There are examples of this VABE in virtually every organization I have ever been in. It manifests itself in many companies. Especially those managed by authoritors who manage by the numbers without being among and relating to their employees. It is manifest in companies in which the authoritors do not recognize the importance of organizational culture and how it affects results. The military is another example of where PWD ... is widespread. Many government bureaucracies also show a disdain for feel. Organized crime is another place where PWD ... dominates.

Diagram

Does how you *feel* affect your performance?

- How many times have you been asked by supervision at work how you want to feel?
- How do you *WANT* to feel? (Do you know?)
- The pervasive management assumption:

PWD WT🚫TD ROHT🚫

- A formula for *mediocrity*.

Challenge

1. Identify the managers in your organization who seem to believe the PWD VABE.
2. How might one engage those managers in a re-examination of that VABE?
3. To what extent do you believe in the PWD … VABE?
4. What would happen if you could let go of this VABE?

80. Influencing at Level Three VABEs

Concept

How does one influence at Level Three? The first thing is to think about influencing what people believe. We *know* from our previous discussion of human habituality that people are not likely to change their VABEs, and they might. The question is not, "Can people change?"—we all know they can and do. The better question is, "What are the odds a person will change his/her VABEs?" The odds are low. We know that—AND it seems to me we should give them the chance. Most people never engage Level Three conversations so they don't even try. Are you willing to have Level Three conversations? Are you willing to engage people at Level Three? To me, most other conversations are just superficial.

Here are some approaches for influencing people at Level Three.

First, if you have identified what looks like another person's VABEs, you can ask if your view is accurate. You can seek to confirm your observations. "I think you have an assumption that people should obey whatever you say. Is that correct?" The *confirmation conversation* can be very powerful and enlightening for both parties. It is important to go into that conversation with an open mind rather than a judgmental, accusatory, or pre-confirmed mindset.

Second, you can seek clarity on the purpose of your organization. "What are we here for? What is our mission or reason for existence?" Some people will roll their eyes at these questions as if they were obvious. Usually, they are taken for granted without any close examination.

Third, you can seek clarity on direction or vision. "Where are we going? What are we trying to create?" These conversations are easier to get into. The danger is that a fuzzy, foggy future is tolerated. Clarity of what we are trying to do brings wonderful focus.

Fourth, you can employ music. I used to think that it was *unprofessional* to play music between classes. My colleague and co-author, Doug Newburg, gently over several years introduced me to the power of music. I began to play music between classes and noticed the impact on the energy in the room. Participants liked it. The energy improved. The tone in the room became less stilted and more open.

Fifth, you can show symbols. The clothes you wear, the facial expressions you show, and the logos you display will all affect the people around you. I changed from wearing white shirts and ties to class to all black turtle necks with black pants and socks and shoes. The impact was dramatic. Everyone noticed and continue to notice. It sets a tone. Some people are condescending, "You look like Johnny Cash." So?

And facial expressions. It's amazing how learning to smile regularly can change your impact on others. A simple smile. I have noticed it can change the whole tone of a conversation or a class. Flags, pictures, logo mugs on the desk, all of these things will also have a subtle impact on the people in the room.

Sixth, you can ask, "What do you want?" I have been struck with how many people don't know. Wealth? Power? Fame? Salvation? Health? Bigger house? Uncovering those things can totally change work relationships and clarify what we are doing here.

Seventh, you can ask what VABEs underlie certain behavior. "I noticed that you have come late to all of our meetings. May I ask what your assumption is about timeliness? Do you assume that walking in late is not affecting the rest of the people in the room?" Be careful here. This can be or sound accusatory. To work at Level Three, we usually need to minimize defensiveness. Defensiveness keeps people from being willing and able to discuss their Level Three VABEs.

Eighth, it is important for you to be confident in who you are. If your self-esteem relies heavily on the opinions of others, it will be more difficult/dangerous for you to work at Level Three. If someone criticizes your VABEs, will that "destroy" you? If someone disrespects your VABEs, will you become combative? The willingness to let others have their VABEs and to express them and remain calm is an important Level Three skill. In my experience, this means you have to know who you are, what you believe (your VABEs) and allow others to have theirs. Disagreement is not an attack on your being. Allowing others to express their VABEs without raising your own defenses and becoming angry will help you work better at Level Three.

Does Level Three influence take a long time? It could, but not necessarily. That depends on your ability to engage with minimal levels of defensiveness sent or received.

In general, I offer this sequence for influence at Level Three:

1. Identify the other person's VABEs by watching their behavior.
2. Confirm your inferences with the other person. "You seem to have a VABE that … Is that correct?" For example, "if you want it done right, do it yourself."
3. Set a probationary time period. Most people won't change, some will. How long can you or your organization afford to give this effort?
4. Begin active coaching. Engage discussions about the functionality of the VABEs in question. For example, "The core VABE of effective managers is that it's best to get things done through other people. *Do It Yourself* is really counter-productive AND you'd never be able to do all the jobs in this plant!" Some managers will say, "I don't have time to coach or hold hands." Hmmm. Okay, what's more important than developing your leadership bench strength?
5. Observe results. If the person is improving, great. If not, it could be for either of two reasons: either you are not a good coach or he or she is not open to changing. They might have a low CQ—see the chapter on Intelligences.
6. If there is no change, and you have reached the end of your probationary period, and you have done your best, make a unilateral decision.

Example

The story of Joshua Chamberlain at Gettysburg is a great example of fast, powerful, Level Three influence. Chapter two in Michael Shaara's book, *Killer Angels*, describes a situation in which one man was able to have a huge, deep Level Three influence on a group of angry felonious deserters and in so doing changed the course of American and world history.[27] I have used that situation to teach Level Three influence all over the world. My teaching note for that exercise is given here—for instructors. Within a matter of a few minutes, Chamberlain was able to convert angry deserters who were at Level 1 of Buy-In into passionate Level 1 Buy-In warriors.

---

[27] Shaara, M. 2010. *Killer Angels*, Ballantine (latest edition).

The John Wolford case (UVA-OB-0167) is a classic case that introduces the challenge of managing at Level Three very well.

Diagram

LPV 3. Courage to Act?
What to do with Different (Difficult) Others?

1. Observe and identify VABEs
2. Confirm VABEs with person
3. Explore validity of VABEs with person
4. Set probationary time period
5. Make Invitations to change VABEs
6. Active coaching
7. If progress, continue;
   if not, make a change (cause = my weak coaching or his weak learning or both)

Levels of Human Activity

1. <u>Visible Behavior</u>

2. Conscious Thought

3. VABEs

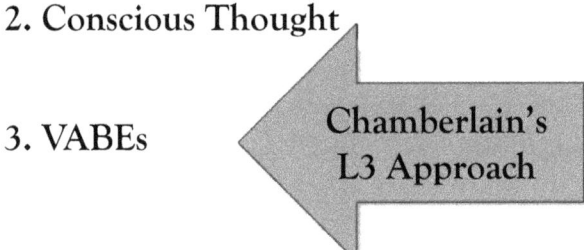

Chamberlain's L3 Approach

Challenge

1. Identify some VABEs held by a subordinate.
2. Have a Level Three conversation with that person to confirm your inferences.
3. Practice describing the purpose of your team/organization.
4. Read chapter two of *Killer Angels*. How did Chamberlain use Level Three techniques?
5. Take the self-assessment tool at https://virginia.az1.qualtrics.com/jfe/form/SV_8kK6FJQBy0InfHS

81. The Dark Side of Level Three Influence with VABEs

Concept

There is a dark side to working at Level Three. Because people tend to rely on their VABEs more than evidence, they are susceptible to those who can tell a good story in a convincing way. Conmen have an advantage in the world because people want to believe a good story. So people for whom *truth, trust,* and *transparency* are not high values can use that tendency to their advantage.

Cults are a nefarious outcome of those who influence others at Level Three by creating false missions and false visions. Cults have a number of characteristics.[28] In part, they have a charismatic leader, joining rituals, rituals of advancement, fantastical views of purpose and direction, separation of members from the rest of the world, elitist dogma, frequent violence, financial contributions, and difficulty in leaving.

Cults can be organized in small groups or even whole nations. The focal dogma can be religious or political in nature. Utopian communes can be cultist as can nations like Leninist Russia, Hitlerian Germany, and Kimian North Korea.

Religious cults get people to join through specialized rituals, isolate them from others including family, demand financial contributions, limit the information members have access to, often change how people dress, demand complete loyalty and devotion, and create significant barriers to escape.

This phenomenon also occurs in business. The stories told by Bernard Madoff, Victor Lustig, and Charles Ponzi drew people in to invest their savings based on promises of larger returns—which never materialize. Business scams often draw in thousands of people susceptible to false promises.

Confidence games, schemes or *cons* usually have several steps or elements: ground work, approach, build-up, mini-payoff, urgency, and

---

[28] Only One Man, *A Song of Humanity: A Science-Based Alternative to the World's Scriptures,* LuLu, 2016, Gods chapter 25.

social proof.[29] The *marks* or potential *gullibles* are not aware of these steps, and given the limited information and a willingness to believe often inflamed by the promise of unusual payoffs (financial or salvation in the next life), they gradually gain confidence or faith in the story being told.

On the consumer's side, we might encourage people confronted with religious, business, or political salespeople to be cautious, to do their homework in finding independent evidence and data, and to check their tendencies to want to believe in unusually wonderful promises. Buddha's advice seems relevant: "Believe nothing, no matter where you read it or who has said it, not even if I have said it, unless it agrees with your own reason and your own common sense."

Example

The People's Temple Agricultural Project or Jonestown is one example of how people can dupe others into a system of VABEs that dominates their lives. The movement founded by Jim Jones in Indiana moved to San Francisco where Jones was active in local politics.[30] Jones then convinced his followers to move to Guyana where Jones promised the establishment of a utopian society. Eventually, 909 of them committed mass suicide on Jones's command.

Bernie Madoff's scam was run through his Wall Street firm, Bernard L. Madoff Investment Securities. He later described it as "one big lie," a lie that involved 4,800 clients and over $64 billion.[31]

---

[29] https://en.wikipedia.org/wiki/Confidence_trick See also http://businessinsider.com/7-tell-tale-signs-of-a-con-artist-2016-3/#6-loan-sharking-6

[30] https://en.wikipedia.org/wiki/Jonestown

[31] https://en.wikipedia.org/wiki/Bernard_Madoff

Diagram

The Dark Side of Level Three Power

<u>CULTS</u>
1. Joining Rituals
2. Esoteric, elitist knowledge
3. Extraordinary promises
4. Isolationist
5. Financial contributions
6. Advancement rituals
7. Frequent use of Violence
8. Demand complete loyalty
9. Barriers to exit

Challenge

1. Describe a time/incident when you felt you had been *had* or *scammed*.
2. How could you have avoided being scammed?
3. Write down the names of the top five scammers that come to your mind.
4. What techniques did they use?
5. Describe the kinds of deceits you see in business practice.
6. Why do business people use deceit or lack of transparency in their business practices?
7. Using the characteristics of cults introduced above, write down the names of cult-like organizations you observe in the world around you.

82. Active Listening

Concept

Effective leaders are good listeners. They collect data from multiple sources and inductively integrate that information into a worldview that drives their strategic thinking. Listeners who focus on a few channels put their grasp of reality at risk.

Most people are not good listeners. Watch how long it takes most people to turn a conversation to their own history, examples, insights, or beliefs. Carl Rogers was a strong advocate for active or reflective listening.[32] Rogerian technique involved listening carefully to two things, content and emotion and then reflecting back that understanding to ensure accuracy. This was a departure from traditional Freudian psychotherapy in which the therapist was to give virtually no stimuli or reaction.

The ability to listen reflectively or actively without over-reaching or under-reaching requires practice. We call over-reaching speculation. Speculation extends what the other has said beyond what they said. Rogerian theory argues that over-reaching will cause defensiveness and therefore a barrier to getting in touch with real, underlying issues.

Under-reaching is often the hallmark of novice reflective listeners and often termed *parroting*. An under-reach indicates low investment in understanding, which also creates barriers to progress. Simply repeating what the other person said indicates a superficial investment to the speaker.

An appropriate reflective or active response recognizes what the speaker was saying and the emotion attached to it in one's own words without speculating or simple mimicking. It takes practice to hit this middle ground consistently and comfortably. To do so, one must exert energy to "hear" what the person is saying and resist the tendency to try to solve the person's issue(s). Rogers argues that only the person can do that.

For many years, the Active Listening technical note was the bestselling note at Darden.[33] One way to think about listening styles is to arrange them on a scale from directive to non-directive. The diagram below shows

---

[32] Rogers, C. 2012. *On Becoming a Person: A Therapist's View of Psychotherapy.* Mariner.

[33] Clawson, J. 1986. *Active Listening.* Darden Business Publishing, UVA-OB-0341.

such a scale. I invite you to read it carefully and think about which technique you tend to rely on. Rogers asserted that non-directive techniques that left choice of solutions to the speaker were ultimately more powerful than techniques that relied on instructions from the listener. Most lay-listeners want to move quickly to solutions and hence tend to use directive techniques, for example, "You should do this." or "Have you tried that?" Psychotherapy is less directive than reflective listening. On the other hand, patients sometimes feel frustrated because they think the psychotherapist isn't doing anything. Rogerian active listening presents a powerful technique between total non-direction and overly invasive directive techniques.

Some people are seeking advice. Many *listeners* yield to that temptation and offer it. All too often that advice is based on the listener's experience and not necessarily what's good for the speaker.[34] Active or reflective listening is a powerful skill that effective leaders use to understand the people they are talking with—at a deeper Level Three level.

Ironically, active listening requires one to suspend judgment based on one's own VABEs while one is listening for and *hearing* the speaker's VABEs. This is probably the main reason it is difficult for lay-people to become good reflective listeners. To become a good listener, one must do four things well:

1. Suspending judgment of the speaker
2. Focusing on emotion as well as content
3. Following, not leading the conversation
4. Reflecting accurately what you understand, so the speaker can *see* it more clearly

Dale Carnegie long ago encouraged people to be good listeners in order to have more influence over others. It was and is good advice.[35]

---

[34] Brain chemistry also enters into this discussion. People with ADD or ADHD in my experience often need help in making decisions. That is different from listening and allowing people with brain chemistry imbalances to reach their own conclusions about their situation.

[35] Carnegie, D. 2010. *How to Win Friends and Influence People.* Simon and Schuster (latest edition).

Example

Here are some examples of the directive to non-directive techniques and how they might be worded.

DIRECTIVE

Commands and threats	↑	Telling a person what to do. Giving orders.
Persuasion		Selling, urging, entreating, building "logical" arguments to persuade the other to your point of view. Arguing is a heated form of persuasion.
Advice		Offering what you think should be done, based usually on your own view and values.
Questioning and focusing		Establishing a focus on what you will talk about next. Can be done through statements or questions.
Giving feedback		Telling the other person your judgments—both positive and negative. Extremely volatile, that is, can be constructive or destructive to the individual and to the relationship. Can be solicited or unsolicited.
Directive probing		Asking leading questions to reach specific conclusions. Effective, if used skillfully, in getting a person to "personalize" joint conclusions.
Role playing		Building skills by allowing the other person to practice saying and behaving in situations that are likely to appear.
Summarizing		Attempting to outline the major points of the discussion.
Self-disclosing		Giving information about yourself. Very powerful in building trust and credibility. Can be overdone.
Exchanging		Undirected exchanges of greeting, social comments. Builds rapport and pleasantries and establishes a socially acceptable base for the conversation.
Problem-solving		Open-ended exploration of alternatives without preconceived notions about how to solve the problem. Brainstorming, or "dialogue" techniques, then evaluating alternatives.
Continuances		"Umm," "Uh-huh," "Yeah," and other means of encouraging the other person to carry on.
Silence		Can be somewhat directive depending on the situation.
Reflective listening	↓	Setting aside personal views and listening to another's content and emotion and then reflecting that understanding back to the speaker. Related to empathy. Extremely useful in building support.

NON-DIRECTIVE

Try to categorize the responses below using the response types above. If you would like more examples, see *Kinds of Responses*, Darden Business Publishing, UVA-OB-0653.

Speaker 1
(Woman, 27)

"I'm concerned about what to do. My husband is looking for a job, too, and it looks like his best opportunities are on the West Coast. But my family lives in New Jersey, and I'd like to be close to them. And my best offer, my dream job, really, is in the same area. So, I'm not sure what to do. What should I say to my husband?"

Responses To Speaker 1

Match the responses below to the Directive/Non-Directive Scale above.

1. What is your next step?
2. You seem a little selfish to me.
3. Staying close to your family is your most important value, isn't it?
4. You should think about other people more. It will help you in the long run.
5. Ooooh! Don't worry! It will turn out all right!
6. Uh, huh. Did you see the ball game last night?
7. It sounds like you feel torn between your family, your job offer, and your husband and can't see yet how to balance all three.

Diagram

Be an Active Listener

1. **Let go** of your own thoughts and VABEs for moment
2. Focus on **what** the Other is saying and on their **emotions**
3. Occasionally **reflect** your understanding of the content and Avoid responding with directive answers. Strive to let the person speak **freely and safely** without fear fo rejection
5. **invite** the Other's recommendation for solutions if any are needed or requested
6. When appropriate **invite** the Other to consider your assessment. Avoid "You should ..."

Challenge

1. Practice mouthing out loud reflective responses at home.

2. Read the "Active Listening" note references above.

3. Listen for the kinds of responses other people use in conversation. Try to categorize them according to the scale introduced above.

4. Become more aware of when you use directive techniques and resolve to use more non-directive responses.

83. The Language of Execution

Concept

There are a lot of managers who don't get much done. Part of the issue is tolerating unexamined reports. Effective executives are able to drill down, press for meaningful answers, dig into the realities, and as a result, they have better information about what's going well and what isn't.

"How to Conduct a Strategy Review," Chapter 8 in Larry Bossidy and Ram Charan's book, *Execution: The Discipline of Getting Things Done*,[36] presents this focal point. The challenge in this kind of discussion is to get below the surface and down to the real issues. Managers ask their subordinates how are things going, and the answer that frequently comes back, "No problems, boss." Whenever I hear "no problem," I know/believe there's a problem. This also happens at the executive level when business leaders present their strategy books and go through them, slide by slide or chart by chart or idea by idea. Frequently, too frequently, the conducting executive doesn't get down to the underlying assumptions hidden in the rhetoric.

Bossidy and Charan assert that the strategy review is the "prime Social Operating Mechanism" in the strategy process. No matter what organization or part of an organization you run, your reviews of what's going on and where that unit is going are the main mechanism you have for keeping on top of things. Lose your ability to see down to the skeleton of that business, and you are soon lost in erroneous inferences and conclusions.

Here are some key concepts and methods Bossidy used to guide his conversations at General Electric and later at Honeywell.

1. The review *should be a creative exercise* not a dry regurgitation of the *book*.
2. The review is also a place to assess and develop younger executives. You teach by what you do and ask.
3. "Tell me about your competition." How well does the business leader understand who he or she is competing against? Quality?

---

[36] Bossidy, L., and R. Charan. 2002. *Execution: The Discipline of Getting Things Done*. Currency.

Supply chain? Marketing and Sales? Reaction to our behavior? Potential acquisitions? Alliances with other competitors?

4. How well do the unit's capabilities match their strategy? Do they have the core capabilities to actually do what they want to? What's the linkage between our capabilities and what we are promising? (See chapters above on Charters and Results.)

5. Is the strategy focused or so diffused that it is not likely to happen? How long will it take to get these things done? If we are more focused, can we get this one done faster?

6. Do we have the linkages between people and processes clear and strong? We have to link strategy, people, and processes. If we re-organize, will we have the people skills to succeed with the new role demands? Who is running each program/initiative?

7. Are we working on the *right* ideas for our industry? Are we falling behind?

8. Follow through after the review to make sure that the ideas agreed upon are being executed.

The thrust of these foci is to drill down and get below the "all's well, boss" superficiality in many management conversations and uncover what's going on and where that is taking us. Clearly closed-ended, yes/no questions are more superficial than open-ended probing questions. "What new products and strategies are your competitors working on?" is much more probing than "Are you prepared to meet your competition." "Describe how your core capabilities match up with your strategy" is stronger than "Do you have the ability to execute your strategy?" "Tell me how you link your strategy with your people and processes" pushes deeper than "Do you have the right people and processes in place?"

Example

The dean's office of a large business school once organized annual review meetings with each of the 10 academic disciplines in the school. These disciplines included finance, operations, decision analysis, strategy, leadership, and organizational behavior, communications, marketing and so on. The dean's office was represented by the dean, the associate dean for the faculty, the assistant dean for intellectual capital, and the assistant dean for degreed programs. That seemed appropriate. So, along with the 5 to 10 people in each discipline, these were meetings of about 15 people gathered around one table for roughly 60 to 90 minutes once a year.

The dean's office held those meetings every spring for four years and then canceled them. When asked why, the answer was, "We don't know what to do with them." I was shocked. How could the C-level officers of any organization run their business without meeting at least annually with the core pools of human capital in the organization? These are the people who deliver the two primary products of the organization, classes for paying students and additions to the pool of worldwide knowledge. "We don't know what to do with them?"

What would you do in such a meeting if you were the dean and associate dean for the faculty? The answer seems clear to me:

1. What did you do last year? How many courses did you teach? What courses? What gaps are there in your offerings? How were your ratings? How many articles and books did you publish?

2. What is your competition doing? How does your area/department compare with our major competitor schools? Offerings? Topics? Research?

3. What are your plans for the next year and five years? What kind of new faculty do you need? What kind of new courses do you need to offer? What new delivery skills (e.g., online) are you developing? How many articles and books do you plan to write? What are the topics?

4. What kind of practitioner contact do you have? How many companies and which companies are you consulting with? Writing cases about? Teaching in executive education? How do you keep in touch with the *real world*?

5. What kind of help do you need from us? When would you like to hire? Do you have any retirements coming up or potential departures?

6. What about your alumni connections? Do you connect when you travel consulting? How can we assist in that?

I don't think 90 minutes a year to discuss in some depth those issues is nearly enough. And certainly important enough to hold the meetings *at least* once a year if not more. What about you?

Diagram

Conducting Business Unit and Strategy Reviews

- Focus on "creation" rather than last year's strategy book
- Assess and develop young talent
- What is the competition doing?
- How do your capabilities match your strategy?
- How focused is your strategy?
- How are your people and processes linked to your strategy?
- What new ideas are you working on to lead your industry?
- Don't tolerate superficial, vague answers

Challenge

1. Develop a list of questions you would ask if you were a C-level executive conducting a strategy review with your subordinate lines-of-business leaders.
2. Read Bossidy and Charan's book.
3. In the next performance review you *receive*, be prepared to answer the questions raised in this chapter and then influence the discussion to ensure you convey your thoughts on all of those. Be a *partner* not a recipient in the performance review.
4. Learn to engage the people you conduct performance interviews with in a way that they *learn* how to conduct similar reviews in their careers.

84. Developing the Next Generation of Leaders

Concept

Executives frequently do things unintentionally that undermine the development of their own bench strength. Then they ask people like me to come present leadership development seminars. I frequently note that we could do that, however, it would be a lot less expensive, more powerful and more long-lasting if they would simply change the way they deal with their subordinates. "What do you mean?" they say.

People respond to the way they are treated, particularly by people in positions of authority, what I call *authoritors*. Frequently, those authoritors assume that their job is to give instructions, demands, commands, and directions. That's one way to look at the role of leadership. And that way tends to develop followers but not leaders. People treated this way for long periods of time *learn* insidiously to wait to be told what to do, they learn to live *outside-in*.

Consequently, as time goes by and the senior leadership are looking for more leadership, they look around and all they see are followers. So, they search for consultants to help them develop the next crop of leaders. The consultants who take this job are facing a big challenge because the culture of the organization as defined and created by the current executive leadership is not going to change as the result of having 25 to 45 people in a room for a week. The other 51 weeks of the year, they will again be immersed in the culture that made them into followers.

Executives who truly want to develop leaders will take that task on themselves. They will think of every encounter between them and their direct reports as more than *getting something done*. Rather, they will think of it as a developmental opportunity, a teaching moment. Doug Mac-Gregor once (famously) noted that every encounter between a boss and a subordinate is teaching the subordinate something—whether the boss intends it or not. How to think, how to communicate, what to do, how much to prepare, how to dress, and a host of other *lessons* are conveyed dozens of times a day. And a frequent lesson is "Do what you're told."

So, I have a discussion with my prospective clients in which I assert that if they would change the way they communicate with their direct reports, they would be developing a whole generation of leaders. But that would mean changing the way the executives behave. Most, in my experience, are not willing to even consider that possibility. "We are not the problem," they will say, "they are. We want you to teach them how to lead."

What the executives do who have a strong bench is teach. They ask questions rather than give directions. "What do you think we should do and why? Here's the information I have and why I'm thinking differently. I invite you to do some more homework and come back to discuss this again. It's important and we need to make a good decision." This approach takes too long in the view of many executives. But like the discussion of team development, too little investment up front leads to major costs and overruns later on. Especially in leadership development.

A few high spirited, high initiating individuals will do their own homework without being asked and have the will to overcome the wet blanket of expected obedient execution. Even these in the face of inexorable pressure to conform will often give in. "Why bother? The boss will tell us what he or she wants done anyway," sets in as the dominant if semi-conscious attitude.

Parents do the same thing. When parents tell their children what to do without ever asking their advice, thoughts, and results of their research, they stunt their children's growth. Teachers in schools can, and often, do the same thing.

If you want to grow capable people, think about it in every interaction you have.

Example

In our First Year required courses, our faculty typically asks the questions. We spend hours pondering and devising the right questions to ask to stimulate our students' thinking. We might have five good questions for a class, each one designed to generate energy for a 10, 15, or 20 minute segment of the class. All well and good.

However, by the time our students get to the Second Year elective curriculum, we have taught them and they have learned a dangerous, implicit assumption, namely, that the instructor asks the questions. I have heard faculty even *joke* about this, "Excuse me, Mr. Jones, you don't understand. WE ask the questions here."

In my Second Year electives, I began asking my students to think about how they would structure the discussion if they were leading the class. Sometimes, I/we would even have students run a class. Usually, they were disasters with disjointed, non-flowing, dead-ended discussions that left everyone frustrated. I realized that this was where the sad saying "That MBA can't think his way out of a wet-paper bag!" came from. Our students had not been prepared to run a discussion—only to participate in one.

The same phenomenon occurs in business. Subordinates are *taught* to respond, to obey, to follow, to listen, and to execute so that when they are asked to lead something, their first thoughts are "Where should I go? What can I do and not do? How much budget do I have? How do you want me to do this?" and so on.

Diagram

You are always teaching.

Every encounter between a superior and a subordinate involves learning of some kind for the subordinate. (It should involve learning for the superior, too, but that is another matter.) When the boss gives an order, asks for a job to be done, reprimands, praises, conducts an appraisal interview, deals with a mistake, holds a staff meeting, works with his subordinates in solving a problem, gives a salary increase, discusses a possible promotion, or takes any other action with subordinates, he is teaching them something .

The attitudes, the habits, the expectations of the subordinate will be either reinforced or modified to some degree as a result of every encounter with the boss. . .The day-by-day experience of the job is so much more powerful that it tends to overshadow what the individual may learn in other settings.

Source: The Human Side of Enterprise, pp. 199–200

Challenge

1. For every class or meeting you go to, AFTER you have done your homework for the content of the meeting, WRITE DOWN the outline you would use if you were the convener for that class or meeting. Think about the flow of the conversation and how it

should be structured: what logically comes first, second, and next and so on. Practice planning for meetings as if you were the leader.

2. After every class or meeting you go to, spend five minutes debriefing what went well, what went not-so-well, and how you could have/would have done things differently to make it better. Be sure to gauge the energy level in the room as a part of your regular assessments.

3. Read books on how to run effective meetings and teach yourself. Don't rely on your leader who may or may not be good at it to be your only guide. (I could give you several references here on books to read—but I am not going to. You can find them yourself, yes?)

85. You Teach What You Tolerate

Concept

Having dinner one evening with a colleague and his wife, she said, in the midst of the conversation, "You teach what you tolerate." I was struck by that insight and its truthfulness. When we allow a behavior to continue, we are, in essence, teaching that behavior. Tolerance is reward.

This is true, I believe, for children, students, employees, and executives. When we, whoever we are, permit others to continue doing something, it is likely to persist. The year 2017 was when sexual harassment came to fore in American society.[37] It became front page news how much our society had tolerated over the decades in terms of sexual harassment—almost totally men on women.

The issue of *tolerance-as-teaching* relates to the "E" in VABEs, expectations. If our expectations are too lax or too strict, in fact, whatever they are, others will sense those boundaries and either live within them or push on them. Our responses to that pushing further defines how much we tolerate and how much we don't. Leaders set those boundaries either intentionally or unintentionally by virtue of the authority they possess.

Clearly those boundaries go a long way to defining who a leader is and what he or she stands for.

Sometimes people who set loose boundaries think they are being *kind* or *compassionate*. Then when things get out of hand, they clamp down and *lay down the law*. This kind of oscillation confuses children and employees. See the chapter on trust and the importance of consistency. Better, I think, to have consistent expectations and set them appropriately for the child's or employee's capabilities.

At the other end of the scale are people who set expectations so high that people live in constant fear of judgment and being found inadequate. This strictness can create a kind of creative paralysis born of the fear of rejection. If you don't tolerate any mistakes, people will pull back until they are sure that everything they do is conservative enough to avoid censure.

What is your stance, your tolerance level, for lying? How about, stealing? Cheating? Skimming? Not meeting goals? Tardiness? Lack

---

[37] http://ajc.com/news/world/from-weinstein-lauer-timeline-2017-sexual-harassment-scandals/qBKJmUSZRJqgOzeB9yN2JK/

of preparation? Flirting? Touching? False advertising? Manufacturing defects? Racial slurs? Drunkenness? Drug use?

What, then, of the impact of *repression*? If an authoritor refuses to tolerate *variation*, will the person so constrained break out later on when in a more tolerant environment—like college or independent living? Or immigration to another country? Or departure from a strict religious culture?

Example

Business people have a lot of meetings. In business school, we also organize students into classes and learning teams so they have a lot of meetings. Business is a social science—it requires meeting with and influencing other people. What is the reaction of your team when people come unprepared for a meeting? Do you say anything? Or do you avoid a potentially unpleasant conversation?

Shrinkage is the term often used to describe pilfering at work. We plan for a *certain amount of shrinkage*. That is, we plan for theft. When it gets to a certain point, our tolerance level, we begin to act. Do we assume our employees are thieves? Corruption is tolerated in many regions—not just countries—of the globe. Leaders there assume that *everyone will be skimming*.

I was told by a tour guide in India once that only 13 percent of Indians pay income tax because they know that if they pay it, most of it, if any, will not reach the government. Another estimate reported by the India Times is only 1.5 percent![38] The country of India took in about US$92 billion in 2007–8 where the individual tax tiers are 0 percent, 5 percent, 20 percent, and 30 percent.[39] There are likely many reasons why the Indian government might *tolerate* such a low tax participation. Here in America, we *tolerate* intense party feuds that seem to undermine the *good of the country*.

---

[38] https://economictimes.indiatimes.com/news/economy/policy/why-income-tax-payers-in-india-are-a-small-and-shrinking-breed/articleshow/56929550.cms
[39] https://en.wikipedia.org/wiki/Income_tax_in_India

Laws against drinking and fornication are very strong in Saudi Arabia.[40] Not only countries, but individual families are also intolerant of inter-ethnic marriages.[41,42]

Diagram

You Teach What you Tolerate

Will you tolerate what you know is incorrect, wrong or dysfunctional?

NOPE.

Challenge

1. How much variation/latitude do you give your children?
2. Your employees?
3. Your spouse?
4. If you were the CEO of your organization, how much variation would you tolerate? (See the chapter on control.)
5. Name the five issues on which you are least tolerant.
6. Name the five issues on which you are most tolerant.
7. Write down your understanding of what your expectations are teaching people.

---

[40] E.g. https://europe-solidaire.org/spip.php?article36517
[41] E.g. https://ncbi.nlm.nih.gov/pmc/articles/PMC2848333/
[42] http://jpost.com/Israel-News/Israeli-Christian-father-allegedly-killed-daughter-over-Muslim-boyfriend-499853

86. The Language of Influence

Concept

Most of us use language bits and pieces that we have made habitually. Many of these phrases, while "accepted" in "normal" conversations, can and often do create defensiveness and shut down any change process. We can think of a conversation like a dance where we want to coordinate our movements to a pleasing outcome. Then, my colleague Alec Horniman, would say we can think of a person's effectiveness in life on a scale from 1 to 5. The "1's" never got to the dance. The "2's" in life got to the dance but never went inside, just hung around outside the door. The "3's" got inside and then sat through it on the walls. The "4's" in life are out on the dance floor enjoying the experiencing and learning new steps. The "5's?" Oh, they are back outside holding hands and maybe kissing. And it was the "6's" who organized the dance.

If you want to become a more effective communicator, I encourage you to heighten your awareness of these dysfunctional phrases and then practice replacing them with something more effective so you can enjoy our dancing conversations ever more. The general goal is avoid saying things that are accusatory and cause the Other to be defensive and use language that is informative, that acknowledges everyone's point of view (this is not "giving in"), and creates a higher probability of effective listening.

Dysfunctional Phrases	More Effective Phrasing
Lose your "buts." When you say, "I agree with everything you've said, but …" you've told a little lie.	Replace your "buts" with "ands." "I agree with everything you've said and I still don't see how that gets us where we want to go."
Avoid using the 2nd person. "Gerry, you have a problem."	"Gerry, I have a problem. Can you help me? I want you to be on time and I'm frustrated."
Don't disguise your opinions as questions. Own your own VABEs. Don't lead the Other. "Don't you think that's right?"	"I believe we should do X. What do you think?"
Seek to understand before you start trying to convince the other.	Just so I'm sure of your point of view, would outline what you see as the problem here?

Don't discount yourself. "Well this may be a stupid question but …"	"Would you please explain the Concept in chapter 94 to me?"
Don't use emotion as your primary influence technique. Emotions are fleeting and unreliable.	Use evidence to present your conclusions and then emotion to dramatize them.
Don't judge, describe. "Hey you jerk!"	"I think when one is pushed out of line, fairness has left the building."
Avoid recreating yesterday. "That's the way we've always done it."	Think creatively. "Here's a better way and why I think it's better."
Don't become a victim. "There's nothing I can do about it."	Accept responsibility for your life and every situation that you are in.

Example

See each one above.

Diagram

Some Rules for a Successful "Dance"

- Target Level Three Influence
- Bring your energy and spread it
- Replace your "buts" with "ands"
- Own your VABEs and Want-Got Gaps
- Don't disguise statements as questions
- Don't present your opinions as facts
- Use evidence and emotion
- Make better invitations

87. Team Life Cycles

Concept

Businesspeople are constantly forming and reforming teams. Wise team leaders understand that teams go through predictable phases or cycles.[43] The traditional model was "forming, storming, norming, and performing" as outlined by Bruce Tuckman in 1965.[44] Later research included a recognition of the frequency with which teams had to dissolve and reform.

Consequently, a more *modern* model of the phases of team development would be:

1. Forming
2. Norming (including *storming*)
3. Performing
4. Re-forming

The first phase, forming, occurs when potential members of a team come together. This might include recruiting and the processes by which people approach the team. Teams might be formed by assignment or natural accrual.

Norming or rule-setting typically follows the early forming phase. In *norming*, members of the team settle on the rules for the team, how we are going to operate. Some theorists suggest that this *phase* is ongoing, however, for teams to function well, these issues need to be largely settled.

Performing refers to actually doing the work/project/program was intended to do. Presumably, the team uses the rules/norms established as they do the work.

Re-forming is meant to help us understand that in today's world of rapid change, teams are not so long-lived as they used to be. Teams are disrupted by many things including completion of work, re-organizations, sell-offs, mergers, change in leadership, technology substitutions, and so forth.

---

[43] For example, https://pmi.org/learning/library/leadership-project-life-cycle-team-character-development-5303

[44] https://en.wikipedia.org/wiki/Tuckman%27s_stages_of_group_development

The central concept here though is that teams, similar to people, go through phases of development and that the wise team leader will understand that and what those phases are. Each phase presents different challenges and issues. (See the next chapter.) To ignore those phases and their issues is to undermine one's own effectiveness as a team leader.

We should also make here a distinction between work groups and teams.[45,46] Workgroups differ from teams in a number of ways. See diagram below. Building a team is much more than simply bringing a group of people together or assigning people to a related job.

We can also make a distinction between functional teams and integrated product development teams. Many organizations have what we might call sequential functional teams that pass a program or project from one to the next in line. These might include design, engineering, pre-production, production, quality control, delivery, and maintenance teams. I had a client once who had 23 such teams in their program process, but you can get the idea of the logic from this simplified list.

An integrated product development team or IPDT includes cross-functional expertise throughout the program process. The intent there is to reduce late stage engineering change requests that are both expensive and schedule delaying.

Example

A company assigns a group of people to design and develop a new helicopter in response to a *request for proposal* (RFP) from the government. Where to begin?

A CEO creates an ad-hoc *team* to research and propose a solution for a business problem.

A group of faculty assigned to teach five different sections of the same required course meet to discuss the course and its delivery.

---

[45] For example, http://onlinelibrary.wiley.com/doi/10.1002/0471264385.wei1214/abstract;jsessionid=4FD4835E991EE2F0E0FD1AB3E3F1533A.f02t04

[46] See primarily Katzenbach, J., and D. Smith. 2015. *The Wisdom of Teams: Creating the High-Performance Organization* Harvard Business Review Press (latest edition).

A major consumer brand product team meets to discuss new competition.

The international team in a global tire company meets to discuss a proposal from a new subsidiary to separate software from hardware as a unique salable product.

Diagram

Group/Team Development

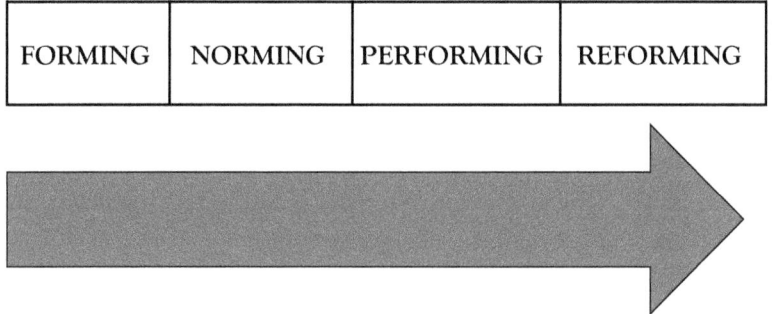

FORMING	NORMING	PERFORMING	REFORMING

Challenge

1. Think about successful teams you have been a part of. What phases did they go through?
2. Think about unsuccessful teams you have been a part of. What phases did they go through (or not)?
3. Think about your current team. What phase are you in now? What's next? How will you know when the next phase comes?
4. Write down what you think the indicators are of each phase transition.

88. Team Activities and Team Life Cycles

Concept

Given the four broad phases in team development introduced in the last chapter, we can turn to the activities necessary in each phase.

The key issues in the forming phase are purpose, membership, and leadership. The first potential confusion is why the group is brought together. I have heard team leaders say, "Okay, you all know why we're here, let's get down to it." Frequently, no, we *don't* know why we are here and unless we sort that out there are to be many different expectations in the room. Sometimes, it seems obvious that even the stated mandate, if there is one, is not the real reason for the group. The stated purpose might be something like "to explore the attractiveness of entering a new market" when in reality the purpose is "to identify how to best enter this market." I have talked with numerous team/group members of various teams who realized either along the way or afterward that the real reason for the group was not the one stated up front.

Effective team builders will have a careful and thorough discussion of the purpose of the group before they jump into action. In fact, not doing that can lead to tremendous difficulty down the road as people mid-stream begin to question increasingly the group's purpose. Group members who seem to have a modest to low commitment to the group can be a drag on later team performance. An effective Level Three group leader will have conversations with these people to assess their commitment to the mission of the group and if necessary to try to build that commitment on the buy-in scale.

The second issue that needs sorting out up front is "Do we have the right people in the room?" Have you ever gone to a meeting and wondered why you were there? I heard that all the time. Effective team leaders will ensure that they have the right people in the room even if they aren't *assigned* to be there. Leaving out key players can almost guarantee a late-schedule torpedo. Make sure the necessary technical skills, customer skills, and internal management skills are in the room.

The final issue to sort out up front is who's in charge? Research has been done about organic groups and naturally emerging leadership. Sometimes the *naturally emerging leader* is self-appointed and is not the same person who has the *legitimate* responsibility for the group. Unless these differences are sorted out, the group is likely to founder on the rocks of conflict. A wise and well-spoken leader can help the group phrase the *right* purpose, enlist the right members, and put to rest any questions about who's making the final decisions. That is not to say such a leader doesn't listen, not at all. See, for example, the Dialogue chapter coming up.

Once the group has settled on purpose, membership and leadership, it can move on to operating guidelines, the *norms* of the group. Unless these are explicitly discussed, the group will migrate toward an amalgam of individual expectations that may inhibit progress. The group should make agreements about preparation for meetings, punctuality, conversation guidelines (see the chapter on the Language of Leadership), and following-up on action items.

A good, standard distributed-in-advance agenda can help. This might include the following:

1. Time, date, place, and invitees
2. Purpose of the meeting
3. Relevant background information and data
4. Report from last meeting's action items
5. Each new item listed in the form of a *question* rather than a topic. This will help ensure forward motion rather than just more talk
6. Recorded action items with person responsible

Note that in my experience, framing each agenda item as a question is far more effective than simply listing topics. With topics, one gets the same items year after year. With questions, you can make progress by continuously coming back to the questions. Be sure you have the right questions.

Camaraderie is an important part of building teams out of work groups. Some team leaders will organize charity outings, low or high ropes exercises or socials to encourage the development of informal more *social* bonds between group members. Sometimes the intensity of the work, as in boot camp in the military, will in and of itself build team cohesion.

Intense training that focuses on the skill sets necessary for the work group have the double advantage of being on-point and bond building.

The third phase, action, means doing the work. Most of this will be done outside of meetings unless the group decides to have workshops or retreats. Here, the agreement about preparation for meetings becomes an important element. If group members come unprepared to report on their assignments, the whole group cum team is set back.

Finally, no team is permanent. Teams come to an end when members turn-over, when the job is done, when the group is outsourced or merged or reorganized. The dissolution of a high performance team can be a traumatic experience for members. A good team leader will plan for this and begin, when the time is *right*, to ease the team into awareness of an impending change. Individual counseling may be necessary. Good team leaders either do that or find the right resources to do so.

Main activities of any team:

1. Purpose? Vision?
2. Membership? Status? Value added?
3. Who's the leader?
4. What's our style? Rules?
5. What's okay? What's not?
6. Working on the task.
7. Getting completion.
8. Letting go, new tasks, new assignments, new relationships.

We can array these activities on a vertical axis in the first column of a table and then add columns for each phase as shown below. As a group morphs into a team, the members— especially the leader—will be aware of the diagonal down-right movement of the group through the table. Jumping to action before the Forming and Norming phases are complete is a formula for failure. Ignoring the fourth stage can leave members de-energized and dispirited.

Example

Program teams in the defense industry will often hand out various objects to help the members identify with the team as they begin. Desktop models, special shirts, mugs with logos, hats, and other paraphernalia are often distributed to build a sense of ownership and membership. Those trinkets are no substitute, however, for the team leader's impassioned description of the team's purpose or mission.

In the undisguised case "The Tough Team Call (A)" team members are arguing late in its project life cycle about who's in charge and the nature of their purpose. The inability to settle these issues early on has led to significant dysfunction and the rising probability of failure.[47]

Diagram

Mapping Design Issues and Team Life Cycles

	1. Forming	2. Norming	3. Performing	4. Reforming
Purpose	X			
Membership	X			
Leadership	X			
Rules		X		
Measures		X		
Task			X	
Disconnecting				X

Challenge

1. Train yourself to watch for and identify the changing, emerging phases of team development.
2. Vow to manage your own teams with that awareness.
3. Develop skills in articulating purpose, identifying key team members, shaping highly functional team norms, managing progress, and managing dissolution.

---

[47] Isabella, L. n.d. *Making the Tough Team Call* (A). Darden Business School Publishing, UVA-OB-0705.

89. Distributed Leadership

Concept

Bicyclists, automobile racers, military teams in the bush, cross-country skiers, and even geese use the concept of rotating leadership. The basic principle is that leading demands more energy than following, so to give the leader a rest, we can rotate that assignment. Of course, in these cases the additional energy burden is largely physical, but it is also psychological. My experience as the CEO of a non-profit organization of 3,000 people and eight different units was enlightening; there is a heavy mantle that descends with those who sit in the last chair. Leadership demands large amounts of physical, psychological, intellectual, and emotional energy. Bureaucratic maintenance requires much less, just do what we have always done. But to *lead* consumes energy.

In the business world, the experiments with self-directed team organizations included rotating leadership.[48] In this arrangement, teams would elect their team leaders from time to time, typically annually. This structure was *self-correcting* in the sense that if a leader began to feel cocky and arrogant, it was relatively easy to vote the person out and select a new, more sympathetic one. This was a way of avoiding the tendency of bosses to become assholes.[49] Informal groups tend to be more self-correcting than assigned groups. Cliques will expel non-conforming members while assigned leaders can often maintain their control by virtue of their legitimate power. (See the chapter on Sources of Influence/Power.) This erodes superior-subordinate trust.[50]

Further, team leaders learned something of the issues and challenges of managing, something many Technical Experts (see the chapter on Career Concepts) don't really understand until they get a managerial job.

---

[48] Clawson, J. *The Aberdeen Experiment.* Darden Business Publishing, UVA-OB-0998.

[49] Sutton, R.I. 2010. *The No Asshole Rule: Building a Civilized Workplace and Surviving One That Isn't,* Business Plus.

[50] For example, http://huffingtonpost.in/debashis-sarkar/being-a-boss-5-deadly-hab_b_9006726.html

That insight tended to dampen misdirected desires to be promoted for reasons of power and compensation.

It's one thing to rotate a team leader's job, it's another thing to rotate or share the chief executive's job. Some companies are experimenting with this arrangement.[51] Some companies have *co-chairmen*.[52] This structure leads to its own challenges—it requires a group of people who can work together without jealousy, backbiting, undermining, and all of the other issues that arise when people share positions of high power. Typically, that situation leads to in-fighting and sabotage that is dysfunctional for the larger organization. The benefit, of course, is sharing the load—assigning parts of the job to one, other parts to another. One could focus on domestic affairs, for example, another on international affairs. Some academics believe that a shared leadership role is more diverse and therefore more robust.[53] The downside is the energy wasted in jockeying for power.[54]

One can argue that the job of the board of directors is to provide a correcting function here. The difference is that the corrections are made by those above the CEO, not those below, and that the CEO is typically the chief selector of those on the board—so the correcting effect is minimized. Further, boards meet only periodically.

One alternative to the co-CEO structure is the "Moses model." Moses in his old age had two main advisors, Aaron and Hur, who stood beside him and held up his arms.[55] This structure implies a single CEO with two main counselors. Of course, there's nothing magical about having two and not four main counselors, which is the more common model.

Rotating leadership is one way of sharing the load, distributing leadership is another. Distributed leadership is power to lead pushed down in the organization. See the next chapter on Empowerment. The willingness to let others make significant decisions is couched in a person's

---

[51] https://forbes.com/sites/rogertrapp/2017/03/20/can-a-ceo-job-share-work/#5c8241de491c

[52] http://businessinsider.com/why-major-companies-have-2-ceos-2014-9

[53] Private conversation with a colleague.

[54] https://fastcompany.com/40473112/why-having-co-ceos-is-a-bad-idea

[55] *Holy Bible*, Exodus 17:10-12.

VABEs about control. (See the chapter on Control.) The constantly shifting balance in such a structure is between delegation and control.

Marriage is another playground for this dilemma. Who makes the major decisions? How are the major decisions made? What is the balance of power between the two partners? (and the children if any) What kind of, if any, conflict arises from this binary arrangement?[56]

Rotating leadership and distributing leadership have as many issues as the single leader. Which is better, in your mind, a single leader or a cadre of leaders? The former pinpoints responsibility, but rests on the abilities and character of that leader. The latter shares a heavy load, but can diffuse responsibility and results.

Example

Tour de France teams and automobile racers frequently draft the leaders to save energy and go faster. They also rotate that leadership to save energy (fuel) and share the burden.

Oracle, Whole Foods, Daimler AG, and Chipotle have all experimented with co-CEOs. At least one company has done this successfully for over seven years.[57]

Diagram

Team Leaders are like chefs: ...

- Whom are we serving?
- What're the right ingredients?
- What flavor does each ingredient add?
- How much to put in and when?
- How long do we cook it and how?
- When do we serve it and how?
- How much did it cost/produce?
- Did they get gas?

---

[56] See, for example, Clawson, J. *Dual Career Decision Making.* Darden Business Publishing, UVA-PACS-0099.

[57] https://forbes.com/sites/amynorman/2016/10/18/theres-no-7-year-itch-in-this-co-ceo-relationship/#2a8a62177f45

Challenge

1. Describe how your team would change if your team elected its leader.
2. What, if any, problems would you anticipate in electing your team leader?
3. What is your opinion about shared leadership at the top of an organization?
4. How do you manage the balance of power in your long-term personal relationships?

90. Empowerment

Concept

The previous chapter on distributing leadership raises the issue of *empowerment*. Empowerment was a hot topic in the 1990s given the surge in popularity of Japanese management practices. Clients, students, and participants often mention the need to *empower* people. When you ask them what that means, they look confused. And they are. Let's break down the concept of empowerment.

What do you intend to empower people to do? Here are some options.

1. Identify problems.
2. Analyze problems.
3. Develop a list of options for dealing with the problems.
4. Choose which option to use.
5. Implement the chosen option.
6. Assess the results of the initiative.
7. Decide whether to proceed or start over.

Many managers reserve all of these activities for management. Having lived in Japan for four years and read several accounts of Japanese management practice, I am convinced that the Japanese *empowerment* did not go all the way down the list, in fact, it was quite limited—it typically stopped at step 3 reserving for management of the choice, implementation, and assessment of solutions. People who chose 25 percent or less on the Control scale (see above), would be willing (in theory) to go much further down the list, perhaps to step 6.

So when you or a colleague begins talking about *empowerment*, I invite you to pause and press down a little to help people clarify just what they mean. Empowerment is not a binary concept, it arrays on an analog scale.

Management cultures that punish variance tend not to be empowered. Introducing an *empowerment* program without creating a safe and trusting culture is a useless waste of time. I once participated in a nominal group in which participants were writing issues on flip charts posted around the room. The leader of the organization was in the room observing. At one point, the leader approached a participant and challenged him for writing something about weak leadership. The process did not match the management culture or the leader's VABEs. Honest opinions were not safe. The fear of rejection continued to seep through the organization. Bad news was minimized; accolades were maximized. Trust eroded.

Example

Nominal groups began to be popular in the United States after the surge in interest in Japanese management. Nominal groups were like extended focus groups conducted among employees. Extended in the sense that they went beyond opinions to identifying problems and proposing solutions. Selecting a decision was often informed by the number of votes (or sticky tabs) a particular solution garnered from the group.[58] The final decision, execution, and assessment was typically reserved for management. You probably have been part of a *nominal group* that generated problems, options, and then voted with sticky spots.

This endnote references several companies, including H&R Block and Tesla, who are using *empowerment* to grow.[59]

A colleague once went into a hotel to register. The desk clerk was wearing a nice looking pin that said "Empowered!" My colleague said, "That's a cool pin! I'm a professor of management. I'd like to have one of those!" The desk clerk said, "Just a minute. I'll have to go ask my boss." ☹

Diagram

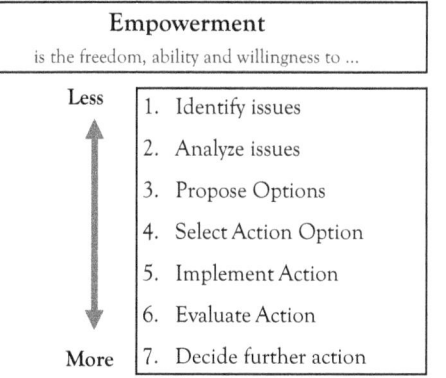

| Empowerment |
| is the freedom, ability and willingness to ... |

Less

1. Identify issues
2. Analyze issues
3. Propose Options
4. Select Action Option
5. Implement Action
6. Evaluate Action
7. Decide further action

More

---

[58] https://en.wikipedia.org/wiki/Nominal_group_technique

[59] https://ibm.com/blogs/watson/2017/03/empowered-employee-6-companies-arming-teams-data/

Challenge

1. How far down the empowerment scale does your team go?
2. How would you assess the empowerment philosophy of your management team?
3. What would be the pros and cons of going further down the empowerment scale?

91. Getting the Right People on the Team

Concept

Whether it's a board of directors, a C-level group, a divisional management, a departmental management, an ad-hoc study group, or a first level production group, getting the right people on the team is as important as any other piece of building world-class teams. If you have a clear mission, good leadership, and the wrong people on the team, the odds are you will fail. The same is true of an organization overall. Hence, in my view, recruiting is one of the most important issues executives face. You can tell the quality of a leader, I think, by the quality of people they choose.

The usual first criterion for selecting team members is expertise. Those assembling teams want to have the right skill set as Jim Collins would say, *on the bus.*[60] Sometimes executives even overlook this issue, eschewing technical people for the sake of having business people in the room who *understand the bigger issues.* As described earlier, the common costs associated with sequential program teams created pressure to develop integrated product development teams early in a program's life cycle. This approach brings a more varied group of skills onto teams than the traditional sequential approach.

A team selection criterion that is often overlooked is social skills. We might have technical skills in the room, but do we have good social skills like listening, process orientation, task orientation, problem solving, and teamwork? Superior technical skills are no guarantee of superior social skills. Wise team builders will include a diversity of social skills—and may even assign social process roles to members so inclined. (See the next chapter for more.) Building a team without paying attention to the key social skills can kill a team before it gets started.

This issue bears on organizational recruiting as well. Organizations that hire primarily Technical Experts (see the chapter on Career Concepts) will find it difficult to select leaders from amongst their midst. Organizations in cyclical industries who don't hire a significant proportion of Transitories will find themselves facing cultural backlash at each

---

[60] Collins, J. 2013. *Good to Great.* op cit.

layoff. Finding the right mix of technical, leadership, and social skills at every level is an important executive skill.

Finally, we might mention energy level. However skilled an individual is, if they have no energy for the group's purpose, they will likely be a drag on the team.

Example

A plant building a *no fear* culture intentionally hires people with strong social skills over technical skills. Their philosophy is "it's easier to teach technical skills than attitude."[61] In that plant, they actually hired a woman to be a welder who had never welded before. She learned to weld and became an extraordinary employee, almost a poster child for the kind of culture they were creating.

Universities typically have a seven-year *probationary* period, tenure track, during which they assess the long-term fit between individuals and their institution. Businesses usually don't take that long, however, they also seldom grant any kind of contractual tenure. They can fire their mistakes. That said, it's often harder to get rid of someone than it is to hire someone. The Chicago Park District, a quasi-governmental agency with the power to levy taxes, once required 81 steps to fire an employee.[62] That reality alone highlights the importance of being very careful in every hire you make.

---

[61] Clawson, J. n.d. *The Aberdeen Experiment*. UVA-OB-0998, Darden Business Publishing.

[62] Clawson, J. n.d. *Chicago Park District* (A). UVA-OB-0618, Darden Business Publishing.

Diagram

Recruiting Team Members

Challenge

1. Assess each member of your team in terms of what they add and what they don't add.
2. What skills does your team have? What skills are missing on your team?
3. Whom would you like to add to your team?
4. Whom would you like to let go from your team?
5. How committed is each member of your team, say, on a scale of 1 to 10?

92. Key Roles in Effective Teams

Concept

If we have the right people on our team, we may or may not have the right *roles* in play. If we have selected the right people, they may play the necessary roles naturally—and they might not. A good team leader will watch for these roles and ensure that they are alive and well. He or she might even explicitly *assign* the roles to individuals to be sure those functions occur.

What roles would you say are key for any high performing team? Write down your thoughts here.

Blake and Mouton gave us the traditional functional axes in the Managerial Grid.[63] These axes are task and process. In other words, somebody has to be thinking about getting the job done and someone *should* be thinking about *how* we get the job done. While we can use this grid to assess managerial style (Jack Welch famously used a nine cell version), we can also apply this to teams. Who on the team is paying

---

[63] https://en.wikipedia.org/wiki/Managerial_grid_model from Blake and Mouton, *The Managerial Grid: The Key To Leadership* Excellence, Gulf Publishing, 1964.

attention to getting the job done? Who is watching our process to ensure we aren't behaving dysfunctionally?

The importance of getting things done, the TASK function, is obvious. If we meet and meet and work and work but never accomplish anything, what good is it?

The process function asks our team to be aware of and manage internal conflicts, dysfunctional communication styles, lack of listening, interrupting, getting everyone's voice heard, and so on. Some people watch these things naturally; many, if not most, do not. The leader's style will influence the process function dramatically. If the team leader is not a skilled facilitator, meetings can devolve into useless exercises.

There are at least two other dimensions that I think are important: creativity and practicality. In today's world in which innovation and creativity are increasingly important,[64] encouraging creative thinking seems critical.[65] With the Internet, instantaneous information sharing, the ability to hide margins and buckets of money have evaporated. The world is much more transparent. The days of making margins on middle men and ignorance have passed. Creativity is critical to success in today's business world.

That said, we could argue that a million new ideas are fine but only if a few of them bring in revenues. We need to balance creativity with practicality.

We could conflate the two axes, task and process, on a single *balance* scale. The middle position would be a good balance between task and process.

Then, we could chart two dimensions, task/process and creativity/practicality, and strive for a balance of both in our meetings and discussions. As mentioned above, organizations tend to recreate themselves. People tend to choose what they know. That leads to a resistance to change and innovation.

---

[64] For example, https://jeanneliedtka.com/ Also, https://ideou.com/pages/design-thinking
[65] For example, http://thecreativemind.net/1268/how-to-be-creative-michael-gelb-on-creativity-and-innovation/

Observing a large sample of executive education teams in educational situations, Belbin argues for nine observable roles.[66] You and I might identify the common roles we see in our own meetings. (See below.) My concern, however, is more for what roles do we need rather than what roles we can commonly observe.

Example

Entrepreneur magazine highlights 10 companies with *fantastic* cultures.[67] They get results with good process, and balance creativity and process. Those companies include Zappos, Warby Parker, and Southwest Airlines. I once heard of a candidate at Southwest Airlines who submitted her resume on a sheet cake. She wrote her resume in icing! AND she got the job!

Diagram

High Performing Team Essential Roles

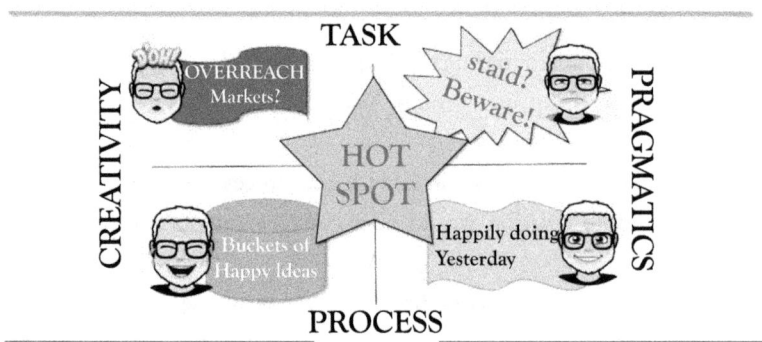

---

[66] Belbin, M. 1981. *Management Teams,* Heinemann, London.

[67] https://entrepreneur.com/article/249174

Challenge

1. In your next team meeting, try assigning the following roles: process monitor, task monitor, creativity monitor, pragmatic monitor, recorder of to-do assignments.
2. You may have to educate your team on what good process looks like. You can find lots of articles online, for example, https://thebalance.com/tips-for-better-teamwork-1919225
3. Periodically ask your monitors how the team is doing.
4. Listen to what your monitors say.
5. Repeat every meeting until it becomes a habit.

93. Dialogue Technique

Concept

Peter Senge and his group at MIT developed a way of ensuring that every team member's insight and perspective could be had in team meetings. They called this process the *dialogue* technique, but it's not dialogue as laypeople know it. Senge's dialogue has a particular meaning and process.[68]

The goal of Senge-dialogue is to avoid group think that is based on the voices of a few and to make transparent the views and opinions of everyone in the room and on the team so that the team can make better decisions. I am sure you have been in meetings in which only a few participate while others sit silently. One way to overcome this phenomenon is to ask the quiet people what they think. That puts them on the spot and they may or may not feel safe and comfortable speaking out. Plus, if interrupting is a norm, the louder people may cut short what the quieter people have to say.

When usual conversation seems to have brought a discussion to halt or a repetitive cycle, team leaders may decide to employ the dialogue technique. The process looks like this:

1. Place a significant object in the center of the table on which people can focus (similar to a campfire).
2. Ask everyone to focus on the object and to listen to their colleagues carefully.
3. Go around the table one at a time in order, asking people to voice their thoughts on the topic in question.
4. Do not allow any comments or reactions to what the speaker(s) is saying. Everyone is to focus on the central object and listen.
5. When everyone has spoken, go around again, one at a time with again no interruptions or comments, this time speaking a last time one's thoughts now modified by what has been said.
6. After the second round, the leader or others summarize the tone of the comments.

---

[68] William, I. Autumn 1993. "Taking Flight; Dialogue, Collective Thinking, and Organizational Learning." *Organizational Dynamics*, pp. 24–39.

This process takes a little time and in the mid-run, it probably saves lots of time. The best thinking of everyone in the room is now "on the table" and available for everyone to consider. Compare this to other meetings where people come and go and have only heard from one or two people in the room. Regular use of the process also encourages preparation since members know that at some point, their voice will be heard—and they will need something to say.

The collective team based dialogue process works best when the members of the team have also been instructed in and accepted good communication skills including active listening, not interrupting, eliminating *buts*, and owning their opinions as opinions rather than presenting them as facts.[69]

When a team uses this process well, the level of trust and safety ramps up, oligarchic domination diminishes, and teams are better prepared to make fully informed decisions.

Example

Here are some situations in which use of the dialogue technique described above would be useful:

1. A program team is trying to decide whether to scrap a lengthy development process and adopt another approach.
2. A teaching team is trying to decide what main topics to include in a required course.
3. A legal team is trying to decide whether to adopt a line of interpretation that might leave the firm at major risk.
4. An executive team is trying to decide whether to buy a company in a significantly different industry. Would you think people at the executive level would be susceptible to *groupthink* or becoming *yes men*?
5. A foundation team is trying to decide whether or not to support a particular initiative.

---

[69] James Clawson, with Jean Kane and Cathryn Harding, "Dialogue," UVA-OB-0633, Darden Business Publishing.

Diagram

Senge's Dialogue Technique

1. Central focal object ala campfire
2. Focus on the object and listen
3. One at a time, what are your thoughts?
4. No reactions or comments, just listen.
5. Go around a second time folding in what's been said.
6. Leader or group summarizes the comments

Source: Adapted from William, I. Autumn 1993. "Taking Flight; Dialogue, Collective Thinking, and Organizational Learning." *Organizational Dynamics*, pp. 24–39.

Challenge

1. Train your team in the dialogue technique, for example, read Isaacs article or my technical note.
2. Try the dialogue technique in a meeting when after significant discussion, the answer is still not clear.
3. Use the principles of the dialogue technique to ensure every voice on your team is fully heard.

94. One World-Class Team

Concept

The "Greenland" case (UVA-OB-0581) describes the history and experience of a group of four Norwegians who set a world record in cross-country skiing pulling 250 pound sleds across Greenland, the globe's largest island. While this is an unusual case for a business school discussion, every one of the 200+ times I have taught this case, people identify 20+ lessons that one can learn about creating world-class teams. I will simply list these insights here and invite interested parties to read the whole case.[70] These insights were also enumerated in a book chapter.[71]

1. **Preparation**. One year of practice trips that were more intense than the actual trip, prep to action ratio, 26:1. You play like you practice. Careful, meticulous planning.

2. **Clear Goal**. Set a world-record. Comes from within, not from someone else.

3. **Recruiting**. By invitation to weekend practice sessions. Fifty percent attrition rate by choice.

4. **Benchmarking**. Interview experts but modify significantly what they did, else you replicate what they did. Benchmarking prepares you for someone else's yesterday, not your tomorrow.

5. **Calculated Risk Taking**. Careful calculation of key variables: weight, location, speed, time, and energy (calories) led to key decisions to leave behind 8# rifle and throw away excess food 2/3 of the way through.

6. **Latest Technology**. Use of pre-commercial military GPS system in order to pinpoint location, which was critical to speed calculations. Not fad gadget, critical to calculations.

---

[70] James Clawson and Morten Lie, "Greenland," Darden Business Publishing, UVA-OB-581.

[71] "Greenland: Creating World Class Teams," in *Extreme Leadership: Leaders, Teams and Situations outside the Norm,* eds. Giannantonio, C.M., and Hurley-Hanson, A.E. Edward Elgar.

7. **Unbending Strategy.** Light = Fast = Safe. Physics is in play; F = ma. More mass means more force to move it, so our central principle is lightweight. Stripping edges from skis, no rifle, re-packaging food, and so on.

8. **Flexible Tactics.** Adapt hourly decisions to local circumstances within inflexible strategy. Jury-rigging a ski pole rather than bringing back-ups.

9. **Social Conflict Planning:** Never waste time blaming (even when fuel leaked into the food causing diarrhea), focus on solutions. Blame game wastes energy.

10. **Rotating Leadership.** Traveling single-file taking turns breaking trail, which required more energy.

11. **Customized Equipment.** They rigged their own harnesses and other bits of equipment to suit their needs rather than relying on off-the-shelf.

12. **Focus on Energy.** They measured energy (in foodstuffs and body fat) carefully.

13. **Competition.** Bedard Ulvang, Olympic gold medalist and national hero, was leading the group right behind them.

14. **Luck.** They didn't encounter any polar bears and had reasonable weather—although they hiked rather than camped in the blizzards they faced.

15. **Short Term Goals.** The once-a-week flight schedule from the west coast pressed them to get there sooner to avoid waiting a week for the next flight.

16. **Social Support.** They would walk beside sick comrade even though that doubled the energy required to break trail. This energy cache is not mysterious (e.g., telepathy), rather social support helps a person unleash energy they already have but which is unavailable because of a clouded mind-body connection.

17. **Persistence.** The longer they were out there, the more dangerous it became, plus their goal was to set a speed record, so they walked when sick and in storms.

18. **Pacing.** They didn't walk as fast as they could because sweat would freeze in the -60°F temperatures, so they paced themselves just below the heavy sweat level.

19. **Restructuring Time.** Two-thirds of the way through, they decided they weren't tired at the end of the day so they began working 30 hour days instead of 24 hour days.

20. **Discipline.** They were deeply committed to their goal especially given the extremely dangerous conditions and environment.

21. **Celebration.** They carried a bottle of cognac with them (the only violation of the core strategy) to celebrate Norway's Independence Day. Survivalists will say never drink alcohol in hypothermic situations and it was heavy. They calculated that the energy release from celebrating would outweigh the cost of carrying the cognac.

22. **Team versus Individual Focus.** Their calculations were team-based rather than individual-based, and they determined to stay together.

23. **Break Up.** Near the end of the trek, as they neared the finish line, they spread out. They later regretted this. That said, no team (or automobile engine) can perform at high RPMs indefinitely. One should anticipate a break-up and plan for it.

This group of unknown Transitory Norwegians not only broke the 28 day previous world record, they **smashed** it in 13 days. There was no band at the end, no newspaper reporter, no cash prize. We might ask why people do things like this. See the chapter on Resonance and Flow.

Example

There are many examples of people who engage in extreme recreations presumably seeking that internal sense of being alive mentioned by Joseph Campbell (below). These recreations include single-breath deep sea diving, technical rock climbing, single-handed circumnavigation of the globe, climbing 8,000 meter peaks, and more.

Diagram

Resonance is a question of harmony between inside and outside

*"I think that what we're seeking is an experience of being alive, so that our life experiences on the purely physical plane will have **resonance** with our innermost being and reality, so that we actually feel the rapture of being alive."*

- Joseph Campbell, *The Power of Myth, 1988*

Challenge

1. What kind of effort does it take to become world-class at something?
2. Where have you noticed organizations giving *lip service* to being world-class?
3. How good do you want your team to be?
4. How could you get your team to "feel the rapture of being alive?"
5. Which of the elements in the list above could you add to your team? Where do you come up short?

95. Planned Team Obsolescence

Concept

The Greenland chapter introduces the concept that high performing world-class teams are not likely to continue indefinitely. Things change. People leave. Projects are completed. Management changes. The concept here is that wise team leaders will plan for this.

For many high-performing teams, the excitement and resonance of being in that high level of excellence pushes out any thoughts of *what's next?* This is dangerous. When the job is done or leadership or membership change and things aren't going so well, the drop can be a catastrophic one. Here are some things team leaders can do to manage this potential pitfall.

First, realize that no good thing goes on forever. All good things come to an end sometime, somewhere. A cursory look at the history of the world shows that sooner or later things will change in a dramatic way.[72] Even in the short run, things will change. Don't let yourself be blindsided by those changes. Anticipate and prepare for them. Do you have a strong and efficient replacement process for those who leave? What would happen if your funding went away? How will you manage your team when the project is completed? Are you assuming someone else will take care of you? Beware.

Second, develop your replacement process before you have to use it. Identify the key skills on your team. Identify in advance sources for those skills. Have them ready to go just in case.

Third, manage your team like a small business. What if your funding disappeared? Would you be able to take your unit out into the big, blue ocean of shark-filled competition if your unit were outsourced?[73]

Fourth, clarify your unit's purpose for existing. If it's a program, what happens when you complete the program? Will you and your people be re-absorbed back into the larger matrix organization assured of jobs on

---

[72] Only One Man, "Genesis," *A Song of Humanity: A Science-Based Alternative to the World's Scriptures*, L3L LLC, 2016.

[73] https://outsourcinginsight.com/outsourcing-trends/

another program? Not so fast. I have had many, many participants who thought their jobs were safe—and ended up depressed and on the job market.[74] One result of the end-of-program phenomenon is *institutionalization*.[75] While this term can refer to the cultural incorporation of a process, it can also refer to the bureaucratization of a unit in organizational theory. In other words, even though the unit's original purpose has been completed, the unit semi- or unconsciously morphs its purpose into *surviving* and continuing. The original purpose can be and often is subverted into simple survival. If you let yourself slip into this whirlpool, you are contributing to the morass of moribund bureaucracies in the world. Maybe you could redefine your unit's purpose in a more positive, energetic, customer serving way. This will likely mean creating a new charter as if you were an entrepreneur.

However you do it, plan for the dissolution of your high-performing team. That plan is your strategic insurance. Make sure it has comprehensive provisions.

Example

A study of the star research teams at the former Bell Labs showed that the only difference between the average teams and the star performers was that the latter had anticipated changes in resources and oiled their supply relationships in advance.[76]

There was a participant in one of my seminars who ran a very profitable but small business within a larger conglomerate. He was crestfallen to learn that the corporate *powers-that-be* were going to sell off his unit—despite their high level of profitability. While an interested observer could easily draw a strategic link between this little business and the bigger one, senior management had decided to slough it off. Clearly, this unit manager had not thought ahead about that possibility and it left him in crisis.

---

[74] https://en.wikipedia.org/wiki/Product_life-cycle_management_(marketing)

[75] https://en.wikipedia.org/wiki/Institutionalisation

[76] https://hbr.org/1993/07/how-bell-labs-creates-star-performers

Diagram

Planned Team Obsolescence

- Members turnover
- Supervising management changes
- Funding disappears
- Unit is outsourced
- Unit completes its mission/program/project
- Economy or demand collapses

Don't be caught off guard! Plan ahead!

Challenge

1. Work through all four issues introduced above for your team.
2. What other contingencies can you foresee?
3. How will you deal with them? Put your plan on paper.
4. Describe the demise of high-performing teams you have observed. What happened? How could it have been different? What do you learn from this? Write your lessons down.

SECTION VII

Organizational Architecture: Can You Organize to Help Not Hinder?

Executives, whether they like it or not, are organizational architects. They make decisions about how to recruit, how to on-board, how to organize work, how to reward, how to keep control, and dozens of other decisions that taken together design their organizations. Sadly, in my experience these decisions too often de-energize employees rather than energize them. This section is about how to design organizations that help not hinder the implementation of a charter. Of course, without a charter, these decisions end up becoming ad-hoc and disjointed, and ultimately energy dissipating.

96. The Southern Ball: Can You Organize to Help Not Hinder?

Concept

A big part of the responsibility of executive leaders is organizational architecture. Existing companies have developed structures and systems, hundreds of systems, over the years that may or may not be helping current employees to do their jobs. Whether executives like it or not, they are organizational architects, yet many of them inadvertently create organizations that hinder rather than help.

Bureaucracy has its place. It puts decision making in systems rather than individuals. It protects large organizations from impulsive leaders. It gives employees and customers a sense of stability. But bureaucracies can also stifle creativity, timely responsiveness to market changes, and innovation.

Stephen R. Covey, author of *Seven Habits of Highly Effective People*, was my first instructor in business school. He told a story in class one day that I have never forgotten—a good example by the way of the effectiveness of a Level Three technique. He said a man went in to buy a suit. The salesman put him in front of a three-way mirror, put a suit on him and said, "What do you think?" The man said, "Hmm. I like it, but the right shoulder looks a little low."

"Hmm," said the salesman. "We could send it off to the alterer. He'd rip the sleeve off, stuff some padding in there, and re-sew it. That would take a couple of days or a week and cost more money. It would be a lot better if you would just raise your right shoulder a little."

"Oh," said the customer, "that looks better." "Well then," mused the salesman, "anything else?" The customer looked at the mirror and said, "Um, yes. There is too much fabric in the body of the suit. It looks floppy." "Ah," said the salesman. "I see. Well, we could send it off to the alterer. He would cut cut cut, snip snip snip, and stitch stitch stitch. That would be more time, more money, more bother. Why don't you just tuck your left elbow in and take that fullness out?" The man complied and liked the look.

"What about the trousers?" asked the salesman. "Hmm. I like the length, like the hem. But there is too much fabric in the seat!" said the man. "Well," said the salesman, "Again, we can send them off, cut cut cut, snip snip snip, stitch stitch stitch! Why don't you just reach behind with your left hand and pull on the seat? That takes that fullness out!"

So the man liked the look of the suit and he bought it. And wore it out the store, shuffling along with one shoulder up, the other elbow tucked in, and his hand behind pulling on the seat of his trousers. Across the street two women were watching this. "Oh my," one said. "I wonder what happened to that poor man!" "I know," the other said. "But look how good his suit fits him!"

The point of Covey's story was that too often management puts employees into jobs that constrain them in so many ways that they can hardly do their jobs. Further, after a year's work, they conduct a performance review. The usual results of those reviews are "Good job! Now, next year do 10 percent better!" So, now the employees have to shuffle faster and faster while wearing the constraints that become more and more debilitating.

Worse, after a few years, one could take the suit (the job) off the man, and he would still walk with one shoulder up, one elbow in, and one hand behind. The job would have *trained* him to work in that way.

Wise executives will study and understand the pros and cons of the various structural alternatives and be very careful about implementing systems without understanding their implications and unintended consequences. We will have more on this topic below.

Examples

City government of Mexico City had a problem some years back, heavy unhealthy smog. Mexico City lies in a bowl surrounded by mountains at 7,382 feet altitude. So the city planners got together and decided to strike a blow at the smog that collected in this natural bowl. They made a law that every car with an even numbered license plate could drive on Monday, Wednesday, and Friday and that every car with an odd numbered license plates could drive on Tuesday, Thursday, and Saturday. *This* they thought will force people to car pool, cut smog in half and solve our problem. What do you think happened?

The result was that the smog in Mexico City *doubled*! Why? Because people went out and bought a second car and because the average income level in Mexico City was—what do you think? High, medium or low? Low, so the second car they bought was cheap, old and a clunker that emitted more exhaust fumes.

Other cities like Beijing and Athens have also tried this system. With the same result.

Gator Financial (a disguised name) had a similar experience. Eighty percent of Gator's revenue came in through telephone switchboards. A few customers complained that they couldn't get through fast enough, so management got together and decided to make a new rule/system. They put an electronic device on every sales representative's phone and told them we want you to answer every phone call within 20 seconds. This device will track how long it takes you to answer your phone. Our goal overall is 80 percent of calls answered within 20 seconds.

What do you think happened? Customer satisfaction went up, flat, or down? Why?

Down. Sales reps started putting the people they were helping on hold so they could answer the new incoming phone calls within the 20 second benchmark.

Both of these examples demonstrate that the problem with poor organizational performance is not always poor employee performance but often the poor design imposed on them by inept management.

Diagram

Don't Make Your
People Wear
ILL-Fitting Suits!
It's bad bonsai!

Challenge

1. Before you engage in designing a system, talk with and engage those who will be using it. This will help you avoid some *obvious* mistakes.
2. Don't take organizational architecture lightly. Bad designs and bad systems can squash human talent.
3. Many consulting firms will offer to help you think through organizational architecture. Be careful. They may not know your organization as well as you do.
4. Think about removing organizational constraints rather than adding to them.
5. Be careful about making blanket rules for single exceptions. Maybe the problem is the individual and not the system.
6. Study organizational architecture carefully.

97. Pyramid Organization: The Common Structure

Concept

Let's begin our discussion of organizational architecture with issues of organizational structure. We can distinguish between structure and design in that, the latter would include the myriad systems that add muscle to the structural skeleton. Jay Galbraith was one of the most prolific scholars on organizational design. If you would like to pursue this issue further, check out his long list of books.[1]

The simplest organizational structure is a pyramid with a large number of employees at the bottom and a single chief executive at the top. Each layer has fewer and fewer managers and managers of managers until the top layer has only one.

One of the primary issues in pyramid organizations is span of control. This was a big topic back in the 1950s and 60s.[2] How many people can one manager manage effectively? Various studies came up with different numbers. The taller the organization, that is the more layers it had, the fewer is the span of control. The flatter the organization, the more is the span of control.[3] Another telling number was the ratio of staff to *in-line* employees.[4] The staff to productive employee ratio could be considered a measure of efficiency. My guess is that would be a curvilinear relationship, too few and too many would be detrimental. What do you think?

The lines of authority in a pyramid could be built around geographic areas, products, functions, or customers. Lines of authority could also be mixed so that in a functional organization, sales could be organized by

---

[1] https://amazon.com/s/ref=nb_sb_noss?url=search-alias%3Daps&field-keywor ds=jay+galbraith+books&rh=i%3Aaps%2Ck%3Ajay+galbraith+books

[2] http://jstor.org/stable/2391262?casa_token=pd6RhnstPK4AAAAA:kiFCNF UWN8Gms-emCcR9ei2BbSmP1HqbXt5RguQXASPO1BqoCMlVPt7ae7T-Fo5e5hsK8mai70_XhZ-Q6OqHEKklb4fqPpGQHkYWBIAspD8Ujo3ggo-c&seq=1#page_scan_tab_contents

[3] Galbraith, J. 1977. *Organization Design*. Addison Wesley Publishing, Reading Mass.

[4] http://jstor.org/stable/2351633?casa_token=KD-cwAcdHpsAAAAA:OstdelL LrrrvnHZXPsefkcfFNCGCY-Ub6wkLClhyPVktNoWVeIJTfecxkpBp5ZNcu L8ne1_-YWypQlCocrfW5gJGPeBTvw5lK-qfqu0yScYwWS53EMA&seq=1#-page_scan_tab_contents

geographic area while engineering could be organized by product line, while marketing could be organized by customer segment.

Some of the benefits of a pyramid organization are clarity of responsibility, simplicity of reporting structures, focus of each unit, and high levels of control. On the other hand, difficulties include slowness of decision making, redundancy of capability investments, and lack of internal coordination across multiple organizational boundaries—which led to a series of constant reorganizations as companies tried to find ways to balance emphasis from area to customer to product to function.

Example

Pyramid organizations are everywhere in human history. Traditional (as opposed to guerrilla) military organizations tend to be pyramidic. Most of the large corporations in the first half of the 20th century were pyramids. Ford Motor Company stands out as does Edison Electric.

Diagram

The Pyramid Organization

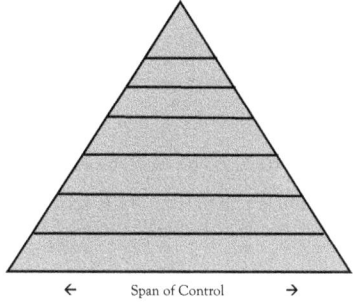

PROS
• Clear Responsibility
• Direct Authority
• Unit focus
• Control

CONS
• Slow Decisions
• Redundancies
• Lack of Coordination

← Span of Control →

Challenge

1. How many people could you manage at once?
2. How many layers are there in your organization? How many, if any, do you think are unnecessary?
3. How long does it take your senior management to make a big decision? Why?
4. How well does your organization coordinate across organizational boundaries?

98. M-Form Organization

Concept

After the pyramid structure, the next step in the evolution of the modern organization is the M-Form, which is constructed by putting several pyramid organizations side-by-side, ^^^, hence the "M" form. Of course, one need not stop at two pyramids, M, one could add as many as one can manage, ^^^^^^. Again, the question is the span of control.[5] Each division is a complete company. How many fully fledged pyramid organizations can a chief executive handle?

Now, if each of those companies also was a conglomerate of several pyramids, we would have a pyramid of pyramids. The "M's" would be growing and getting bigger and bigger. In this larger view, a company becomes a conglomerate with no single focal business, rather multiple businesses in multiple industries. The difficulty in managing something like this is well stimulated in part Peters and Waterman's book, *In Search of Excellence*, in which one of their key principles was "Stick to Your Knitting."[6] The concept was that when an organization diversifies *too much*, it gets into businesses it doesn't really understand or know how to compete effectively. That desire to grow overwhelms the details of success—and is based in the belief that management skills are transferable from one industry to another. They frequently are not.[7,8]

This brings us back to the growth issue.[9,10] Many executives and pundits believe that a company must grow or die. This is a stock-price,

---

[5] http://journals.uchicago.edu/doi/abs/10.1086/467039?journalCode=jle

[6] https://amazon.com/Search-Excellence-Waterman-January-Hardcover/dp/B014GG9H5W/ref=sr_1_2?ie=UTF8&qid=1514649121&sr=8-2&keywords=in+search+of+excellence+tom+peters

[7] https://cambridge.org/core/journals/journal-of-management-and-organization/article/onboarding-externally-hired-executives-avoiding-derailment-accelerating-contribution/D9324122CD5F117E45616F0EEE6E751B

[8] http://gref.org/nuevo/socios/docs2p_priv/hbr_171206_2.pdf

[9] http://emeraldinsight.com/doi/abs/10.1108/eb039992?journalCode=jbs

[10] http://sciencedirect.com/science/article/pii/S0024630198001332

Wall Street oriented perspective. In nature, when one part of an eco-system grows too large, it collapses.[11] Consider wolves and mice in the northern tundra. When wolves overeat, they sow the seeds of their own destruction. When the wolves die off from starvation, the mice proliferate. So in that way, most ecosystems create a natural equilibrium. When humans come in and unwittingly upset that balance, the ecosystems get out of balance.[12]

So, are there limits to the scalability of the M-Form? What do you think? What are your VABEs about growth? Is good management transferable to any kind of organization?

Example

General Electric in the 1990s was a conglomerate of several hundred companies organized into several divisions including jet engines, locomotives, consumer products, financial products, and so on.

One famous example of the lack of transferability of management skills from one industry to another would be the Apple story, in particular, the story of John Sculley's move from Pepsi.[13] Eventually, Steve Jobs was called back to rescue the company.

---

[11]   http://jstor.org/stable/1380725?casa_token=tVAwkqM17NAAAAAA:
j7Lpd4aVbrvYlAuzZYFPC_EiB2AhZl_Zzk8ght2VwqGQhj4_gK4qF-
plkq4eBNnMj7zj5bKHS52Q3bKaWHey4fuGff-pn8sZnPpEflKTV1t-
fQMHACNRc&seq=1#page_scan_tab_contents

[12]   https://books.google.com/books?hl=en&lr=&id=rn8SDAAAQBAJ&oi=f
nd&pg=PA155&dq=wolves+and+mice+balance&ots=I3wL0M1sf3&sig=T_
denTrco-mxlu_lx1F2amwL-J8#v=onepage&q=wolves%20and%20mice%20
balance&f=false

[13]   https://thenextweb.com/apple/2011/08/25/a-look-at-apples-ceos-from-
1977-to-2011/

Diagram

The M-Form Organization

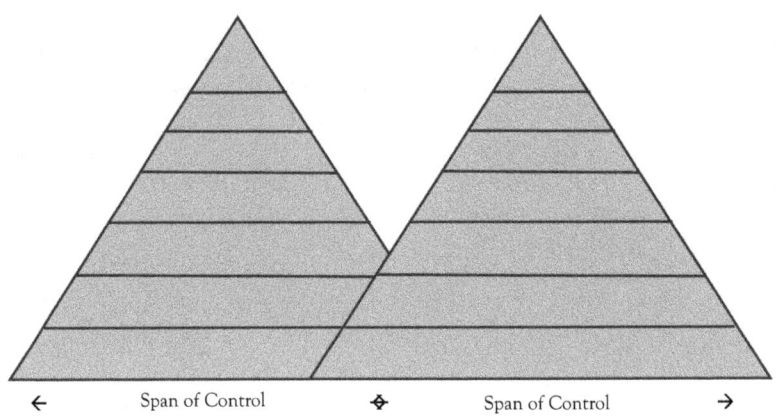

Challenge

1. How many "M's" are there in your company? How are they coordinated, if at all?

2. What functions, if any, should be centralized in an M-Form organization?

3. What are your beliefs about the *grow or die* principle?

4. What are your beliefs about the transportability of executive management skills?

99. The Matrix Organization

Concept

In the post-World War II defense industry, TRW came up with an innovative way to save costs in the development of large budget programs, the matrix organization. The idea was to merge M-Form organizations to reduce redundancies of expensive technical skills like engineers and have those engineers working as needed on more than one program/project at a time. The functional managers would control the talent (engineers), while the program managers (say a missile or an aircraft) would control the budget. The two managers would then negotiate (or have decided for them by management) a pay scale and hours needed.

Matrix organizations ramped up significantly the complexity of large organizations. Now, there were two or more hierarchies, multiple executive managers, and fuzzier lines of authority. Engineers would report to two bosses—the functional manager who would have influence over their careers and the program managers who would have input into their performance reviews and pay scales.

Matrix organizations have a number of benefits when compared to M-Form organizations. Matrices use human resources more efficiently by reducing redundancies and down time, provide financial responsibility to program managers, allow greater customization for customers, reduce costs, raise utilization of key resources, and through the program manager create greater coordination across organizational boundaries.[14]

Matrix organizations also have concomitant difficulties: role ambiguity for technicians and managers, confusion in authority structures, complexity in management, loss of control, fights over control, and susceptibility to economic cycles.[15]

Successful matrix organizations, many of them in the defense industry because of the size and complexity of the programs, rely heavily on their program managers. These people must navigate large organizations

---

[14] https://mckinsey.com/business-functions/organization/our-insights/revisiting-the-matrix-organization

[15] https://hbr.org/1978/05/problems-of-matrix-organizations

and entrepreneurially gather the resources they need to complete their programs. Matrix management skills include salesmanship, good communications, broad perspective, attention to details, budgeting, negotiating, and more. Program managers often have to sell their programs to both internal and external customers.[16] Because of this, they often come from unusual sources and typically not from highly esoteric technical functions.

Example

The Comanche program is a good example of a large program that required the use of a matrix organization ("Organizing the Comanche Program A," Darden Business Publishing, UVA-OB-0432).

Most defense companies employ matrix organizations. These include BAES, Elbit Systems, Northrop Grumman, Lockheed Martin, and more.

A client once was a program manager on a large navy contract. He was recognized as superior among his peers—yet he was hired from the ranks of high school music teachers. Perhaps his ability to lead a band of teenagers stood him in good stead.

Diagram

The Matrix Organization

FUNCTIONS	DESIGN	ENGINEERING	PRODUCTION	MARKETING
PROGRAMS				
Product A	DESIGNER	ENGINEER	MACHINIST	ANALYST
Product B				
Product C				
Product D	←———————	ENGINEER		
Product E				
Product F				

---

[16] https://forbes.com/sites/georgebradt/2017/01/10/%EF%BB%BF12-ways-to-make-matrix-organizations-more-effective/#48bbf89a4066

Challenge

1. Describe any matrix elements in your organization. What are the pros and cons?
2. Would you like to be a matrixed manager? Why or why not?
3. What skills are necessary for a matrixed manager to succeed?

References for Further Reading

1. https://amazon.com/Designing-Matrix-Organizations-that-Actually/dp/0470316314/ref=sr_1_1?s=books&ie=UTF8&qid=1514662061&sr=1-1&keywords=the+matrix+organization
2. https://amazon.com/Matrix-Addison-Wesley-organization-development-Stanley/dp/0201011158/ref=sr_1_2?s=books&ie=UTF8&qid=1514662061&sr=1-2&keywords=the+matrix+organization

100. Organizational Control

Concept

As soon as two people agree to work together, issues of control arise. We introduced this basic concept in an earlier chapter. When there are 200,000 people, the control issues are paramount and more complex, so let's add a little detail. How does one *control* a large organization? Control systems are essential to good management. Good systems are a boon, while badly designed control systems can be worse than nothing.

There are many things to control: budgets, expenses, hiring, firing, promotions, graft and corruption, regulatory compliance, taxation, quality control, culture, and much more.

Accounting is the usual financial control system. Those systems vary widely from firm to firm. Standardized accounting principles in most industrialized nations yield a certain confidence in the accuracy of the numbers reported. Those numbers are important for internal management ("How are we doing?") and for outside investors.

Good control systems have several characteristics:[17,18,19]

1. **Accuracy**. If one cannot trust the data provided by a control system, why have it?
2. **Timeliness**. If the system's data is too old to be of use, why have it? Many control systems are *ex post facto* when what management demands more and more of in the modern world are real-time *in vivo* systems that report results while they can still be altered.
3. **Comprehensiveness**. If a control system overlooks or ignores important parts of the business, one is vulnerable to being blindsided.
4. **Objectivity**. Good control systems are not susceptible to political influences, rather report the data as they are without shadings.

---

[17] http://smallbusiness.chron.com/qualities-effective-control-system-48590.html

[18] http://smallbusiness.chron.com/qualities-effective-control-system-48590.html

[19] https://scribd.com/doc/77854138/Characteristics-of-Effective-Control-Systems

5. **Relevance**. Control systems are built to collect and report data. If the data collected is irrelevant to the running of the business, it is useless.

6. **Fitted to the Organization**. There is no one control system to fit all organizations. One's industry, business, and strategy all influence the design and application of control systems.

7. **Somewhat flexible**. Most businesses will have surprises of one kind or another. A good control system will have enough flexibility built in to *account* for those variations.

8. **Manageability.** Good control systems are manager-friendly; they present in a way that managers can understand and act.

9. **General Acceptance and Approval.** Control systems are designed to give confidence to managers, investors, customers, and regulators alike. Unless they lend general confidence, they are not doing their *job*.

A robust control system is an essential architectural tool for the executive. Given their complexity and all the issues they address, good control systems are a product of intense and evolving design efforts.

Example

One plant manager in the tire business had 64 measurements imposed on him by his management. He felt like he was paralyzed.

The LIBOR scandal in banking was the result of several banks, notably Barclays, submitting false interest rate numbers to the London Interbank Offered Rate offices.[20] A whistleblowing employee reported the behavior.[21] That resulted in the resignation of the Barclays CEO and the layoff of thousands of employees. The control system overlooked a check-and-verify tic on a system that controlled trillions of dollars of derivatives.[22]

---

[20] https://en.wikipedia.org/wiki/Libor_scandal
[21] http://telegraph.co.uk/business/2017/04/10/whistleblowing-scandal-barclays-unfolded/
[22] https://dealbook.nytimes.com/2014/05/15/head-of-barclays-investment-banking-in-asia-to-step-down/

Diagram

Control Systems: Key to Good Management

- Accurate
- Timely
- Comprehensive
- Objective
- Relevant
- Fitted
- Relevant
- Flexible
- Manageable
- Accepted

Challenge

1. What kind of controls do you have on your own life? Health? Finances? Relationships?
2. What controls in your organization do you deal with regularly?
3. What controls are missing in your organization?
4. Where do you draw the line between control and creativity?
5. What kind of controls do you think a government should have on the private sector?
6. Why did unions arise?

101. A General Model of Organizational Architecture

Concept

Edwards Deming,[23] the famous system designer who was widely accepted in Japan before his approach became popular in the United States, once said, "Every organization is perfectly designed to produce the results it's producing." One of the principles of this volume is that executive managers need robust frameworks that are easy to remember, powerful in application, and flexible enough to incorporate new insights. Here, I offer another such framework, a model of how to think about the huge field of *organizational design and architecture.* I will introduce the framework here and then offer some details in subsequent chapters—one concept per chapter.[24]

The elements of the Organizational Architecture Model (OAM) are background factors, leadership philosophy, design decisions, organizational culture, and results. The first broad concept is that the context in which one designs an organization will have a strong influence on the design. The second idea is that the VABEs of the designing executive (including founders and subsequent remodelers) will shape the design. Third, those executives, given their VABEs, make a long series of decisions on a host of systems. Fourth, when you put people into those designs, the resulting collision of behavior becomes the organization's culture. And finally, it's the *culture* that produces the results of the organization.

The overarching impact of this is that leadership only has an *indirect* influence on results through the design decisions they make. Standing on a podium and imploring, shouting, begging, and directing will not overcome the effects of their design decisions. We will explore each of these elements in subsequent chapters.

---

[23] https://en.wikipedia.org/wiki/W._Edwards_Deming
[24] Like all of the concepts in this volume, this one evolves from *Level Three Leadership: Getting Below the Surface, 5th edition,* by James Clawson.

Example

The *Aberdeen Experiment* (UVA-OB-0998), an undisguised case about a defense supplier, describes these elements in detail.

The *SAS Institute A* case (by Jeff Pfeffer at Stanford GSB) does a great job as well introducing all of these elements.

Diagram

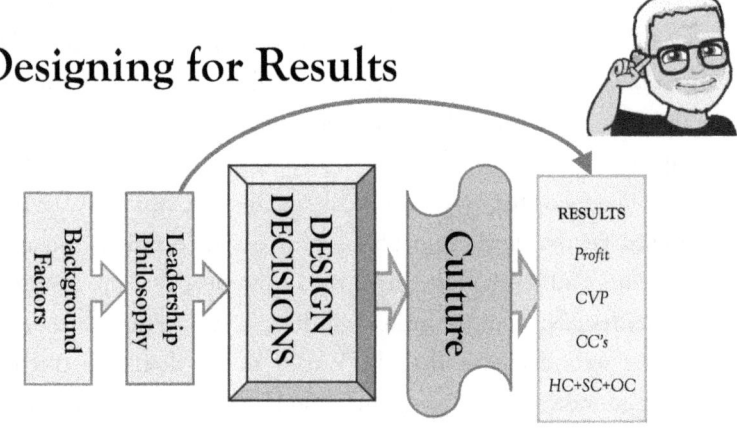

Designing for Results

Challenge

1. How does your organization's design affect its results?
2. What organizational remodeling has your company done recently?
3. How would you describe your organization's culture?

102. Background Factors

Concept

Every organization exists in a context that includes regulatory environment, labor markets, competition, macro and micro economic climates, political backdrop, and many other factors. When one begins to design or redesign an organization, one ignores these factors at their own risk.

Economic conditions will affect numerous elements of design including capital structure, borrowing capacity, investment opportunities, and much more.

Labor markets will affect the ability of the organization to find the kind of employees needed to populate the business.

Proximity to corporate headquarters will affect a plant's ability to innovate new processes.[25]

Awareness of the competitive environment in the company's industry will also affect design decisions.[26]

The political environment will also affect a company's design decisions.[27]

The size of an organization will also affect its design and success. As will the company's customer base. A company with one customer will face different design issues than a company with 1,000 customers or one with one million.

I doubt that any model of background factors would be comprehensive enough to apply to all situations. That said, any executive making design decisions should be aware that the contextual factors surrounding them will affect their results, so they should analyze them carefully as they make design decisions—often without a careful awareness of their own VABEs and the way they shape their assessment of the linkage between background factors and design options.

---

[25] http://tennessean.com/picture-gallery/news/local/williamson/spring-hill/2014/03/23/history-of-saturn-plant-in-spring-hill/6798363/

[26] https://scholar.harvard.edu/files/aghion/files/causal_effects_of_competition.pdf

[27] https://bizfluent.com/info-8377458-effects-political-environment-business-organizations.html

Example

At least one Japanese car manufacturer looking to build a plant in the southeastern part of the United States where wage rates were lower, climate was better, and tax conditions were favorable had to construct an intensive training program in order to bring the skill level of the local labor market up to their standards.[28,29,30]

Coca-Cola found that the introduction of products in Japan was shaped dramatically by the Japanese business context and cultural expectations.[31]

Companies wanting to start businesses in the Middle East must learn many new ways of thinking about organizational design. Sharia law along with different assumptions about payments are but two key issues to understand.[32] I once conducted a seminar for a client in the Middle East and was informed afterward, to my surprise, that I would be paid when the organizer was paid. Final payment didn't arrive until over a year later.

Diagram

Background Factors

ECONOMICS

LABOR POOL

POLITICS

COMPETITION

ARGH!

DESIGN DECISIONS

Challenge

1. What are the important background factors in which you are conducting business?
2. How do they affect your design decisions?

---

[28] https://charlestonbusiness.com/news/automotive/72801/
[29] https://charlestonbusiness.com/news/automotive/72801/
[30] https://toyota.com/usa/tten/
[31] http://coca-colacompany.com/coca-cola-unbottled/innovation-resilience-key-to-coca-cola-heritage-in-japan
[32] https://businessknowhow.com/manage/middleeast.htm

103. Leadership Design VABEs

Concept

The design assumptions of company founders and remodelers have a huge impact on organizational design. Some of these assumptions will be explicit; the owners will be aware of these. Others will be implicit; the owners will be unaware of these. If an executive believes in *one man, one boss*, that will affect his or her decisions. If an executive believes in *less than 10 subordinates*, that will affect the design.

Some other design related assumptions include the following:

1. The organization should *face* its customers.
2. We need to be 100 percent sure our employees don't do anything unethical or illegal.
3. Our competitive advantage has been and will be delivering the highest product quality.
4. We will only hire the smartest people.
5. We will let our people hire from their alma maters.
6. People respond to financial incentives.
7. Everyone is upwardly motivated; everyone wants to be and should want to be promoted.
8. We should organize ourselves around self-leading teams.
9. A little bit of fear is good.
10. We owe our employees' stability of employment (or not).
11. Reducing cost is more important than any *implied contract* to our older employees.
12. We should avoid paying as much tax as we possibly can.
13. Too many layers slow down our decision making.
14. That's the way we have always done it and that's the way we will continue doing it.
15. One should never act without getting permission first.
16. We will be the industry leader, not the second follower.

And so on. Hundreds of VABEs about how an organization should look and work. Hundreds of them unexamined, even with hundreds of them explicitly stated.

Example

Bob Lancaster, the founder of the Aberdeen Plant at FMC had several unusual VABEs.[33] They included these:

- People should be able to work without fear. I want an organization devoid of fear.
- Peer groups create as much fear as management.
- People talk mindlessly in ways that make others defensive.
- Skill is easier to teach than attitude.
- Not everyone wants to be promoted.
- We should pay people for their skills, not their time, seniority, or piecemeal production.
- We should hire people based on their personalities more than on their skills.
- We want people who are learners, problem solvers, team players, and initiators.
- We should let teams decide whom to hire and who will lead them.
- We should let people decide how long and when they will work.
- Choice is more powerful and energizing than obligation.
- People should *own* their work.
- Not everyone can work in an environment that emphasizes choice and ownership.
- People need to know everything about the business if they are to own it.
- Our organization should allow for natural human tendency.

With those assumptions in mind, Lancaster built an extra-ordinary organization that has persisted with high profits, high customer satisfaction, low turnover, high productivity, high quality, and frequent benchmarking from others for four generations of leadership. Two of

---

[33] Clawson, J. n.d. *The Aberdeen Experiment*. UVA-OB-0998, Darden Business Publishing.

those CEOs appeared in my seminars in which I was teaching that case—and confirmed the accuracy and comprehensiveness of the material.

Diagram

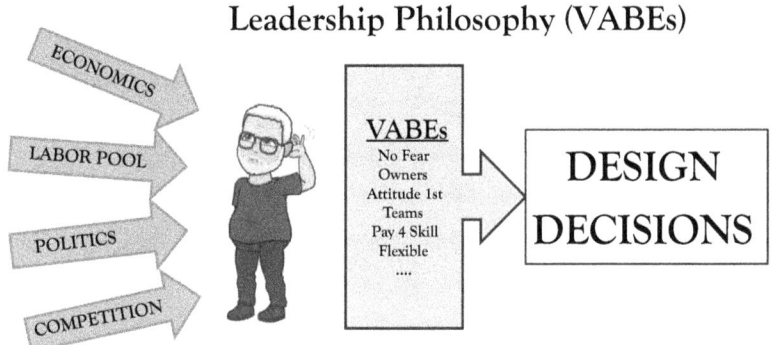

Leadership Philosophy (VABEs)

Challenge

1. Write down as many of your design VABEs as possible. You can begin by agreeing or disagreeing with the ones listed above.
2. Based on both policy (stated VABEs) and behavior (implicit VABEs), what are the apparent design VABEs in your organization?
3. How, if at all, do your design VABEs differ from those apparent in your organization?

104. Design Decisions

Concept

Every organization has been *designed* either consciously or unconsciously. Decisions are made from the beginning about a multitude of things only one of which is organizational structure. We can compare the reporting structure of an organization to a skeleton and the various systems that hang on that structure to the organs and muscles that hang on a skeleton.

There are too many design decisions to enumerate them all here. A cursory list would include structure, recruiting, hiring, job design, control, performance appraisal, reward, learning, design, research, production, quality, and marketing.

Example

One company hires from employees' alma maters while another advertises widely. One company outsources design activities while another hires internal designers. One company pays by the hour while another pays by output. One company has 10 layers top to bottom while another company has three. One company gives year-end bonuses while another does not. One company lobbies legislators while another doesn't. One company has an automated assembly line while another uses autonomous teams. And on and on and on and on.

Diagram

SO Many Design Decisions

- Recruiting
- Hiring
- Work
- Control
- Research
- Marketing
- Production
- Etc....

Challenge

1. Identify 20 systems in your company.
2. Assess each system in terms of its usefulness.
3. How if at all would you remodel those systems?
4. If you were starting your own business, what are the first 10 systems you would design?

105. Human Resource Related Systems

Concept

Every organization, consciously or not, deals with a predictable set of human resource related systems. Those are:

1. **Recruiting**. Where are we going to look for our next candidates?
2. **Selection**. How will we select from among all the candidates we generate?
3. **Hiring**. How will we hire people?
4. **On-Boarding**. How will we introduce new hires to our way of doing things?
5. **Work Design**. What kind of work will we give our employees to do?
6. **Performance Appraisal**. How will we assess the performance of our people?
7. **Rewards**. How will we reward or compensate our people?
8. **Learning**. What kind of training and learning opportunities will we offer?
9. **Outplacement**. How will we terminate unsatisfactory employees?

This list pertains only to human resource systems. Some companies ignore various pieces like on-boarding or what academics call *socialization*.[34] Others will have an intensive on-boarding process designed to bring people *up-to-speed* quickly. The point is that every organization, whether they attend to them or not, must deal with these nine processes.

Example

SAS Institute in Cary, NC often hired single working mothers because they worked hard, were dependable, and did good work.[35]

John Van Maanen and Ed Schein in the MIT Organizational Behavior group described a process for organizational socialization. (See endnote.)

---

34 https://dspace.mit.edu/bitstream/handle/1721.1/1934/?sequence=1
35 *SAS Institute A* by Jeff Pfeffer, Stanford GSB.

Employees in the BAES Aberdeen plant are paid by skill while sales people in many organizations are paid a base salary (high or low) and a commission bonus.

Assembly line workers typically do a short list of tasks while pod-based production systems require employees to be skilled at a wide range of tasks.

Diagram

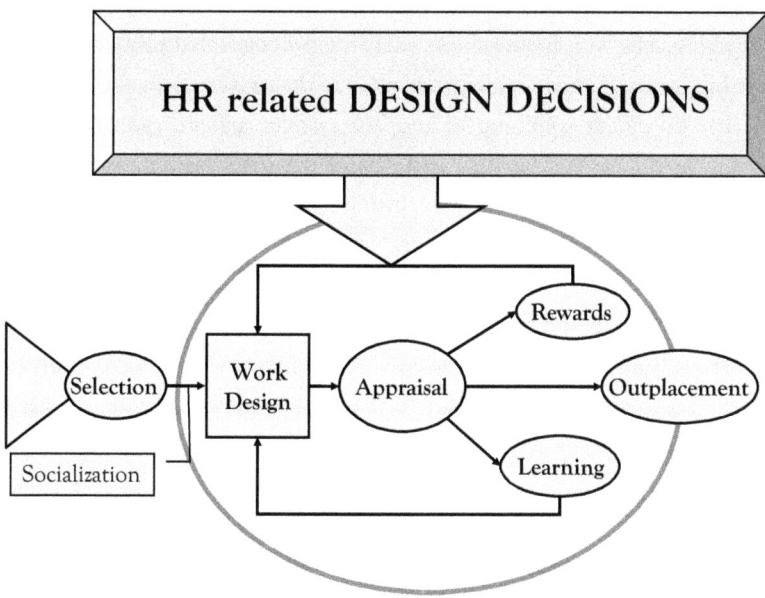

Challenge

1. Describe your organization's hiring process. What are its strengths and weaknesses? What is its error rate?
2. How much latitude do you and your colleagues have in what you do in your job?
3. How often and how are you and your colleagues assessed?
4. What learning opportunities does your organization offer?
5. How are you and your colleagues compensated? How effective is that system?

106. Systems Theory and Organizational Behavior

Concept

The broader concept of *systems theory* informs our view of organizational design. Many opined on the *necessary systems* in organizations.[36,37] James Thompson's classic book also informs us.[38]

In Thompson's view, organizations have several common systems: boundary spanning in, adaptive, production, managerial, maintenance, and boundary spanning out. In this view, we can think of organizations like living cells with membranes. There are processes that bring things in, get things out, and several internal systems that govern behavior.

The boundary spanning in and out systems are processes by which people or materiel move into and out of the organization. For human resources, these would include recruiting and outplacement. For materiel they include procurement (supply chain is a whole discipline) and distribution.

The adaptive subsystem faces the background factors mentioned earlier and guides the organization in its resistance to or adaptation to external forces. The managerial subsystem *controls* or instructs the other subsystems in their activities.

The maintenance subsystem strives to coordinate all of the other systems and to ensure that the organization internally has what it needs to function. The adaptive subsystem focuses on external forces, the maintenance subsystem focuses on internal forces.

The production subsystem does the *work* of the organization whether that be service execution or physical manufacturing.

Thompson's perspective gives us a nice high-level view of what's happening in organizations and thus a reminder of meta-systems we should be thinking about.

---

[36] https://bizfluent.com/info-8509346-types-organizational-systems.html
[37] http://springer.com/us/book/9783642191084
[38] Thompson, J. 1967. *Organizations in Action*. McGraw Hill.

Example

- How does Proctor & Gamble or General Mills decide what new products to bring to market?
- How does General Electric coordinate and share information internally?
- How does Northrop Grumman adapt to changing demands from their customers amidst a stern regulatory environment?

Diagram

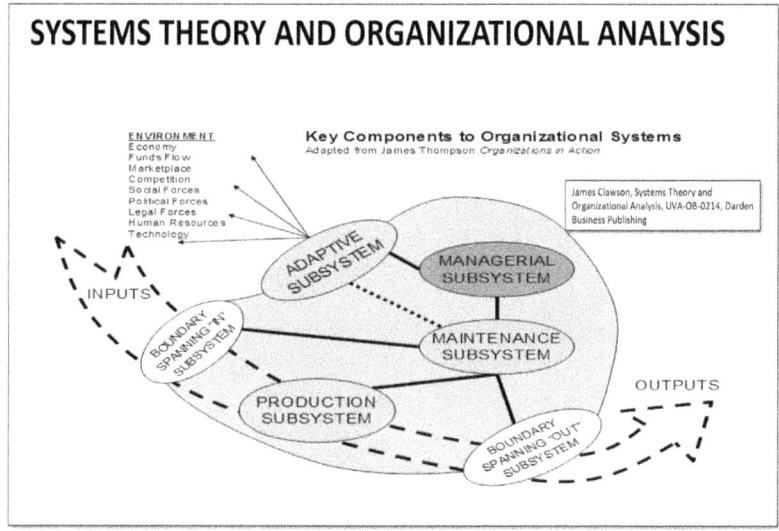

Challenge

1. Describe your organization's supply chain.
2. Describe your organization's distribution system.
3. Describe your organization's maintenance system.
4. Describe your organization's adaptive system.
5. What if any changes would you recommend?

107. Recruitment and Selection

Concept

The decision to bring people into your organization is one of the most important decisions you make. Because they are the people who will implement your purpose, vision, and strategy, and because once in, it's harder to get them out.

There are several phases to *hiring*. First is recruitment. How do you develop a pool of reasonable candidates from which to choose? You can advertise, but that will get you a wide range of candidates many of whom are not at all suitable. Recruiters may get hundreds of resumes a day from advertising and then they have to sift through them. You could use an online recruiting service,[39] but then you are delegating the winnowing of your pool to someone else. You could rely on current successful alumni to recruit for you at their alma maters, but then you may be unnecessarily limiting your scope, plus you are putting recent graduates who are not professional recruiters on the front line of an important function. You could send a cadre of recruiters to the top schools, but then there is significant expense attendant. You could delegate your recruitment to a recruiting firm who will interview you about desired characteristics and then do the pool generation and winnowing for you. Big data techniques are becoming more popular as firms try to sift through multiple sources and large pools of *matches*.[40] Finally, more and more companies are using social media to find good candidates.[41]

Second is selection. Once you have a reasonably manageable pool of candidates, how do you winnow and finally select the *right* candidate. Most companies use a variety of interviews, remote and on-site at headquarters. These interviews might include psychological testing, one-on-one, one-on-many, presentations, or action/behavioral assessments. All of which can be and often is intimidating to the young candidate.

---

[39] https://inc.com/john-rampton/9-ways-to-recruiting-top-talent-that-grow-businesses.html

[40] https://thebalance.com/data-driven-decision-making-to-improve-recruiting-4153980

[41] https://betterteam.com/social-recruiting-tips

Psychological testing attempts to measure key personality characteristics requested by the employer. One-on-many interviews save time for the employer and may be used intentionally to measure reaction to stress. Behavioral interviews may include time in job, problem solving, and time with teammates to see how candidates actually think and work.[42]

One thing many recruiters and candidates overlook is how well the candidate knows him or herself and how well they can present that knowledge in the midst of the recruiting processes. Candidates who try to "fake it until they make it"[43] or who don't know what they really want/need to succeed can make the process even more difficult than it inherently is. A candidate who has taken a course like "Self-Assessment and Career Development"[44] and has a data-based list durable *life themes* is well-armed and deeply prepared to be a ***partner*** in the recruiting process—in which the goal is to find a good ***fit*** between candidate skills and employers' job demands. When either candidate or recruiter enter interviews believing that the other is trying to deceive the other, it's hard to find good fits.

Recruiting deception is not limited to candidates trying to *give them what they want*. Recruiters also try to put their *best foot* forward, and in so doing, too often disappoint new hires who find out later that the full-court press including time with the C-Level officers was just for the courtship—and evaporates post marriage. The realization of having been *had* or manipulated is not a good way for any relationship to begin.

I once made a study of recruiter forms. They varied from a blank page to 10 pages of detailed criteria.[45]

The hiring process is not over when an offer is made. Both sides still need to hammer out the details. There are lots of details. Things like signing bonuses, moving expenses, health care, vacation time, working

---

[42] https://thebalance.com/behavioral-interviews-525761

[43] I've had MBA students declare this as their strategy in job-hunting and early career financial success. I always advised against this approach and was surprised at how many students adopt this avenue.

[44] https://faculty.darden.virginia.edu/clawsonj/FindingFIT.html

[45] Clawson, J. et al. 1990. Chapter 27 "Interviewing." In *Self-Assessment and Career Development*, 3 ed. Englewood Cliffs: NJ, Prentice-Hall.

conditions, location, salary, immediate boss,[46] and more. Once both parties agree to those details, and a handshake or signature is given, the candidate is *in*. He or she has crossed the organizational boundary/ membrane and gone inside.

Third is on-boarding or socialization. Once a new hire arrives at work, many things begin. Whether they are planned or not varies widely from firm to firm. Where does the candidate go?[47] Oh, there's fingerprinting? Papers to sign for health care and retirement funds? Meeting your boss? Getting supplies? Learning what's acceptable behavior and what's not? How to dress? Where the rest rooms are? Cafeteria? Fitting into the corporate culture. This process, partly planned, partly not planned, goes on until the new hire feels that they have become aware of how to work in the firm. That might take weeks, months, or years. Dalton, Thompson, and Price called this stage the *apprenticeship*.[48] Employers might say it has a finite end, however, in reality, the end of the socialization process is usually not recognized on either side. It just emerges into awareness when one day the newbie is no longer a newbie—and recruitment is over.

Example

A student in my careers class one fall came to me late term and said, "I had a job when I came back from my summer internship. I got a huge signing bonus. After developing my life themes and using them to analyze my job, I've realized I've made a bad decision. I've sent back my signing bonus and informed the firm that I won't be coming. I wish I'd had this information before I went recruiting." That was a big event for that student and for me. It underscored the importance of the well-informed partnership necessary in effective recruiting. [49]

---

[46] Dissatisfaction with bosses is the cause of enormous financial and energy losses and turnover, https://usnews.com/news/blogs/data-mine/2015/04/03/why-workers-hate-their-bosses

[47] You would think this would be a no brainer, but I have had many MBA students who reported for work and no one knew they were coming and had no space for them.

[48] https://sciencedirect.com/science/article/pii/009026167790033X

[49] https://blog.capterra.com/top-15-recruiting-statistics-2014/

Another student called me six months into his job complaining that despite the excitement he had while interviewing with the chief executive and the fancy dinners, he was now stuck in a small windowless room with a boring assignment and wishing he had paid more attention to the *details* instead of the prestige and money.

Diagram

Hiring: Recruitment, Selection & On-boarding

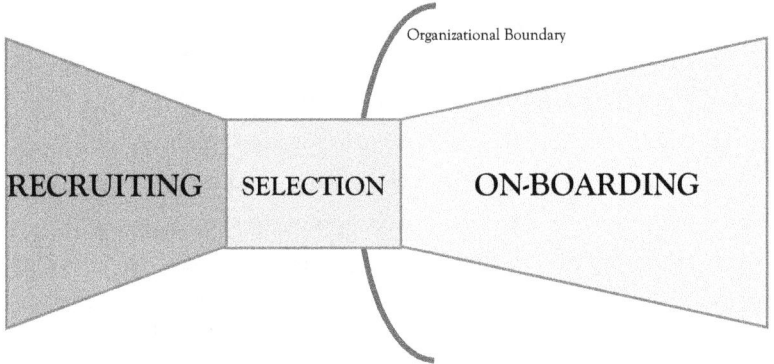

Challenge

1. Describe your organization's recruiting process.
2. Describe your company's selection process.
3. Describe your company's socialization process.
4. What is the average job satisfaction rating of your company's employees?
5. How if at all would you modify those processes?

108. Job Design

Concept

An important element of organizational architecture is job design. What kind of work do you give your employees to do? Yes, it varies widely. And, what are the typical parameters? What parameters do you imagine make a difference in job design?[50]

Hackman and Lawler[51] gave us what has become the classic model of job design. The elements of their model were:

1. **Variety**. Jobs with more variety were more interesting and engaging to people than those that were narrow and repetitive.
2. **Task Identity.** The *wholeness* of the task so that workers could see the whole of what they were doing.
3. **Task Significance.** The perceived importance of the job. Trivial jobs were less engaging.
4. **Autonomy.** The more choice workers had the more engaged they were.
5. **Direct Feedback.** Workers wanted to know how well they were doing from the work itself.

The premise was that any job could be diagnosed on these five dimensions and that varying these dimensions would affect worker/employee satisfaction with the work. Subsequent research showed that *variety* and *autonomy* were the most important of the five. The authors created a job richness score[52] based on their diagnostic tool calculated by:

$$MPS = (\text{Variety} + \text{Identity} + \text{Significance}) \times (\text{Autonomy}) \times (\text{Job Feedback})$$

I wonder how many candidates and recruiters look at the first assignment for a new hire and assess those five dimensions. I am guessing it's a

---

[50] See Turner, A., and P. Lawrence. 1965. *Industrial Jobs and the Worker.* HBS Publishing.

[51] Hackman, J.R., and E.E. Lawler. 1971. "Employee Reactions to Job Characteristics." *Journal of Applied Psychology Monograph* 55, pp. 259–286.

[52] More recently, Hackman, J.R, and G.R. Oldham. 1975. "Development of the Job Diagnostic Survey." *Journal of Applied Psychology* 60, pp. 159–170.

very low number. I believe that over the last 40 years of my career, autonomy has improved, but I am not sure.[53],[54] At least one study suggests that autonomy is important worldwide not just in the United States.[55]

Example

Automobile assembly line workers in the first half of the 20th century were notoriously frustrated by low variety, low autonomy, and lack of direct feedback. (Was that bolt fully seated?) Indeed, Henry Ford designed those jobs to be more suited to robots, which eventually took them over.

What about brick laying? Highly repetitive, not a lot of variety, but good identity and feedback.

Management? One could argue that the more responsible and multi-functional the job, the more the job maxes out on these five dimensions. And I have on tape an interview with a powerful corporate attorney who argues that the significance of his job (Which company will make more money?) paled in comparison to his volunteer work at the Chicago Park District.

Diagram

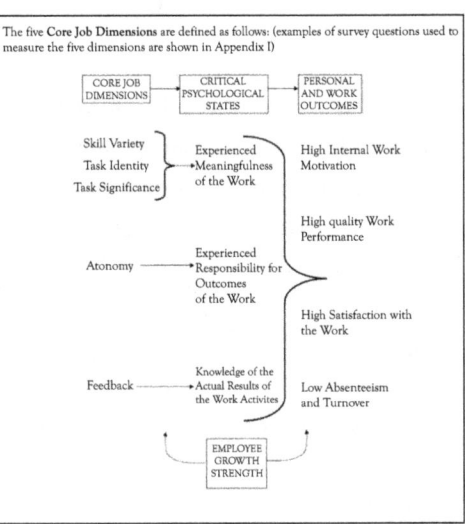

---

[53] http://journals.sagepub.com/doi/abs/10.1177/089124191020001003
[54] http://journals.sagepub.com/doi/abs/10.1177/001872679104400102
[55] https://link.springer.com/chapter/10.1007/978-90-481-9667-8_8

Challenge

1. Rate your job 1 to 10 on all five dimensions
   a. Variety
   b. Identity
   c. Significance
   d. Autonomy
   e. Real Feedback
2. How do your company's jobs *rate* on average? How could you find out?
3. If it were your company, how would you manage the design of work?

109. Performance Appraisal

Concept

Every organization needs to assess internal and external performance in some way. External performance is usually left to the financial reports. Earlier, I recommended an adaptation to the Kaplan & Norton Balanced Scorecard as a better, more robust way of assessing external results by mixing in internal capabilities and intangible asset pools (human, social, and organizational).

Measuring internal results, employee performance or core capability performance, is also critical to constant improvement and dependability. How does one measure individual and team performance? Most companies use a periodic, top-down (now modified with some peer and subordinate *360°* feedback) performance appraisal system. These typically involve filling out forms, gathering *data*, making judgments, having interviews, getting signatures, and submitting to a human resource function. This usually occurs at all levels and in a repeated cycle annually. The forms may have a scale usually with five or ten points on various dimensions. CollierBroderick, a consulting firm, suggests 10 dimensions: quantity, quality, punctuality, efficiency, customer impact, self-reliance, department contribution, work habits, learning, and compliance.[56] That's a reasonable list; every company has their own.

Jack Welch famously used a nine cell grid to assess his managers on dimensions of performance and style. He separated those reviews so that the style/process half got equal billing as tangible results. That, of course, doubled the time and energy put into performance evaluation. One could argue that's appropriate when one relies on executives to get things done. What could be more important than working with your incumbent leaders? The GE system reinforces a point made in the literature: performance reviews should be both evaluative and developmental.[57]

---

[56] See, for example, https://collierbroderick.ie/info-centre/hr/performance-management/10-performance-dimensions/

[57] For example, http://smallbusiness.chron.com/purpose-performance-appraisal-systems-1921.html

To that end, we could summarize some key points for assessor and assessee like this:

Giving Feedback	Receiving Feedback
Intend to HELP?	Don't be defensive
Understandable?	Seek clarifications
Willing to receive?	Summarize for accuracy
Specific?	Express your feelings at the END
Doable?	Confirm with others
Recent?	It's just data
Trusted?	You decide who you are
Caring?	
Descriptive not just judgmental?	

Well . . . Jim Goodnight at SAS Institute has another view. With regard to performance reviews, he said in essence, nobody likes to give them, nobody likes to receive them, they tend to be *after the fact*, they tend to be inaccurate, they tend to be heavily skewed to recent events, AND they cost a lot to do. So, he said, we aren't going to do them. And he doesn't.[58] And his company has outperformed its competitors significantly.

Pundits of all kinds have argued long and hard about the pros and cons of positive and negative feedback.[59] The positivist research stream pushes giving positive feedback only saying that negative feedback is not helpful. Others argue for negative feedback.[60]

It seems that there are different skills involved in giving and receiving feedback. You might be interested in two technical notes I wrote, "Some Principles of Giving and Receiving Feedback" (UVA-OB-0322)[61] and "360* Systems." (UVA-OB-0861) By the way, we talk about 360* systems that gather feedback from peers and subordinates as well as bosses. We should talk about *spherical systems* that also gather feedback from suppliers and customers.

---

[58] Jeff Pfeffer, "SAS Institute A," Stanford GSB.
[59] http://nytimes.com/2013/04/06/your-money/how-to-give-effective-feedback-both-positive-and-negative.html
[60] For example, https://hbr.org/2013/09/the-benefits-of-negative-feedback
[61] Adapted from a note by Anderson, J. n.d. "Giving and Receiving Feedback." Internal Document of Proctor & Gamble Corporation.

Example

One of my former students was kind enough to write a fairly detailed account of his first performance review after graduating with his MBA.[62] He reported a common phenomenon: major surprise. He had been given a 5 percent raise and couldn't believe that his efforts weren't more valued than that.

We have been in an interesting situation on occasion where the state mandated annual performance reviews but had no resources with which to give raises—so the exercise was time- and energy-consuming but irrelevant.

Another system I am aware of sends out short notes with an outline of raises but eschews personal conversations. So, one in that system didn't get any details on what went into the percent raise calculation.

Diagram

<u>Performance Appraisals</u>

- Results?
- Style Development?
- When?
- From whom? 360*?
- Accuracy? Recency effect?
- Transparency?
- Cost?
- Usefulness?

Performance Reviews

<u>Giving Feedback</u>
- Intended to help?
- Understandable?
- Willing to receive?
- Doable?
- Specific?
- Recent?
- Trustworthy?
- Do I care?
- Descriptive not evaluative?
- Timing?

<u>Receiving Feedback</u>
- Don't be defensive.
- Seek clarification
- Summarize for accuracy
- Express your feelings at the end
- Confirm with others
- It's just data
- You decide who you are.

---

[62] "My First Annual Review," UVA-PACS-0082, Darden Publishing.

Challenge

1. Describe the best performance review you have received. The worst?
2. Describe your feelings about giving and receiving performance reviews.
3. What are the most important principles, to you, of giving and receiving feedback?

110. Reward Systems

Concept

How are you going to reward your people? Money? Stock options? More benefits? (Pensions, health care, dental care, etc.) Promotion? Pride of purpose? Recognition? Gold stars? More time off? Do you let them decide what they want or do you decide what you will offer? Or some balance of both? Do you want to pay more than your competition or less? That will affect the quality of talent you attract.

You have to reward them *somehow*. Your appraisal system (see the last chapter) will inform how much you *want* to reward them. Reward systems are difficult to design well; there are many considerations.[63] Here are some options:

1. Pay by the hour.
2. Pay by output.
3. Pay by commission.
4. Pay annual salary.
5. Pay for skill.
6. Pay for time.
7. Add flexible work schedule.
8. Add health care benefits (general, eye, dental, etc.)
9. Add ownership options.
10. Pay with stock. (Beware, stock price can vary widely.)
11. Add recognition. (Company newsletters, podcasts, executive speeches)
12. Add bonuses.
13. Add expensive pre-paid vacations.

And the possibilities are endless.

The issue is tied up broadly in the huge field of *motivation*. Why do people do what they do? What would make them do what I want them to do? How much is genetic? How much is learned? How much is internal?

---

[63] http://accaglobal.com/content/dam/acca/global/PDF-students/2012s/sa_jan13_p5_reward_a.pdf

How much is outside-in? Why are some people goal-oriented and others are not? Who should set those goals?[64]

Herzberg argued that money is only a *hygiene* factor—after a certain level, more money doesn't mean much.[65] Yet I know executives who have hundreds of millions and still seek to make more. They seem to enjoy the deal making rather than counting.[66] Who *needs* their second hundred million much less second billion?

Victor Vroom argued that a person's energy will be affected by how much they *value* a reward times the *probability* of getting that reward. Expectancy Theory remains a big influencer of reward system designers.[67] Expectancy Theory says that you must account for the *value* of any reward to the recipient. (The "V" in VABEs.) Steve Covey argued for *win-win* reward systems in which boss and subordinate negotiated performance contracts and then everyone who fulfilled their contracts got the rewards.[68]

How much should you pay people? How much should you spend on their working conditions? Benefits? What kind of reward system would you design?

Example

Howard Schulz once noted in a speech to a group of marketers in San Francisco in 2002 that when Starbucks was a small company with 10 stores and 100 employees, he wanted to give his *part-time* (Transitory) employees stock options and comprehensive medical benefits. The reason he noted was based on an incident when he was seven and his

---

[64] See the classic article by Levinson, H. n.d. "Management by Whose Objectives?" https://hbr.org/2003/01/management-by-whose-objectives

[65] See his classic article, "One More Time: How do you Motivate Employees?", https://hbr.org/2003/01/one-more-time-how-do-you-motivate-employees

[66] https://forbes.com/forbes/welcome/?toURL=https://forbes.com/billionaires/&refURL=https://google.com/&referrer=https://google.com/

[67] http://yourcoach.be/en/employee-motivation-theories/vroom-expectancy-motivation-theory.php

[68] Covey, S.A. 1989. *Seven Habits of Highly Effective People*. Rosetta (latest edition after 1989).

father was injured at work.[69] Imagine you were on the Board of Directors when Howard walked in and asked for this. How would you have voted? (No one else is doing it, it's expensive, and these are part-time baristas!)

In my first OB class in business school, Steve Covey gave us performance contracts. There were lists of things to learn in order to earn Cs, Bs, and As. There were significant differences between the lists. Each student chose what they wanted to work for, and committed. In essence, students *chose* the reward they wanted—and how hard they wanted to work.

Diagram

<u>Reward Systems</u>

Challenge

1. What do you like/dislike about your current compensation system?
2. How would you remodel it if at all?
3. If it were your company, how would you design the reward system?

---

[69] Film recording of the event made by Linkage, Inc.

111. Learning Systems

Concept

Arie deGeus and Jack Welch agree: *learning* is the main if not the only source of sustainable strategic competitive advantage. Organizations who want to avoid becoming ossified bureaucracies must learn how to learn and make it a habit. Without learning systems, companies become dinosaurs. Many scholars including Peter Senge at MIT have worked hard in defining and creating learning organizations.[70] Senge argued that there were five key elements in the creation of a learning organization: Personal Mastery, New Mental Models, Team Building, Building Shared Visions, and Systems Thinking. Marcia Conner and I convened a conference at one point in which scholars working on learning organizations shared their insights. The conference proceedings and invited papers are included in *Creating a Learning Culture.*[71] McGill and Slocum asserted powerfully that organizations who learn have to *unlearn* many of the things they had *learned* historically.[72]

There are many ways to learn organizationally:

1. **Hire younger people** from different disciplines. Of course, if you socialize them into your way of doing things, you just negate the value of new and diverse hires.
2. Support **Off Site Education** short and degree programs. This can be expensive and there's no guarantee that people will stay after they finish the program and get their degrees. The U.S. military does this but with a commitment of some number of years after graduation. With regard to short (1–21 days) programs, what are the odds that a one week program off-site will change the behavior of the home company the other 51 weeks?

---

[70] Peter Senge's model is presented quickly here: https://toolshero.com/management/five-disciplines-learning-organizations/ See his original work, *The Fifth Discipline: The Art and Practice of the Learning Organization*, Crown, 1990, 2010 (for later edition).

[71] Conner, M., and J. Clawson, ed. 2004. *Creating a Learning Culture.* Cambridge University Press.

[72] McGill & Slocum. 1993. "Unlearning the Organization." *Organizational Dynamics*, Autumn.

3. **Rotational assignments**. Many companies use this approach, accepting lower levels of productivity while people rotate through various functions and locations to learn the scope of the business.

4. **In-House Training.** This is more focused than open-enrollment programs offered by consulting firms and business schools, and it requires the expense of hiring in-house designers and trainers. Some companies develop their own *universities* with comprehensive facilities and curricula to address their *unique* needs. One potential pitfall is that the focus of in-house designs tends to be repetitive and inbred; one could argue for more outside intercourse to ensure innovation.

5. **Open Enrollment Outside Training.** These programs are usually offered by business schools and are focused on a topic rather than on a company. Participants from many companies attend further fertilizing the insight of each individual. Some of these programs orient toward *experiential* learning—high ropes, low ropes, raft building, crew rowing, hiking, and so on. These programs also wrestle with the "what's my return?" questions.

6. **Customized Outside Training.** These are offered by consulting firms and business school executive education programs. Every group has a distinctive set of skills and educational VABEs so this approach, too, can become repetitive.

7. **Hiring Executives from Other Industries.** New leadership can instigate change and new insight. If only one person comes, however, the odds are that the existing culture will continue to dominate. And the outside other-industry perspective may not be appropriate for your company.

8. **Action Learning Programs.** Here, companies engage instructors to help employees work on real projects sponsored by internal managers. This provides participants the opportunity to learn about various parts of the company in a direct way, supposedly raising efficiency levels. Chris Argyris of the Harvard School of Education was a major proponent of this approach.[73]

---

[73] https://en.wikipedia.org/wiki/Chris_Argyris

9. **Create a "Learning Culture."** This approach has perhaps the biggest promise of results and requires the most comprehensive effort from the top to the bottom.

There are other learning systems, some of them hybrids of a combination of those listed above. Companies invested in learning often develop a curricular grid with organizational level on the rows and topics on the columns. Finding the right programs for each cell in the grid is important—and the more cells one populates, the more expensive it becomes.

Companies are rightfully concerned about the return-on-investment with learning systems. How much return do we get from these programs? Do people really learn? (See the chapter on Habituality.) How is that learning manifest, if at all, in improved corporate results? Most companies use post-program participant evaluations as a primary indicators. Meanwhile, clients and providers alike strive to find better ways.[74]

These investments in a company's human capital pool will largely be a waste of time and money unless the topics are directly related to developing and fertilizing the company's core capabilities as outlined above in the chapters on Results and Strategy Maps.

Example

General Electric has been a leader in in-house corporate education. Its facility in Crotonville, NY included a leading edge facility with a variety of learning rooms, team discussion *break out* rooms, a hotel and a restaurant to serve their participants. Jack himself noted, "An organization's ability to learn—and [rapidly] turn that learning into action—is the ultimate competitive advantage."

---

[74] https://books.google.com/books?hl=en&lr=&id=yZFHBAAAQBAJ&oi=fnd &pg=PR4&dq=evaluating+corporate+training+programs&ots=GMmxXHTHp E&sig=pVPoxnE2aAYZGsaSliaeqN5PQ-Q#v=onepage&q=evaluating%20cor- porate%20training%20programs&f=false

Some companies outsource the cost of facilities to university business school organizations like Harvard, Duke, or the Darden School.[75] [76]

The BAES Aberdeen plant referred to earlier has a powerful learning culture.

Diagram

Change and Learning

In a world of change, **learners** will inherit the earth, while the **learned** shall find themselves perfectly suited for a world that no longer exists.

Eric Hoffer, Ordeal of Change

Challenge

1. Describe your personal learning habits. Do you have a personal learning strategy?
2. Describe the learning activities in your company. How are they integrated? How do they apply to your strategic core capabilities?
3. What gaps can you identify in your corporate learning systems? If it were up to you, how would you fill those gaps?

---

[75] https://ft.com/content/1e17b87e-2c47-11e7-bc4b-5528796fe35c

[76] https://businessbecause.com/news/mba-rankings/3973/the-top-50-schools-for-executive-education

112. Organizational Culture

Concept

Culture is a set of shared VABEs. The VABEs can have to do with lots of things: food, dress, manners, religion, laws, marriage, relationships, business, and more. Organizations have cultures, too. And those cultures are enormously influential in the firm's results. Effective executives understand and manage organizational culture. Lou Gerstner at IBM noted that culture wasn't part of the problem, it **was** the problem.

Culture is what happens when you put people in your organizational design. People react to the organizations into which they are put, we could say they *collide* with the design. While your organizational architecture will influence organizational culture, it is the culture that produces results as we introduced above.

People tend to try to describe organizational culture in single words like patriarchal, rigid, staid, and so on. Ed Schein asserted, and I agree, that a more robust description comes from a listing of the underlying assumptions evident in behavior.[77] Ed visited our school once and walking around began making notes on its apparent cultural features. A skilled observer, he gleaned a page and a half of VABEs describing how we functioned in a day and half.

In my consulting practice, I have visited dozens and dozens of companies. Some of the more common cultural VABEs I have noticed are:

1. Professionals will do what they have to do regardless of how they feel.
2. You must get permission before you act.
3. My superiors don't seem to know what's going on down here, management does not care about us.
4. We don't have a clear purpose or direction, management doesn't know where we are going.
5. Management knows best.
6. We protect our own data and clients—even from each other.

---

[77] Schein, E. 2016. *Organizational Culture and Leadership*, 5th ed. Jossey-Bass/Wiley.

7. It's okay to yell and scream at your subordinates.
8. Smiles and laughter indicate a lack of seriousness.
9. We only hire and promote white men.
10. Management is just trying to make their numbers whether they reflect reality or not.
11. We love this company because of the benefits.
12. Documentation takes too much time and energy; paperwork is odious.
13. We never say anything negative about anyone—in public.
14. Information is on a "need to know" basis only.
15. Slow down, you are making the rest of us look bad.
16. Never leave the office before the boss and even then; expect to spend all nighters.
17. The way you dress reflects your value to the firm.
18. Rank has its privileges.
19. Good ideas only come from the top.
20. We are the best and all we need to do is keep doing what we've been doing.

What would be the implicit VABEs of your organizational culture?

Example

One company doesn't accept returns, another pays for postage in both directions.

One company has *table thumping debates*, while another never raises voices or directs personal criticism.[78]

One company organizes internal focus groups to gather information while another tells employees what to do based on management's perceptions alone.

One company allows managers to manage as entrepreneurs while another requires approvals for all expenses.

---

[78] Descriptions on taped clips accompanying "The Life and Career of a Divisional CEO: Bob Johnson at Honeywell," UVA-OB-0872.

Peter Browning at Continental White Cap[79] had a significant impact on the White Cap culture by changing one thing in their management meetings. Instead of listening to complaints about how much better things were in the good old days, he refused to tolerate complaints *unless* the speaker had done his homework and came with a well-thought out proposal for how to fix the issues in question. This one thing changed the way senior executives thought about their work and *taught* them to stop complaining unless they had designed a reasonable solution. THAT one thing alone builds bench strength. Companies who complain that they don't have enough leaders coming up should review their own management culture as mindlessly conveyed by their superiors who tolerate whining.

Diagram

Organizational Culture is the result of putting people in your design ...

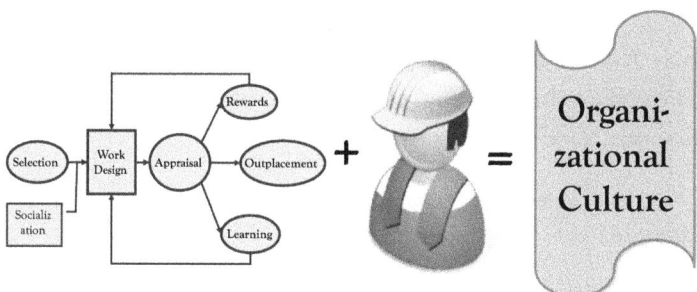

Challenge

1. List the top ten VABEs that describe your organization's culture.
2. What VABEs would you like your organization to have that it doesn't?
3. How would you go about making them a part of your culture?

---

[79] "Peter Browning at Continental Whitecap (B)," HBS case 9-486-091 rev 2000.

113. System Alignment

Concept

Organizations are able to gain more momentum and produce better results when their design decisions are internally consistent. When one system seems to be pointed in one direction and another system is pointed in another vector, the organization wastes energy tugging against itself. It's as if the organization was being drawn and quartered. When all systems are aligned, that is, pointed in the same direction with the same cultural intentions coming manifest, the organization is likely to have more energy, more focus, more productivity, and better results.

One could argue that competing vectors in system design provide checks and balances that keep an organization from going way off line. Perhaps. So here is another paradox of management—how to balance system alignment with insurance against lurching toward disaster.

System alignment is more difficult to get in matrix organizations that are *designed* to have competing interests usually between program managers with budgets and functional managers with human resource pools. Balancing a matrix organization is a bit like flying a B2 bomber, a flying wing that is inherently unstable but works with constant ultra-fast computer based flight trimming.[80]

Example

One of the most common systemic divergences comes when the reward system pays for individual performance while executive rhetoric, a communication system, presses for working together as a team. This divergence is in reality self-defeating. To which influence is the employee to respond? Clearly, the odds lie in favor of the tangible nature of the pay system.

Systems that encourage cost control while at the same time demanding more emphasis on innovation or customer focus also fall into this category.

---

[80] https://en.wikipedia.org/wiki/Flying_wing

Diagram

System Mis-alignment drains Organizational Energy

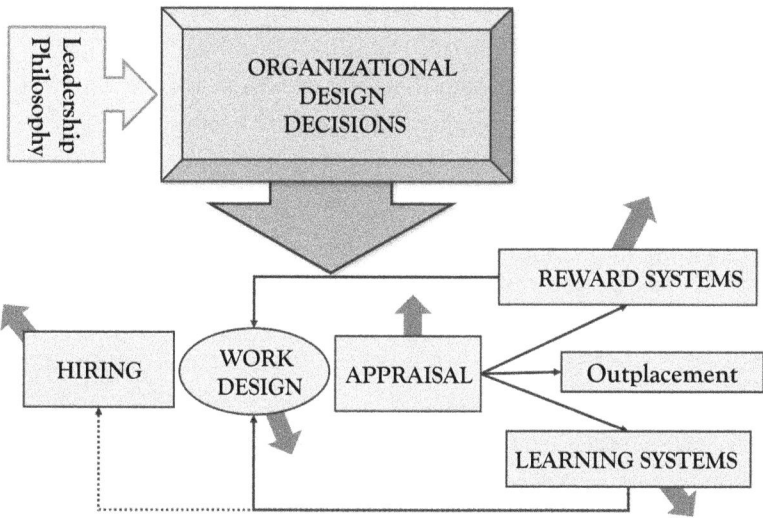

Challenge

1. Identify as many system mis-alignments as you can in your organization.
2. How would you propose remodeling them?
3. Identify as many pros and cons as you can for each proposed remodel.

114. Organizational Glue

Concept

What holds a company together? What is the cohesive mortar or glue that keeps an organization from flying apart? This question lingers today.[81,82] My colleague Bill Zierden, years ago, developed this concept from his experience in the nuclear submarine force and his consulting and executive practice. He argued there were four kinds of *organizational glue* that held an organization together: charismatic leadership, Rules and Regulations, Reward Systems, and Common Values (VABEs).

Bill's idea was that whatever held an organization together, we could call 100 percent and then allocate that 100 percent among these four forces. Further, he would argue that the distribution of glue would have a big effect on the organization's energy level and culture. Organizations that were held together primarily by charismatic leaders could easily turn into cults—AND when the leader died or left, would face a succession crisis. Organizations that relied heavily on rules and regulations would likely be less innovative and more vulnerable to substitutions in their industries. Organizations that relied more on reward systems would develop a *mercenary* culture and be susceptible to having their talent hired away by better offers. Finally, organizations that were held together by common VABEs would be resilient, high energy, and likely to be high performing.

Example

Cults like Jonestown and religions like Islam (Mohammed), Scientology (L. Ron Hubbard), and Mormonism (Joseph Smith) relied heavily on charismatic leaders. The passion, rhetoric, and stories of the leaders were so powerful that people would sell all they have and move to be near them.

---

[81] https://hbr.org/1996/11/what-holds-the-modern-company-together

[82] http://thepracticalleader.com/consistence-the-glue-that-holds-organizations-together/

Rule-oriented organizations like the military and government agencies (created by self-defining and constraining statutes) tend to be large, slow-moving, and ponderous.

Rewards-oriented businesses rely primarily on financial compensation to keep their employees at home. Wall Street firms are notorious for the magnetic draw they create by the promise of big incomes.

Non-profit organizations and religions tend to rely on common VABEs to keep people coming back.

Diagram

Organizational Glue

	CO A	CO B	CO C	Your Co
Charismatic Leadership	10	60	30	
Rewards	40	10	0	
Rules and Regulations	20	10	20	
Common Values and Purpose	30	20	50	
TOTAL GLUE	100%	100%	100%	100%

Challenge

1. Rate your company on the glue grid above. What are the implications of your assessment?
2. What do you think the glue mix of your organization should be? Why?
3. How strong is the glue in your company? What would it take for your company to fly apart?

115. Organizational Life Cycles

Concept

Observers notice the development of humans through largely predictable life stages.[83] We have outlined above the common phases that groups-to-teams go through. Typically, product life cycles are viewed in terms of four phases: introduction, growth, maturation, and decline. This simple model is usually based on a calculus-oriented analysis of sales curves by identifying the inflection points.

Larry Greiner of HBS and USC business schools proposed a theory of phases in a typical organizational life cycle.[84] Greiner's insight was that each chapter in an organization's growth produced answers to predictable questions, which in turn create a crisis that fomented movement or birth into the next chapter.

Greiner's phases were:

1. **Creativity**. During founding and establishment, an organization must create something new. Typically, this is based on a founder or founders' vision. Those founders will shepherd the company until they retire, die, or sell out. At that point, the organization faces a crisis of direction or one might say of leadership. Who will take over now? Where do we go from here?

2. **Direction**. Once the leadership succession crisis has been solved and a new direction is developed, the organization continues to grow until … the direction and focus of the second generation becomes stifling and subordinates begin to chafe. This creates a crisis of autonomy. Too much direction! We need some latitude! Give us some slack!

3. **Delegation**. The solution to the autonomy crisis is delegation. Give people more authority. Empower them. And the organization continues to grow. But this delegation incrementally compounded eventually creates a crisis of control. To rein in the expanding sense

---

[83] For example(s), Erikson, E. n.d. *Childhood and Society*. Judith Simon, *Five Life Stages*, Levinson, George Vaillant, and Neugarten's theories, https://study.com/academy/lesson/theories-of-adult-development-levinson-vaillant-neugarten.html
[84] Greiner, L. May-June 1998. "Evolution and Revolution as Organizations Grow." *Harvard Business Review* (classic reprint).

of being out of control, the organization begins to enforce more processes of coordination and integration.

4. **Coordination**. The way to solve the out-of-control crisis is to instill more controls. The organization makes more rules, constraints, guidelines, oversights, and permission signatories. In time, this leads to a red-tape crisis. We are drowning in bureaucracy! Too much red tape! Too many signatures!

5. **Collaboration**. The solution to the red-tape crisis is to cut back, slim down, clean out, and emphasize internal coordination across now expanding number of divisions and functions. Be more productive! Cut waste! Work together! Share resources! And the company continues to grow. Increased collaboration internally leads to a crisis of growth. Whoa, we need to continue growing despite cutting back.

6. **Alliances**. Greiner's last phase is the formation of alliances—this is the way to solve the growth problem created by focusing on internal coordination of a large number of divisions. So, the company acquires companies and creates alliances with other firms. Both activities create a new crisis—who are we? A crisis of identity.

Greiner was, no doubt, influenced by his colleagues, Paul Lawrence and Jay Lorsch, at Harvard, who had published the classic analysis of organizational growth issues.[85] They described how as organizations grew, they naturally became more complex and that complexity created a concomitant problem (*crisis* if you will) of internal integration. It seems to me that Greiner took that idea and applied it to shorter time periods and devised what has become now a classic article on how each growth phase in an organization creates the next, predictable, crisis and how each growth phase creates its own unique crisis.

Example

Apple fires Steve Jobs and hires John Sculley.

As at Apple, Starbucks' CEO Howard Schulz passes the baton and then later must return to right the ship.

---

[85] Lawrence, P., and J. Lorsch. 1967. "Differentiation and Integration in Complex Organizations." *Administrative Science Quarterly* 12, pp. 1–30.

Jack Welch spent five intense years on his "Work-Out" effort to reduce red-tape and bureaucratic behavior at GE.[86]

Pick your favorite example of large companies who have grown by acquisition and alliance until they changed their names and logos—trying to find/create a new identity. Time-Warner? Accenture? BAES? Lockheed-Martin? Daimler-Chrysler? Chrysler-Fiat? Yum Brands?

Diagram

There are a number of representations of Greiner's model. A few of them are shown below.

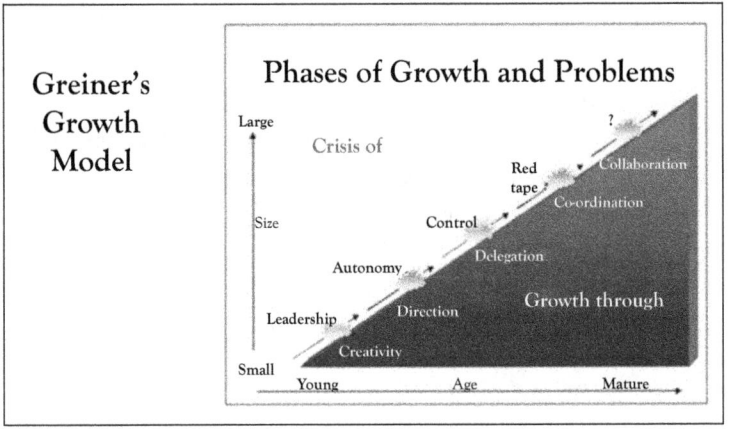

Challenge

1. Identify as many of the Greiner crises as you can in your own organization's history. How did your organization deal with them?
2. What phase is your organization in now? What is the next impending crisis? How can your organization prepare for it?
3. Can you identify organizations that are stuck or paused in one or another of Greiner's phases? How would you explain that?

---

[86] https://strategy-business.com/article/03403?gko=cf5d2 I was a consultant on the GE Work Out team for three years, meeting regularly in Crotonville with Jack Welch and his executive team. There were four consultants in the inner circle (Including Len Schlesinger, Noel Tichy, and Steve Kerr) and another ~15 on the execution consulting team of which I was a part.

SECTION VIII

Mastering the Change Process: Are You a Change Master?

The South-East Axis of our Diamond Model represents the need to adapt to changing environmental conditions. By the time the executive has developed a strategic story, sold it, designed a functional organization, and learned to complement their talents, the world has evolved. With a robust charter, one can continue to drive forward and at the same time learn to adapt to short-term speed bumps. Like any of the other elements of our model, leading and managing change is based on one's VABEs. In my experience, most executives do not have a clear model of the change process, they fly from the hip. This section will introduce principles that will help you move from a *white belt* to a *black belt* in managing change, toward becoming a Change Master.

116. The Southeast Axis: Leading Change

Concept

The fifth main element in our diamond model is leading change. We began by saying that leadership is really about leading strategic change. I assert that any effective executive must be as Bob Johnson, former CEO of Honeywell Aerospace, once said, "a Change Master."[1] Before we jump into the topic, please diagram your current mental model of what you think the change process is. Winston Churchill among others used the principle of forming personal opinions on every matter as a way of training his mind. Churchill's practice

> ... was not to read any particular debate "until I have recorded my own opinion of the subject on paper, having regard only to general principles. After reading I reconsider and finally write", setting out in pencil, on small pieces of paper, his own views on each subject, which he then pasted into the volumes.[2]

Diagram your model in the space below.

---

[1] From taped interviews accompanying, "The Life and Career of a Divisional CEO: Bob Johnson at Honeywell Aerospace." UVA-OB-0872, Darden Business Publishing.

[2] Gilbert, M. 2014. *Churchill: A Life*. Rosetta Books.

In the chapters that follow, I will introduce you to some of the common models of change out and about in the world.

Example

I ask this question of the participants in my seminars. It's fascinating to watch people strive to put their semi-conscious VABEs on paper and then to see what they came up with. We would call out a random number and then ask that person to explain their change model as if they were the CEO explaining it to your employees. When the person was done, we would open it up for questions. Again, a fascinating sequence. Here's one of those chalkboard drawings just FYI.

Diagram

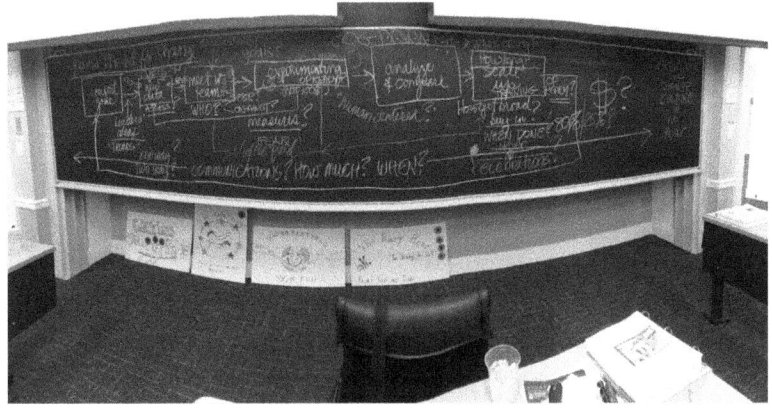

Challenge

1. What's your model of change as of today? Draw it out on paper. Remember the discipline of translating your thoughts at Level Two out to Level One Visible Behavior.
2. Ask a colleague to review your model and note questions or comments (based on *their* model).
3. Keep this model handy as you review the rest of the chapters in this module.

117. The Anti-Change Bowstring

Concept

As we said earlier, people are creatures of habit.[3] Most people assess in their experience that people tend to be as much as 90 percent creatures of habit. See the earlier chapter on Habituality. So when we approach the topic of understanding and managing change, we need to take this habituality into account.

Habituality is like a bowstring; when you pull against someone's habits, they tend to want to snap back to their established way of doing things. Modern research sometimes calls this *set points*.[4] If there are set points in *fat carriage*, perhaps also in other aspects of human behavior. The set point is the least tension in a bowstring, the straight line. When we try to change our habits, the tension of our historical habits pull us back toward our previous *equilibrium*.[5]

When we think about understanding and managing change, we need to be aware of and respect this natural tendency to *snap back* to our previously, established, baseline of behavior.

Example

Set theory in obesity research shows that when people try to change their weight, their bodies tend to want to return to a previous stable weight—and that this *set point* may have genetic roots.

Economics also asserts an equilibrium among the major macro-economic factors, a *resting point* where the factors are in balance.

Our previous chapter on organizational culture also pointed out that "culture eats strategy for breakfast." Attempts to change an organization must take into account the settling or equalizing role of

---

[3] James, W. n.d. "Habit." https://amazon.com/Habit-William-James-ebook/dp/B0 75NFD22D/ref=sr_1_4?s=digital-text&ie=UTF8&qid=1515077688&sr=1-4&keywords=james+habit

[4] https://medical.mit.edu/sites/default/files/set_point_theory.pdf

[5] https://en.wikipedia.org/wiki/General_equilibrium_theory

the organization's culture, like an obesity set point or an economic equilibrium.

Research shows that most change efforts fail.[6,7,8]

Diagram

Baseline Behavior
The Starting Point for Change

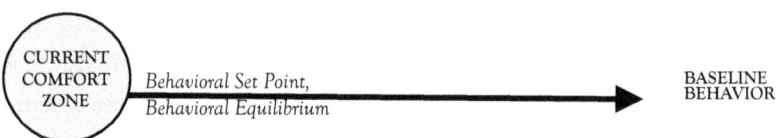

Challenge

1. What is your weight set point?
2. What is your economic equilibrium?
3. What is your comfortable daily routine? Write it down.
4. What things about your life are you determined *not* to change? Why?

---

[6] https://hbr.org/1995/05/leading-change-why-transformation-efforts-fail-2

[7] https://inc.com/lee-colan/10-reasons-change-efforts-fail.html

[8] https://processexcellencenetwork.com/organizational-change/columns/eight-reasons-change-efforts-fail

118. Change Roles

Concept

There are many roles that occur in the change process. We can name at least the following:

1. Change Leader
2. Change Designer
3. Change Agent
4. Change Manager
5. Changee

Change leaders see the pain, envision the need, and start things rolling. Change designers lay out the plan, the process, the mechanisms for making the change. Change agents organize and begin the change program in part by assembling a change team. Change managers are the people in the middle of the effort, experiencing and executing the change process. Frequently, change managers are reacting to the requests or directions of the change agents. Changees are the people who are affected by and must adapt to the elements of the change process.

People can be in several of these roles, perhaps even all of them. An awareness of the different functional roles in the change process can help designers ensure they have the right people involved. In *top down* change efforts, senior executives are the change leaders, internal consultants or senior level managers play the role of change designers, and lines of business (LOB) managers become the managers of the change process.

Example

C-level executives reviewing periodic reports identify a variance from plan. They decide something needs to be done to rectify the results emerging from the organization. They hire consultants or bring in internal consultants from their organizational development department or human resources department to help them design the change effort. Once the program is designed, the plan is rolled out to the in-line LOB leaders for implementation; their job is to make it happen. Those reporting the LOB leaders are tasked with implementing the program. The people reporting to them find themselves having to change their daily routines and activities to fit into the requests.

In a mid-level or lower-level model, as suggested by Senge, a few employees with initiative see a need and begin to design a fix. They may seek guidance or simply go about designing and making changes without involving senior management.

The organization's control systems and resulting culture will determine whether and how often mid and lower level change efforts pop up.

Diagram

Change Roles

- Change Leader
- Change Designer/Planner
- Change Agent
- Change Manager
- Changee

Challenge

1. Which change roles have you played in your career?
2. How should Change Leaders think about the other roles?
3. Who ensures the success of any change effort?
4. What are the skills associated with each role?

119. Types of Change

Concept

There are many types of change. These include the following:

1. Incremental
2. Quantum Leaps
3. Inside-Out
4. Outside-In
5. Top Down
6. Bottom Up
7. Middle Out

to name a few.

Each of these types of change, we could imagine, might have different processes that would work better. I don't know that, and it seems logical to me. What do you think? Would you manage a top-down effort differently from a bottoms-up effort? Probably.

Example

Some companies seek to improve 10 percent a year. Others find themselves in need of a transformation. The Chicago Park District decided it needed a *big bang* approach despite what pro-bono consulting firms were recommending. They didn't know how many employees they had, they were hemorrhaging money, they were paying bills alphabetically out of a shoe box, and had been mired in a *moribund bureaucracy* for over 70 years. If you were in Forrest Claypool's position as the new Superintendent, what approach would you take?

Diagram

Types of Change

- Quantum Jump
- Incremental
- Top Down
- Bottom Up
- Middle out
- Outside-In
- Inside-Out

Challenge

1. What types of change have you experienced?
2. Which did you prefer? Why?
3. Which types of change does your organization employ/tolerate/ encourage?

120. Resistance to Change

Concept

Most people resist change. They like their historical, habitual comfort zones. Why? There are a number of reasons. They include:

1. Habit
2. Genetics
3. Comfort
4. Waiting for others to lead
5. Logic for the change is unconvincing
6. Too many cries of *wolf*! (false sense of urgency)
7. Don't see the value or benefit of the change (cost > benefits)
8. Have no role to play, it's irrelevant
9. Lack of involvement in the planning
10. Change Overload
11. Trust in management is low
12. Don't believe it's the right thing to do
13. Believe it's too expensive
14. Not in my skill set

There are others.[9,10]

This has been an issue for a long time. Paul Lawrence in 1969 wrote an article on "How to Deal with Resistance to Change."[11] Since before then and still today, managers wrestle with resistance to change. Any *change master* must understand and be able to manage the various forms of resistance to change. On our buy-in scale, we want to move people from levels 5, 6, and 7 up to levels 1, 2, and 3.

I used to question whether people could change. Eventually, after observing some people who had changed, I adapted my main question

---

[9] https://thebalance.com/what-is-resistance-to-change-1918240

[10] https://torbenrick.eu/blog/change-management/12-reasons-why-people-resist-change/

[11] January 1969, *Harvard Business Review*.

from "Can people change?" (Yes, they can) to "What are the *odds* that a person will change?"

Example

A company introduces a new computer system. A year later, no one is using it.

A government agency introduces a new, expensive computer-based knowledge management system. Years later, a small minority are using it.

A company asks people to augment their behavior (make more client visits), but a year later, nothing has changed.

Diagram

Why People Resist Change

- Habit
- Comfort
- Waiting for others to set vision
- Logical models: "Right data will convince" but it doesn't (VABEs>data)
- Too may cries of "Wolf!" (false cries of urgency)
- Dont't see the value or benefit
- Have no part to play
- Don't know how
- Wrong thing to do
- Don't trust management

Challenge

1. Identify changes you have resisted or resist now. Why?
2. In your experience, why do change efforts fail?
3. Have you tried to change your spouse/significant other? How did that go? Why?
4. Has your spouse or significant other tried to change you? How did that go? Why?

121. Kurt Lewin's Model

Concept

Kurt Lewin was an early pioneer in applied social-psychology—something that hits at the heart of management. Lewin's work added a rich understanding to the field of management. He added force field analysis, a theory of human behavior (behavior is a function of the person in his or her environment—a precursor to contingency theory ala Lawrence and Lorsch), gestaltism, systems thinking (contextual analysis), action research (later expanded by Chris Agryris), leadership styles (authoritarian, democratic, and laissez-faire), and managing change.[12] By all accounts, Lewin significantly influenced many aspects of modern management thinking. The persistence of VABE-based conflicts in the 21st century underlie the depth of Lewin's insights. His history emigrating from Poland through Nazi Germany to the United States underlies and informs, I believe, his understanding of the importance of context, VABEs and human behavior.

With regard to change, Lewin proposed a simple but powerful three-step model: unfreeze, retrain, and freeze. His approach recognized the power of historical, habitual behavior. One must *unfreeze* that mass of habits before one could make a change. He argued that unfreezing involved dissembling the historical paradigm or mindset. The second step was, now facing a more malleable, open-minded audience, re-educating, or reshaping the person/people into a new perspective, and then third, before that new mindset evaporated, resetting it, gelling it, freezing it into a new habitual way of being and doing. Lewin used the term *freezing* for phase three; later pundits called it, reasonably given phase one, *refreezing*.

The devil is in the details, of course, of how one unfreezes, retrains, and refreezes habitual behavior. Which of the forces of influence does one use in each phase? Force? Rewards? Punishments? Level Two techniques of evidence and logic? How does one unfreeze VABEs? Refreezing probably has something to do with repetition—at all three levels.

As the speed of change increased with new technologies and information sharing globally, one could argue that Lewin's model should be *unfreeze*, *retrain*, and *retrain*. To the extent that learning is critical to

---

[12] For a summary, see https://en.wikipedia.org/wiki/Kurt_Lewin

success in the 21st century, and we no longer have the luxury of waiting for the old paradigms to (literally) die off, *refreezing* takes too much time. Lewin would probably be on the leading edge of that discussion if he were still with us.

Lewin also introduced the notion of Force Field analysis—identifying and assessing the strength of forces that are *for* and *against* the intended change. With this concept, managers could strengthen the *for* forces and weaken the *against* forces.

Example

A company acquires several new subsidiaries. More than eight years later, despite new logos and management, the acquired units still refer to the *old* way we used to and still should be doing things.

Ford Motor Company: "Culture eats strategy for breakfast."

Participants in my Power and Leadership (Level Three Leadership) week-long seminars frequently complain about the rapidity of change in their companies. "We never have time to settle in to the new changes before more changes come!" "We haven't finished the last change and already the next one is cascading over us!" "Every day it's something new! Stop already!"

Diagram

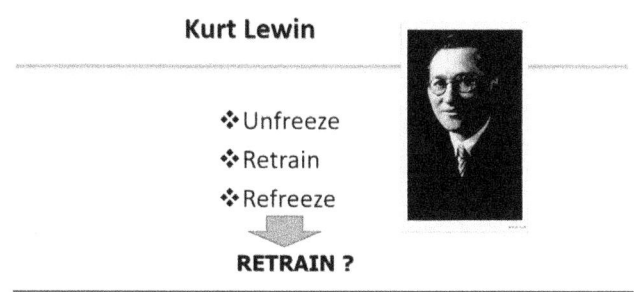

Kurt Lewin

❖ Unfreeze
❖ Retrain
❖ Refreeze

RETRAIN ?

Source: https://google.com/search?q=images+Kurt+Lewin&tbm=isch&ved=2ahUKEwikpPWp0L zuAhXST98KHa35CbEQ2-cCegQIABAA&oq=images+Kurt+Lewin&gs_lcp=CgNpbWcQA zIGCAAQCBAeOgIIADoGCAAQBRAeUO2tBFj8vQRg7MUEaABwAHgAgAGnAYgBng WSAQM5LjGYAQCgAQGqAQtnd3Mtd2l6LWltZZ8ABAQ&sclient=img&ei=aqERYKTHB tKf_Qat86eICw&bih=578&biw=1366&rlz=1C1GCEB_enUS910US910#imgrc=ytXUSy8Nds9 GXM

Lewin's Force Field Analysis

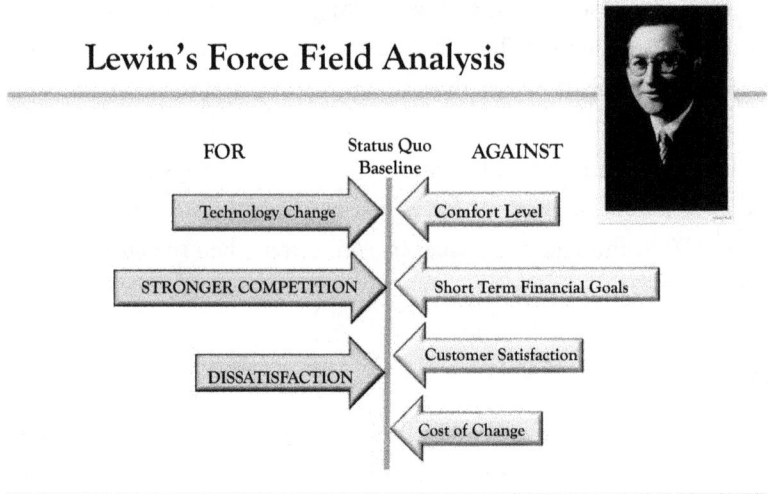

Challenge

1. Identify as many VABEs in your company that would have to *unfreeze* and change for your company to move forward as you can.
2. Do the same for yourself.
3. Describe your attitude toward the changes taking place in your company.

122. Mike Beer's Model of Change

Concept

Mike Beer was a senior executive at Corning Glass who then joined the faculty of the Harvard Business School where I became acquainted with him. Mike had a wonderful balance/mixture of theoretical education and practical experience.[13] And he is a warm, generous human being.

Mike developed a theory of change that he summarized in an equation, something which engineers might find attractive. Mike's equation was:

$$Cp = (D \times M \times P) > C$$

where Cp was the probability of change happening, D was dissatisfaction with the status quo, M was the clarity of a model and vision of the future and where we want to go and P was a process for managing the change. The *C* represented the cost of making the change. You can see the influence of Lewin's Force Field Analysis[14] in that dissatisfaction, vision, and process are pushing for change while the cost of the change is a force pushing against. I think we all stand on the shoulders of those who went before. (Of course, that's the premise of every research study, which begins with a thorough literature review.)

Beer surmised that the relationship among the positive forces was multiplicative; if any of them went to zero, the whole of them went to zero and therefore so did the probability of making a change. The relationship between the positive and negative forces was consistent with force field logic—the stronger force will win.

Measuring the elements of Beer's model was not always that easy, however, being able to conceptualize them was an important starting point. How does one measure dissatisfaction in an organization? (Yes, surveys. And?) How does dissatisfaction among senior managers relate to that among lower level employees? How does one measure the clarity of a future vision/goal? (Aha, my answer would be a charter!) And what is a *clear* model for managing change? Hmmm. Can you put it on paper? (See the earlier chapter on Introduction to the Change Module.) How does one measure resistance to change? The *costs* of making the change? What are the values of discarded VABEs?

---

[13] https://hbs.edu/faculty/Pages/profile.aspx?facId=6421
[14] https://en.wikipedia.org/wiki/Force-field_analysis

Example

Senior management wants to reorganize with more emphasis on centers of competence distributed across its geographic footprint. The site managers in the system resist sharing their resources. The e-mails and phone numbers of the site managers are not readily available online. Employees feel loyalty to their location and its historical expertise and product line. Customers begin to experience confusion about whom to call for problem solving. The center leaders are focused on building their expertise but without a specific program budget. Investors including primarily the parent company want short-term profits and more efficiency in product/cost ratios.

Diagram

Beer's Change Equation

$$Cp = D \times M \times P > C$$

Cp   = Probability of Change

D   = Dissatisfaction with Status Quo

M   = Clear Model or Vision of the Future

P   = Clear Process for Managing the Change

C   = Cost of Making the Change

Source: from Leading Change, Michael Beer, HCS

Challenge

1. Use Beer's equation to assess the last change you or your company made. How, if at all, did this explain what happened?
2. How could you use Beer's model to plan the next change for you or your company?

123. John Kotter's Model of Change

Concept

John Kotter's model of change is probably the most widely used model in the world. John used multi-faceted research models—on-site visits, interviews, survey data, record analysis and more—to develop the eight step model in his best-selling book, *Leading Change*.[15] Based on his research, John has built a worldwide reputation and a major consulting firm. It was a privilege to have been his colleague for a short while.

John's model of change begins with his field-based identification of eight pitfalls in change efforts:

1. Allowing complacency
2. Failure to create a guiding coalition
3. Underestimating the power of vision
4. Under-communicating the vision
5. Failing to create short-term wins
6. Declaring victory too soon
7. Neglecting to anchor changes in the culture

One can recognize vestiges of other models. That's a good sign, because it suggests that the people conceiving the models are observing the same phenomena. We can link complacency with dissatisfaction. Partner with Whom and guiding coalition. Vision and Charter. Under-communicating with Unfreeze. And so forth. The linkages are, to me, reinforcing.

Kotter's eight errors in leading change point directly to the positive side, what to do:

1. Create a sense of urgency (a way to *unfreeze*)
2. Create a guiding coalition (similar to Senge's small team)
3. Develop a strong vision and strategy (Charter and Beer's M and P)
4. Over-communicate the vision and strategy (a way to *retrain*)

---

[15] https://amazon.com/Leading-Change-New-Preface-Author-ebook/dp/B00A07F-PEO/ref=sr_1_1?ie=UTF8&qid=1515172462&sr=8-1&keywords=leading+change+by+john+kotter

5. Redesign to encourage broad-based action (organizational architecture)

6. Generate short-term wins (STOGs)

7. Consolidate gains in redesign and human resources

8. Anchor changes in the culture ("Culture IS the issue." Gerstner)

Example

President Bush declaring "MISSION ACCOMPLISHED."

You Teach What You Tolerate

Focusing on short-term financial goals instead of mission and vision and values.

Executives who change their message every time they speak.

Diagram

Kotter's Eight Stage Process for Creating Transformation

1. Establish a sense of urgency

2. Create a guiding coalition

3. Develop strong vision and strategy

4. Over communicate the vision and strategy

5. Redesign to encourage broad-based action

6. Generate short-term wins

7. Consolidate gains in redesign and HR

8. Anchor changes in the culture

Source: Adapted from Leading Change, John Kotter, HBS Press, 1996
https://google.com/search?q=images+John+Kotter&tbm=isch&ved=2ahUKEwjuu5_O0LzuAh-
WCPt8KHc8jCUoQ2-cCegQIABAA&oq=images+John+Kotter&gs_lcp=CgNpbWcQAzoECC
MQJzoCCABQpZ0FWKWuBWCotAVoAHAAeACAAUaIAfEEkgECMTGYAQCgAQGqA
Qtnd3Mtd2l6LWltZ8ABAQ&sclient=img&ei=tqERYO6IEoL9_AbPx6TQBA&bih=578&biw
=1366&rlz=1C1GCEB_enUS910US910#imgrc=4nMoNRE1XY-H_M

Challenge

1. Analyze your last organizational change effort using Kotter's eight steps. What went well? What didn't go well?

2. Read *Leading Change* and Kotter's metaphor book, *Our Iceberg is Melting.*[16]

---

[16] https://amazon.com/HSA/pages/default?pageId=CD149802-0170-4236-879C-AC392C22D604&store_ref=SPONSORED_SEARCH_AC2CQ227 2ZB3XY4&store_ref=SPONSORED_SEARCH_AC2CQ2272ZB3XY4&pf_rd_m=ATVPDKIKX0DER&pf_rd_p=3365067662&pd_rd_wg=9nage&pf_rd_r=6S0RX2XASZ7RCYFD4QZN&pf_rd_s=desktop-sx-top-slot&pf_rd_t=301&pd_rd_w=hPSdd&pf_rd_i=john+kotter&pd_rd_r=f233e4a4-a977-4e0a-a5db-02513665912f&hsa_cr_id=7862263120101

124. Tim Gallwey's Model of Change

Concept

Tim Gallwey wrote a series of books with the title "The Inner Game of …."[17] In these books, he argued for awareness of the difference between Self 1 and Self 2. Self 1, he said, were the *should* we carry around with us, the *oughts* we garnered over the years from other people. Self 2 was our *inner* self, the self we believed and wanted. He noted, I think accurately, that it is often difficult to distinguish between the two.

With regard to management, in the *Inner Game of Work*, Gallwey argued that finding the right measures was an important part of finding a better way. He said this was a way of focusing attention. At the same time, it was important to listen to one's inner self, Self 2.

I have encountered this concept in several places including *Leadership and Self-Deception: Getting Out of the Box*.[18] In both, I have a question about the *correctness* or *functionality* of one's inner voice. From a religious point of view, there are those who believe that mankind is imbued with a *spirit of godliness*, or an infallible conscience or the Holy Spirit whispering. In my experience, it is hard to trust this voice—it varies from person to person. One person's conscience says do this while another's conscience says, do that. This relates to me to the fundamental attribution error, the concept that people tend to blame others for their failures and take credit for their successes.[19]

Example

Gallwey tells of a consulting assignment from a large dental office. They were concerned about the number of patients who were complaining about the wait time. Gallwey asked the office if they could track the actual wait times. They said they could, and he went home. Three days later, the dental office called and said, "How did you do that?" "Do what?" Gallwey

---

[17] https://google.com/search?q=gallwey+books&oq=gallwey+books&aqs=chrome..69i57j0l3.2183j0j4&sourceid=chrome&ie=UTF-8

[18] 2010. *Leadership and Self-Deception: Getting Out of the Box*. Arbinger Institute.

[19] https://en.wikipedia.org/wiki/Fundamental_attribution_error

replied. "Well," they said, "the first day the average wait time was 30 minutes. The second day it was 15 minutes. The third day it was down to five minutes. How did you do that?" Gallwey smiled. When people have the right information and focus, things happen.

Diagram

Inner Game of Change

Self 1 (Shoulds) and Self 2 (Inner Self)

❖ Select the right measures

❖ Focus attention and see what happens

❖ Listen to Self 2 (inner voice)

Source: Adapted from Tim Gallwey, Inner Game of Work
https://google.com/search?q=images+Tim+Gallwey&tbm=isch&ved=2ahUKEwjmnf740LzuAh
VFB98KHfqJBocQ2-cCegQIABAA&oq=images+Tim+Gallwey&gs_lcp=CgNpbWcQAzoCCA
A6BAgAEB46BggAEAgQHlCxuAVY8ssFYN_TBWgAcAB4AIABRogBigWSAQIxMZgBAK
ABAAoBC2d3cy13aXotaW1nwAEB&sclient=img&ei=D6IRYKbaOMWO_Ab6k5q4CA&bih=
578&biw=1366&rlz=1C1GCEB_enUS910US910#imgrc=zfdaTzxR4iZIzM

Challenge

1. What measures do you pay attention to?
2. How does focusing make things change?
3. Does accurate information affect your assessment of others and yourself?

125. The MIT (Nevis) Change Model

Concept

A team of researchers led by Edwin Nevis at MIT developed a *life cycle* model of the change process.[20] They characterized the change process as a progression from complacency through turbulence, resistance, small wins, consolidation, and a new baseline. Again, one can immediately see similarities with pieces of the other change models. Complacency and a lack of urgency. Turbulence and disconfirming data. Resistance and denial. Small wins and small wins(!). Consolidation and consolidation. And New baseline and anchoring. I infer that these writers are observing the same phenomena and applying somewhat different labels and perhaps somewhat different transition boundaries. Transitions are likely to be the least clear while the middle of a phase or stage would be the clearest and therefore most observable.

Nevis's team (Anthone DiBella and Janet Gould) thought of the change process as a learning process. Learning is change, change is learning. Again, major overlaps with other authors' views as introduced in the Organizational Learning chapter above. The MIT group argued that a learning organization had three main elements: strong bases for developing new products and services, a culture of continuous improvement, and the ability to renew itself.[21]

They also argued that there were seven learning *orientations*: knowledge source, product-process focus, documentation mode, dissemination mode, learning focus, value-chain focus, and skill development focus. One can see how a company might be oriented toward one of these or another—and still be a learning organization. Whatever the orientation, the team observed that the successful organizations actively supported the learning systems in their companies.

Example

Many companies go bankrupt by not recognizing the changes in the world around them. Buggy whips, carriages, tube-based televisions, and others.

---

[20] https://sloanreview.mit.edu/article/understanding-organizations-as-learning-systems/

[21] Outlined in the article above and in their book. 1996. *Intentional Revolutions*, Jossey-Bass.

Companies experience turbulence when they begin to get disconfirming data: declining sales, declining profits, customer dissatisfaction, and so on.

Companies who wither and die are usually stuck in denial, another form of resistance. Detroit's response to the smaller, more efficient Japanese car invasion is an example.

Small wins perhaps overlooks an *experimentation* phase from which those small wins emerge. IDEO currently emphasizes the importance of running small experiments to find the right solutions.

Getting a company to change permanently by consolidating changes and small wins into a larger culture is a challenge. I had one client who made a major organizational change and then five years later went back to its original design. The *bowstring* snapped back.

Diagram

Nevis' MIT Phases of Change

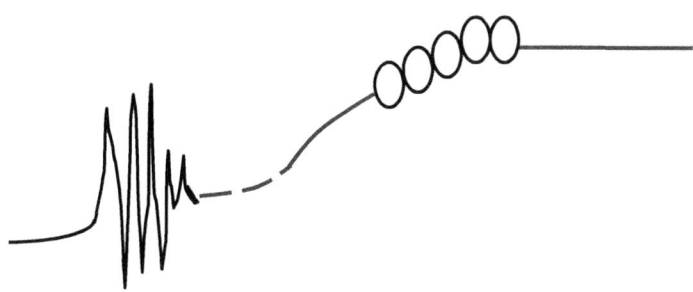

Complacency/ Turbulence / Resistance / Small Wins / Consolidation / New Baseline

Challenge

1. Can you map the MIT model on your company's last change effort?
2. What do you think about the lack of an experimentation phase?
3. What are your thoughts on "learning is change, change is learning?"

126. Change Is Like Dying Little Deaths

Concept

Elizabeth Kubler-Ross (EKR) pioneered the study of near-death experiences. Her book, *On Death and Dying*, became a classic.[22] In it, she outlined a series of steps or phases through which she had observed the dying to progress.

These phases were:

1. **Denial**. The person refuses to believe the impending diagnosis.
2. **Anger**. When forced to accept the diagnosis, anger sets in.
3. **Bargaining**. When the anger subsides, she said, people try to change the diagnosis by promising to do this or that if only they could live longer.
4. **Depression**. When it becomes clear that the diagnosis is not going to change, the emotional state turns to depression, a sad acknowledgment of the looming reality.
5. **Acceptance**. When the person realizes that the end is what it is and no behavioral or emotional reaction will change it, they move to accepting reality.

Progression through these phases could take considerable time. People could linger or even become stuck at one phase or another. The transitions were defined by the person's behavior, not a pre-determined period.

EKR applied this model not only to the dying but also to those who had experienced a significant loss. A person losing a loved one or experiencing a divorce or even failing at business would go through these phases.

My reflection on the EKR model suggested some possible adjustments. First, *denial* is, I suppose, in reaction to some news, probably disconfirming data. The news might be, "You have cancer," or "Your department is being sold off," or "Your position is no longer needed," or "I'm leaving you." Once one gets some disturbing data, the EKR process can begin.

---

[22] Kubler-Ross, E. 1969. *On Death and Dying*. Scribner.

Once the person has progressed to depression or despair, it seems to me if they move on, they are going to try something different. That means experimentation. Experimentation with new thoughts, new emotions, and perhaps new behaviors. When one leaves depression and begins trying new things, the natural, related emotion is hope. Without hope, there is no experimentation.

The experimentation with thoughts, feelings, or behavior may lead to EKR's acceptance, what we might call an integration with one's view of one's position in the world.[23] Erik Erikson's theory of dichotomous life phases ended with the dilemma between despair and integrity, the sense of things didn't work out or whew, it all came together. It seems to me there's an analogous structure here to EKR's concept of acceptance.

Looking at the progression, it looked to me like a cascading pendulum between behavior and emotion. So, my adaptation of the EKR model looks like the one in the diagram below. People have diagramed EKR's theory in different ways. One used two axes of energy and satisfaction to chart the progression.[24] Another used a simple time line.[25] To me, the five steps reflect an oscillation between behavior and emotion—denial leads to anger, bargaining to depression, and acceptance to peace.

Example

A manager's division is sold off. He can't believe it. He calls for confirmation. Then he rants, he screams, he throws things, he kicks the garbage can. Then he calls back and argues for a reversal if he promises to reduce expenses. When that is not granted, he goes home in a blue funk. His spouse tries to comfort him. Months later, managing the business for a new owner, he gradually forgets his disappointment at the hands of his former owner. Or not.

---

[23] I'm combining here with Erik Erikson's notion of dichotomous dilemmas in his eight ages or stages of mankind. See *Childhood and Society*, W.W. Norton & Company, 1993, first edition 1950.

[24] https://en.wikipedia.org/wiki/K%C3%BCbler-Ross_model#/media/File:K%C3%BCbler_Ross_grieving_curve.png

[25] https://en.wikipedia.org/wiki/K%C3%BCbler-Ross_model#/media/File:K%C3%BCbler_Ross%27s_stages_of_grief.png

An elderly parent wants to stay in her home despite her declining health. Gradually, she is limited to a wheelchair because her legs are weakening. Then she breaks an ankle trying to do exercises on the handicapped bar in her hallway. Then a neighbor pushes her down the sidewalk and hits a curb launching her into midair on to the pavement, breaking both femurs. She refuses to stay in the rehab center, demanding to go home. She is so abusive to in-home care providers that they refuse to return. So she begins advertising for live-in help hoping to find a single nursing student who will live with her free of charge in return for helping with bathing, hygiene, and shopping. She invites a homeless person into her home. When he threatens her, she calls 911. She continues to advertise and interview itinerants trying to find a live-in nurse-aid.

Diagram

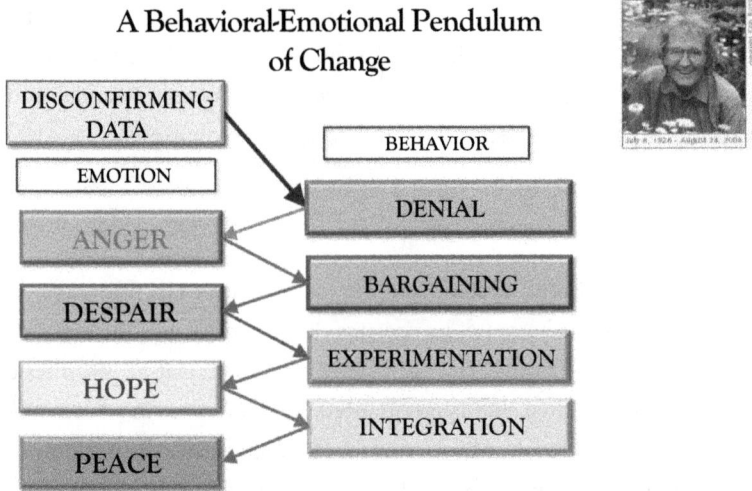

Source: Adapted from Elizabeth Kubler-Ross by (c) James G. Clawson
https://google.com/search?q=images+Elizabeth+Kubler-Ross&tbm=isch&ved=2ahUKEwiD6tSl
0bzuAhVNNd8KHc0VDXkQ2-cCegQIABAA&oq=images+Elizabeth+Kubler-Ross&gs_lcp=-
CgNpbWcQAzoCCAA6BggAEAgQHjoECCMQJzoFCAAQsQM6BAgAEB5Qj60HWNLtB2D
f8AdoBnAAeACAAV2IAcgNkgECMjmYAQCgAQGqAQtnd3Mtd2l6LWltZ8ABAQ&sclien
t=img&ei=baIRYMP_Jc3q_AbNq7TIBw&bih=578&biw=1366&rlz=1C1GCEB_enUS910US9
10#imgrc=rT32z1ReTTJDnM

Challenge

1. Reflect on a change you made in your life. How well does the EKR revised model match what you did and felt? Did you get *stuck* at any of the phases? Which and why?

2. Reflect on big changes you have seen others make. How well does the EKR revised model fit what they did and felt? Did they get stuck or bogged down at any of the phases?

3. Think about a change that was made in your organization. How well, if at all, does the revised EKR model describe what happened?

127. The Many Faces of Denial

Concept

Denial is the first step in the EKR model introduced in the last chapter. Sometimes people get *stuck* in denial. They wrestle with acknowledging reality. Jack Welch once asserted that his managers should "Face reality as it is, not as it was or as you wish it were."[26] Jim Collins's version of this principle was "Confront the Brutal Facts."[27] Clearly, lots of people can get bogged down in denying the reality changing around them.

My colleague, Alec Horniman, once noted that there are many kinds of denial.

1. One can deny the message, the data, the information. "That's not correct!" or "That information is spurious."
2. **If** one is forced by time or some other means to acknowledge the accuracy of the information, one can then deny the messenger. "Well, you're not a real doctor!" or "You don't know what you're talking about!"
3. **If** one is forced to acknowledge that the messenger is telling the truth, then one may deny the relevance of the message to them. "Well, that won't happen to me!" or "I'm going to beat the odds, they don't apply to me."
4. **If** one is forced to acknowledge the relevance of the message, then one may deny one's ability to do anything about it. "Well, that's just the way things, are, I can't do anything about it." Or "I can't fix it, so I'm going to ignore it."

It's easy to see how denial can be a big roadblock to forward movement and adaptation.

Example

"Don't worry about it. Those blips are just our bombers coming in from the mainland."

---

[26] Welch, J., N. Tichy, and S. Sherman. 1994. *Control Your Destiny or Someone Else Will.* HarperPB.

[27] Collins, J. 2011. *Good to Great*, HarperBusiness (latest edition).

"You got your degree from Mossy Rock University. What do you know?"

"So prices are falling in Europe. That's nothing to us."

"Let's just stay the course. We can't really affect the market anyway."

"I'm doing fine." (Despite the surrounding squalor)

"People will always want to read hardcopy newspapers."

"They will always need pilots."

"They will always need drivers."

"There will always be enough oil/fish/food."

"What global warming?"

Diagram

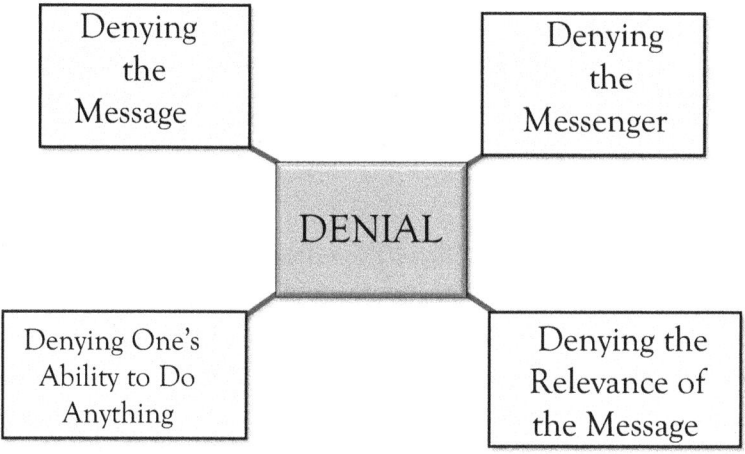

Challenge

1. Describe a time when you were in denial.
2. Describe a time when someone you knew was in denial.
3. Describe a time when someone rejected what you knew was good information you were giving.
4. How can you help a person out of denial? If beliefs trump evidence (as outlined in earlier chapters), how can you help someone accept a disconfirming reality?
5. If you cannot get someone to get out of denial, what do you do?

128. Prochaska's Model of Change

Concept

JO Prochaska was a clinical psychologist who focused on addictive behavior. His experience in dealing with addicts led him to conclude that that kind of deeply entrenched habitual behavior was likely to be so strong that attempts to change it would be cyclical, that is, steps forward and then steps backward. One could therefore expect a kind of spiraling around growth and retreat in the change process.

When one adds hard-wiring genetics to early childhood developmental habits, human behavior becomes hard to change. The DRD2 gene has been closely linked to alcoholism and other addictive behaviors.[28] Prochaska concluded from his clinical practice that one must first *contemplate* and desire a change and then engage a series of cycles until, if successful, one might become able to *maintain* the new non-addictive state and carry on from there.

Example

I remember where I was and what I was doing the day they announced the discovery of the DRD2 gene and its impact. It was significant to me because my father was an alcoholic. And his father was an alcoholic. And so was his father. One roasted himself after crawling out of a bar and resting on a warm spot—that turned out to be a pile of coal locomotive clinkers on which he roasted himself. Given that, what are the odds that I had/have the DRD2 allele? High, yes? As a result, I determined to break that chain of alcoholism. Although I didn't drink, I found carbohydrates an *easy* substitute. Fighting my tendency toward sweets has been a life-long battle—marked by successes and failures over and over again.

---

[28] https://ncbi.nlm.nih.gov/pmc/articles/PMC3180592/#:~:text=The%20D2%20dopamine%20receptor%20(DRD2,use%2C%20gambling%2C%20and%20overeating

Diagram

Prochaska's Spiral of Change

Recycling is likely for as many as 85%.

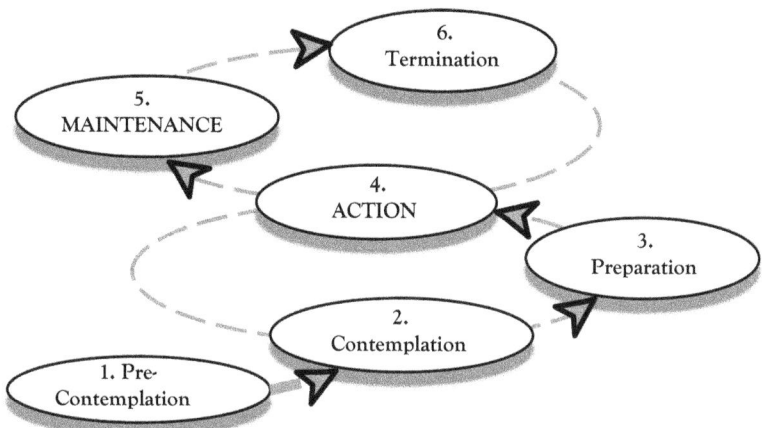

Challenge

1. What changes have you tried to make in your life?
2. How if at all have you encountered the spiraling/cyclical process Prochaska described?
3. How have you experienced or observed others getting to the "maintenance" stage of Prochaska's model?

129. Peter Senge's Model of Change

Concept

Peter Senge of MIT is one of the 50 most influential management thinkers in the world.[29] Peter visited Darden once and explained his model of leading change. His model had two axes, time bifurcated by today and internal-external. On the time axis, he argued that most people focus on the past and struggle to think about the future. On the internal-external axis, he said his anchor points were going it alone versus (external) searching for and using partners.

This two axis model creates four quadrants each with a central question. The northwest quadrant (future/internal) question was "What do we need to do tomorrow?" The northeast quadrant (future/external) question was "Whom do we need to partner with?" The southwest and southeast questions were "What are we doing today?" and "Whom do we partner with today?"

These four questions are high level. Again, the devil is in the details. As Peter explained his model, he made a number of comments, which I have summarized on the second diagram below. That list will give you a much richer insight into his thinking.

Example

Many companies strive to do what they've been doing better when what they need to do is learn to do something new and different—at which they might not be skilled. The *In Search of Excellence* model included *stick to your knitting*, which seems counter to Senge's advice.

---

[29] http://economist.com/node/12552876

Diagram

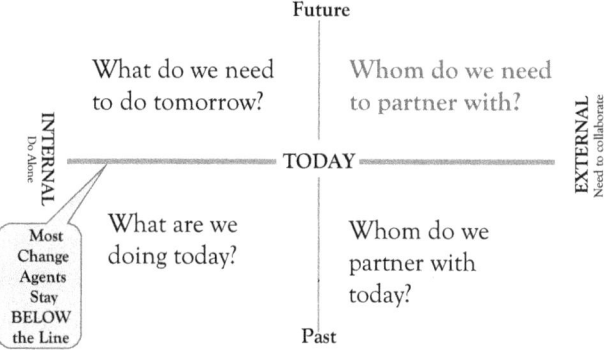

Senge's Model of Change

Future

What do we need
to do tomorrow?

Whom do we need
to partner with?

INTERNAL
Do Alone

──────────── TODAY ────────────

EXTERNAL
Need to collaborate

Most
Change
Agents
Stay
BELOW
the Line

What are we
doing today?

Whom do we
partner with
today?

Past

Source: The Necessary Revolution, Peter Senge, 2008
https://google.com/search?q=images+Peter+Senge&tbm=isch&ved=2ahUKEwiYtdfj0bzuAh
WnVt8KHeHhDHwQ2-cCegQIABAA&oq=images+Peter+Senge&gs_lcp=CgNpb-
WcQAzoECCMQJzoFCAAQsQM6AggAOgYIABAIEB5QoKgJWJq5CWDtvgloA-
HAAeACAAW-IAaoFkgEEMTAuMZgBAKABAaoBC2d3cy13aXotaW1nwAEB
&sclient=img&ei=76IRYNiBKqet_Qbhw7PgBw&bih=578&biw=1366&rlz=1C1G
CEB_enUS910US910#imgrc=6vl-AHzmPAfVGM

Challenge

1. How much of your time do you spend in the present or past? How
   much of your time do you spend *in* the future?
2. When you have made changes in yourself or your company, with
   whom did you partner/ally (if anyone at all)?
3. Identify the small team of change initiators in your company
   today, who are they? How, if at all, are you supporting or joining
   those people?
4. How robust is your network at the company? Do you enjoy
   building your network? How do you do that?

130. The Five P's

Concept

The CEO of a large American insurance company, USAA, used what he called the "Five P's" to design and implement change initiatives. The Five P's were Pain, Purpose, Picture, Plan, and Personal Part. Continuing our theme of linking similar elements between models, we can relate Pain to Beer's Dissatisfaction, yes? Purpose of the change effort had to do with what are we trying to do? (Mission) USAA's Picture is similar to Kotter's vision. The Plan links to Beer's Process. And Personal Part meant everyone should be able to see what their role in the change process was.

Part of the power of this model was its simplicity—not too many elements and alliteratively easy to remember.

Example

Customers are complaining about wait times on the telephone. (pain)
We want to keep customer dissatisfaction to an absolute minimum. (purpose)
Our customers should never have to wait more than twenty seconds to get through. (picture)
We are going to monitor customer wait times on every customer representative phone line. (plan)
Every customer representative and their managers and the IT department have a part to play here. (part)

Diagram

5 P's of Leading Change

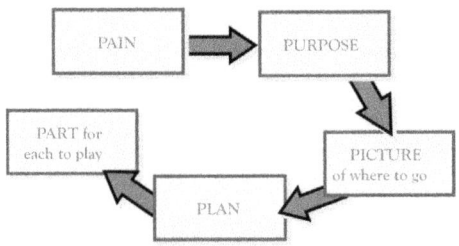

Source: Adapted from USAA Group

Challenge

1. What pain do you feel or observe in your organization today?
2. If you were designing a change process to fix that pain, what would the purpose be?
3. If your change effort were successful, what would the end result look like?
4. What plan would you create to make that change?
5. What part would each person affected by the change play?

131. The GE Model of Change

Concept

Between roughly 1988 and 1993, General Electric under the guidance of Jack Welch and a team of consultants engaged in an effort to reduce bureaucratic red-tape and speed adaptation to changing economic conditions. Welch called this the "Work Out" initiative. He thought the company needed a work-out to get rid of organizational cholesterol.[30] I was fortunate enough to be a member of the second tier of consultants hired to support that effort. The subsidiary I was assigned to was later named to be one of the top 10 plants in the country by *Industry Magazine*.[31]

Welch's inner group of four consultants devised a change process that was extraordinarily successful. This process had five phases or steps.

1. Describe the current system.
2. Describe the current results.
3. Describe a better system.
4. Describe expected results.
5. Describe a plan for execution.

The concept was that line managers would work with assigned consultants to generate internally a list of things that needed to be done to move the company forward. In this way, the process was both top-down and bottoms-up in design. The process included a series of consultant-led seminars that (a) introduced the theory of managing change (see this whole module), (b) asked participants to work together to develop a list of needed changes, (c) to develop the five overhead slides suggested by the process above, (d) present those initiatives to senior management, e) who in turn would decide on the spot whether to proceed/accept or not.

The power of this process lay in its involvement of research (the consultants), changes (the participants), and senior management *and* in the directive to decide the fate of each project *on the spot.*

---

[30] There are many articles and books on this effort. For example, https://amazon.com/dp/B000QUCO9Y/ref=dp-kindle-redirect?_encoding=UTF8&btkr=1

[31] https://automation.com/automation-news/industry/ge-fanuc-automation-celebrates-15-year-anniversary

Example

In the attempt to demonstrate his division's progress, one GE divisional CEO piled up stacks of paper—bureaucratic red-tape that they had *eliminated*—in the entry way to his headquarters. In our subsidiary, we identified 205 *projects* or issues recommended by employees over the course of two years. These projects ranged in importance from changing the uniforms on the softball team to redesigning and shortening the methods by which the company brought new products to market. Can you imagine standing up in front of your senior management and proposing a change in the softball uniforms as your *big insight*? One proposal described more than a dozen steps required to get a hammer out of the supply room— and a proposal to shorten the process significantly. The larger projects required major planning and additional support mechanisms.

Diagram

Five GE Slides for Continuous Change

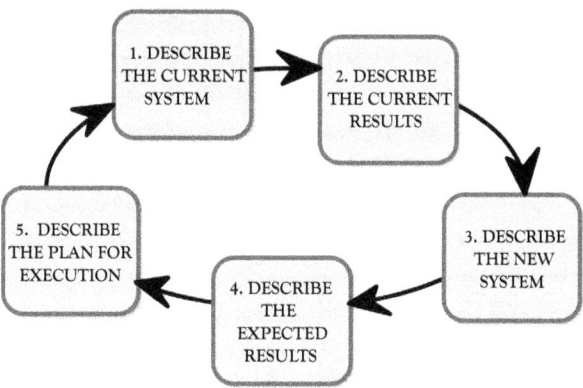

Challenge

1. Describe a current system in your organization that you think needs redoing.
2. Describe the results this system produces.
3. Describe a system that you think would improve the current system.
4. Describe the results you would expect the new system to produce.
5. Design a plan to implement this new system, step-by-step.

132. Susan Campbell's Model of Change

Concept

Susan Campbell, a Washington DC consultant, developed her model of change in her book, *From Chaos to Confidence*.[32] In it, she posited eight stages:

1. **Feeling Unsettled.** "Something isn't right."
2. **Denial.** "It's not that bad."
3. **Facing the Present.** "I see things as they are."
4. **Letting Go.** "The past isn't working. The future is unclear."
5. **Envisioning.** "I now know what I want."
6. **Exploring Options.** "We could do it this way or that way."
7. **Committing to Action.** "Okay, I'm going to do this."
8. **Integrating the Change.** "I AM doing it."

Yet again, the overlaps with other models jumps out. I won't beat that dead horse, rather let you draw the connections.

Example

Let's consider a hypothetical automobile company and how they might express themselves using Campbell's model.

"Our sales are flat."
"Flat's not too bad. They aren't declining."
"AH! The Japanese are stealing our sales!"
"Our big, gas guzzling cars aren't selling anymore."
"We need to develop smaller, more fuel efficient cars."
"We could copy theirs, we could design our own, we could leapfrog them, we could build a new plant."
"Let's get our own more efficient designs out on the road."
"We are selling smaller, more efficient cars and they are going well!"

---

[32] Campbell, S. 1995. *From Chaos to Confidence*. Simon & Schuster.

Diagram

Susan Campbell's
Stages of Change

1. **Feeling Unsettled:** Something isn't right.
2. **Denial:** It's not that bad.
3. **Facing the Present:** I see things as they are.
4. **Letting Go:** The past isn't working; the future is unclear.
5. **Envisioning:** I know what I want.
6. **Exploring new Options:** Maybe I can do it.
7. **Committing to Action:** I can do it.
8. **Integrating the Change:** I am doing it.

Source: Adapted from *From Chaos to Confidence*, Susan Campbell, Simon & Schuster, New York, 1995
https://google.com/search?q=images+Susan+Campbell&tbm=isch&ved=2ahUKEwjB3a6u0rzuA
hWIA98KHTP2BPgQ2-cCegQIABAA&oq=images+Susan+Campbell&gs_lcp=CgNpbWcQA
zoECCMQJzoCCAA6BggAEAUQHjoGCAAQCBAeUNKbDVjwrg1gwLYNaABwAHgAgA
FTiAGAB5IBAjE0mAEAoAEBqgELZ3dzLXdpei1pbWfAAQE&sclient=img&ei=jKMRYMH
nEoiH_Aaz7JPADw&bih=578&biw=1366&rlz=1C1GCEB_enUS910US910#imgrc=IywKWK
GMho0PdM

Challenge

1. Apply Campbell's model to the last change you or your organization made. How well does it fit?
2. What do you like about this model?
3. What do you dislike about this model?

133. Jim Clawson's Model of Change

Concept

We began this module by asking you to make a diagram of your personal model of change. If you did this, you had to stop and think about your VABEs, about what change is, and how the change process works. The premise there, and I believe it is very important, is that people learn better and deeper when they plumb their own understanding, bring that to Level One (paper or voice) and then discuss it. I always asked my students/participants to come to class having formed opinions about the issues, analyses, and action plans for every case. I noted recently from reading a biography of Winston Churchill[33] that he used that principle to educate himself: Churchill's practice "... was not to read any particular debate 'until I have recorded my own opinion of the subject on paper, having regard only to general principles. After reading I reconsider and finally write', setting out in pencil, on small pieces of paper, his own views on each subject, which he then pasted into the volumes." I have asked you to do the same throughout this volume. It's too *easy* to listen to someone else's views and then conclude, "I knew that." When in fact, if asked *a priori* to state your views, the vast majority of people could *not* have said that.

Then, we outlined a double handful of change models active in the world today. That double handful was just a sampling. There are many, many more models out there. In the ones we introduced, you noticed many overlaps, an indication of the triangulation on a commonly observed phenomenon.

So, lastly, I will share my model with you. First, I think people live in their **comfort zones,** their accumulated set of habitual behavior, thinking, and VABEs. Second, so long as people continue to receive or perceive confirming feedback data, they will persist in their behavior. We can call that behavior their *baseline* behavior. People consider deviating from their baseline for one or both of two reasons: they get bored or they get disconfirming data—which hurts.

When people get *disconfirming data*, they can do one of four things: ignore it, deny it, distort it, discount it, or ignore it altogether, in which

---

[33] Gilbert, M. 2014. *Churchill: A Life*. Rosetta Books.

case they will continue doing what they have always been doing. If the pain of the disconfirming data is strong enough, they may begin to search for other ways of doing things.

People who get *bored* with their lives will begin to *search for alternatives* but with some enthusiasm or hope instead of pain. The search for alternatives may be difficult. Some won't know how to search. They simply know they don't like the status quo. If they have a bit of built-in confidence, they may know to read, to ask, to invite, to explore, to search for different ways of doing things.

The search for alternative ways of doing and being leads to some *experiments*. Experiments by their nature involve breaking old habits. Eat less? Exercise more? Stop smoking? Change our recruiting process? Change our reward system? Change the way we design work? Change our business model? Change the reason we are in business? Change our VABEs about how to organize and manage?

These experiments, like the baseline behavior, will return some *results*. If the experiments fail, if the data coming back are negative, SNAP, we go back to our original baseline behavior. Often we deep down don't really want to change and we set up the experiments to fail.

If the experiment works, yay, we will continue doing it. Maybe. The payoff of a successful experiment might be good reinforcement for the new behavioral alternative, but if the payoffs aren't strong enough to overcome our baseline tension, then, snap, back we go again to yesterday. If the payoffs are strong enough and our determination is strong enough, we may form *a new baseline* that includes the new, alternative behavior.

Each of the elements or *states* listed above represent opportunities for leaders to influence the change process. These opportunities are shown as red "L's" in the diagram below.

Example

Some people actively seek new ways of doing things. They probably have a semi-conscious VABE "There's always a better way." Some people just do the same thing over and over again, day after day, week after week, year after year. And are happy. No problem. Until and unless they get fired or their spouse comes and says, "Goodbye." Same for companies. They do the same thing and go bankrupt. As outlined above over and over again, the value of being a "learning being or a learning organization."

Companies with declining numbers (or growing cost ratios), search for alternatives. Often they rely on consulting firms to help them if management doesn't know what to do. They try the new thing and if it works, they continue. If not, they go back to what they were doing. Many management teams will pay a lot of money for a consulting report and then it lies fallow on the credenza. Their VABEs are dominating their ability to try something new.

Daimler buys Chrysler thinking to use it to gain a larger foothold in America. Chrysler was losing money and not very healthy and needed a capital infusion, so they were happy about this investment. Later, Daimler divests Chrysler when the expected results didn't materialize. Culture eats strategy for breakfast. This is not a rare phenomenon. The vast majority of mergers and acquisitions fail.[34]

Motorola reinvents itself over and over again and survives today.[35]

Diagram

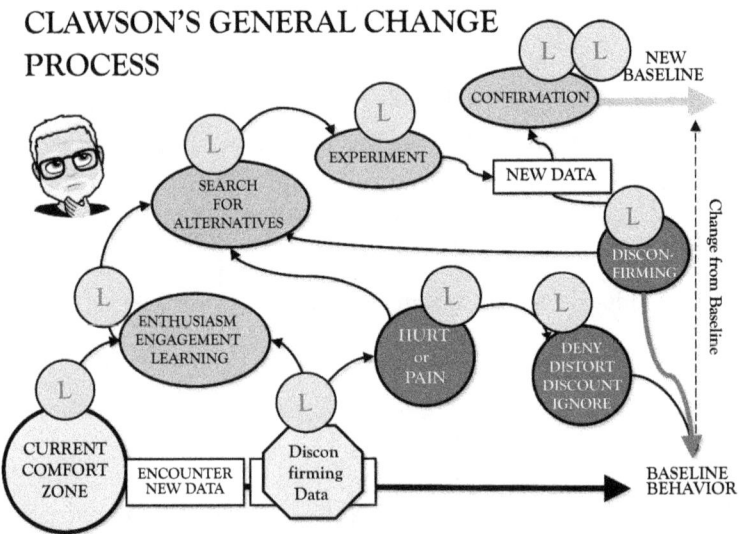

CLAWSON'S GENERAL CHANGE PROCESS

---

[34] http://lakeletcapital.com/blog/2017/3/15/success-and-fail-rate-of-acquisitions
[35] http://bgr.com/2011/11/11/rebirth-of-an-icon-motorola-reinvents-the-razr/

Challenge

1. How often are you looking for a new and different way of doing things?
2. How do you respond to disconfirming data?
3. How good are you at creating different alternatives?
4. How many experiments did you run last year? What new things did you do? What did you learn? Which of those have become a part of a new baseline?

134. Managing Mergers and Acquisitions

Concept

Most mergers and acquisitions fail.[36] Typically, that means not meeting their stated financial goals within five years. In my consulting, I have worked with many companies who as a part of their strategic plans acquire and sell subsidiaries. The two main strategic growth patterns are by acquisition and by internal sales growth. At the same time, I have been surprised by apparent lack of a disciplined process for merging a new company into the parent.

I found a company once that had made 23 acquisitions in 18 years and in which four of those acquisitions were larger than the parent company itself. I spent two years interviewing people and learning how they had managed to be so successful in their efforts. They had a unique process, which I will describe here.[37] I came to believe that the process was extraordinary, well planned, and highly successful.

First, the senior management determined that they would never make a hostile takeover. They didn't want to deal with employees of a company that didn't want to be acquired.

Second, senior management wanted to manage the social aspects of the merger as well as the financial ones.

Third, the acquiring management team wanted to shorten the window of uncertainty for employees on both sides as much as possible. Their VABE was that the uncertainty about whether one had a job was de-energizing and detrimental to the firm.

Fourth, management wanted to use the best talent from both sides. They did not accept the usual notion that only the acquiring side's managers would be in charge. They interviewed managers from both sides for every possibly redundant function to find the best talent.

Fifth, in order to keep the window of uncertainty as short as possible, they designed cross-company merger teams for every function or activity

---

[36] http://lakeletcapital.com/blog/2017/3/15/success-and-fail-rate-of-acquisitions
[37] The case ultimately was not released, so I will leave the name of the company anonymous.

that was implicated in the merger as a possible redundancy. The team members were already being socialized into the new larger parent company.

Sixth, the merger teams, as many as 23 in one acquisition, began meeting as soon as the merger was agreed upon, but well in advance of the actual signing.

Seventh, they chose leaders of the merger teams from both sides depending on the perceived superiority of the individuals. Thus, the teams were led by managers from both companies, not just the acquiring company.

Eighth, the merger teams made plans to merge their corresponding departments that could and would be implemented within two weeks of the final, formal signing.

Ninth, when the final agreement was signed, the merger teams sprang into action. The guideline was, "if you have a job after two weeks, you can relax, the layoffs will be over."

Tenth, the senior management of the acquiring firm (the COB and the CEO) visited every unit of the acquired firm. In these visits, they distributed to all employees a handbook describing the charter of the parent company. Then they held an all-hands meeting in which they introduced themselves and went through the charter of the parent company: its mission, its vision, its values, its strategies, and its measurements. Then in the afternoon, they went around the plant and shook hands with all the employees and answered questions. They repeated this process for every acquired unit, perhaps 30 to 40 times. You can see that this might take six months after the acquisition was finalized.

As a result of this process, the company's acquisitions all folded into the parent company with a minimum of disturbance and resistance, passive or otherwise. One plant manager said, "This plant was built 50 years ago. This is the first time since then that a senior officer has set foot in the place. It's really refreshing! They actually know who we are!"

My takeaway from this research project was that while most acquisitions fail, they don't have to. And they are in fact likely the result of inadequate management preparation and planning. I worked with the

MAC Group at one point, developing this sequence into a model for use in other firms, a summary of which appears below in the Diagram section.

There is a lot of interest these days in *post-merger integration*. See the additional references below. To my mind, the very phrase indicates the problem: *post-merger* is too late. The process outlined above shows that successful mergers begin well before the merger formally occurs. Of course, in some cases, one must comply with regulatory constraints about coordination with potential acquisitions.

Example

I had a client once who was growing by acquisition. Yet in the seminars, participants frequently mentioned how the acquired units seldom seemed to work well with their counterparts or the parent company. They described what seemed to me a rather ad-hoc and helter-skelter plan for the post-merger acquisitions. Like most companies, they focused on the financial redundancies, let the acquiring company managers dominate, and paid little attention to the collision of cultures that took place each time—the assumptions being ours is the best way, and *they* will become like *us*.

After one seminar in which there were many participants from various acquisitions, I submitted my invoice as usual. My counterpart came back asking me to prepare 23 invoices because they didn't have a centralized way of billing for all of the new subsidiaries. That was very unusual for me. When I asked for their addresses, I was told that they didn't have them. Hmm. So, I am supposed to find out on my own how to bill 23 different participants with no known address or contact information—because the firm had not adequately planned the post-merger integration of each acquisition.

On a larger scale, I am reminded of the events following the second Iraq war. The President declared "Mission accomplished" when in fact, the hard work was just beginning. Our apparent lack of planning seemed to magnify the problems that arose subsequently to the end of military operations.

Diagram

THE MAC MODEL OF MANAGING MERGERS AND ACQUISITIONS

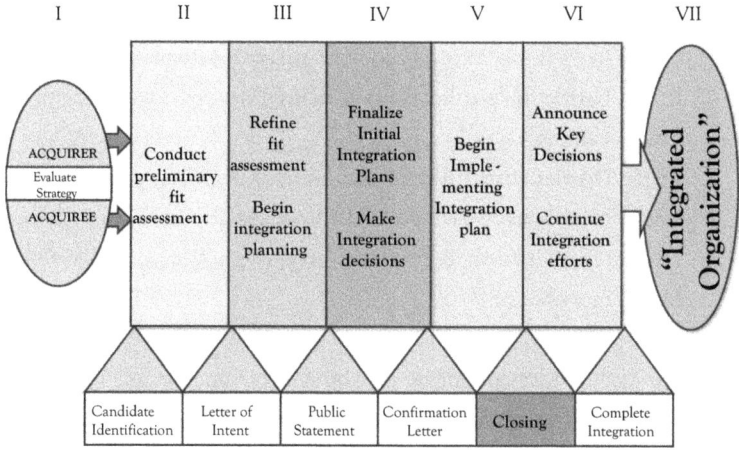

Source: Adapted from consulting work done by Jim Clawson with the MAC Group

Challenge

1. What is the process that your company uses to merge acquisitions?
2. How successful has your company been with its post-merger processes?
3. What changes would you recommend?

Additional References

1. http://info.midaxo.com/post-merger-integration-guide?utm_campaign=AW%3A%20TOFU%20-%20PMI&utm_source=ppc&ads_cmpid=720196695&ads_adid=41786944733&ads_matchtype=b&ads_network=g&ads_creative=238473957119&utm_term=m%26a%20integration%20strategy&ads_targetid=kwd-298481535502&utm_campaign=&utm_source=adwords&utm_medium=ppc&ttv=2&gclid=CjwKCAiAhMLSBRBJEiwAlFrsTjcC9uyfkOuX6ZNxUCBhYABZk3XFIzL0K-5jhLeXlrSItl0C4oOJeKBoCv04QAvD_BwE

2. https://macouncil.org/event/art-ma-integration/san-diego-ca/feb-2018?gclid=CjwKCAiAhMLSBRBJEiwAlFrsTnMEvJ48d607 7Ek1L-0bgswxrfcexIiP_s-w6uSO4ICeEDTPCH4E4BoC8E-sQAvD_BwE
3. https://en.wikipedia.org/wiki/Post-merger_integration
4. http://bain.com/publications/articles/10-steps-to-successful-ma-integration.aspx
5. https://forbes.com/forbes/welcome/?toURL=https://forbes.com/sites/mattporzio/2016/08/04/four-ways-to-succeed-with-post-merger-integration/&refURL=https://google.com/&referrer=https://google.com/

In the end, leadership must be about creating results. What those results should be has become an increasingly challenging question. First, what are the *intangible asset pools* I have mentioned. Second, what do we mean by *results*?

Kaplan and Norton at the Harvard Business School developed a powerful way of thinking about the primary role of executives—the ability to transform intangible asset pools into tangible financial results. In the end, this is where the rubber meets the road, where an executive's worth becomes apparent. This section will introduce the basics of recognizing what your intangible asset pools are and how you can think about converting them into financial results.

135. Results of the Leadership Diamond

Concept

In an earlier chapter, we introduced a Diamond Model of Leadership comprised of individual leadership characteristics, strategic story, the ability to sell that story, organizational architecture, managing change, and the various links between each of these four key elements. Now, we turn to *results*, a consideration of what comes out of that model. Before we do, write down *your view* of what the best measures of leadership success should be:

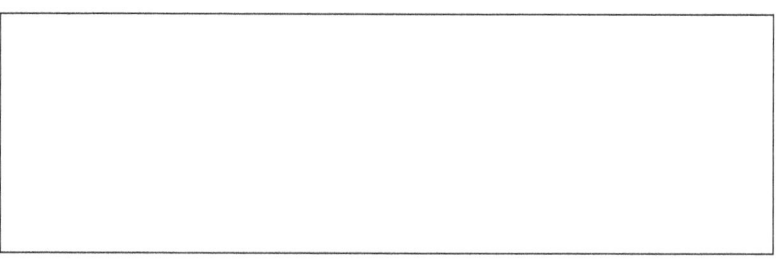

Building and adapting from the strategy planning research of Kaplan and Norton, we argue here for four key elements of results. The first, of course, is what everyone wants to think of as results, *profitability*. Effective leadership should indeed be profitable. If one *only* thinks of profits, however, one can make decisions that will endanger the long-term viability of the firm. So we will consider here results for a sustainable business, one that is intended to continue functioning and functioning robustly going forward. Those who only want to acquire firms, strip them of their assets, and realize the profits on sales of those assets won't find this approach interesting.

Consider then where profits come from. Profits are the positive result of revenues minus costs, $P = R - C$. Effective leaders pay attention to both parts of this equation. Of course, paying attention to cost alone is fruitless if revenues are shrinking, so the main issue then is where do we get revenues? And the answer is the second level of results, *customers*.

Happy, satisfied customers will give you more money. Therefore, the primary question facing us at results level two is "what is your customer value proposition?" In other words, what are you promising your customer that you will deliver? Yes, there are customer segments, and we must consider those, but overall, what do you promise your customers? Price? Quality? Dependability? Convenience? Consistency? Image? Value per dollar? Some combination of all of these? Whatever that combination is, the leadership of the firm must be clear on what they are trying to deliver to their customers. Especially when they engage in advertising. One channel reports the trust level in American CEOs to be around 17 percent! [38] How important is trust to you compared with profits?

This clarity is important for multiple reasons. Without a clear customer value proposition (CVP), potential customers won't have a reason to try what you offer. Without a clear CVP, *existing* customers won't know why they should stay. And without a clear CVP, *employees* won't know what they are trying to deliver.

The third level of results to consider is whether or not your organization has *the capability of delivering on the promises to your customer*. There may be three to six key core capabilities that you will need to have or develop in order to come through on your promises to your customers. If quality is key, you will need excellent engineering, quality control, and manufacturing capabilities. If image is critical, you will need a robust marketing department and easily recognized symbols (like the Tri-Star). If durability is important, you will need a strong procurement function that can find the best materials and superb operations. If price is central, you will need to have lean processes and high levels of productivity.

Notice that these *capabilities* do not appear on your balance sheet. These are easily imagined, but not easily measured clusters of skills.

The fourth and last level of scrutiny in leadership results is a triad of conceptual pools: human capital, social capital, and organizational capital. The key point here is that the assets at levels two to four are all *intangible*. They exist in our ability to imagine them, but they don't appear on the balance sheet or income statement. Profits are tangible; you can see them and measure them in formal documents. *So, the issue is how does one convert intangible asset pools (HC+SC+OC) into tangible assets (profits, revenues, and costs)*. Further, how does one invest effectively in one's intangible asset pools in a thoughtful and strategic way so that the

---

[38] http://marketingcharts.com/traditional/us-trust-in-business-hits-10-year-low-only-17-trust-ceos-7718/

connections between investments in levels four, three, and two actually result in increased revenues and profits?

Employee training, for example, is an investment in HC. That investment is wasted unless it contributes directly to the development of an HC pool that contributes directly to key core capabilities (CC) that in turn serve a specific CVP so that customers will buy more goods and services. The cost of reorganizing is a waste unless that reorganization results in a positive increase in SC that contributes to key CCs that serve customers. The cost of new information technology is a waste unless it contributes to SC and CCs in ways that fulfill the CVP. Likewise, the lack of investment in deficient intangible asset pools can also undermine customer trust and satisfaction and in turn depress revenues while in the short run reducing costs.

Examples

At one point, rocket scientists at NASA's Goddard Space Flight Center had to rummage through project files stored in *cardboard boxes* in a concrete basement in order to find answers to critical technological issues. We interviewed a project leader who knew that someone in the organization had solved the air-turbulence-over-skin-rivets problem previously, but the information could not be found. The PhD in astrophysics thought she could solve the problem in about six months and that it would take her three months to sort through all the project paper files stored in boxes. She chose the shorter alternative. The organization's lack of ability to store, retrieve, and utilize important knowledge was a drag on its ability to move forward. She found the answer, by the way, after about two and a half months of searching.

In a large global defense company, communications between different geographic sites, between functions in the company, and between program managers was at one time slow and sluggish. The lack of communication viscosity in the company resulted in its losing some important bids and being unable to bring the talents of its engineers to bear on current programs. That same organization was re-organized three times in 10 years, changes that resulted in enormous losses of employee morale and energy—especially when the last re-org went back to the way it had been.

Starbucks, it could be argued, has four core capabilities upon which their success is based: procurement, roasting, store management, and real estate. The company has invested millions of dollars in finding and educating the best coffee bean producers so they can have the best raw materials. They have a proprietary roasting process as secret as the Coca-Cola formula. They obviously manage their stores in unique ways. And with all those sites, they must have real expertise in managing real estate. Yes/no?

Leaders who cannot describe in some detail, and with some clarity, the strategic linkages between their intangible assets and their tangible outcomes are not, frankly, doing their jobs. Those who see and manage the direct linkages between all four levels—HC+SC+OC→C→CVP→PFTs— are doing their job; they are strategically savvy and results oriented. Those who focus only on short-term profits are likely to make big long-term mistakes.

Diagram

Converting Intangible Assets to Tangible Results

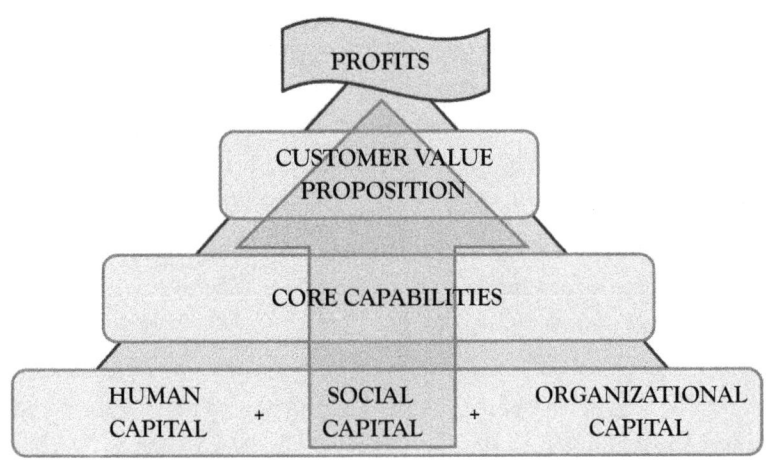

Challenge

1. When you think of results, go beyond the common answer of *profits*.
2. Think about where profits come from and how you can build an organization that is sustainable and has an NPV higher than its PV.
3. Try to articulate clearly and succinctly your customer value proposition.
4. Try to articulate the short list of core capabilities your organization must have in order to fulfill your promises to your customers.
5. Try to understand and articulate the health of your HC and SC and OC.
6. Judge the value of every investment by how well it serves the strategic linkages between the four levels outlined above.
7. Read more about the Balanced Scorecard described by Kaplan and Norton (e.g., *Strategy Maps*).
8. Encourage your organization to be more careful, intentional, and strategic in the investments it makes by using this four level model.

136. Human Capital

Concept

Human Capital is the imaginary sum of what all of your employees can do. A stack of resumes is a poor approximation of an organization's human capital; note that an MBA is not an MBA is not an MBA. As you can imagine, it's difficult to measure a person's abilities much less add those together with others'. Hence, it's an intangible asset pool.

Example

Supposing you own a title company, which reviews and *clears* real estate titles for transfer to a buyer. After a couple of months, you could record how many titles your 30 employees could *clear*. Adding those up, you would have a rough estimate of the *value* of your human capital pool.

Diagram

Human Capital Asset Pool

Challenge

1. How many humans are in your organization?
2. What kinds of human skills are essential to your organization's functioning?
3. How would you summarize the value of the human asset pool of your organization?

137. Social Capital

Concept

Social Capital refers to the incremental value added by the way your people interact. This incremental value added can be positive or negative. Social Capital can enhance or detract from an organization's assets. Negative social capital erodes a company's effectiveness. Positive social capital can accelerate an organization's productivity.

Social capital is affected by organizational structure, systems, bureaucracy, layers of authority, culture, hiring practices, and the local labor market among other things.

Wise executives will realize that it's easier to teach skills than attitude and hire for goodness of fit with their intended organizational culture. Hiring the best skill set/resume may add to one's human capital pool but if they detract from social culture, the net result can be a big negative for the company overall.

Example

If you want to hire a welder, whom do you look for? The best resume? The widest range of skills? Do you hire the *best* welder? The Aberdeen Plant at FMC (now BAES) realized that they could teach people to weld but not to change their attitudes. So they hired people based on their cultural fit rather than their welding skills to the point that they hired a woman as a welder who had never welded before—but she had the burning desire to learn, got on well with others, loved to solve problems, and was a good team player.

Diagram

Social Capital Asset Pool

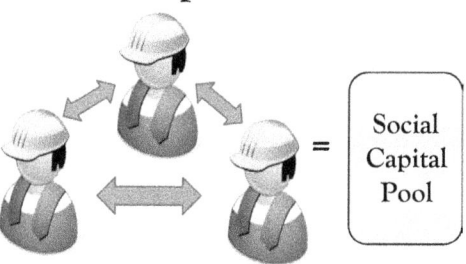

Challenge

1. On a scale of 1 to 10, how would you rate the quality of relationships in your organization? Do people like each other?
2. Have you ever gone to a team building exercise (high ropes and/ or low ropes)? Did it help build and strengthen your social capital?
3. What in your organization erodes your social capital?
4. Think about your most frequent relationships in the organization? What could you do to enrich the social capital in your personal network?
5. What if any VABEs in your de facto organizational culture erode your social capital?

138. Organizational Capital

Concept

Organizational Architecture can either enhance or inhibit an organization's ability to perform. The contribution made by organizational architecture, positive or negative, can be conceived of as *organizational capital*.[39] Some confuse this term with social capital (already introduced).[40,41,42] It's an intangible asset. Organizational architecture, that is, how you are organized can either release latent energy or clog it up. As you noted above in Larry Greiner's description of organizational evolutions and revolutions, the solutions to yesterday's problems often become tomorrow's bureaucracy. Sludge. Cholesterol.

We cannot really measure the effectiveness or efficiency of an organization with any exactitude. We can count layers. We can count steps in a process. We can note the time to make significant decisions. We can note the time to market for new products. All of these things contribute to or detract from organizational capital, another imaginary asset pool based on the *quality* of our organization. So, while we cannot really measure it[43] (like human capital or social capital) we can conceive of organizational capital as a pool of intangible assets that either help or hinder the achievement of our strategies.[44] And like human and social capital, organizational capital should contribute to the development and fertilization of our core corporate capabilities.

Example

The organizational capital of the BAES Aberdeen plant (previously introduced) is significantly positive. The organizational capital of large, slow bureaucracies (pick your favorite) is significantly negative. I was fortunate to be involved in the GE "Workout Process" in the late 80s and

---

[39] https://en.wikipedia.org/wiki/Organizational_capital

[40] http://johntomer.com/organizational-capital/

[41] https://hbr.org/2004/02/measuring-the-strategic-readiness-of-intangible-assets

[42] https://managementmania.com/en/organizational-capital-structural-capital

[43] http://cjournal.cz/files/121.pdf

[44] http://emeraldinsight.com/doi/abs/10.1108/14691930610681438

early 90s. The goal of that effort was to enhance the organizational capital pool by discovering and removing *organizational cholesterol* that was slowing the company down. I knew of one unit that required 23 steps to get a hammer out of the store room. Other units would pile up *standard operating manuals* in their entryways to show how much bureaucratic red tape they had gotten rid of. The Workout Effort was an enormous project—and very insightful in its focus on improving that intangible asset pool—organizational capital.

Diagram

One Way to Measure Organizational Capital

Survey your employees on the following:
- How much does your organizational **structure** contribute to getting your job done? (-5 to +5)
- How much does your organization's systems contribute to getting your job done? (-5 to +5)
- How much does your organization's **information systems** contribute to getting your job done? (-5 to +5)

Challenge

1. If perfect organizational efficiency is *100* percent, how efficient would you rate your organization capital?
2. Rate how much your organization's architecture contributes to you getting your job done? (−5 to +5)?
3. How much does your organization's systems contribute to you getting your job done? (−5 to +5)?
4. How much does your organization's information technology infrastructure contribute to you getting your job done? (−5 to +5)
5. How would you *measure* your organizational capital?
6. How long do big decisions take in your organization?
7. How many layers are there in your company?
8. Identify a system or process that adds sludge to your organization and design a better way. Then see if you can sell it to your management. Use the principles in the Change section to help you.

139. Core Capabilities

Concept

Investments in the three intangible asset pools are useless unless they contribute directly to the enhancement of an organization's core capabilities. By core capabilities, we mean the imaginary but real clusters of skills that form the basis for an organization's ability to compete in the market place. Training programs for *human capital* and *social capital* and re-organizations for *organizational capital* won't be anything more than money down the drain unless the corporation's core competitive capabilities are fertilized and grown.

Example

In the post-WWII years, Komatsu in Japan had a difficult time until its management realized that unless they could build with the quality that Caterpillar had, they couldn't compete. Whatever it was that produced the *legendary* Caterpillar strength and dependability, they had to figure that out and duplicate or exceed it if they wanted to compete against their American industry leader. That effort took the company some ten years or more. Building a *core capability*, in this case high quality manu-facturing systems, isn't something that can be done overnight. There was a time when Japanese products were viewed as "cheap, poorly built and undependable" in the United States. Same with Chinese products. Today, both countries along with South Korea are producing high quality highly competitive products. See again the chapter on the Innovator's Dilemma.

Starbucks is another example of *core capabilities*, which are usually a handful of abilities that define the company's strength. Often these have to do with the supply-chain management skills. In Starbucks case (see the case written by Scott Snell at Darden Business Publishing), the handful of capabilities were acquisition of highest quality coffee beans, proprietary roasting process, store design and management down to inches of move-ments for baristas, and real estate. The company invested over $10mm in a Central American agricultural school to educate bean growers on how to produce better beans. The roasting facilities are closely guarded. Starbucks' store management is legendary (like McDonald's). And with the global network of stores, real estate management is a critical focus.

Diagram

Creating Core Capabilities

- The building blocks of corporate strategy are not products and markets but business processes.
- Competitive success depends upon transforming a company's key processes into strategic capabilities that consistently provide superior value to customers
- Companies create these capabilities by making strategic investments in a support infrastructure that links together and transcends traditional functions.
- Capability-based strategies, because they cross functions, must be championed by senior leadership.

Source: Stalk, Evans, and Shulmand (1992)

Challenge

1. Write down the handful of core capabilities essential to your organization's ability to compete and survive.
2. Assess how your organization's investments in HC, SC, and OC have contributed to those core capabilities. How would you adjust those investments if at all?
3. Assess the core capabilities of your major competitors.
4. What are they better at than you?
5. What are you better at than them? How could you protect those advantages?

140. Customer Value Proposition

Concept

The necessary linkages between the intangible asset pools and core capabilities should seem obvious by now. The next level of linkages are equally important. We are building a larger picture here. IF your core capabilities are directly linked to and supportive of your customer value proposition (CVP), you are wasting time and money.

What do you promise your customers? Note your understanding here.

Companies can promise customers lots of different things. Quality. Convenience. Price. Brand identity. Dependability. Serviceability. Image. And some combination of those. As noted earlier, these decisions depend on management's VABEs, the company's target audience(s) the balance of speed, quality, and cost along with what we can or cannot do (core capabilities) and what the competition is doing. These issues apply to both products and services.

Example

If you buy a Mercedes Benz, what are the promises that you are buying? The Tristar on the front of the car is one thing, a status symbol, a statement of your identity. Lowest cost is not one, neither in purchase price or maintenance.

The experience I mentioned earlier about my Japanese haircuts is an example of a service-oriented CVP for customers. The promises there were highest quality, reasonable price, and supreme experience. Not the lowest cost.

Diagram

Customer Value Proposition

- Price?
- Value?
- Dependability?
- Maintenance?
- Durability?
- Guarantees?
- Identity?
- Convenience?
- Sustainability?
- Experience?

Challenge

1. Identify and write down your organization's promises to its customers.
2. Draw the linkages from your core capabilities to the CVPs that they support.
3. Are the linkages and investments clear and strong?

141. Tangible Financial Results

Concept

Most executives seem to behave the core VABE of *maximizing profits*. In fact, most business schools teach the importance of the *core capitalist* principle of maximizing profits. This, people say, is why investors give their capital to the corporation—to maximize their returns on their investments. Even when I ask "What is the purpose of your company?" the most common answer is, "Are you nuts? To maximize profits of course." And usually, they mean *maximizing short-term profits* that raise the share price, delight their investors, and guarantee rewards from their performance contracts.

As we near the end of our time together (on first reading anyway), I invite you to consider the proposition that *maximizing profits* in today's world is a defunct and in fact morally bankrupt VABE. The alternative is *maximizing sustainable profits*.

By *sustainable profits* I mean profits that respect and protect rather than abuse the *Commons*. By Commons I mean air, water, soil, flora, fauna, and the underprivileged—the things we all share regardless of where we live and in what level of congregation. Historically, business in general has sought to maximize profits at the expense of the Commons— by dumping into the air, the water, the soil, by choosing profits over flora and fauna and the well-being of the underprivileged.

The world is slowly turning in this direction as we debate the consequences of global warming, over-flowing landfills, the hundreds of millions of tons of plastics being dumped into the *oceanfills*, the destruction of flora that feed the atmosphere and our lungs, the fishing and hunting to near extinction, and widespread poverty and homelessness that plague various cities, regions, and countries in the world. The debate rages about whether it's too late or whether we should do anything different. *Conservatives*, in general, oddly tend to favor maximizing profits at the expense of conservation. One might think that *conservatives* would be in favor of saving the world and *liberals* would be more in favor of economic freedoms, but it's the opposite.

It seems to me that every person, every family, every company, every country throughout the globe share a *responsibility of citizenship* to protect and not abuse the Commons. Ethicists often talk about the *tragedy of the Commons*, the notion that people, companies, and nations just don't care about the Commons, at least not as much as they do about maximizing profits and minimizing costs.

Consider recycling. What if corporations were responsible for the end-of-life recycling of their products and packaging? Imagine how changes in product design and packaging design and materials would blossom. Now, those considerations are out of mind as too expensive.

With regard to the *underprivileged*, every society decides what it will do with those born with severe birth defects, mental illness, and absent parents. No one can say "they chose their lot" as some do with the poor. In a society, who if anyone, should care for these unfortunate souls? One billionaire said to me, "Put them on the hillside with the predators, like the Indians did." Hmmm. Every society makes those decisions and world wide we have starvation, homelessness, and illiteracy *issues*.

So, can you trace the *red threads* in the diagram below from intangible asset pools right through to tangible profits in your organization? If not, perhaps expensive decisions are being made without an awareness of the linkages we have described.

Example

I have mentioned earlier the example of the Japanese auto industry shipping 10-year-old cars to Central Africa where they pile up when they die. India has a *ship breaking* industry in which rusting out old freighters are driven up on shore and then cut to pieces for scrap by barefoot workers. Brazil and many other countries have homeless people who live off of the trash deposited in landfills. China's two main rivers dump 300 million tons of plastic each into the Pacific Ocean. The debates over fracking continuing in the United States along with the arguments about drilling in wildlife refuges and off-shore sites. Meanwhile, several companies are mapping the ocean floor in the Pacific and dredging there, digging up five feet of sludge looking for precious metals. And the Japanese continue to hunt whales, while New England cod and sword fishermen have been so successful as to destroy their own industries.

Diagram

Strategy Maps and Investment Linkages

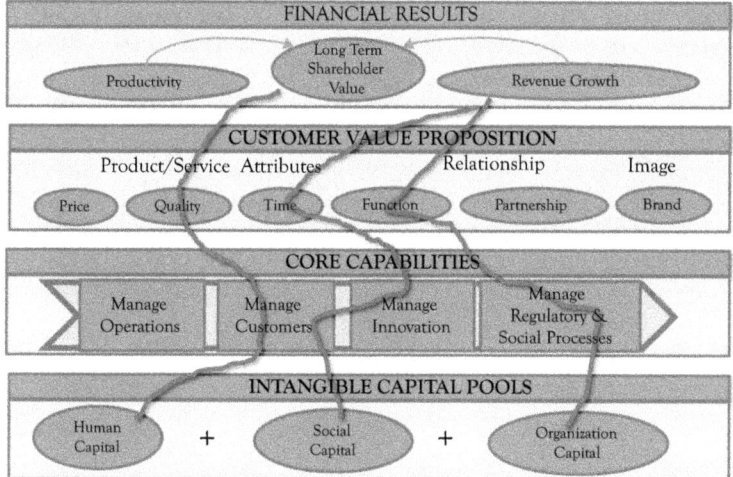

Source: Adapted from Strategy Maps, Kaplan & Norton, HBRP, 2004

Challenge

1. What do you think about the maximizing profit VABE?
2. What do you think about the responsibility, if any, of individuals, companies, and nations with regard to the Commons?
3. What do you think Adam Smith meant when he noted that capitalism relied on men of good character?
4. What's your view of people who litter?
5. If you were head of a nation-state, what would your policies about the Commons be?
6. How much *freedom* does a *citizen* have? (Neighborhood, city, state, nation, globe?)
7. How much if any *responsibility* does a *citizen* have?

SECTION IX

Conclusion

This book was written with short chapters introducing and explaining a single concept each, and then showing examples and diagrams and inviting you to some seriously challenging thoughts. I wanted to give new insights or increased clarity in every chapter. Have I done so? Believing that hope is not a strategy, I hope so. I have tried to summarize at a high level here the integration I have made of my lifetime study of leadership and human behavior in organizations.

May I leave you with two additional thoughts?

142. Zoysia Grass

Concept

If you have read or browsed your way to here, you have encountered concepts related to all the main elements of our Diamond Model: Who am I? What's my strategic story? Can I sell my story? Can I organize to help not hinder? Can I lead change like a Change Master? And how do I think of results?

As I said at the beginning, the Diamond Model represents a generalized, flexible, robust model onto which you can add/integrate new insights without having to change your basic paradigm. I may, indeed, add chapters as time goes by. If you have suggestions for such, let me know. I hope you find the framework useful and easy to remember, hurray. If you have suggestions, again, let me know.

At the end of my week-long seminars, people often ask some variant of this question, "What if my boss hasn't been here?" In other words, if you aren't getting support, what do you do? It's a big question. Remember that Senge (and others) recommended allowing change to emerge from any layer in the organization.

So, what can one do if one is not the CEO and yet wants to make change? Here's my answer.

Be a Zoysia Plug!

Zoysia grass is an unusual kind of grass:

1. It grows so thick it crowds out all the weeds (i.e., energy sucking nay sayers!).
2. It doesn't need a lot of water so it is drought resistant.
3. It grows slowly so it needs less mowing.
4. It has no seeds so you have to buy some to get it started, it grows by sending out runners.
5. It goes dormant after a hard freeze.
6. It turns white when it goes dormant.
7. It is hard to get rid of.
8. It is self-healing, burn it, gouge it, dig in it, and it just grows back.

Some people don't like the *turns white in winter* thing, but I love this stuff. My lawn was full of weeds one year, so I bought some zoysia grass and began planting it in the various mud holes here and there in my yard. Every January, I could see the white patches where the zoysia plugs had taken root. Every year, those white patches had expanded and spread out. For me, that was like an annual income statement—I could see my results year after year.

Once my *mother patch* was well established, I didn't have to buy any more—I could just transplant from her and fill in the holes with soil/potting mix. Zoysia grass is self-repairing, self-healing.

SO, in your organization, look around. Find a mud hole, something that needs improving. Don't ask for more budget. Don't ask permission. Don't tolerate the mud and weeds. Take the initiative and build a high-energy, high-producing unit within your immediate purview. Like zoysia grass, let your enthusiasm and vision crowd out all the nay-sayers, and fill in the eroded spots. Don't be in a big hurry. Take your time. Build a team. Show *them* how to be something better.

I will not say this approach is without risk. (See my example below.) One day I was burning leaves and I went into watch the Masters golf tournament. Suddenly, my neighbor was pounding on my front door, "Your lawn's on fire!" A smoldering leaf had jumped from my burn pile to my hibernating zoysia grass. Small inch high flames, easily knocked out with a broom. My wife looked at the burned patch and said, "Jim, I'm sorry. After all that effort, your zoysia grass is dead!" Academic geek that I am, I said, "Nope. Level Three grows deep!" And one month later, that patch had grown back in, lush, thick, green, and weed-free. The roots (Level Three) were still there and alive and well.

It turns out because zoysia grass is so thick, they recommend that you de-thatch it periodically. Rather than use a rake, I have found a faster way to de-thatch! Now, every two to four years, I burn my lawn!

Be a zoysia plug. Fix your part of the organizational lawn. If you do, pretty soon your influence will spread and if you have one or two colleagues, their patches will spread and soon you will have a lush, green, productive organizational lawn.

Example

At various times in my career, I have consulted with General Electric. At one point, we were working through 10 contracted programs on Level Three Leadership principles. After four sessions, each with ratings through the roof, and two weeks before the next session, I got a phone call. "We have to cancel the program," they said. What? Why?

> Well, one of our senior executives was having a large meeting and during the Q&A, someone asked him what his VABEs were on some topic. He didn't know what a VABE was and it annoyed him and he told us to cancel the program. He said, "we have our own language."

Hmm.

That's another example of several things:

a. Working with top level executives helps (but is not necessary).
b. Leadership development programs *should* be consistent with senior management VABEs—and most senior managers have no idea what's being taught in their sponsored programs because they don't attend them.
c. Culture dominates and language is a part of culture.
d. People who have insights must be careful as they *educate* others of their views lest they get rejected out-of-hand.
e. People who lead change from the middle must be especially sensitive to their cultural context and of their role to educate effectively.

On the other end of the scale, you can watch and learn from Pike's Place Fish Market, BAES Aberdeen plant, SAS Institute, Google, Southwest Airlines, and other similarly high energy, high achieving organizations. They are in the minority in their industries. And they are hard to copy, they have sustainable strategic competitive advantage. Their VABEs about how to manage are difficult to copy. They manage at Level Three.

Diagram

Challenge

1. Find something that needs fixing.
2. Fix it.
3. Don't wait to be told to.
4. Don't ask for budget.
5. Just do it!
6. Crowd out the energy-sucking nay-sayers!
7. Do your homework, build a charter, ramp up your energy, make it happen!
8. Then help others in your team and your network to do the same.

143. Be the Captain of Your Ship

Concept

Former U.S. Navy Captain, Michael Abrashoff, wrote a provocative book about how to transform an under-performing organization into a top-ranked one.[1] There were a number of lessons in that book but the central, and to me the most important, one was to take control of your life and career in the same spirit that he took control of his new command. Remember Jack Welch's invective, *Control Your Destiny or Someone Else Will!*[2]

At the very end of the seminars, when people are thinking about how if at all they can lead strategic change from their mid-level positions, I encourage them to take control of their lives and careers. Live more inside-out and less outside-in. Create your own charter and a charter for your department. Define the purpose of your life and spend the rest of your life implementing that. Create a vision and work toward it. Clarify what you stand for. Clarify your strategies for reaching your vision. Find your resonance and let it flow. Infect others with your enthusiasm. Energy/mood is contagious. Be a net-energy contributor, not an energy sucker. Forget about "what's in your wallet," think about "what's in your wake?" How do you leave people hour by hour, day by day?

Building on the concept Captain Abrashoff clarified, I list the following premises:

1. Your life and your career are your *ship*.
2. You are the Captain of your ship.
3. You decide the purpose of your ship.
4. You decide the rules on board your ship.
5. You decide whom to invite on board your ship.
6. You decide how fast to go. (Faster uses up more fuel.)
7. You decide what ports to put into.
8. You decide the condition of your ship when you step off.

---

[1] Abrashoff, M. 2007. *It's Your Ship!*. Grand Central Publishing.
[2] Welch, J., N. Tichy, and S. Sherman. 1994. *Control Your Destiny or Someone Else Will*. Harper PB.

Abrashoff and Welch's advice line up with the advice of many writers in psychology.[3]

Example

You. Who decides the purpose of your life, if not you? Who decides who you will be when you are 70 if not you? Who decides what compromises you make if not you? Who decides how much to learn if not you? Who decides how hard to work if not you? Who manages your energy level if not you?

Diagram

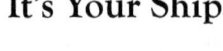

It's Your Ship!

- Your life and your career are your ship
- You are the captain of your ship
- You decide the purpose of your ship
- You decide the destination of your ship
- You decide the rules of your ship
- You decide whom to let on board your ship
- You decide how fast you go
- You decide where to put into port
- You decide how to leave your ship

Challenge

1. Determine to live more *inside-out* than *outside-in*.
2. Decide your purpose in life.
3. Write the rest of your personal Charter.
4. Make those last six decisions in the *It's Your Ship* list above.
5. Visit my website to see video clips of these same concepts: http.nadobimakoba.com
6. Write me with your comments: jimclawson@virginia.edu

---

[3] Glasser, W. 2010. *Choice Theory*. HarperCollins (latest edition).

About the Author

James Clawson is the Johnson & Higgins Emeritus Professor of Leadership and Organizational Behavior at the Darden Graduate School of Business Administration at the University of Virginia. He has degrees from Stanford University, Brigham Young University and Harvard University. His areas of expertise include Leadership, Organizational Behavior, Leading Change and Career Management. He has authored 23 books and more than 300 business cases and technical notes, taught in MBA, doctoral and executive education programs and consulted with scores of Fortune 500 corporations world-wide. His vita and publications list along with a summary of his life's work are found on his website at www.nadobimakoba.com

Index

OTHER TITLES IN THE HUMAN RESOURCE MANAGEMENT AND ORGANIZATIONAL BEHAVIOR COLLECTION

Michael Provitera, Editor

- *Civility at Work* by Lewena Bayer
- *Lean on Civility* by Christian Masotti and Lewena Bayer
- *The Successful New CEO* by Christian Muntean
- *Breakthrough* by Saundra Stroope
- *Agility* by Michael Edmondson
- *Strengths Oriented Leadership* by Matt L. Beadle
- *Competencies at Work* by Enrique Washington and Bruce Griffiths
- *Manage Your Career* by Vijay Sathe
- *Leader Evolution* by Alan Patterson
- *Creating a Pathway to Your Dream Career* by Tom Kucharvy
- *Designing Creative High Power Teams and Organization* by Eric W. Stein
- *Fostering Creativity in Self and the Organization* by Eric W. Stein
- *You're A Genius* by Steven S. Taylor
- *Leading The Positive Organization* by Thomas N. Duening, Donald G. Gardner, Dustin Bluhm and Andrew J. Czaplewski
- *The Search For Best Practices* by Rob Reider
- *Effective Interviewing and Information Gathering* by Tom Diamante
- *Mastering Self-Motivation* by Michael Provitera

Concise and Applied Business Books

The Collection listed above is one of 30 business subject collections that Business Expert Press has grown to make BEP a premiere publisher of print and digital books. Our concise and applied books are for...

- Professionals and Practitioners
- Faculty who adopt our books for courses
- Librarians who know that BEP's Digital Libraries are a unique way to offer students ebooks to download, not restricted with any digital rights management
- Executive Training Course Leaders
- Business Seminar Organizers

Business Expert Press books are for anyone who needs to dig deeper on business ideas, goals, and solutions to everyday problems. Whether one print book, one ebook, or buying a digital library of 110 ebooks, we remain the affordable and smart way to be business smart. For more information, please visit www.businessexpertpress.com, or contact sales@businessexpertpress.com.

www.ingramcontent.com/pod-product-compliance
Lightning Source LLC
Chambersburg PA
CBHW070601141224
18965CB00008B/72